*A few acres*

*of snow*

# A few acres of snow

DOCUMENTS IN PRE-CONFEDERATION CANADIAN HISTORY    *3rd edition*

EDITED BY THOMAS THORNER WITH THOR FROHN-NIELSEN

UNIVERSITY OF TORONTO PRESS

LIBRARY AND ARCHIVES CANADA CATALOGUING IN PUBLICATION

    A few acres of snow : documents in pre-confederation Canadian history / edited by Thomas Thorner; with Thor Frohn-Nielsen.—3rd ed.

First ed. published 1997 under title: "A few acres of snow" : documents in Canadian history, 1577–1867. Includes bibliographical references.

ISBN 978-1-4426-0029-4

    1. Canada—History—1763–1867—Sources.  2. Canada—History—To 1763 (New France)—Sources. I. Thorner, Thomas  II. Frohn-Nielsen, Thor, 1955–

FC18.F49 2009        971        C2009-904156-1

We welcome comments and suggestions regarding any aspect of our publications—please feel free to contact us at news@utphighereducation.com or visit our Internet site at www.utphighereducation.com.

*North America*
5201 Dufferin Street
North York, Ontario, Canada, M3H 5T8

*UK, Ireland, and continental Europe*
NBN International
Estover Road, Plymouth, PL6 7PY, UK
tel: 44 (0) 1752 202301

2250 Military Road
Tonawanda, New York, USA, 14150

FAX ORDER LINE: 44 (0) 1752 202333
enquiries@nbninternational.com

ORDERS PHONE: 1-800-565-9523
ORDERS FAX: 1-800-221-9985
ORDERS E-MAIL: utpbooks@utpress.utoronto.ca

The University of Toronto Press acknowledges the financial support for its publishing activities of the Government of Canada through the Book Publishing Industry Development Program (BPIDP).

This book is printed on paper containing 100% post-consumer fibre.

Book design by Black Eye Design.

Printed in Canada.

This book has been printed on 100% post consumer waste paper, certified Eco-logo and processed chlorine free.

# *Contents*

NOT ANOTHER EDITION

## (Preface to the Second Edition)

**M**any publishers annually incorporate relatively minor changes to produce yet another edition of their textbooks. This usually prevents students from selling their old editions and from purchasing cheaper used books for courses. In this case well over half of the material is entirely new. The idea of a revised edition originated with a number of specific problems. First, one of the most compelling documents in the original collection turned out to have been fabricated. Without any hint of its fictional nature, Gerald Keegan's diary can still be found in one of the best anthologies concerning the Irish in Canada. Yet its authenticity sparked a major controversy in Ireland during the early 1990s. The "diary" turns out to have been written as a short story by a Scottish immigrant 50 years after the events it describes and was not the account of a genuine Irish famine victim. The Keegan material also leaves the impression that the main motives for migration centred upon dispossession, nationalism, and Anglo-phobia, a version sharply contradicted by the De Vere account which now forms part of this new edition. Second, students wanted to hear more from the perspective of Native peoples. Therefore a new opening chapter comparing cultural perspectives as well as an entire chapter devoted to Native dissent was added to the volume dealing with pre-Confederation documents. Third, some critics thought that a single chapter on the early Maritime colonies was grossly inadequate. In its place are four new chapters. With the volume covering the period after 1867, many readers sought more material on classic Canadian issues and coverage beyond 1982 (which still remains the termination date for our post-Confederation history at Kwantlen University College). Another common suggestion was to include study questions, which previously had been available only in the study guides provided to instructors.

The first edition also failed to provide sufficient acknowledgement to the library staff at Kwantlen—in particular Margaret Giacomello and Jean McKendry—as well as Karen Archer, Jacinta Sterling, Kathie Holloway, Ann McBurnie, Judy Isaac, and Nancy Smith—who always managed to keep the interlibrary loan material, upon which so much of this book was based, flowing.

Finally, this project would never have been possible without the steady support of Michael Harrison, Vice-President and Editor of Broadview Press.

YET ANOTHER EDITION

## (Preface to the Third Edition)

C ritics of the second edition told us that many of the chapters were too long, included too many points of view and focused too much on economics. They also wanted more information about the context in which each document was written and biographical details of each author. The result is a trimmer third edition that includes new chapters on the disappearance of the Beothuck, the War of 1812, and the Loyalists in *A Few Acres of Snow* and new chapters on Victorian Canada's attitudes to sex, treaties in the far north, drugs, and the counterculture of the 1960s in *A Country Nourished on Self Doubt*. These revisions would not have been possible without a research grant from Kwantlen Polytechnic University.

GENERAL INTRODUCTION

## (First Edition)

*"You realize that these two countries have been fighting over a few acres of snow near Canada, and they are spending on this splendid struggle more than Canada itself is worth." —Voltaire, Candide, 1759*

Voltaire's remark, although unflattering, remains one of the best-known descriptions of early Canada. The modern reader must find it ironic that one of the leading thinkers of the Enlightenment could utterly dismiss an area, which he never visited, that would come to be one of the world's wealthiest and most highly developed societies. Published in 1759, when French dreams of a religious utopia or commercial success in North America lay in shambles, the remark could be attributed to bitterness or Eurocentrism. Yet many high-ranking French government officials shared his assessment of Canada. With this short incisive remark, Voltaire also satirized his fellow philosophers such as Montaigne and Rousseau who romanticized about the garden paradise and natural goodness found in the New World. But four years after *Candide* Voltaire published another novel, *L'Ingénu*, that contradicted his earlier views. Its protagonist, a French Canadian raised by the Huron, employs his morality and ingenuity to rise above the corrupt Parisian environment he is forced to confront.[1]

Nonetheless, Voltaire's image has served as and still remains a powerful characterization of this country. Whether they wrote exploration diaries, natural histories, guide books, immigration tracts, or essays, early Canadian writers often concentrated upon the physical environment. As the ink froze in her pen, Anna Brownell Jameson recorded that human character and behaviour "depend more on the influence of climate than the pride of civilized humanity would be willing to allow" and went on to pity the poor immigrants who were as "yet unprepared against the rigour of the season."[2] While some such as Catharine Parr Traill experienced "infinite delight...contemplating these pretty

---

1    Greg Gatenby, *The Wild is Always There* (Toronto: Alfred A. Knopf, 1993) 177, 458-59. For some the qualifier "near Canada" in the famous *Candide* quote has also been taken to invalidate its wider application. On this debate, Gatenby cites "L'Opinion de Voltaire sur le Canada," *Séances et Travaux de L'Académie des Sciences Morales et Politiques: Compte Rendu* (Paris, 1900). Even if the *Candide* remark did not refer exclusively to Canada, the association between Canada and snow is unequivocal in Voltaire's remark of October 13, 1759: "We French had the bright idea of establishing ourselves in Canada, on top of the snow between the bears and the beavers."

2    Anna Brownell Jameson, *Winter Studies and Summer Rambles in Canada*, Vol. 2 (London: Saunders and Otley, 1838) 27-28.

frolics of Father Frost,"[3] many other Canadians perceived their relationship with winter in hostile terms. One is reminded of Thomas Keefer's lament that "from Canada there is no escape: blockaded and imprisoned by Ice and Apathy."[4] A partial explanation for these varying opinions may be that Canadian winter meant different things to different people. According to Judith Fingard, "To the successful merchant and his family winter represented a time of entertainment, sport, cultural activity or, at worst, boredom," while to the labourer winter was "synonymous with hardship, cold, hunger, and gloomy unemployment or underemployment."[5] What meaning Indigenous people placed upon winter is not as well documented, but they too experienced vast differences. The winter village ceremonies of the West Coast, for example, contrasted sharply with those of the Cree hunting bands of the prairies.

The bleakness inherent in the image of "a few acres of snow" is also in harmony with the disappointment and subsequent transiency of the colonial population. Some, like Susannah Moodie, described Upper Canada as a "prison house." Whether it was groups such as Black Loyalists who chose Sierra Leone over Nova Scotia or individuals such as Samuel Cunard or Thomas Chandler Haliburton, many sought to escape the limitations of Canada and moved elsewhere. For the Irish arriving at Grosse-Île or the gold mines of British Columbia, as the following accounts reveal, the promise of a better life was often illusionary.

What follows is a volume that attempts to bring together compelling excerpts of divergent eyewitness perspectives on specific topics in Canadian history. The fascination of primary sources like the Voltaire quote lies in their personal perspective and the immediacy of experience they convey. However lacking in objective insight they may be, they were written by people at or close to the source of the events they describe.

Many collections of Canadian readings on the market today reprint articles from academic journals as models of scholarship. Although such articles may certainly be of great value, they naturally tend to be written with a scholarly audience in mind. Coupled with standard survey texts, the near-total reliance upon secondary sources has had wide-ranging consequences. A student registering for a course on the Victorian novel would, no doubt, expect to read Victorian novels, not simply digest what secondary sources had to say about them. Even if the raw materials were as dense, drab, and dull as the popular perception of Canadian history makes them out to be, bypassing them would be disturbing. But the primary sources are far from dull. What historians usually find most enjoyable

---

3    Catharine Parr Traill, *The Backwoods of Canada* (London: Charles Knight, 1836) 245.

4    Thomas Keefer, *Philosophy of Railroads* (Montreal: Armour and Ramsay, 1850) 1.

5    Judith Fingard, "The Winter's Tale: The Seasonal Contours of Pre-Industrial Poverty in British North America, 1815-1860," *Canadian Historical Association Papers* (1974) 65.

about the craft is research—the labyrinthine quest in primary sources for answers about the past. In the same way, readers of this book are encouraged to analyze the arguments and information in the sources for themselves.

This is still very much a book aimed at those largely unfamiliar with the subject. In order to make available the greatest possible amount of original material that is interesting and important, some less pertinent passages have been deleted. Exercising even a minimal shaping hand will sacrifice some dimensions of the past, but even if the occasional reader feels uncomfortable that the integrity of some documents has been violated, one hopes that in the interests of engaging a wider readership and lifting the veil of boredom from Canadian history, the end will have justified the means.

Some may also wish to hear less in a volume such as this one from the voices of white men. Despite efforts to the contrary, the unfortunate fact is that for many topics one has to rely upon the opinions of the white male elite. Even those women who did provide detailed records of their experiences in early Canada often reflected their origin and class more closely than their gender. On the rare occasions when one comes upon a substantial native commentary, it has invariably been transcribed by Europeans, rendering its contents highly suspect.

Editors of document collections must also be sensitive to Emma Larocque's criticism that reproducing historical documents such as these perpetuates negative images, particularly about Native people, and as such constitutes hate literature.[6] Without a doubt many documents written by ethnocentric Europeans, with their emphasis on Native violence, are elements of a literature of hate written to justify white domination. But it hardly follows that reprinting these inaccuracies constitutes disseminating hate literature. Instead, these documents may provide a means of exposing these lies, of demonstrating the basis of intolerance, and of understanding that prejudice is commonplace. In some respects these documents may be used to confront the current complacency or smugness of Canadians who assume that, especially compared to the United States, ours has been a kinder, gentler history and therefore lacks the foundation for bigotry and racism.

---

6    Emma Larocque, "On the Ethics of Publishing Historical Documents," in *"The Orders of the Dreamed"*: *George Nelson on Cree and Northern Ojibwa Religion and Myth 1823*, ed. J. Brown and R. Brightman (Winnipeg: University of Manitoba Press, 1988).

## USING PRIMARY HISTORICAL SOURCES

When first approaching history texts, students are usually overwhelmed by the amount of new information and find it difficult to distinguish key points or determine the author's main thesis. They have no reason to doubt authors' veracity and assume that any published account must contain a measure of truth since it would otherwise not be an assigned text. As their understanding of history increases, they will find that historians divide source materials into two categories. Textbooks, written by contemporary authors who never experienced the historical events themselves, are referred to as secondary sources, while any accounts or material that was recorded when an event in the past occurred are known as primary sources. In other words eye witnesses are distinguished from those who may have studied the event but did not observe or participate directly in its occurrence. Considerable debate exists between the utility of secondary sources as opposed to primary sources. Secondary sources are often able to take a broader, more objective perspective. Much like the expert witness in court, secondary sources evaluate many of the first-hand accounts and offer an overall assessment, usually by a distinguished professional historian. However, most textbooks also project a sense of completeness and authority that suggests a lack of controversy. Even when standard historical textbooks deal with debatable points, they imply that there is one "right" answer and one linear narrative. As in life, historical events were never simple or viewed from the same perspective. One could even suggest that the fatal flaw in most secondary historical writing comes from the disadvantage of hindsight. Later writers knew the outcomes that were unknown to the participants. Textbooks are also written in tune with the cultural norms of their age. Much of what was said in the past is now excluded as "hate literature" since it is no longer politically correct and would offend many groups within our society. Our society also equates objectivity with a lack of emotion. Few textbooks probe the human characteristics that link us directly to people in the past.

Courts, as well as historians, invariably prefer eye witnesses to experts. Primary documents contain a sense of intimacy with the past that simply does not exist in most secondary accounts. The difficulty for students is that historians read primary sources as pieces of conflicting testimony, not as overviews or stories of the past. Just as one would cross-examine a witness, primary documents call for series of litmus tests in order to assess their credibility. At the outset one needs to consider the type or kind of document itself. Diaries, journals, letters, official reports, speeches, census returns, newspaper editorials—all have their own strengths and limitations. Do diaries contain mostly fantasies or our deepest personal thoughts? Surprisingly in the nineteenth century when many Canadians still maintained diaries they simply recorded the weather. Would someone have been more likely to tell the truth in a letter to their mother or in an official report to their employer?

Some argue that the best types of documents are the least intentional, in other words those that someone scribbles without giving a second thought to who might eventually read it or respond to it. Others argue that publicly available or published documents are more credible since they would be subject to wider scrutiny and confirmation.

Next, it is useful to consider the place where the primary source was created. Was it composed in close proximity to the events it describes? If so, that suggests that the author had an appropriate vantage point from which to observe the events in question. One also needs to address the issue of time. Did the author write the document immediately after or during the event in question? Alternatively, did years go by before anything was recorded? Generally speaking, the longer the interval between observation and recording, the more likely that some details have been forgotten or adjusted to coincide with subsequent developments. Many memoirs or autobiographies suffer from this problem. While place and time may be relatively easy to determine, the prevailing cultural milieu in which a document was produced is far more problematic. Nowhere is this more obvious than in the area of language. A seventeenth-century French Canadian did not use the term "sauvage" in the same sense that we use the term "savage," nor did the Hudson's Bay Company mean what we understand when its officials commented upon having a "gay time" at New Year's.

Much less daunting is the basic question: what was the purpose of this document? Why did someone bother to create it? Did they need to convince someone of something, set the record straight, or justify an action? If there was a clear intent, it may indicate obvious bias. Next one looks at the audience for whom the document was intended. Different recipients may have conditioned the formalities of language, the way the events are described, and even the contents of the document. For example, in the highly competitive travel literature market, the publisher of James Cook's voyages inserted references to cannibalism among Natives of the West Coast simply due to the expectations of his European readers. He also turned what was a rather tedious ship's log into an adventure story.

However, nothing may be more important than the authors themselves. One needs to know how familiar they were with the subject being described and their ability to articulate their observations. Knowing that the average Canadian soldier in World War I had a grade six education has led to a number of comments about the limitations of their wartime journals. The position or occupation of authors may have also had an impact on their observations. Consider the document by the lawyer Charles Fitzpatrick, whose job it was to provide Louis Riel with the best defence possible. Lawyers are notorious for putting their clients' actions in the best light and arranging the facts to help their clients. To make matters still more complicated, one finds that age, gender, ethnicity, and class may have had a direct bearing on the contents of a primary document. Sociologists suggest that people tend to dwell disproportionally upon events that occurred in late adolescence or early adulthood. Would women have experienced the Great Depression differently than men? Evidence suggests that the pressure to maintain their role as breadwinner drove far more men to suicide in the 1930s than women. The document by HDP in Volume 2 also indicates that working-class women saw suffrage differently than their middle-class neighbours.

Next, one moves to the document itself. Does it provide facts or opinions? Does it rely on logic or emotional appeal? Does it exaggerate, distort, or omit vital information? Does it include details or generalizations? Does it contain contradictions? Does it demonstrate narrow-mindedness? Afterwards, and still much like adversarial legal proceedings, the historian considers corroborative evidence from other primary sources. Do they verify or contradict the account in question? With older documents, particularly from the Middle Ages, one confronts the question of authenticity. How do we know a particular document was not forged, plagiarized, or ghost written? Questions of accurate translation or transcription usually surround ancient documents, but a close look at the works of noted Canadian author Thomas Chandler Haliburton indicates how nineteenth-century Canadian authors shamelessly plagiarized from their British counterparts. In the end, we even need to ask questions about ourselves. Are modern biases and preconceptions distorting our view of historical documents? In other words, do we only accept what makes sense to us and fits our culture? Does our desire to explain the present distort our view of the past? Will different readers in our society get different impressions from this document? Do these documents have any relevance today? Why are they worth reading or saving?

Since history has often been referred to as a "soft "or "inexact" science, historians are deeply concerned with developing critical tests to justify not merely their interpretations but also their methods of arriving at them. Most students do not ordinarily question the historian's authority to explain what happened in the past and why. Yet, confronted with examples of divergent perspectives, they will realize the difficulty of creating history. Through primary sources students confront three essential facts. First, every document is created in a context—a particular place, a particular time, a particular culture, a particular situation—and must be examined with that context in mind. No document can be understood on its own, in a vacuum. Second, one must accept the fact that there is always more than one version of what actually happened. Third, students bring to the sources their own biases, created by their own personal situations and the social environments in which they live. In the end students need to realize that any history reflects an author's interpretations of past events. Therefore, it is subjective in nature. Finally, it may be worth adding that the ability to understand and make appropriate use of many sources of information is not restricted to historical research: it requires constant cultivation in our society where a sophisticated mass media assumes that advertising and political images can manipulate passive recipients.

# CHAPTER I

# "So Blind and So Ignorant"

## LOOKING INTO OTHER EYES

### INTRODUCTION

When did Canadian history begin? Certainly not with the arrival of Europeans. White contact was a pivotal event, but Indigenous cultures existed across the width and breadth of the continent for centuries prior. Thus, a volume of primary research materials on Canada's history should surely start with an examination of the cumulative knowledge Native people passed orally from generation to generation. Historians dealing with this early period, however, face a dilemma: some accept oral history as the Native equivalent to European documents and the sole means to reconstruct Native perspectives. Others demand traditional European "hard evidence," and therefore argue that the Indigenous interpretation of events is unknowable because documentation simply does not exist. In a recent landmark case, the Supreme Court of Canada ruled in favour of the legitimacy of Native oral history previously rejected as mere hearsay. Many historians remain uncomfortable with this legal precedent. Primary sources are typically eyewitness accounts created by specific individuals at specific times. They remain static in their original form for subsequent generations to assess. Oral history, meanwhile, evolves over time through its retelling and, for some historians, should be categorized as secondary, not primary evidence. Whether non-Natives are even capable of assessing the cultural context of Native oral history also raises serious evidentiary questions. Often classified as sacred and personal, some Native groups are now reluctant to share their histories with historians or anthropologists. Therefore, for better or worse, the documentary analysis in this volume begins with European accounts.

Unlike early explorers who had limited contact with North America and its inhabitants, French missionaries, soldiers, and administrators spent long periods not only observing and commenting upon the culture of local Native groups but also recording the words spoken by individual Natives.

But can two wildly different cultures accurately perceive or interpret one another? If they can, what are the limitations to using their evidence? What did Natives and Frenchmen see when they gazed upon each other for the first time? Early French records portrayed Native North Americans as "Noble Savages" from whom Europeans could learn much, but who could learn even more from Europeans—particularly about Catholicism and "civilization." Some adherents of this interpretation even stressed the "noble" prefix and elevated Native culture above French. Early eighteenth-century writers like Baron Lahontan, for example, transformed the Huron from a people who tortured their captives to "children of nature" and "noble savages" who lived in a blissful state of natural grace and harmony, unencumbered by the stultifying trappings of French culture. Historical descriptions changed with time. The "noble savages" imagery slowly gave way to pejorative depictions of a people who were "ruthless heathens" and not noble at all.

The extremely few recorded Native observations from this period remain highly suspect since they had to be translated and may reflect more what the recorder wished to hear than what truly represented the Native perspective. While "Adario" and the "Micmac Chief" may have been real, most historians contend that their discourses were most likely invented as a subtle means for their French authors to critique their own societies while evading censorship. Nor is this issue merely about the dangers of motivation. Native spoken words may have lost nuances when translated into written French and semantics evolve over time. The French word "sauvage," or "savage," for example, carried fewer negative connotations, and indeed some positive implications, in the seventeenth century. However, when we read the word with our modern sensibilities, we wince at what we perceive as European bigotry and cultural imperialism—which may be grossly unfair. As well, the voluminous annual missionary reports sent to Rome were heavily edited by priests who had never visited the New World and who wished to encourage further missionary endeavours.

Post-modernist historians claim that there is no objective "truth" because truth exists in the eye of the beholder and is therefore relative to everyone else's truth. They argue that it is impossible to distinguish between truth and falsehood since reality is up to the individual perceiving it, and ethnocentrism, among other things, hopelessly biased the Jesuit and other early accounts of Native people. To this group, the Jesuits' effort to understand Indigenous culture is entirely unacceptable and amounts to "cognitive imperialism" and "academic colonization." This post-modernist approach, not surprisingly, wholeheartedly supports using Native oral history, even by itself, because the oral tradition gives equal voice to players who were traditionally silenced. Furthermore, they say, because missionaries and their historians were, and are, cultural imperialists, oral history is an essential tool to correct the distorting biases promulgated by centuries of one-sided and agenda-laden interpretations.

It is, however, possible to make some tentative observations on the Native view. Historians can ascertain, for example, that some Natives converted, abandoning their traditional religious values for a new world view. Others accepted aspects of Christianity, though often not the central tenets, either for ideological reasons or because lip service to Catholicism improved trade. Most Indigenous people, however, generally clung to their religion as tenaciously as the missionaries tried to convert them. They repeatedly reaffirmed their own pantheon and strenuously resisted Christianity, either by avoiding the missionaries or by refusing to accept their teachings. They remained deeply suspicious of the message preached by the "Black Robes" and clearly recognized the cruel irony of an ideology that promised them heaven but delivered hell on both conceptual and physical levels as deadly European diseases, against which Natives lacked immunity, often arrived with the European clergy.

### DISCUSSION POINTS

1. Which aspects of Native society did Le Clerq and Lahontan admire? Which did they dislike? Did their descriptions serve to justify French domination and the conversion of Native people to Christianity?

2. Some argue that early Europeans never understood anything about Natives. Do the documents by Le Clerq and Lahontan tell us more about French society and its values than about Native culture?

3. From the perspective of the Micmac Chief and Adario, what impact did French colonization have upon the North American Native population?

4. What indicates that these Native speeches may have been fabricated?

5. Consider the audience for whom these accounts were published. At that time who had the ability to read? What would these readers have expected to find in literature from the New World? Would the characteristics of the reading public and their expectations have affected these accounts?

DOCUMENTS

### 1. Christien Le Clerq, *New Relations of Gaspesia*, 1691

*Le Clerq (1641-1700?), a Recollect priest, arrived in New France in 1675 and began an 11-year relationship with the Micmac in the Gaspé Peninsula, a people he called the "Gaspesians." Though not very successful at converting Natives to Christianity, and driven by doubts because of this, Le Clerq learned the local dialect, created a syllabic written version of it, and wrote the best early ethnographic study of these people.*

No matter what can be said of this reasoning, I assert, for my part, that I should consider these Indians incomparably more fortunate than ourselves, and that the life of these barbarians would even be capable of inspiring envy, if they had the instructions, the understanding, and the same means for their salvation which God has given us that we may save ourselves by preference over so many poor pagans, and as a result of His pity; for, after all, their lives are not vexed by a thousand annoyances as are ours. They have not among them those situations or offices, whether in the judiciary or in war, which are sought among us with so much ambition. Possessing nothing of their own, they are consequently free from trickery and legal proceedings in connection with inheritances from their relatives. The names of sergeant, of attorney, of clerk, of judge, or president are unknown to them. All their ambition centres in surprising and killing quantities of beavers, moose, seals, and other wild beasts in order to obtain their flesh for food and their skins for clothing. They live in very great harmony, never quarrelling and never beating one another except in drunkenness. On the contrary, they mutually aid one another in their needs with much charity and without self-seeking. There is continual joy in their wigwams. The multitude of their children does not embarrass them, for, far from being annoyed by these, they consider themselves just that much the more fortunate and richer as their family is more numerous.... [T]hey are also free from all those anxieties which we give ourselves in connection with the accumulation of property for the purpose of elevating children in society and in importance.... This duty, which in Europe is considered too onerous, is viewed by our Indians as very honorable, very advantageous, and very useful, and he who has the largest number of children is the most highly esteemed of the entire nation. This is because he finds more support for his old age, and because, in their condition in life, the boys and girls contribute equally to the happiness and joy of those who have given them birth....

It is certainly true that our Gaspesians had so little knowledge of bread and wine when the French arrived for the first time in their country, that these barbarians mistook the bread which was given them for a piece of birch tinder, and became convinced that the French were equally cruel and inhuman, since in their amusements, said the Indians, they drank blood without repugnance. It was thus they designated wine. Therefore they remained some time not only without tasting it, but even without wishing to become in any manner intimate, or to hold intercourse, with a nation which they believed to be accustomed to blood and carnage. Nevertheless, in the end, they became accustomed gradually to this drink, and it were to be wished that they had still today the same horror of wine and brandy, for they drink it even to drunkenness, to the prejudice of their salvation and of Christianity; and it makes them commit cruelties much greater than those which they had imagined in the conduct of the French....

The months of January and February are for these barbarians, as a rule, a time of involuntary penitence and very rigorous fasting, which is also often very sad as well, in view of the cruel and horrible results which it causes among them. Nevertheless they could very easily prevent its unfortunate consequences if they would but follow the example of the ants, and of the little squirrels, which, by an instinct as admirable as it is natural, accumulate with care in summer the wherewithal to subsist in plenty during the winter. But, after all, our Gaspesians are of those people who take no thought for the morrow, though this is much more because of laziness in collecting good provisions than through zeal in obeying the counsel which God has given thereon in His Holy Gospel. They are convinced that fifteen to twenty lumps of meat, or of fish dried and cured in the smoke, are more than enough to support them for the space of five to six months. Since, however, they are a people of good appetite, they consume their provisions very much sooner than they expect. This exposes them often to the danger of dying from hunger, through lack of provision which they could easily possess in abundance if they would only take the trouble to gather it. But these barbarians, being wanderers and vagabonds, do not plough the ground, nor do they harvest Indian corn, or peas, or pumpkins, as do the Iroquois, the Hurons, the Algonquins, and several other nations of Canada. In consequence they are sometimes reduced to so great need that they have neither the strength nor the spirit to leave their wigwams in order to go seek in the woods the wherewithal for living. It is then impossible to behold without compassion the innocent children, who, being nothing more than skin and bone, exhibit clearly enough in their wholly emaciated faces and in their living skeletons, the cruel hunger which they are suffering through the negligence of their fathers and mothers, who find themselves obliged, along with their unhappy children, to eat curdled blood, scrapings of skin, old moccasins, and a thousand other things incompatible with the life of man. All this would be little if they did not come sometimes to other extremes far more affecting and horrible.

...Those who imagine a Gaspesian Indian as a monster of nature will understand only with difficulty the charity with which they mutually comfort one another. The strong take pleasure in supporting the feeble; and those who by their hunting procure many furs, give some in charity to those who have none, either in order to pay the debts of these, or to clothe them, or to obtain for them the necessaries of life. Widows and orphans receive presents, and if there is any widow who is unable to support her children, the old men take charge of them, and distribute and give them to the best hunters, with whom they live, neither more nor less than as if they were the actual children of the wigwam. It would be a shame, and a kind of fault worthy of eternal reproach, if it was known that an Indian, when he had provisions in abundance, did not make gift thereof to those whom he knew to be in want and in need....

For it is true that these people are distinguished in their manner of living by an uncleanness which turns the stomach. I cannot believe that there is any nation in the world so disgusting in its manners of drinking and eating as the Gaspesian, excepting, perhaps, some other peoples of this new world. Hence it is true that of all the troubles which the missionaries suffer at first in order to accustom themselves to the manner of life of the Indians for the sake of instructing them in the maxims of Christianity, this is without a doubt one of the most difficult to endure, because it very often causes a rising of the stomach. Our Gaspesians never clean their kettles except the first time they use them, because, they say, they are afraid of the verdigris [copper sulphate], which is in no danger of attaching itself to them, when they are well greased and burnt. Nor do they ever skim it off, because it seems to them that this is removing grease from the pot, and just so much good material is lost. This causes the meat to be all stuffed with a black and thick scum, like little meat balls which have nearly the appearance of curdled milk. They content themselves with removing simply the largest moose hairs, although the meat may have been dragged around the campfire for five or six days, and the dogs also may have tasted it beforehand. They have no other tables than the flat ground, nor other napkins for wiping their hands than their moccasins, or their hair, on which they sedulously rub their hands. In a word there is nothing that is not rough, gross and repellent in the extraordinary manner of life of these barbarians, who observe neither in drinking nor in eating any rules of politeness or of civility....

The Gaspesians do not know how to read nor how to write. They have, nevertheless, enough understanding and memory to learn how to do both if only they were willing to give the necessary application. But aside from the fickleness and instability of their minds, which they are willing to apply only in so far as it pleases them, they all have the false and ridiculous belief that they would not live long if they were as learned as the French. From this it comes that they are pleased to live and to die in their natural ignorance.... [A]nd it can be said with truth that there are seen in Gaspesia as fine children, and persons as well built, as in France; whilst among them there are as a rule neither humpbacks nor crippled, one-eyed, blind, or maimed persons.

They enjoy a perfect health, not being subject to an infinity of diseases as we are. They are neither too stout nor too thin, and one does not see among the Gaspesians any of those fat bellies full of humours and of grease. Consequently the very names of gout, stone, gravel, gall, colic, rheumatism, are entirely unknown to them.

They all have naturally a sound mind, and common sense beyond that which is supposed in France. They conduct their affairs cleverly ... our Gaspesians can call themselves happy, because they have neither avarice nor ambition—those two cruel executioners which give pain and torture to a multitude of persons. As they have neither police, nor taxes, nor office, nor commandment which is absolute (for they obey, as we have said, only their head men and their chiefs in so far as it pleases them), they scarcely give themselves the trouble to amass riches, or to make a fortune more considerable than that which they possess in their woods. They are content enough provided that they have the wherewithal for living, and that they have the reputation of being good warriors and good hunters, in which they reckon all their glory and their ambition. They are naturally fond of their repose, putting away from them, as far as they can, all the subjects for annoyance which would trouble them. Hence it comes about that they never contradict anyone, and that they let everyone do as he pleases, even to the extent that the fathers and the mothers do not dare correct their children, but permit their misbehaviour for fear of vexing them by chastising them.

They never quarrel and never are angry with one another, not because of any inclination they have to practice virtue, but for their own satisfaction, and in the fear, as we have just said, of troubling their repose, of which they are wholly idolaters.

*"So Blind and So Ignorant": Looking into Other Eyes*

Indeed, if any natural antipathy exists between husband and wife, or if they cannot live together in perfect understanding, they separate from one another, in order to seek elsewhere the peace and union which they cannot find together. Consequently they cannot understand how one can submit to the indissolubility of marriage.... In a word, they hold it as a maxim that each one is free: that one can do whatever he wishes: and that it is not sensible to put constraint upon men. It is necessary, say they, to live without annoyance and disquiet, to be content with that which one has, and to endure with constancy the misfortunes.... In a word, they rely upon liking nothing, and upon not becoming attached to the goods of the earth, in order not to be grieved or sad when they lose them. They are, as a rule, always joyous, without being uneasy as to who will pay their debts....

It is not the same, however, when they are ill-treated without cause, for then everything is to be feared from them. As they are very vindictive against strangers, they preserve resentment for the ill-treatment in their hearts until they are entirely avenged for the injury or for the affront which will have been wrongly done them. They will even make themselves drunk on purpose, or they will pretend to be full with brandy, in order to carry out their wicked plan, imagining that they will always be amply justified in the crime which they have committed if they but say to the elders and heads of the nation, that they were tipsy, and that they had no reason or judgment during their drunkenness....

They are so generous and liberal towards one another that they seem not to have any attachment to the little they possess, for they deprive themselves thereof very willingly and in very good spirit the very moment when they know that their friends have need of it. It is true that this generous disposition is undergoing some alteration since the French, through the commerce which they have with them, have gradually accustomed them to traffic and not to give anything for nothing; for, prior to the time when trade came into use among these people, it was as in the Golden Age, and everything was common property among them.

They are naturally fickle, mockers, slanderers, and dissimulators. They are not true to their promises except in so far as they are restrained either by fear or by hope; and they believe any person would have no sense who would keep his word against his own interest.

...[I]n fact they do not know what civility is, nor decorum. Since they consider themselves all equal, and one as great, as powerful, and as rich as another, they mock openly at our bowings, at our compliments, and at our embracings. They never remove their hats when they enter our dwellings....

They are filthy and vile in their wigwams, of which the approaches are filled with excrements, feathers, chips, shreds of skins, and very often with entrails of the animals or the fishes which they take in hunting or fishing. In their eating they wash their meat only very superficially before putting it upon the fire, and they never clean the kettle except the first time that they use it. Their clothes are all filthy, both outside and inside, and soaked with oil and grease, of which the stink often produces sickness of the stomach. They hunt for vermin before everybody, without turning aside even a little. They make it walk for fun upon their hands, and they eat it as if it were something good. They find the use of our handkerchiefs ridiculous; they mock at us and say that it is placing excrements in our pockets. Finally, however calm it may be outside of the wigwam, there always prevails inside a very inconvenient wind, since these Indians let it go very freely, especially when they have eaten much moose....

There is no one, however, more to be pitied than the sick persons, who endure without complaint the hubbub, the noise, and the fuss of the juggler [somewhat analogous to a shaman] and of those in the wigwam. It seems indeed that our Gaspesians, who in other respects seem sufficiently humane and kindly, are lacking in regard to charity and consideration for their sick. It can in fact be said that they do not know how to take care of them, they give them indifferently everything which they desire, both to drink and to eat, and whenever they ask it. They take the sick persons along, and carry or embark them with themselves on their voyages when there is any appearance of recovery. But if the recovery of the sick man is wholly despaired of, so that he can no more eat, drink, nor smoke, they sometimes break his head, as much to relieve the suffering he endures as to save themselves the trouble which they have in taking him everywhere with them.

Nor have they any better idea what it means to comfort a poor invalid, and from the moment when he no longer eats or smokes any more tobacco, or when he loses speech, they abandon him entirely, and never speak to him a single word of tenderness or comfort....

## 2. Micmac Chief's Speech in Christien Le Clerq, *New Relations of Gaspesia*, 1691

*The dates and name of the "Micmac Chief" are unknown. Within Le Clerq's two-volume memoir of his long apostolate among the Micmac were a number of transcriptions of Native speeches, such as the following attributed to a local leader.*

I am greatly astonished that the French have so little cleverness, as they seem to exhibit in the matter of which thou hast just told me on their behalf, in the effort to persuade us to convert our poles, our barks, and our wigwams into those houses of stone and of wood which are tall and lofty, according to their account, as these trees. Very well! But why now, do men of five to six feet in height need houses which are sixty to eighty? For, in fact, as thou knowest very well thyself, Patriarch—do we not find in our own all the conveniences and the advantages that you have with yours, such as reposing, drinking, sleeping, eating, and amusing ourselves with our friends when we wish? This is not all, my brother, hast thou as much ingenuity and cleverness as the Indians, who carry their houses and their wigwams with them so that they may lodge wheresoever they please, independently of any seignior whatsoever? Thou art not as bold nor as stout as we, because when thou goest on a voyage thou canst not carry upon thy shoulders thy buildings and thy edifices. Therefore it is necessary that thou prepares as many lodgings as thou makest changes of residence, or else thou lodgest in a hired house which does not belong to thee. As for us, we find ourselves secure from all these inconveniences, and we can always say, more truly than thou, that we are at home everywhere, because we set up our wigwams with ease wheresoever we go, and without asking permission of anybody. Thou reproachest us, very inappropriately, that our country is a little hell in contrast with France, which thou comparest to a terrestrial paradise, inasmuch as it yields thee, so thou sayest, every kind of provision in abundance. Thou sayest of us also that we are the most miserable and most unhappy of all men, living without religion, without manners, without honour, without social order, and, in a word, without any rules, like the beasts in our woods and our forests, lacking bread, wine, and a thousand other comforts which thou hast in superfluity in Europe. Well, my brother, if thou dost not yet know the real feelings which our Indians have towards thy country and towards all thy nation, it is proper that I inform thee at once. I beg thee now to believe that, all miserable as we seem in thine eyes, we consider ourselves nevertheless much happier than thou in this, that we are very content with the little that we have; and believe also once for all, I pray, that thou deceivest thyself greatly if thou thinkest to persuade us that thy country is better than ours. For if France, as thou sayest, is a little terrestrial paradise, art thou sensible to leave it? And why abandon wives, children, relatives, and friends? Why risk thy life and thy property every year, and why venture thyself with such risk, in any season whatsoever, to the storms and tempests of the sea in order to come to a strange and barbarous country which thou considerest the poorest and least fortunate of the world? Besides, since we are wholly convinced of the contrary, we scarcely take the trouble to go to France, because we fear, with good reason, lest we find little satisfaction there, seeing, in our own experience, that those who are natives thereof leave it every year in order to enrich themselves on our shores. We believe, further, that you are also incomparably poorer than we, and that you are only simple journeymen, valets, servants, and slaves, all masters and grand captains though you may appear, seeing that you glory in our old rags and in our miserable suits of beaver which can no longer be of use to us, and that you find among us, in the fishery for cod which you make in these parts, the wherewithal to comfort your misery and the poverty which oppresses you. As to us, we find all our riches and all our conveniences among ourselves, without trouble and without exposing our lives to the dangers in which you find yourselves constantly through your long voyages. And, whilst feeling compassion for you in the sweetness of our repose, we wonder at the anxieties and cares which you give yourselves night and day in order to load your ship. We see also that all your people live, as a rule, only upon cod which you catch among us. It is everlastingly nothing but cod—cod in the morning, cod at midday, cod at evening, and always cod, until things come to such a pass that if you wish some good morsels, it is at our expense; and you are obliged to have recourse to the Indians, whom you despise so much, and to beg them to go a-hunting that you may be regaled. Now tell me this one little thing, if thou hast any sense: which of these two is the wisest and happiest—he who labours without ceasing and only obtains, and that with great trouble, enough to live on, or he who rests in comfort and finds all that he needs in the pleasure of hunting and fishing? It is true, that we have not always had the use of bread and of wine which your France produces; but, in fact, before the arrival of the French in these parts, did not the Gaspesians live much longer than now? And if we have not any longer among us any of those old men of a hundred and thirty to forty years, it is only because we are gradually adopting your manner of living, for experience is making it very plain that those of us live longest who, despising your bread, your wine, and your brandy, are content with their natural food of beaver, of moose, of waterfowl, and fish, in accord with the custom of our ancestors and of all the Gaspesian nation. Learn now, my brother, once for all, because I must open to thee my heart: there is no Indian who does not consider himself infinitely more happy and more powerful than the French.

### 3. Baron Lahontan, *Some New Voyages to North America*, 1703

*Louis Armand Lom D'Acre, Baron Lahontan (1666–prior to 1716) arrived in New France in 1683 as a member of the French Marine Corps. A restless adventurer, Lahontan aided Natives in their wars, explored, fought against the British, and finally deserted. Exiled to Holland, he wrote a very popular account of life in the New World. Although considered by many to be a combination of fact and fiction, the book was repeatedly republished.*

All the savages are of a Sanguine Constitution, inclining to an Olive Color, and generally speaking they have good Faces and proper Persons. It is a great rarity to find any among them that are Lame, Hunch-backed, One-eyed, Blind, or Dumb. Their Eyes are large and black as well as their Hair; their Teeth are White like Ivory, and the Breath that springs from their Mouth in expiration is as pure as the Air.... They are neither so strong nor so vigorous as most of the French are in raising of Weights with their Arms, or carrying of Burdens on their Backs; but to make amends for that, they are indefatigable and inured to Hardships, insomuch that the Inconveniences of Cold or Heat have no impression upon them; their whole time being spent in the way of Exercise, whether in running up and down at Hunting and Fishing, or in Dancing and playing at Football, or such Games as require the Motion of the Legs.

The Women are of an indifferent Stature, and as handsome in the Face as you can well imagine; but then they are so fat, unwieldy and ill-built, that they'll scarce tempt any but Savages. Their hair is rolled up behind with a sort of Ribbon, and that Roller hangs down to their Girdle; they never offer to cut their Hair during the whole Course of their Lives, whereas the Men cut theirs every Month.

The Savages are very Healthy, and unacquainted with an infinity of Diseases, that plague the *Europeans*, such as the *Palsey*, the *Dropsey*, the *Gout*, the *Phthisick*, the *Asthma*, the *Gravel*, and the *Stone*: But at the same time they are liable to the *Small-Pox*, and to *Pleurisies*. If a Man dies at the Age of Sixty Years, they think he dies young, for they commonly live to Eighty or an Hundred; nay, I met with two that were turned of an Hundred several Years. But there are some among them that do not live so long, because they voluntarily shorten their Lives by poisoning themselves....

The Savages are utter Strangers to distinctions of Property, for what belongs to one is equally another's. If anyone of them be in danger at the Beaver Hunting the rest fly to his Assistance without being so much as asked. If his Fuse bursts they are ready to offer him their own. If any of his Children be killed or taken by the Enemy, he is presently furnished with as many Slaves as he hath occasion for. Money is in use with none of them but those that are Christians, who live in the Suburbs of our Towns. The others will not touch or so much as look upon Silver, but give it the odious Name of the *French Serpent*. They'll tell you that amongst us the People Murder, Plunder, Defame, and betray one another, for Money, that the Husbands make Merchandize of their Wives, and the Mothers of their Daughters, for the Lucre of that Metal. They think it unaccountable that one Man should have more than another, and that the Rich should have more Respect than the Poor. In short, they say, the name of Savages which we bestow upon them would fit ourselves better, since there is nothing in our Actions that bears an appearance of Wisdom. Such as have been in France were continually teasing us with the Faults and Disorders they observed in our Towns, as being occasioned by Money. It is in vain to remonstrate to them how useful the Distinction of Property is for the support of a Society: They make a Jest of what's to be said on that Head. In fine, they neither Quarrel nor Fight, nor Slander one another. They scoff at Arts and Sciences, and laugh at the difference of Degrees which is observed with us. They brand us for Slaves, and call us miserable Souls, whose Life is not worth having.... That we degrade our selves in subjugating our selves to one Man who possesses the whole Power, and is bound by no Law but his Own Will; That we have continual Jars among our selves; that our Children rebel against their Parents; that we Imprison one another, and publically promote our Own Destruction. Besides, they value themselves above any thing that you can imagine, and this is the reason they always give forth, *That one's as much Master as another, and since Men are all made of the same Clay there should be no Distinction or Superiority among them.* They pretend that their contented way of living far surpasses Our Riches; that all Our Sciences are not so valuable as the Art of leading a peaceful calm Life. That a Man is not a Man with us any farther than Riches will make him; but among them the true Qualifications of a Man are to run well, to hunt, to bend the Bow and manage the Fuse, to work a Canoe, to understand War, to know Forests, to subsist upon a little, to build Cottages, to fell Trees, and to be able to travel an hundred Leagues in a Wood without any Guide, or other Provision than his Bow and Arrows. They say, we are great Cheats in selling them bad Wares four times dearer than they are worth, by way of Exchange for their Beaver skins: That our Fuses are continually bursting and laming them, after they have paid sufficient Prices for them.

The greatest Passion of the Savages consists in the Implacable Hatred they bear to their Enemies; that is, all Nations with whom they are at Open War: They value themselves mightily upon their Valour; insomuch that they have scarce any regard to any thing else. One may say that they are wholly governed by Temperament, and their Society is perfect Mechanism. They have neither Laws, Judges, nor Priests; they are naturally inclined to Gravity, which makes them very circumspect in their Words and Actions. They observe a certain Medium between Gayety and Melancholy. The *French* Air they could not away with; and there was none but the younger sort of them that approved of our Fashions.

They are as ignorant of *Geography* as of other *Sciences*, and yet they draw the most exact Maps imaginable of the Countries they're acquainted with, for there's nothing wanting in them but the Longitude and Latitude of Places: They set down the True *North* according to the *Pole Star*; The Ports, Harbours, Rivers, Creeks and Coasts, of the Lakes; the Roads, Mountains, Woods, Marshes, Meadows, and counting the distances by Journeys and Half-journeys of the Warriors, and allowing to every Journey Five Leagues. These *Chorographical Maps* are drawn upon the Rind of your Birch Tree; and when the Old Men hold a Council about War or Hunting, they're always sure to consult them.

This People cannot conceive that the *Europeans*, who value themselves upon their Sense and Knowledge, should be so blind and so ignorant as not to know that Marriage in their way is a source of Trouble and Uneasiness. To be engaged for one's Life time, to them is matter of Wonder and Surprise. They look upon it as a monstrous thing to be tied one to another without any hopes of being able to untie or break the Knot.

### 4. Adario's Conversation in Baron Lahontan,
*Some New Voyages to North America*, 1703

*This speech appeared in Baron Lahontan's memoir and may be an invention to facilitate criticism of French society without facing prosecution. More likely, "Adario" is a partial anagram for "Kondiaronk" (1649-1701), the great Huron diplomat whose orations Lahontan attended. Kondiaronk brokered treaties between Iroquois and other tribes, and Lahontan accused him of conspiring with the Iroquois against the French. Kondiaronk's skills, however, played a major role in the Great Peace of 1701, and, unlike Adario, he converted to Catholicism. Guests at his funeral mass included French soldiers, Huron and Ottawa warriors, clergymen, and even Montreal's governor.*

I am ready to hear thee, my dear Brother, in order to be informed of a great many things that the Jesuits have been Preaching up for a long time; and I would have us to discourse together with all the freedom that may be. If your Belief is the same with that of the Jesuits, it is in vain to enter into a Conference; for they have entertained me with so many Fabulous and Romantic Stories, that all the credit I can give them, is to believe, that they have more Sense than to believe themselves.

How do you mean, without the Knowledge of the True God? What! are you mad? Do thou believe we are void of Religion, after thou hast dwelt so long amongst us? Do'st not thee know in the first place, that we acknowledge a Creator of the Universe, under the Title of the Great Spirit or Master of Life; whom we believe to be in every thing, and to be unconfined to Limits? That we own the Immortality of the Soul. That the Great Spirit has furnished us with a Rational Faculty, capable of distinguishing Good from Evil, as much as Heaven from Earth; to the end that we might Religiously observe the true Measures of Justice and Wisdom.... This my dear Friend is Our Belief, and act up to it with the greatest Exactness. We believe that we shall go to the Country of Souls after death; but we have no such apprehension as you have, of a good and bad Mansion after this Life, provided for the good and bad Souls; for we cannot tell whether every thing that appears faulty to Men, is so in the Eyes of God. If your Religion differs from ours, it does not follow that we have none at all. Thou knowest that I have been in *France, New York* and *Quebec*; where I Studied the Customs and Doctrines of the *English* and *French*. The *Jesuits* allege, that out of five or six hundred sorts of Religions, there's only one that is the good and the true Religion, and that's their own; out of which no Man shall escape the Flames of a Fire that will burn his Soul to all Eternity. This is their allegation: But when they have said all, they cannot offer any Proof for it.

How do you mean, *without contradicting one another!* Why! That Book of Holy Things, is not it full of Contradictions? These Gospels that the Jesuits speak of, do not they occasion discord between the *French* and the *English*? And yet if we take your word for it, every Period of that Book Sprung from the Mouth of the Great Spirit. But if the Great Spirit meant that his Words should be understood, why did he talk so confusedly, and clothe his Words with an ambiguous Sense? One or two things must follow from this advance. If he was born and died upon the Earth, and made speeches here, why, then his discourses must be lost; for he would certainly have spoke so distinctly and plainly, that the very Children might conceive his meaning. Or, if you will have the Gospels to be his genuine Words, and contain nothing but what flowed from him; why, then he must have come to raise Wars in the World instead of Peace; which cannot be. The *English* have told me that though their Gospels contain the same Words with the French, yet there's as great a difference between their Religion and yours, as between Night and Day. They say positively that their's is the best; and on the other hand, the

Jesuits allege, that the Religion of the *English*, and of a thousand Nations besides, is good for nothing. If there be but one true Religion upon Earth, who must I believe in this case? Who is it that do's not take their own Religion to be the most perfect? How can the Capacity of Man be able to single out that Divine Religion from among so many more, that lay claim to the same Title? Believe me, my dear Brother, the Great Spirit is Wise, all his Works are perfect; 'tis he that made us, and he knows perfectly well what will become of us. It is our part to act freely, without perplexing our thoughts about future things. He ordered thee to be Born in *France*, with intent that thou shouldest believe what thou neither seest nor conceivest; and me he has caused to be Born a *Huron*, to the end that I should give credit to nothing but what I understand, and what my reason teaches me.

I perceive then, the words of the Son of the Great Spirit are chargeable with self-contradiction or obscurity; for as much as you and the *English* dispute about his meaning with so much heat and animosity: And this seems to be the principal spring of the hatred that these two Nations bear to one another. But that is not what I insist upon.

As for my own part, I have always maintained that if it were possible that the Great Spirit ... to descend to the Earth, he had shown himself to all the In-habitants of the Earth; he had descended in Triumph, and in public view, with Splendor and Majesty; he had raised the dead, restored sight to the blind, made the lame to walk upright, cured all the diseases upon the Earth: In fine, he had spoke and commanded all that he had a mind to have done, he had gone from Nation to Nation to work these great Miracles, and to give the same Laws to the whole World. Had he done so, we had been all of the same Religion, and that great Uniformity, spread over the face of the Earth, would be a lasting Proof ... the truth of a Religion that was known and received with equal approbation in the four Corners of the Earth. But instead of that Uniformity, we find five or six hundred Religions, among which that Professed by the *French*, is according to your argument the only true one, the only one that is good and holy.

For when they allege that God, ... could produce a Son under the Figure of a Man: I am ready to reply, that a Woman can't bring forth a Beaver; by reason that in the course of Nature, every species produces its like. Besides, if before the coming of the Son of God all men were devoted to the Devil, what reason have we to think that he would assume the form of such creatures....

In the next place, as for working on the days set apart for worship, I do not find that you make any difference between Holy-Days and Work-Days; for I have frequently seen the *French* bargain for Skins on your Holy-Days, as well as make Nets, Game, Quarrel, beat one another, get Drunk, and commit a hundred extravagant Actions.

And as to the business of lying, I affirm it for a truth, that there is not one Merchant in this Country that will not tell you twenty Lies in felling the worth of a Beaver's Skin in Goods....

You feel we have no Judges; and what's the reason of that? Why? We neither quarrel nor sue one another. And what's the reason that we have no Law Suits? Why? Because we are resolved neither to receive nor to know Silver.

Ha! Long live the Hurons; who without Laws, without Prisons, and without Torture, pass their Life in a State of Sweetness and Tranquility, and enjoy a pitch of Felicity to which the French are utter Strangers. We live quietly under the Laws of Instinct and innocent Conduct, which wise Nature has imprinted upon our Minds from our Cradles. We are all of one Mind; our Wills, Opinions and Sentiments observe an exact Conformity; and thus we spend our Lives with such a perfect good understanding, that no Disputes or Suits can take place amongst us....

[T]he *French*, who like Beasts, love only to eat and to drink, and have been brought up to Softness and Effeminacy. Pray thee, tell me what difference there is between lying in a good Hut, and lying in a Palace; between Sleeping under a Cover of Beaver-Skins, and Sleeping under a Quilt between two Sheets; between Eating Boiled and Roast Meat, and feeding upon dirty Pies, Ragou's, and dressed by your great Scullions? Are we liable to more Disorders and Sickness than the French, who are accommodated with these Palaces, Beds and Cooks? But after all, how many are there in *France* that lye upon Straw in Garrets where the Rain comes in on all hands, and that are hard put to find Victuals and Drink? I have been in France, and speak from what I have seen with my Eyes. You rally without reason, upon our Clothes made of Skins, for they are warmer, and keep out the Rain better than your Cloth; besides, they are not so ridiculously made as your Garments....

You conclude, in pretending that the *French* prevent our Misery by taking pity of us. But pray consider how our Ancestors lived an hundred years ago: They lived as well without your Commodities as we do with them; for instead of your Fire-Locks, Powder and Shot, they made use of Bows and Arrows, as we do to this day: They made Nets of the Thread of the Barks of Trees, Axes of Stone; Knives, Needles and Awls of Stag or Elk-Bones; and supplied the room of Kettles with Earthen Pots. Now, since our Ancestors lived without these Commodities for so many Ages; I am of the Opinion, we could dispense with them easier than the *French* could with our Beaver Skins; for which, by a mighty piece of Friendship, they give us in exchange Fuses, that burst and Lame many of our Warriors, Axes that break in the cutting of a Shrub, Knives that turn Blunt, and lose their Edge in the cutting of a Citron; Thread which is half Rotten, and so very bad that our Nets are worn out as soon as they are made; and Kettles so thin and slight, that the very weight of Water makes the Bottoms fall out....

What signifies your Pepper, your Salt, and a thousand other Spices, unless it be to murder your Health? Try our way of living but one fortnight, and then you'll long for no such doings. What harm can you fear from the Painting of your Face with Colors? You daub your Hair with Powder and Essence....

Ay, most certainly, you are of a different Mould from us; for your Wines, your Brandy, and your Spices, make us Sick unto death; whereas you can't live forsooth without such Drugs: Besides, your Blood is Salt and ours is not; you have got Beards, and we have none. Nay farther; I have observed that before you pass the Age of thirty five or forty, you are Stronger and more Robust than we; for we can't carry such heavy Loads as you do till that Age; but after that your Strength dwindles and visibly declines, whereas ours keeps to its wonted pitch till we Count fifty five or sixty years of Age. This is a truth that Our young Women can vouch for. They tell you that when a young *French-man* obliges them six times a night, a young *Huron* do's not rise to above half the number; and with the same Breath they declare, that the *French* are older in that Trade at thirty five, than the *Hurons* are at fifty years of Age.

### FURTHER READINGS

Anderson, K. *Chain Her by One Foot: The Subjugation of Women in Seventeenth-Century New France*. London: Routledge, 1991.

Axtell, J. *After Columbus: Essays in the Ethnohistory of Colonial North America*. New York: Oxford University Press, 1988.

Axtell, J. *The Invasion Within: The Contest of Cultures in Colonial North America*. New York: Oxford University Press, 1985.

Blackburn, C. *Harvest of Souls: The Jesuit Missions and Colonization in North America, 1632-1650*. Montreal and Kingston: McGill-Queen's University Press, 2000.

Delage, D. *Bitter Feast: Amerindians and Europeans in Northeastern North America, 1600-1664*. Vancouver: University of British Columbia Press, 1993.

Dickason, O. *The Myth of the Savage and the Beginnings of French Colonialism in the Americas.* Edmonton: University of Alberta Press, 1984.

Goddard, P. "Converting the Sauvage: Jesuit and Montagnais in Seventeenth-Century New France." *Catholic Historical Review* 84, 2 (April 1998): 219-39.

Grant, J. *Moon of Wintertime: Missionaries and the Indians of Canada in Encounter since 1534.* Toronto: University of Toronto Press, 1984.

Jaenen, C. *Friend and Foe: Aspects of French-Amerindian Cultural Contact in the Sixteenth and Seventeenth Century.* Toronto: McClelland and Stewart, 1976.

Morrison, K. *The Embattled Northeast: The Elusive Ideal of Alliance in Abenaki-Euramerican Relations.* Oakland: University of California Press, 1984.

Morrison, K. "Montagnais Missionization in Early New France." *American Indian Culture and Research Journal* 10, 3 (1986): 1-23.

Rhonda, J. "We Are As We Are: An Indian Critique of Seventeenth-Century Christian Missions." *William and Mary Quarterly* 3, 34 (1977): 66-82.

Richter, D. *The Ordeal of the Longhouse: The Peoples of the Iroquois League in the Era of European Colonization.* Chapel Hill: University of North Carolina Press, 1992.

Sayre, G. *Les Sauvages Americaines: Representations of Native Americans in French and English Colonial Literature.* Chapel Hill: University of North Carolina Press, 1997.

Trigger, B. *The Children of Aataentsic: A History of the Huron People to 1660.* Montreal and Kingston: McGill-Queen's University Press, 1976.

Trigger, B. *Natives and Newcomers: Canada's Heroic Age Reconsidered.* Montreal and Kingston: McGill-Queen's University Press, 1985.

Warkentin, G., and C. Podruchny, Eds. *Decentering the Renaissance: Canada and Europe in Multidisciplinary Perspective, 1500-1700.* Toronto: University of Toronto Press, 2001.

# CHAPTER 2

# "Advantages and Inconveniences"

## THE COLONIZATION OF CANADA

### INTRODUCTION

W hat role did France see for its North American possessions within the context of the wider French empire and the geo-political realities of the seventeenth and eighteenth centuries? The answer depends upon many factors and changes with time. Thus, Champlain's aims and objectives in 1608, when he founded New France on the banks of the St. Lawrence, varied considerably from Denonville's more than half a century later. New rulers, circumstances, and philosophies shifted world views and led to different emphasis and opportunities. The following documents, however, illustrate the evolution of common threads that cumulatively weave a tapestry of French aspirations, successes, fears, and failures with their colony of New France.

Samuel de Champlain returned to Canada in 1608 after an abortive attempt to settle in present-day Nova Scotia. This time he and his crew settled at what is now Quebec City where they founded New France. It was a logical location: defensible, hopefully at the entrance to the transcontinental passage, close to Native allies, and with good agricultural potential. Problems immediately emerged, however. As with the first settlement efforts at Port Royale, the newcomers suffered terribly from scurvy, cold, hunger, isolation, and internal conflict. Then Champlain supported his new Huron friends by launching a series of raids against their Iroquois enemies, thereby embroiling New France in a desperate conflict that raged for the next half century. It was indeed an inauspicious beginning, and while his promotionally minded dispatches outlined his hopes and dreams for New France, their realization is a matter for debate. Certainly settlement began, but to what extent? His little post clung to life and even disappeared entirely for several years after an attack by English privateers led by the Kirke brothers. Agriculture essentially did not exist by the end of Champlain's life, despite his best efforts, but the fur trade did expand and became New France's economic lifeblood.

The crux of the problem was the fundamentally ambiguous and contradictory nature of the colony's purpose: to be settled and Frenchified under the king's auspices while simultaneously generating profit for private companies that received a monopoly over the area with the proviso that they absorb the expenses. The king followed this policy in order to save state funds, but the system virtually guaranteed colonial development that put profit before investment, despite the trade monopoly stipulation. Simply put, colonizing was expensive, requiring a significant investment in finding, transporting, and settling immigrants, who then needed an extensive and costly support infrastructure at the other end. A handful of traders in a fort, however, could generate huge dividends from the fur trade with minimal investment.

Nor were entrepreneurs the only ones balking at settling New France. Emigration, too, remained a hard-sell. North America, after all, generated horror stories of "savages," monsters, and desperate winters, and was far removed from the perceived security and community of France. To be uprooted from their known world remained frightening to an overwhelmingly illiterate and superstitious French populace. And those who did come? They faced two alternatives: years of lonely, backbreaking work creating economically marginal farms or the siren call of the fur trade with its *bonhomie*, romance, and supposed easy profit. The cumulative result was desperately slow settlement and a transient, male-dominated French population out to make a quick buck before retiring back to France. This was unlike the situation in the New England colonies to the south where settlement proceeded apace and along very different lines.

Prevailing seventeenth-century economic models also discouraged a vibrant New France. Mercantilism held that colonies supplied raw materials and never competed against home-country businesses. Thus, economic diversification along the St. Lawrence remained very difficult as French businessmen zealously guarded their interests and encouraged colonial administrators to shut down perceived competitors. New France thereby had to rely upon French imports for virtually everything but the homegrown bare essentials. This led to a debilitating negative cash flow from the colony to the motherland just as French commercial leaders demanded. Mercantilism indeed tolled the death knell to any chance of colonial self-sufficiency. If that was not bad enough, transportation costs drove prices upward, and the St. Lawrence froze for many months, halting most trade for a good part of every year. Last, but certainly not least, interminable raids by the Iroquois, culminating in the brutal destruction of Huronia in the 1640s, all but killed New France by strangling the fur trade.

Things improved when Louis XIV, the dynamic and aggressive young "Sun King," made New France a royal province in 1663 after repeated pleas of support from settlers. Regal sanction constituted a major psychological, financial, and sociological boost to the fledgling settlement and guaranteed a measure of stability heretofore unknown. The royal province of New France received access to state funds, security forces, and the same administration as French provinces. This affected the little colony's administrative tone because religious grounds for maintaining New France became secondary to commerce. The new structure did foster growth, and the boundaries of the colony ballooned for commercial and military reasons. Intendant Jean Talon established an exploration program that annexed the heart of modern Canada, the Ohio country of the present United States, and the river network flowing southward to the Gulf of Mexico and France's possession of Louisiana. The expansion offered New France a back door to the St. Lawrence, prevented England from moving westward, and opened up new trade areas with Native people. It also meant, at least in theory, that New England found itself hemmed in by hostile French territory.

Mercantilism remained the economic order of the day throughout this phase, but in a slightly different guise: private enterprise, not the state, took more responsibility to fund and fuel trade and progress. Government still encouraged expansion, but not at the expense of the royal purse. This was, in other words, an era of cutbacks, restraint, cost-cutting, and His Majesty's bureaucrats doing more with less. The emphasis became political stability and peaceful commercial rivalry and coexistence with the old foe England, despite suspecting the illusory nature of that peace. Commercial success should now spring from a closely integrated empire with vibrant trade between all French Atlantic possessions, plus less emphasis on the fur trade in favour of agriculture and industry. This policy did, in fact, see some success.

### DISCUSSION POINTS

1. List the potential benefits colonization of Canada had for France. What impediments had to be overcome?

2. Did the French image of Canada remain the same or change between 1618 and 1737? What trends, if any, emerged in these views?

3. According to these documents, in what respect was life in New France different from that in France? Would an average French citizen have been better off in Canada or not?

4. Which of these accounts seem most reliable? Least?

DOCUMENTS

### 1. Samuel de Champlain, "To the King and the Lords of His Council," 1618

*Samuel de Champlain (1570?-1635) was an excellent cartographer, experienced explorer, and an ardent French patriot who wanted to see France expand. From his post at Quebec he set about establishing both a sustained fur trade and permanent settlement. The former led to an alliance with the Huron and Algonkians against the Iroquois. Never learning to swim, he still crossed the Atlantic 21 times in his quest to generate support for New France since there was always a shortage of settlers, money, and royal support. He was among the first Europeans to place an emphasis on Canada's obvious natural resources rather than the gold and diamonds that men like Cartier expected to find. Despite considerable hardship he also preferred to live in Canada rather than France, although his wife spent only four years with him at Quebec.*

Sire: The Sieur de Champlain represents to you most humbly that for sixteen years he has toiled with laborious zeal as well in the discoveries of New France as of divers peoples and nations whom he has brought to our knowledge, who had never been discovered save by him; which peoples have given him such and so faithful report of the north and south seas that one cannot doubt but that this would be the means of reaching easily to the Kingdom of China and the East Indies, whence great riches could be drawn; besides planting there the divine worship ... in addition to the abundance of merchandise from the said country of New France.... Should this said country be given up and the settlement abandoned, for want of bestowing upon it the needed attention, the English or Flemings, envious of our prosperity, would seize upon it, thereby enjoying the fruits of our labours, and preventing by this means more than a thousand vessels from going to the dry and green fisheries, and for whale-oil....

　　Firstly.—His said Majesty will establish the Christian faith among an infinite number of souls, who neither hold nor possess any form of religion whatsoever, and nevertheless wish only for the knowledge of divine and human worship, according to the reports of all those who have made the voyage to the said New France.

Secondly.—The King will make himself master and lord of a country nearly eighteen hundred leagues in length, watered by the fairest rivers in the world and by the greatest and most numerous lakes, the richest and most abundant in all varieties of fish that are to be found, and full also of the greatest meadows, fields, and forests, for the most part of walnut-trees, and very pleasant hills upon which there is found a great abundance of wild vines, which yield grapes as large as or larger than ours, cultivated as these are.

Thirdly.—The Sieur de Champlain undertakes to discover the South Sea passage to China and to the East Indies by way of the river St. Lawrence, which traverses the lands of the said New France, and which river issues from a lake about three hundred leagues in length, from which lake flows a river that empties into the said South Sea, according to the account given to the said Sieur de Champlain by a number of people, his friends in the said country; whom he has visited and become acquainted with, having ascended the said river St. Lawrence for more than four hundred leagues into the said lake of three hundred leagues in length, on which voyage he found numerous fortified towns, encircled and enclosed with wooden palisades ... which towns can furnish two thousand men armed after their fashion; others less.

That His said Majesty would derive a great and notable profit from the taxes and duties he could levy on the merchandise coming from the said country, according to the memorial submitted, as likewise from the customs' duties on the merchandise that would come from China and from the Indies, which would surpass in value at least ten times all those levied in France, inasmuch as all the merchants of Christendom would pass through the passage sought by the Sieur de Champlain, if it please the King to grant them leave to do so, in order to shorten the said journey by more than a year and a half, without any risk from pirates and from the perils of the sea and of the voyage, on account of the great circuit it is necessary now to make, which brings a thousand inconveniences to merchants and travellers....

The Sieur de Champlain humbly begs to be heard concerning certain facts which he wishes to present to you for the honour and glory of God, for the increase of this realm and for the establishment of a great and permanent trade in New France, as is specified in the following articles:

The advantage that would accrue in the first place from the cod-fishery, which would be carried on annually thanks to the permanent settlement of the people inhabiting the said country of New France, where salt could be made in considerable quantity, and two kinds of fishing could be carried on, namely dry and green, ... and through the industry of the fishermen more than a million livres would be earned annually.

Likewise the salmon fishery, which fish are in such abundance in the harbours and rivers that one could produce annually 100,000 livres.

Likewise the sea-sturgeon fishery, as also that of the sea-trout, which are so abundant in most places that they might be sold ... in regions where this fish is much in demand, annually for 100,000 livres.

Likewise eels, sardines, herrings and other fish are so plentiful that there could be obtained annually for 100,000 livres.

Likewise the whale-oils, in which the country abounds of which one can make in the said country annually to the value of 200,000 livres.

Likewise whale-bone from the said whales, and walrus-tusks, which are better than elephant's teeth ... and an abundance of seals; and of these commodities there might be taken annually to the value of 500,000 livres.

Likewise from the forests, which are of marvellous height, a number of good vessels might be built, which could be laden with the above-mentioned merchandise and other commodities, as will be stated below. From the said forests could be made ships' masts of several sizes, beams, joists, planks of many varieties, such as oak, elm, beech, walnut, plane, maple, birch, cedar, cypress, chestnut, hemlock, pine, fir and other woods; there could be made stave-wood, sawed oak for window frames and wainscoting and for other interior decoration, for which the most part of the said woods are suitable; and there would be obtained from them annually to the value of 400,000 livres.

Likewise there could be obtained a quantity of gum, the smell of which resembles incense.

Likewise of the useless woods one could make ashes, from which there could be obtained annually to the value of 400,000 livres.

From the pines and firs could be obtained pitch, tar and resin to the value annually of 100,000 livres.

As for the nature of the soil, it is certain that it yields to the native tillers corn, maize, beans, peas, roots the dye of which makes a colour similar to cochineal; and if the said root were cultivated one could obtain from it annually to the value of 400,000 livres.

Likewise a notable profit could be gained from the hemp, which the same soil yields without cultivation and which in quality and texture is in wise inferior to ours; and there could be obtained from it annually to the value of 300,000 livres.

In addition is to be considered the profits to be derived from several kinds of mines, such as those of silver and iron which yields 45 per cent., lead which yields 30 per cent., copper 18 per cent., and whatever other minerals, or things not yet come to our knowledge which a permanent settlement in the country may discover; and there could be derived from the said mines annually more than 1,000,000 livres.

Likewise cloths, such as sail-cloths, could be made from the hemp of the said country; as well as cables, ropes, and rigging for all sorts of vessels, to the value of more than 400,000 livres.

Likewise the traffic and trade in furs is not to be scorned, not only marten, beaver, fox, lynx and other skins, but also deer, moose and buffalo robes, which are commodities from which one can derive at present more than 400,000 livres.

Likewise from the said country can be obtained marble, jasper, alabaster, porphyry and other kinds of valuable stones; and a notable profit may be made therefrom.

Vines are in abundance in the said country, which the soil yields of itself; and if they were cultivated they would yield great profits; as likewise corn and other things, which the permanent settlements will be able to supply through the industry of the inhabitants of the said country.

Besides all these things one may expect in the future the same abundance of cattle that is seen in Peru since the Spaniards introduced them there ... and from the Spaniards' account more than a million in gold is obtained annually from the hides. For New France is so well watered everywhere that the fertility of the meadows ensures the feeding and multiplying of the said cattle, whenever they are introduced here....

### 2. Pierre Boucher, *True and Genuine Description of New France Commonly Called Canada*, 1664

*Boucher (1622–1717) arrived in New France in 1635 and assisted the Jesuits in Huronia until 1644. He learned Native languages and became the interpreter for the French garrison, rising through the ranks to become governor of Trois Rivière in 1661. That year he also brought the appeals of New France Habitants to the king of France, the young Louis XIV, who made the colony a royal province in 1663. Thus, Boucher was instrumental in saving the colony from oblivion. He returned to New France and remained a central figure for the rest of his long life. Boucher believed that Frenchmen should unite with Native people and set an example by marrying a Huron woman.*

... But how can we make money there? What can we get out of it all? This is a question that has often been put to me, and that gave me an inclination to laugh every time it was put to me; I seemed to see people who wanted to reap a harvest before they had sowed any thing. After having said that the country is a good one, capable of producing all sorts of things, like France, that it is healthy, that population only is wanting, that the country is very extensive, and that without doubt there are great riches in it which we have not been able to bring to light, because we have an enemy who keeps us pent up in a little corner and prevents us from going about and making discoveries; and so he will have to be destroyed, and many people will have to come into this country, and then we shall know the riches of it; but some one will have to defray the cost of all this; and who shall do it if not our good King? He has shown an inclination to do it, and may God be pleased to keep him still of the same mind.

Our neighbours, the English, laid out a great deal of money at the outset on the settlements they made; they threw great numbers of people into them; so that now there are computed to be in them fifty thousand men capable of bearing arms; it is a wonder to see their country now; one finds all sorts of things there, the same as in Europe, and for half the price. They build numbers of ships, of all sorts and sizes; they work iron mines; they have beautiful cities; they have stage-coaches and mails from one to the other; they have carriages like those in France; those who laid out money there, are now getting good returns from it; that country is not different from this; what has been done there could be done here....

It seems to me that I hear some one say: "you have told us much about the advantages of New France but you have not shown us its disadvantages, nor its inconveniences, yet we know well that there is not a country in the world however good it may be, in which something that is disagreeable is not met with." I answer that you are right. It has been my study all along to make these things known to you; but in order to enable you to understand them more clearly, I shall here specify in detail what I consider the most troublesome and disagreeable things....

The first is that our enemies, the Iroquois keep us so closely pent up that they hinder us from enjoying the advantages of the country. We cannot go to hunt or fish without danger of being killed or taken prisoners by those rascals; and we cannot even plough out fields, much less make hay, without continual risk: They lie in ambush on all sides, and any little thicket suffices for six or seven of those barbarians to put themselves under cover in, or more correctly speaking in an ambush, from which they throw themselves upon you suddenly when you are at your work, or going to it or coming from it. They never attack but when they are the strongest; if they are the weakest they do not say a word; if by accident they are discovered they fly, leaving every thing behind them; and as they are fleet of foot it is difficult to catch them; so you see we are always in dread, and a poor fellow does not work in safety if he has to go ever so little a way off to his work. Wives are always uneasy lest their husbands, who have gone away to their work in the morning, should be killed or taken prisoners and they should never see them again; and these Indians are the cause of the greater number of our settlers being poor, not only through our not being able to enjoy the advantages of the country as I have just said, but because they often kill cattle, sometimes hinder the gathering in of the harvest, and at other times burn and plunder houses when they can take people by surprise. This is a great evil, but it is not beyond remedy, and we expect one from the benevolence of our good King, who has told me that he wishes to deliver us from it. It would not be very difficult to do so, for there are not among them more than eight hundred or nine hundred men capable of bearing arms. It is true they are warlike men, and very dexterous at fighting in the woods; they have given proof of this to our Commanders from France who despised them; some of these were killed and others were forced to admit that one must not neglect to take precautions when one goes to war with them, that they understand the business, and that on this score they are not barbarians; but after all a thousand or twelve hundred men well led would give occasion for its being said, "they were but they are not"; and to have exterminated a tribe that has caused so many others to perish and is the terror of all these countries, would raise the reputation of the French very high throughout New France....

Here is another set of questions that have been put to me, namely: how we live in this country whether justice is administered, if there is not great debauchery, seeing that numbers of worthless fellows and bad girls come here, it is said.

I will answer all these questions one after the other, beginning with the last. It is not true that those sort of girls come hither, and those who say so have made a great mistake, and have taken the Islands of Saint Christophe and Martinique for New France; if any of them come here, they are not known for such; for before any can be taken on board ship to come here some of their relations or friends must certify that they have always been well-behaved; if by chance there are found among those who have, some who are in disrepute, or who are said to have misconducted themselves on the voyage out, they are sent back to France.

As for the scapegraces, if any come over it is only because they are not known for what they are, and when they are in the country they have to live like decent people, otherwise they would have a bad time of it; we know how to hang people in this country as well as they do elsewhere, and we have proved it to some who have not been well behaved.

Justice is administered here, and there are Judges; and those who are not satisfied with their decisions can appeal to the Governor and the Sovereign Council, appointed by the King, and sitting at Quebec.

Hitherto we have lived pleasantly enough, for it has pleased God to give us Governors who have all been good men, and besides we have had the Jesuit Fathers who take great pains to teach the people what is right so that all goes on peaceably; we live much in the fear of God, and nothing scandalous takes place without its being put to rights immediately; there is great religious devotion throughout the country.

Several persons after having heard me speak of New France, whether they felt inclined to come to it or not, have put these questions to me: "Do you think I would be fit for that country? What would have to be done in order to get there? If I took four or five thousand francs with me, could I with such a sum make myself tolerably comfortable?" And after these several other questions which I shall mention after having answered these.

You ask me in the first place whether you are fit for this country. The answer I make you is that this country is not yet fit for people of rank who are extremely rich, because such people would not find in it all the luxuries they enjoy in France; such persons must wait until this country has more inhabitants, unless they are persons who wish to retire from the world in order to lead a pleasant and quiet life free from fuss, or who are inclined to immortalize themselves by building cities or by other great works in this new world.

The people best fitted for this country are those who can work with their own hands in making clearings, putting up buildings and otherwise; for as men's wages are very high here, a man who does not take care and practice economy will be ruined; but the best way is always to begin by clearing land and making a good farm, and to attend to other things only after that has been done, and not to do like some whom I have seen, who paid out all their money for the erection of fine buildings which they had to sell afterwards for less than the cost.

I am supposing myself to be speaking to persons who would come to settle in this country with a view to making a living out of it, and not to trade.

It would be well for a man coming to settle, to bring provisions with him for at least a year or two years if possible, especially flour which he could get for much less in France and could not even be sure of being always able to get for any money here; for if many people should come from France in any year without bringing any flour with them and the grain crops should be bad here that year, which God forbid, they would find themselves much straitened.

It would be well also to bring a supply of clothes, for they cost twice as much here as they do in France.

Money is also much dearer; its value increases one third, so that a coin of fifteen sous is worth twenty, and so on in proportion.

I would advise a man having money enough to bring two labouring men with him, or even more if he has the means, to clear his land; this is in answer to the question whether a person having three thousand or four thousand francs to employ here could do so with advantage; such a person could get himself into very easy circumstances in three or four years if he choose to practice economy, as I have already said.

Most of our settlers are persons who came over in the capacity of servants, and who, after serving their masters for three years, set up for themselves. They had not worked for more than a year before they had cleared land on which they got in more than enough grain for their food. They have but little, generally when they set up for themselves, and marry wives who are no better off than they are; yet if they are fairly hard working people you see them in four or five years in easy circumstances and well fitted out for persons of their condition in life.

Poor people would be much better off here than they are in France, provided they are not lazy; they could not fail to get employment and could not say, as they do in France, that they are obliged to beg for their living because they cannot find any one to give them work; in one word, no people are wanted, either men or women, who cannot turn their hands to some work, unless they are very rich.

Women's work consists of household work and of feeding and caring for the cattle; for there are few female servants; so that wives are obliged to do their own house work; nevertheless those who have the means employ valets who do the work of maidservants....

The land is very high in relation to the river, but quite level. The little of it that is under cultivation produces very good grain and vegetables but is not fit for fruit trees that do not grow in clayey soil. There is eel fishing, but it is not plentiful. There are all types of wood, which are sold at Quebec....

In relation to the great size of the settlement, there is not one-quarter of the workmen required to clear and cultivate the land.

Farmers do not cultivate the land with enough care. It is certain that one *minot* as sown in France would produce more than two as sown in Canada.

Since the seasons are too short and there is much bad weather, it would be desirable that the Church allow the performance of essential works on feast days. There are not ninety working days left from May, when sowing begins, to the end of September, after allowance is made for holy days and bad weather. Yet, the strength of the colony hinges on that period.

It would be necessary to compel neglectful habitants to labor on the land by depriving them of the right to go on voyages, which exempt them from work. They earn thirty or forty écus on a voyage of two or three months but waste the farming season, and land remains fallow as a result....

Oblige the seigneurs, in order to facilitate the establishment of their seigneuries, to give sufficient common land at low prices and to build mills and other public conveniences. Many persons lose up to a third of their time traveling fifteen or twenty lieues to mill their flour....

Order the grand voyer to apply himself to building the roads and bridges necessary for the public, which is something very essential....

The subordination of the vassal to his seigneur is not observed. This error is the result of seigneuries being granted to commoners, who have not known how to maintain their rights over their tenants. Even the officers of militia, who are their dependents, have for the most part no consideration for their superiority and wish on occasions to be regarded as independent.

### 3. Jean Talon, "Memoir on Canada," 1673

*Jean Talon (1626–94) came to New France as Louis XIV's Intendant, the official chiefly responsible for economic development. Indefatigably enthusiastic for the colony's potential, he was innovative and able, establishing ship building, hemp growing, beer brewing, and mineral exploration. Though best known for his* Filles du Roi *program, which improved the perilous gender imbalance, he also expanded the French empire in North America and set the fur trade on firm footing—partly by allowing alcohol as a trade medium. Talon regularly squabbled with both the governor and the bishop, both of whom he accused of interference. He served twice in New France, from 1665 to 1668 and again from 1670 to 1672.*

... It has appeared to me that one of the principal intentions of His Majesty was to form over the years a large and populous colony, full of men suited for all types of professions in the army, the navy, and the fisheries, and strong enough to engage in all types of work.

The girls sent from France by the king and the marriages they contracted with the soldiers who have voluntarily chosen to settle in the colony have so greatly increased the number of settlers that when taking the census in 1671 I found by the birth certificates that seven hundred children had been born in that year. At present I have reason to believe that one hundred marriages between young men and girls born in the colony are possible annually....

His Majesty further intended that the settlers of his colony of New France should enjoy the felicity of his reign to the same degree as his subjects of the old; that ... the southern part of America should be supported by the northern part, which can produce clothing and the necessities of life of which the southern part finds itself deprived by its exposure to the sun and a tropical climate; that stationary fisheries be established, so that the kingdom may not only do without the fish it buys from foreign countries for considerable sums, but also send to the Levant the dried fish that is consumed there in great quantities....

He also had in view the support of his navy with the wood that grows in Canada, the iron that could be discovered there, the tar that could be manufactured, and the hemp that could be grown for the making of ships' riggings. With these four products, he would no longer have to obtain from the princes of the Baltic, with an appearance of dependence, what is necessary to sustain his navy, which is such an important element of his glory and of his state's support.

In all this Canada seems to have responded well enough to the hopes of His Majesty. Hemp is being cultivated with success, cloth is being woven, cable and rope are being produced. The tar which has been manufactured has been tested both here and in France and found to be as good as that drawn from the north. Iron has been discovered, which master forgers consider to be suitable for all purposes. Vessels, which have now been sailing for six years, have been built for individuals who opened up the trade of Canada with the islands. At present there is one of 450 tons and forty-two guns being built for the king, which will put to sea next summer, and there is almost enough material in the yards for another. Before leaving, I established two workshops. During the present winter the first, of twenty-eight men, should produce 1,000 to 1,200 pieces of lumber suitable for the construction of a vessel of 600 to 700 tons, of which his Majesty has seen the model; from the labors of the second, we may hope for 25,000 to 30,000 feet of sheathing....

Stationary fisheries, which are so useful since dried cod is consumed almost everywhere in Europe, have been started before my departure....

Opening a trade between Canada and the Antilles is no longer considered a difficult thing. It was done by me in 1668 with a vessel built in Canada which successfully carried a cargo of this country's products. From there it sailed to Old

France with a load of sugar and then returned to the New with the products of the kingdom of which this country stands in need. Every year since, as a result of this example, this commerce has been carried out by two or more vessels....

This commerce is made up of the excess quantities of peas, salmon, salted eels, green and dried cod, planks and cask wood, and will be increased by excess wheat which will be converted into flour. It is estimated that Canada could export 30,000 *minots* each year if the crops are not ruined by bad weather. Peas could amount to 10,000 *minots*, and salted beef and pork will not in the future make up the smaller portion of this trade. Sales in the islands being favorable, I expect that Canada could soon supply pork, since it now does without that of France from which it formerly drew up to 1,200 barrels annually. The inhabitants of Port Royal in Acadia could supply salted beef. I obtained sixty quintals at twenty-two deniers a pound from there two years ago, which was as good as that of Ireland.

Beer could also profitably enter into this trade. I can guarantee 2,000 barrels a year for the islands and more if the consumption is greater, without altering the supply to the colonists of New France. It is by these methods that His Majesty will succeed in his aim of destroying the trade of the Dutch with our islands, without depriving his subjects residing there of the support they derived from it.

With all the provisions, which Canada will be able to supply in proportionately greater quantities as she develops, the islands will be provided with the necessities of life and will only lack a few accessories like spices, olive oil, wine, and salt. There is even the possibility of establishing salt works in Acadia if the king judges that it would not be prejudicial to Old France to make this new colony self-sufficient in this respect and to enable it to provide by itself for all its needs. I say all its needs not even excluding clothing which, we may hope, will be manufactured not only for the Canadians but in a few years for the islanders as well. For crafts have already been established for the fabrication of cloth, linen, and shoes; we already have enough leather to manufacture on the average 8,000 pairs of shoes annually; we will have as much hemp as we will care to grow; and the sheep which His Majesty sent have bred very well and will provide the material for the sheets and other cloths which we have begun to weave.

And all these things taken together will form the essence of a trade that will be useful to all His Majesty's subjects and will make for the happiness of those of New France. Thanks to the king's care and support, they live in peace and no longer suffer from those pressing needs which they felt for almost everything when his troops first landed in the colony.

Potash, which has successfully undergone a series of tests, can be used to wash linen or can be converted into a soft soap for bleaching or for cleaning silks and sheets. It can be produced in Canada in sufficient quantities to enable Paris to do without Spanish sodium, on which it spends a considerable sum. It could also enable Douay, Lille, Tournay, Courtrai, and other cities in Flanders and even in France where cloth is bleached to dispense with the potash of Muscovy and Poland, which increases the trade of the Dutch who accept this product in partial exchange for the beaver and spices they trade in those countries.

Potash should be received all the more favorably in Paris since all laundry-women know very well that Spanish sodium is very acrid and wears out the cloth, something which potash does not do....

Such, approximately, are the results of His Majesty's first attempt to make of a country that is crude, savage, and pagan the commencements of a province, and perhaps of a kingdom, that is refined, happy, and Christian.

### 4. Jacques-Rene de Brisay de Denonville, "Memoir Respecting Canada Prepared for the Marquis de Seignelay," January 1690

*Jacques-Rene de Brisay de Denonville (1637-1710) was governor of New France from 1685 to 1689 during which time he defeated both the English and the Iroquois. This he did by marching northward against the Hudson's Bay Company territory and by capturing and enslaving 50 Iroquois chiefs. Though these actions could be construed as major victories, the ensuing Native reprisals along the St. Lawrence almost destroyed New France. Denonville liked neither the colony, which he considered indefensible, nor the French Canadians, whom he thought arrogant and debauched. His criticisms may have stemmed from a perfectionist and self-righteous psyche, which in the end earned the displeasure of both the Québécois and the king.*

... Exclusive of the inability of the Governor-General to protect the country when obliged to act on the defensive, the great difficulty in controlling the people arises from the Colony being allowed to spread itself too much; and from every settler maintaining himself, isolated and without neighbours, in a savage independence. I see no remedy for this but to concentrate the Colony, and to collect the settlers, forming good enclosed villages. Whatever obstacle may be encountered herein, must be overcome if we would not hazard the destruction of the entire population....

The weakness of that country arises from isolated settlements adjoining interminable forests. If under such circumstances it be desired to continue the occupation of remote forts, such as that of Cataracouy or Fort Frontenac, it will add to the weakness of the country and increase expenses which cannot be of any use to us, whatever may be alleged to the contrary; for those posts cannot do injury to hostile Indians but to ourselves, in consequence of the difficulty of reaching, and the cost of maintaining, them.

Nothing is more certain than that it was a great mistake to have permitted, in time past, the occupation of posts so remote that those who occupy them are beyond the reach of the Colony and of assistance. The garrisons have thus been necessitated to enter into the interests of those Tribes nearest to them, and in that way to participate in their quarrels in order to please and conciliate them. We have, thus, drawn down on ourselves the enmity of their enemies and the contempt of our friends, who not receiving the assistance they were made to expect or might desire, have on divers occasions embarrassed us more than even our enemies. This has been experienced more than once.

It had been much better not to have meddled with their quarrels, and to have left all the Indians to come to the Colony in quest of the merchandise they required, than to have prevented their doing so by carrying goods to them in such large quantities as to have been frequently obliged to sell them at so low a rate as to discredit us among the Indians and to ruin trade; for many of our Coureur de bois have often lost, instead of gained, by their speculations. More-over, the great number of Coureurs de bois has inflicted serious injury on the Colony, by physically and morally corrupting the settlers, who are prevented marrying by the cultivation of a vagabond, independent and idle spirit. For the aristocratic manners they assume, on their return, both in their dress and their drunken revelries, wherein they exhaust all their gains in a very short time, lead them to despise the peasantry and to consider it beneath them to espouse their daughters, though they are themselves, peasants like them. In addition to this, they will condescend no more to cultivate the soil, nor listen, any longer, to anything except returning to the woods for the purpose of continuing the same avocations. This gives rise to the innumerable excesses that many among them are guilty of with the Squaws, which cause a great deal of mischief in consequence of the displeasures of the Indians at the seduction of their wives and daughters, and of the injury thereby inflicted on Religion, when the Indians behold the French practicing nothing of what the Missionaries represent as the law of the Gospel.

The remedy for this is, not to permit, as far as practicable, the return of any person to the Indian country except those who cannot follow any other business, nor to allow ill conducted persons to go thither; to oblige all to bring to the

Governor and Intendant a certificate of good behaviour and good morals from the Missionaries; to find employment for the youth of the country; which is a very easy matter, for the cod and whale fisheries afford a sure commerce, if closely attended to and made a business of. There is reason to believe that the wisest and oldest merchants of the country are tired of sending into the bush, but there will be always too many new and ambitious petty traders, who will attempt to send ventures thither, both with and without license. It is very proper that an ordinance be enacted holding the merchants responsible for the fault of unlicensed Coureurs de bois, for did the merchants not furnish goods, there would not be any Coureurs de bois....

As regards Acadia, that country is in great danger inasmuch as it has no fort of any value, and the settlers there are scattered and dispersed, as in Canada. It would be desirable that the King had a good fort at La Havre for the security of ships. That post would be much more advantageous than Port Royal, which it is not easy to get out of to defend the Coast from pirates, and to be more convenient to the Islands of Cape Breton and Newfoundland as well as the Great Bank.

Fish is so abundant on all the coasts of the King's territory, that it is desirable that the King's subjects only should go there to catch them, and that his Majesty were sufficiently powerful in that Country to prevent Foreigners fishing on the Great Bank. They ought to be deprived, at least, of fishing on the King's coasts. The Spaniards go every year to those of Labrador adjoining the Straits of Belle Isle. The English trade there more than we.

Hitherto, all the people of Acadia as well as those of Canada have paid more attention to the Beaver trade and to the sale of Brandy than to the establishment of Fisheries, which, nevertheless, afford the most certain and most durable profit, and are best suited to the inhabitants of the country, and to the augmentation of the Colony. For what each settler might realize annually would supply him most abundantly with clothes; and as the fishing season being only after the sowing and terminates before the harvest, every individual of any industry would find means to drive a profitable business, without abandoning agriculture, as the Coureurs de bois do. The Canadians are adroit and would become in a short time as expert as the Basques in whaling, were they to apply themselves to it. If the establishment of this fishery be persevered, there is reason to hope that they will turn their attention to it, being encouraged by the stimulus of gain. But he who is desirous of commencing it, is not wealthy, and will find it difficult to defray its expense....

FURTHER READINGS

Altman, I., and J. Horn, Eds. *To Make America: European Emigration in the Early Modern Period.* Berkeley: University of California Press, 1991.

Benes, P., Ed. *New England/New France, 1600–1850.* Boston: Boston University, 1992.

Bishop, M. *Champlain: A Life of Fortitude.* Toronto: McClelland and Stewart, 1962.

Bosher, J. *Business and Religion in the Age of New France.* Toronto: Canadian Scholar's Press, 1994.

Bosher, J. *The Canadian Merchants, 1713–1763.* Oxford: Clarendon Press, 1987.

Brandao, J. *"Your Fyres Shall Burn No More": Iroquois Policy toward New France and its Native Allies to 1701.* Lincoln: University of Nebraska Press, 1997.

Charbonneau, H., *et al. The First French Canadians: Pioneers in the St. Lawrence Valley.* Newark: University of Delaware Press, 1993.

Dechene, L. *Habitants and Merchants in Seventeenth Century Montreal.* Montreal and Kingston: McGill-Queen's University Press, 1992.

Eccles, W. *Canada Under Louis XIV.* Toronto: McClelland and Stewart, 1964.

Eccles, W. *Canadian Frontier 1534–1760.* Rev. ed. Albuquerque: University of New Mexico Press, 1984.

Eccles, W. *France in America.* New York: Harper and Row, 1972.

Hamilton, R. *Feudal Society and Colonization: The Historiography of New France.* Ganonoque: Language Press, 1988.

Harris, R. *The Seigneurial System in Early Canada: A Geographical Study.* 2nd ed. Montreal and Kingston: McGill-Queen's University Press, 1982.

Miquelon, D. *New France 1701–1744: "A Supplement to Europe."* Toronto: McClelland and Stewart, 1987.

Moogk, P. *La Nouvelle France: The Making of French Canada*. East Lansing: Michigan State University Press, 2000.

Trudel, M. *The Beginnings of New France*. Toronto: McClelland and Stewart, 1973.

Trudel, M. *Introduction to New France*. Toronto: Holt, Rinehart and Winston, 1969.

# CHAPTER 3

# "An Afflicted People"

## THE ACADIANS

### INTRODUCTION

The forcible expulsion of the Acadians during the Seven Years' War still generates controversy among historians and the public. Most recent interpretations of the event, be they monographs, journals, or conferences, cast the British as imperialistic bullies attacking innocent victims and use loaded words like "genocide" and "ethnic cleansing" in their analysis. Nor is such inflammatory language mere hyperbole: the International Court in the Hague presently prosecutes soldiers and politicians for similar crimes that have occurred in such places as Bosnia, Rwanda, and the former Yugoslavia. A conviction, apart from causing national humiliation, logically also raises the issue of restitution for the victims, even long after the incident transpired. Canada set a precedent of sorts, too, by compensating Japanese-Canadians for what we now perceive as their unjustified relocation during World War II. Why not offer similar restitution to Acadian descendants if the expulsion can be proven to have been unwarranted—to have been genocide rather than a legitimate act of war.

France claimed and settled Acadia with a smattering of immigrants during the seventeenth century. The colony encompassed present-day peninsular Nova Scotia and the north shore of the Bay of Fundy, Île Royale, and Île Saint-Jean, now respectively Cape Breton and Prince Edward Islands. The inland borders of contemporary New Brunswick remained vague because nobody cared sufficiently to define them. French administrators considered Acadia less important than New France on the St. Lawrence River and consequently tended to ignore the colony prior to 1713. Thus, communication between the two areas, such as it was, remained slow and infrequent. Though nominally administrated from Quebec, Acadia evolved rather autonomously, generating a culture of self-sufficiency among its officially French population. The people, who originated from a small corner of southwest France and spoke a dialect distinct from New France's, established working relationships with Britain's New England colonies to the south, the Native people in their midst, and their motherland's New France to the north.

While religion, language, and history bound the Acadians far more to France than to Britain, their location compromised that allegiance because Acadia was the geographical buffer zone separating New England from New France. Such zones tend to hold strategic value and often end up as geo-political flash points, particularly when the protagonists are such mortal enemies and competitive imperialists as were Britain and France. The expedient solution to avoid becoming a battlefield, the Acadians believed, was to nurture their independent spirit based upon a centrepiece of declared neutrality. This potentially offered significant dividends. Neutrality, for example, should double their economic activity by allowing trade with both British and French colonies. As well, France and Britain had a history of squabbling over Acadia and nonalignment should keep the Acadians themselves uninvolved or at least from ending up on the wrong side after an official ownership swap, which seemed to occur with monotonous regularity.

Most of Acadia again changed hands in the armistice Treaty of Utrecht in 1713 as a result of France's defeat in its war with Britain. The Union Jack once more fluttered over the Acadian peninsula, which Britain dubbed New Scotland or "Nova Scotia," though Îles Saint-Jean and Royale remained French, as did the north shore of the Bay of Fundy and land stretching into what is today the American state of Maine. An uneasy no-man's border zone emerged at the northern end of the isthmus of Chignecto, both nations eventually building fortifications that allowed French soldiers in Fort Beauséjour to face their British counterpoints at Fort Lawrence, a short distance away.

Britain faced a dilemma in 1713: what to do with the population in its newly acquired territory. On the one hand, a stable population of farmers such as the Acadians could furnish agricultural products to the new British garrison and would encourage later growth through the community's very existence. Expelling the Acadians would disrupt the established trade between Acadia and New England, and their presence assured a modicum of colonial self-sufficiency. And what if the Acadians left? It would presumably be to France's other North American possessions where their number would strengthen the French, something a British strategist should not encourage. Finally, the Acadians seemed sufficiently docile and friendly not to constitute a threat.

On the other hand, however, France was Britain's traditional enemy. The Acadians were culturally French and Catholic, they had weapons, and France busily built forts in the vicinity that the Acadians willingly provisioned. To make matters worse, Catholic priests sent from Quebec repeatedly incited the Acadians and the Micmac against their new masters. Meanwhile, the British garrison was initially so small that a determined band of rebellious subjects could possibly push it into the Atlantic. Did the benefits of the Acadian presence outweigh the dangers?

For their part the Acadians, most of whom were multi-generational settlers, did not wish to leave an area they considered home, regardless of its official ownership. They simply wished to get on with life. The only ones, in fact, who definitely wanted the Acadians out, now that the area was British, were the French who did not want to provide the British with a useful servile population. No, the French argued, the Acadians should do the right thing and remove themselves to French Île Royale (Cape Breton Island), where they could support France's massive new fortifications of Louisburg.

Local British administrators ultimately concluded that the advantages of keeping the Acadians on site did, in fact, outweigh the dangers—as long as they hedged their bets. Britain would treat the Acadians magnanimously *if* their new subjects swore an oath of fidelity to the Crown. The most contentious aspect of the oath, as far as the Acadians were concerned, was the implication that "fidelity" might force them to take up arms for Britain, and presumably against France, which the former Frenchmen patently refused to consider. The two sides overcame the ensuing diplomatic impasse through a tacit agreement, scribbled on the margin of the document, whereby the Acadians swore the oath with a proviso exempting them from military service. This did not sit well in London when the document reached there. To Westminster, new citizens were either loyal or disloyal, period, though in the case of the Acadians it chose not to force the issue. The modified oath was good enough for the "neutral" Acadians, however, who naively settled down to their new reality as British subjects, seemingly oblivious to their status as expendable pawns in a much bigger geo-political game.

Time caught them out, and their neutrality became a liability. France and Britain stood poised for war by the 1740s, and both manoeuvred for the Acadians' loyalty. Britain increasingly believed that "neutral" meant "enemy" in wartime, particularly after a number of suspicious incidents in which Acadians appeared to support French military efforts. British governors therefore repeatedly pushed for the original oath of complete fidelity, which the Acadians refused without their traditional caveat. Tensions escalated. Finally, rather than evict them and thereby strengthen the enemy, Governor Lawrence had the Acadians rounded up, packed onto waiting ships, and dispersed in small groups throughout the Thirteen Colonies where, in theory, they were to be integrated into the local population and disappear as a distinct people. The expulsion began in 1755 and lasted for several years until virtually the entire Acadian population disappeared. Some Acadians did successfully flee to Île Royale or Île Saint-Jean during the initial evacuation, but their luck ran out when British forces overran both islands and expelled them from there as well. It was not until after the end of the war that Britain permitted them to return, and when they did, the Acadians typically found New England immigrants holding legal title to their old homesteads.

### DISCUSSION POINTS

1. Who or what bears primary responsibility for the Acadian dilemma? How much was Britain to blame? The Acadians? The French?

2. Was Britain justified in its final actions, or did the Acadians deserve different treatment? Were there other solutions? Was deportation inevitable?

3. Galerm raises the issue of compensation for Acadian losses. Is the Acadian deportation another example of an historical injustice for which we (or the British government) should provide compensation or an apology?

4. Historians often use the term "history from below" when discussing the perspectives of ordinary people like Galerm. In what respects would documents left by such people be better and/or worse historical sources than accounts from prominent government officials such as Lawrence?

### DOCUMENTS

### 1. Acadians, "Memorial to Nova Scotia Governor Charles Lawrence," June 10, 1755

To His Excellency Charles Lawrence, Governor of the Province of Nova Scotia or Acadie,

Sir,—We, the inhabitants of Mines, Pisiquid, and the river Carard, take the liberty of approaching your Excellency for the purpose of testifying our sense of the care which the government exercises towards us.

It appears, Sir, that your Excellency doubts the sincerity with which we have promised to be faithful to his Britannic Majesty.

We most humbly beg your Excellency to consider our past conduct. You will see, that, very far from violating the oath we have taken, we have maintained it in its entirety, in spite of the solicitations and the dreadful threats of another power. We still entertain, Sir, the same pure and sincere disposition to prove under any circumstances, our unshaken fidelity to his Majesty, provided that His Majesty shall allow us the same liberty that he has granted us. We earnestly beg your Excellency to have the goodness to inform us of His Majesty's intentions on this subject, and to give us assurances on his part.

Permit us, if you please, Sir, to make known the annoying circumstances in which we are placed, to the prejudice of the tranquillity we ought to enjoy. Under pretext that we are transporting our corn or other provisions to Beauséjour, and the river of St. John, we are no longer permitted to carry the least quantity of corn by water from one place to another. We beg your Excellency to be assured that we have never transported provisions to Beauséjour, or to the river St. John. If some refugee inhabitants at the point have been seized, with cattle, we are not on that account, by any means guilty, in as much as the cattle belonged to them as private individuals, and they were driving them to their respective habitations. As to ourselves, Sir, we have never offended in that respect; consequently we ought not, in our opinion, to be punished; on the contrary, we hope that your Excellency will be pleased to restore us the same liberty that we enjoyed formerly, in giving us the use of our canoes, either to transport our provisions from one river to the other, or for the purpose of fishing; thereby providing for our livelihood. This permission has never been taken from us except at the present time. We hope, Sir, that you will be pleased to restore it, especially in consideration of the number of poor inhabitants who would be very glad to support their families with the fish that they would be able to catch. Moreover, our guns, which we regard as our personal property, have been taken from us, notwithstanding the fact that they are absolutely necessary to us, either to defend our cattle which are attacked by the wild beasts, or for the protection of our children, and of ourselves.

Any inhabitant who may have his oxen in the woods, and who may need them for purposes of labour, would not dare to expose himself in going for them without being prepared to defend himself.

It is certain, Sir, that since the savages have ceased frequenting our parts, the wild beasts have greatly increased, and our cattle are devoured by them almost every day. Besides, the arms which have been taken from us are but a feeble

guarantee of our fidelity. It is not the gun which an inhabitant possesses, that will induce him to revolt, nor the privation of the same gun that will make him more faithful; but his conscience alone must induce him to maintain his oath. An order has appeared in your Excellency's name, given at Fort Edward June 4th, 1755, and in the 28th year of his Majesty's region, by which we are commanded to carry guns, pistols etc. to Fort Edward. It appears to us, Sir, that it would be dangerous for us to execute that order, before representing to you the danger to which this order exposes us. The savages may come and threaten and plunder us, reproaching us for having furnished arms to kill them. We hope, Sir, that you will be pleased, on the contrary, to order that those taken from us be restored to us. By so doing, you will afford us the means of preserving both ourselves and our cattle. In the last place, we are grieved, Sir, at seeing ourselves declared guilty without being aware of having disobeyed. One of our inhabitants of the river Canard, named Pierre Melançon, was seized and arrested in charge of his boat, before having heard any order forbidding that kind of transport. We beg your Excellency, on this subject, to have the goodness to make known to us your good pleasure before confiscating our property and considering us in fault. This is the favour we expect from your Excellency's kindness, and we hope that you will do us the justice to believe that very far from violating our promises, we will maintain them, assuring you that we are very respectfully,
Sir,
Your very humble and obt. servants,
Signed by twenty-five of the said inhabitants.

## 2. Governor Charles Lawrence, "To the Governors on the Continent," August 11, 1755

*Charles Lawrence (1709–60), a professional soldier, came to Nova Scotia in 1749 as company commander of the 40th Foot Regiment and eventually became governor in 1756. He sent troops against the French forts on the Isthmus of Chignecto, the strategic land buffering French and British forces, where they found Acadians supporting the French troops. Lawrence thought the Acadians dangerous and hoped to dominate the colony with British immigrants. In July 1755 he demanded the Acadians swear an unconditional oath of loyalty to Britain. The Acadian refusal was the last straw: Lawrence ordered them deported to the British colonies further south. Despite the fact that no orders came from Britain to support the expulsion, no reprimand was forthcoming from his superiors, only complaints from the Thirteen Colonies who objected to these unwelcome immigrants being deposited on their doorsteps.*

Sir: The success that has attended his Majesty's arms in driving the French from the Encroachments they had made in this province furnished me with a favorable Opportunity of reducing the French inhabitants of this Colony to a proper obedience to his Majesty's Government, or forcing them to quit the country. These Inhabitants were permitted to remain in quiet possession of their lands upon condition they should take the Oath of allegiance to the King within one year after the Treaty of Utrecht by which this province was ceded to Great Britain; with this condition they have ever refused to comply, without having at the same time from the Governor an assurance in writing that they should not be called upon to bear arms in the defence of the province; and with this General Philipps did comply, of which step his Majesty disapproved and the inhabitants pretending therefrom to be in a state of Neutrality between his Majesty and his enemies have continually furnished the French & Indians with Intelligence, quarters, provisions and assistance in annoying the Government; and while one part have abetted the French Encroachments by their treachery, the other have countenanced them by open Rebellion, and three hundred of them were actually found in arms in the French Fort at Beauséjour when it surrendered.

Notwithstanding all their former bad behaviour, as his Majesty was pleased to allow me to extend still further his Royal grace to such as would return to their Duty, I offered such of them as had not been openly in arms against us, a continuance of the Possession of their lands, if they would take the Oath of Allegiance, unqualified with any Reservation whatsoever; but this they have most audaciously as well as unanimously refused, and if they would presume to do this when there is a large fleet of Ships of War in the harbor, and a considerable land force in the province, what might not we expect from them when the approaching winter deprives us of the former, and when the Troops which are only hired from New England occasionally and for a smalltime, have returned home.

As by this behaviour the inhabitants have forfeited all title to their lands and any further favor from the Government, I called together his Majesty's Council, at which the Honble. Vice Adml. Boscawen and Rear Adml. Mostyn assisted, to consider by what means we could with the greatest security and effect rid ourselves of a set of people who would forever have been an obstruction to the intention of settling this Colony and that It was now from their refusal to the Oath absolutely incumbent upon us to remove.

As their numbers amount to near 7000 persons the driving them off with leave to go whither they pleased would have doubtless strengthened Canada with so considerable a number of inhabitants; and as they have no cleared land to give them at present, such as are able to bear arms must have been immediately employed in annoying this and neighbouring Colonies. To prevent such inconvenience it was judged a necessary and the only practicable measure to divide them among the Colonies where they may be of some use, as most of them are healthy strong people; and as they cannot easily collect themselves together again it will be out of their power to do any mischief and they may become profitable and it is possible, in time, faithful subjects.

As this step was indispensably necessary to the security of this Colony, upon whose preservation from French encroachments the prosperity of North America is esteemed in a great measure dependent, I have not the least reason to doubt of your Excellency's concurrence and that you will receive the inhabitants I now send and dispose of them in such manner as may best answer our design in preventing their reunion.

### 3. John Winslow, Journal, 1755

*Colonel John Winslow (1703–74) was born in the Massachusetts Bay Colony. He served in the 40th Foot Regiment, which went to Nova Scotia in 1755. There, as commander, he led a local regiment against French forces at Forts Beauséjour and Gaspereau. Governor Charles Lawrence entrusted Winslow with rounding up and deporting the Acadian population to the eastern seaboard colonies of New England. He did so in a remarkably peaceful operation, perhaps testament to both his sensibilities and skills and to Acadian compliance.*

September 5th—At three in the afternoon the French inhabitants appeared agreeable to their citation at the church in Grand Pre, amounting to 418 of their best men. Upon which I ordered a table to be set in the centre of the church and, being attended with those of my officers who were off guard delivered them, by interpreters, the King's orders in the following words: ... "Gentlemen ... The part of duty I am now upon is what, though necessary, is very disagreeable to my natural make and temper, as I know it must be grievous to you ... That your lands and tenements, cattle of all kinds and livestock of all sorts are forfeited to the Crown with all other of your effects, saving your money and household goods, and you yourselves to be removed from His Province....

I shall do everything in my power that all those goods be secured to you and that you are not molested in carrying off them and also that whole families shall go in the same vessel and make this remove, which I am sensible must give you a great deal of trouble, as easy as His Majesty's service will admit, and hope that in every part of the world you may fall you may be faithful subjects, a peaceable and happy people.

I must also inform you that it is His Majesty's pleasure that you remain in security under the inspection and direction of the troops ... and then declared them the King's prisoners...."

September 10th—..., that it would be best to divide the prisoners and that, as there was five transports idle which came from Boston, it would be good ... that fifty men of the French inhabitants be embarked on board of each of the five vessels, taking first all their young men...

I sent for father Landry, their principal speaker who talks English, and told him the time has come for part of the inhabitants to embark and that the number concluded for this day was 20, and that we should begin with the young men. And desired he would inform his brethren of it. He was greatly surprised. I told him it must be done, ... and, as the tide in a very little time favoured my design, could not give them above an hour to prepare for going on board, and ordered our whole party to be under arms and post themselves between the two gates and the church, ... which was obeyed.... I then ordered Capt. Adams with a lieutenant, 80 non-commission officers and private men to draw off from the main body to guard the young men ... and order the prisoners to march. They all answered they would not go without their fathers. I told them that was a word I did not understand, for that the King's command was to me absolute and should be absolutely obeyed, and that I did not love to use harsh means, but that the time did not admit of parleys or delays. And then ordered the whole troop to fix their bayonets and advance towards the French, and bid the four right hand files of the prisoners, consisting of 24 men, ... to divide from the rest. One of whom I took hold on (who opposed the marching) and bid march. He obeyed and the rest followed, though slowly, and went off praying, singing, and crying being met by the women and children all the way (which is 1/2 mile) with great lamentations, upon their knees, praying etc.

I then ordered the remaining French to choose out 109 of their married men to follow their young people.... They readily complied ... So that the number embarked was but 230 and thus ended this troublesome job, which was scene of sorrow....

September 12th—I yesterday received a memorial in French from the Neutral inhabitants.... No. 1 is a petition from the inhabitants to General Phillips praying that all those who should take the oath of fidelity to His Majesty King George may be allowed the free exercise of their religion and that missionaries may be allowed them, praying also a guarantee of their estates and possessions on paying the customary quit rents. The answer signed by General Phillips is that the prayer of their petition is granted and accordingly follows the oath in these words:

"Dated April 25th, 1730

I promise and swear sincerely by the faith of a Christian that I will be truly faithful and will submit myself to His Majesty King George whom I acknowledge to be the Lord and Sovereign of Nova Scotia.

So Help Me God."

Then follows a certificate from Monsieur de la Goudalie and Alexandre de Noinville priests, who certify that General Phillips did promise to the inhabitants that they should be exempted from bearing arms against either the French or Indians, and that they, on their part did promise that they would not take up arms against the Kingdom of England or its government.

No. 2 is a petition to John Winslow esq., Lieut. Col. of His Majesty's troops commanding at Grand Pre, representing that the evils which seem to threaten them on all sides oblige them to beg your protection on their behalf, and that you intercede with His Majesty to consider those who have inviolably kept the fidelity and submission promised to his said majesty. And, as you have given them to understand that the King has ordered them to be transported of this province, they beg, at least, if they must quit their estates, that they may be permitted to go to such places where they will find their kindred, and that at their own expense, allowing them a convenient time for that purpose, ... by that means they will be able to preserve their religion which they have very much at heart, and for which they are content to sacrifice their estates, etc.

17th September, ... I believe they did not then nor to this day do imagine that they are actually to be removed.

September 29th, ... I advise from Capt. Lewis of the 25th instant that the inhabitants of Cobequid have entirely deserted that country and that he began to burn and lay waste on the 23rd.... The French are constantly plying me with petitions and remonstrances.

October 6th—With the advice of my captains, made a division of the villages and concluded that as many of the inhabitants of each as could be commoded should proceed in the same vessel and that whole families go together, and sent orders to several families to hold themselves in readiness to embark with all their household goods, etc., but even now could not persuade the people I was in earnest....

October 7th— ... In the evening twenty-four of the French young men deserted from on board....

October 8th—began to embark the inhabitants who went off very solemntarily and unwillingly, the women in great distress, carrying off their children in their arms. The others carrying their decrepit parents in their carts and all their goods moving in great confusion and appeared a scene of woe and distress ... filled up Church and Milbury with about eighty families, and also made the strictest inquiry I could how those young men made their escape ... found one Francois Hebert was either the contriver or abettor ... who I ordered ashore, carried to his own house and then, in his presence, burned both his house and barn. And gave notice to all the French that, in case these men did not surrender themselves in two days I should serve all their friends in the same manner and ... confiscate their household goods.

October 12th—Our parties, being reconnoitring the country, fell in with one of the French deserters who endeavoured to make his escape on horseback. They hailed him and fired over him, but he persisted in riding off when one of our men shot him dead off his horse. And also meeting with a party of the same people, fired upon them, but they made their escape into the woods....

October 19th, ... I have five hundred people more to embark than the nine mentioned can carry, which will fall some short of 1500. Have had two bad months placed in the centre of Nova Scotia without any fortification or cannon and only 360 men, ... the difficulty is most over and be assured I am heartily tired of it....

### 4. John Baptiste Galerm, "A Relation of the Misfortunes of the French Neutrals, as laid before the Assembly of the Province of Pennsylvania," 1758

*Historians know nothing about John Baptiste Galerm, a displaced Acadian, except for what can be gleaned from this address to the legislative assembly of Pennsylvania.*

About the Year 1713, when Annapolis Royal was taken from the French our Fathers being then settled on the Bay of Fundy, upon the Surrender of that Country to the English, had, by Virtue of the Treaty of Utrecht, a Year granted to them to remove with their Effects; but not being willing to lose the Fruit of many Years Labour, they chose rather to remain there, and become Subjects of Great Britain, on Condition that they might be exempted from bearing Arms against France (most of them having near Relations and friends amongst the French, which they might have destroyed with their own Hands, had they consented to bear Arms against them). This Request they always understood to be granted, on their taking the Oath of Fidelity to her late Majesty Queen Anne; which Oath of Fidelity was by us, about 27 Years ago, renewed to his Majesty King George by General

Philipse, who then allowed us an Exemption of bearing Arms against France; which Exemption, till lately (that we were told to the contrary) we always thought was approved of by the King. Our Oath of Fidelity, we that are now brought into this Province, as well as those of our Community that are carried late into the neighbouring Provinces, have always inviolably observed, and have, on all Occasions, been willing to afford all the Assistance in our Power to his Majesty's Governors in erecting Forts, making Roads, Bridges, &c., and providing Provisions for his Majesty's Service, as can be testified by the several Governors and Officers that have commanded in his Majesty's Province of Nova Scotia; and this notwithstanding the repeated Solicitations, Threats and Abuses which we have continually, more or less, suffered from the French and French Indians of Canada on that Account; particularly, about ten Years ago, when 500 French and Indians came to our Settlements, intending to attack Annapolis Royal, which, had their intention succeeded, would have made them Masters of all Nova Scotia, it being the only Place of Strength then in that Province, they earnestly solicited with us to join with, and aid them therein; but we persisting in our Resolution to abide true to our Oath of Fidelity, and absolutely refusing to give them any Assistance, they gave over their Intention and returned to Canada. And about seven Years past, at the Settling of Halifax, a body of 150 Indians came amongst us, forced some of us from our Habitations, and by Threats and blows would have compelled us to assist them in Way laying and destroying the English, then employed in erecting Forts in different parts of the Country; but we positively refusing, they left us, after having abused us, and made great Havoc of our Cattle, &c. I myself was six weeks before I wholly recovered of the blows I received from them at that time. Almost numberless are the Instances which might be given of the Abuses and Losses we have undergone from the French Indians on Account of our steady Adherence to our Oath of Fidelity; and yet notwithstanding our strict Observance thereof, we have not been able to prevent the grievous Calamity which is now come upon us, which we apprehend to be in a great Measure owing to the unhappy Situation and Conduct of some of our People settled at Chignecto, at the bottom of the Bay of Fundy, where the French, about four Years ago, erected a Fort; those of our People who were settled near it, after having had many of their Settlements burnt by the French; being too far from Halifax and Annapolis Royal to expect sufficient Assistance from the English, were obliged, as we believe, more through Compulsion and Fear than Inclination, to join with and assist the French; which also appears from the Articles of Capitulation agreed on between Colonel Monckton and the French Commander, at the Delivery of the said Fort to the English, which is expressly in the following Words.

"With regard to the Acadians, as they have been forced to take up Arms on Pain of Death, they shall be pardoned for the Part they have been taking." Notwithstanding this, as these People's Conduct had given just Umbrage to the Government and erected Suspicions, to the Prejudice of our whole Community, we were summoned to appear before the Governor and Council at Halifax, where we were required to take the Oath of Allegiance without any Exception, which we could not comply with because, as that Government is at present situate, we apprehend that we should have been obliged to take up Arms; but we are still willing to take the Oath of Fidelity, and to give the strongest Assurance of continuing peaceable and faithful to his Britannic Majesty, with that Exception. But this, in the present Situation of Affairs, not being satisfactory, we were made Prisoners, and our Estates, both real and personal, forfeited for the King's Use; and Vessels being provided, we were some time after sent off, with most of our Families, and dispersed amongst the English Colonies. The Hurry and Confusion in which we were embarked was an aggravating Circumstance attending our Misfortunes; for thereby many, who had lived in Affluence, found themselves deprived of every Necessary, and many Families were separated, Parents from Children, and Children from Parents. Yet blessed be God that it was our Lot to be sent to Pennsylvania, where our Wants have been relieved, and we have in every Respect been received with Christian Benevolence and Charity. And let me add, that not withstanding the Suspicions and Fears which many here are possessed of on our Account, as tho' we were a dangerous People, who make little Scruple of breaking our Oaths. Time will manifest that we are not such a People: No, the unhappy situation which we are now in, is a plain Evidence that this is a false Claim, tending to aggravate the Misfortunes of an already too unhappy People; for had we entertained such pernicious Sentiments, we might easily have prevented our falling into the melancholy Circumstances we are now in, viz: Deprived of our Subsistance, banished from our native Country, and reduced to live by Charity in a strange Land; and this for refusing to take an Oath, which we are firmly persuaded Christianity absolutely forbids us to violate, had we once taken it, and yet an Oath which we could not comply with without being exposed to plunge our Swords in the Breasts of our Friends and Relations. We shall, however, as we have hitherto done, submit to what in the present Situation of Affairs may seem necessary, and with Patience and Resignation bear whatever God, in the course of his Providence, shall suffer to come upon us. We shall also think it our Duty to seek and promote the Peace of the Country into which we are transported, and inviolably keep the Oath of Fidelity that we have taken to his gracious Majesty King George, whom we firmly believe, when fully acquainted with our Faithfulness and Sufferings, will commiserate our unhappy Condition, and order that some Compensation be made us for our Losses. And may the Almighty abundantly bless his Honour the Governor, the Honourable Assembly of the Province, and the good People of Philadelphia, whose Sympathy, Benevolence and Christian Charity have been, and still are, greatly manifested and extended towards us, a poor distressed and afflicted People, is the sincere and earnest Prayer of John Baptiste Galerm.

FURTHER READINGS

Arsenault, G. *The Island Acadians, 1720-1980.* Charlottetown: Ragweed, 1989.

Barnes, T. "'The Dayley Cry for Justice': The Juridical Failure of the Annapolis Royal Regime." In *Essays in the History of Canadian Law,* Vol. 3, ed. P. Girard and J. Phillips. Toronto: Osgoode Society, 1990.

Barnes, T. "Historiography of the Acadians' Grand Derangement, 1755." *Quebec Studies* 7 (1988): 74-86.

Blanchard, J. *The Acadians of Prince Edward Island.* Ottawa: LeDroit and LeClerc, 1976.

Daigle, J., Ed. *The Acadians of the Maritimes: Thematic Studies.* Moncton: Centre for Acadian Studies, 1982.

Faragher, J. "'A Great and Noble Scheme': Thoughts on the Expulsion of the Acadians." *Acadiensis* 36, 1 (Autumn 2006): 82-92.

Faragher, J. *A Great and Noble Scheme: The Tragic Story of the Expulsion of the French Acadians from their American Homeland.* New York: Norton, 2005.

Griffiths, N. *The Contexts of Acadian History 1686-1784.* Montreal and Kingston: McGill-Queen's University Press, 1992.

Griffiths, N. *From Migrant to Acadian: A North American Border People, 1604-1755.* Montreal and Kingston: McGill-Queen's University Press, 2005.

Griffiths, N. "The Golden Age: Acadian Life 1713-1748." *Social History* 17, 33 (May 1984): 21-34.

Johnston, A. "The Acadian Deportation in a Comparative Context." *Nova Scotia Historical Journal* 1 (2007): 114-31.

Plank, G. *An Unsettled Conquest: The British Campaign Against the Peoples of Acadia.* Philadelphia: University of Pennsylvania Press, 2001.

Reid, J. *Acadia, Maine and New Scotland: Marginal Colonies in the Seventeenth Century.* Toronto: University of Toronto Press, 1981.

# CHAPTER 4

# "The Ruin of Canada"

## LAST DECADES OF NEW FRANCE

### INTRODUCTION

The mid-eighteenth century battle for North America between France and Britain, despite erupting two years before the war officially began in 1756, was a sideshow to the greater European struggle. Thus, the two home governments tended to let local commanders take charge of their American theatres of operation, often without supplying sufficient logistical support. This served New England far better than New France. The former had a population vastly greater than the latter, concentrated in one major area, and with a diversified economy that promoted a high degree of self-sufficiency. New France, on the other hand, stretched for miles along the St. Lawrence, a river frozen solid for months at a time during which outside communication stopped. Though agricultural, the colony's economic mainstay remained the fur trade, and mercantilism discouraged both diversification and self-sufficiency. Thus, New France, unlike New England, depended for its survival upon its umbilical cord to Europe, a cord the British Royal Navy largely severed in the mid-Atlantic.

As if this were not bad enough, all manner of internal strife racked New France during its final years. The locally born governor, Vaudreuil, and the French aristocratic senior military commander, Montcalm, hated one another, squabbled incessantly over strategy, and periodically sabotaged each other's efforts. The militia and professional forces disliked and distrusted each other, and Native allies proved highly unreliable. The economy was in shambles, partly because Intendant Bigot and his partners in the "Grand Society" pilfered much of the few imported goods and resold them at extortionate prices. Locally produced supplies disappeared as a result of hoarding and from too many Habitants serving in the militia when they were needed on their farms. Meanwhile, critical imports dried up due to the British blockade, inflation ran rampant, and last, but certainly not least, a pall of defeatism and fear hung over New France's population.

The British, on the overall offensive, eventually chose a three-pronged pincer along the traditional invasion routes into the heart of New France: via the Great Lakes, up the Richelieu River, and by sea through the Gulf of St. Lawrence. Campaign season by campaign season they fought their way northward until General Wolfe stood opposite Quebec on the south shore of the St. Lawrence in the summer of 1759. Then began a summer-long cat-and-mouse game as Wolfe attempted to force the French into battle. He repeatedly probed for a beachhead on the north shore, knowing this would compel the French to leave the protection of the massive fort at Quebec to prevent it. Quebec itself he pounded with artillery, reducing much of it to rubble. French General Montcalm, however, deftly parried every thrust, never giving the British an opportunity to land until Wolfe, desperate for an advantage as winter freeze-up loomed, took a catastrophically dangerous gamble. He landed on the beach in the dead of night on September 12, slightly west of the citadel, and successfully scaled the cliffs below the Plains of Abraham. Montcalm, shocked to find approximately 3,300 British troops on his doorstep next morning, hastily responded by hurling some 3,500 men against them. The disciplined British regulars, the cliffs of the St. Lawrence at their backs, held their fire until the enemy was within 20 meters, then opened with a series of withering volleys that decimated the charging troops that turned into a French rout. Wolfe died within minutes, living sufficiently long to hear that he had won the battle. Montcalm succumbed to his wounds the next night.

Although the town of Quebec and its fort surrendered on September 18, that was not quite the end of New France. What remained of the French forces retreated to Montreal after the Plains of Abraham debacle, hoping for reinforcements the following spring—reinforcements that never came. Several fierce but unsuccessful battles fought in the spring of 1760 failed to dislodge the British and New France formally surrendered on September 8. But that was still not quite the end. This war was, after all, primarily a European conflict, which still raged on the other side of the Atlantic. New France, despite now being under

British control, might revert to France through a French victory in Europe or through postwar diplomatic settlement. In the meantime, the British garrison and the local Canadians eyed each other suspiciously but generally resigned themselves to waiting. The Habitants, however, should have remembered Voltaire's dictum that New France was a mere "few acres of snow." Had they done so, their future might have been clearer—though no more comforting. France not only lost the war in 1763 but then bargained away New France at the peace table in favour of more desirable properties elsewhere. By the Peace of Paris signed in that year, Habitants found themselves officially ruled by their traditional enemy, the nation that had aided the Iroquois in the seventeenth century, had expelled their brethren in Acadia, scorched the agricultural lands south of Quebec, and bombarded their city into rubble.

### DISCUSSION POINTS

1. In the 1750s France again had to assess the value of its colonies in North America. Summarize the pros and cons of retaining New France.

2. Some historians hold Montcalm directly responsible for the collapse of New France. To what extent were other factors more significant?

3. How did Sister Marie's account differ from those of the various government officials? Could these differences be attributed to gender, occupation, personal experience, or other factors?

### DOCUMENTS

### 1. Louis-Joseph de Montcalm, "To Marshal de Belle Isle," Montreal, April 12, 1759

*Louis-Joseph de Montcalm (1712–59) became major-general of French forces in New France in 1756. There he scored decisive victories against the British, especially at Fort Carillon where he defeated a force five times larger. However, he hated New France with its coarse Québécois society and unreliable Native allies. Montcalm also bickered with Quebec-born governor Vaudreuil and bombarded France with letters demanding everything from reinforcements and a higher salary to being made the supreme commander of forces in New France—which was originally the governor's position. The king responded by making Montcalm superior to the governor.*

Canada will be taken this campaign, and assuredly during the next, if there be not some unforeseen good luck, a powerful diversion by sea against the English Colonies, or some gross blunders on the part of the enemy.

The English have 60,000 men, we at most from 10 to 11,000. Our government is good for nothing; money and provisions will fail. Through want of provisions, the English will begin first; the farms scarcely tilled, cattle lack; the Canadians are dispirited; no confidence in M. de Vaudreuil or in M. Bigot. M. de Vaudreuil is incapable of preparing a plan of operations. He has no activity; he lends his confidence to empirics rather than to the General sent by the King. M. Bigot appears occupied only in making a large fortune for himself, his adherents and sycophants. Cupidity has seized officers, store-keepers; the commissaries also who are about the River St. John, or the Ohio, or with the Indians in the Upper country, are amassing astonishing fortunes. It is nothing but forged certificates legally admitted. If the Indians had a fourth of what is supposed to be expended for them, the King would have all those in America; the English none.

This expenditure, which has been paid at Quebec by the Treasurer of the Colony, amounts to twenty-four millions. The year before, the expenses amounted only to twelve or thirteen millions. This year they will run up to thirty-six. Everybody appears to be in a hurry to make his fortune before the Colony is lost, which event many, perhaps, desire, as an impenetrable veil over their conduct. The craving after wealth has an influence on the war, and M. de Vaudreuil does not doubt it. Instead of reducing the expenses of Canada, people wish to retain all; how abandon positions which serve as a pretext to make private fortunes? Transportation is distributed to favorites. The agreement with the contractor is unknown to me as it is to the public. 'Tis reported that those who have invaded commerce participate in it. Has the King need of purchasing goods for the Indians? Instead of buying them directly, a favorite is notified, who purchases at any price whatever; then M. Bigot has them removed to the King's stores, allowing a profit of one hundred and even one hundred and fifty percent, to those who it is desired to favor. Is artillery to be transported, gun-carriages, carts, implements to be made? M. Mercier, commandant of the artillery, is the contractor under other people's names. Everything is done badly and at a high price. This officer, who came out twenty years ago a simple soldier, will be soon worth about six or seven hundred thousand livres, perhaps a million, if these things continue. I have often respectfully spoken to M. de Vaudreuil and M. Bigot of these expenses; each throws the blame on his colleague. The people alarmed at these expenses, fear a depreciation in the paper money of the country; the evil effect is, the Canadians who do not participate in those illicit profits, hate the

Government. They repose confidence in the General of the French; accordingly, what consternation on a ridiculous rumor which circulated this winter that he had been poisoned....

If the war continue, Canada will belong to the English, perhaps this very campaign, or the next. If there be peace, the Colony is lost, if the entire government be not changed....

The general census of Canada has been at last completed. Though it has not been communicated to me, I think I'm correct, that there are not more than 82,000 souls in the Colony; of these, twelve thousand, at most, are men capable of bearing arms; deducting from this number those employed in works, transports, bateaux, in the Upper countries, no more than seven thousand Canadians will ever be collected together, and then it must not be either seed time or harvest, otherwise, by calling all out, the ground would remain uncultivated; famine would follow. Our eight battalions will make three thousand two hundred men; the Colonials, at most, fifteen hundred men in the field. What is that against at least fifty thousand men which the English have!

### 2. Michel-Jean-Hughes Péan, "Memoir on the Condition of Canada"

*Quebec-born Michel-Jean-Hughes Péan (1723[?]-82) rapidly rose through the ranks of the army in New France and was a commissioned officer in the regular colonial troops by the time of the Conquest. A classic opportunist and ne'er-do-well, Péan created a lucrative alliance with the corrupt Intendant Bigot. The two made fortunes selling scarce imports meant as gifts for France's Native allies. Péan fled to France in 1760, one step ahead of the law and military defeat, but was arrested in 1761. Found guilty, the French judiciary banished him for nine years and levied a fine of 600,000 livre.*

... [I]n the month of August last, the Colony remained in the most critical situation; the farmers, after having furnished the last bushel of their wheat for the subsistence of the troops which were marching against the enemy, were supporting themselves only by the aid of some vegetables and wild herbs; eighteen months ago the people, without excepting a single officer, had to be reduced to four ounces of bread a day; they have been reduced of late to two ounces only. During the winter it had become necessary to deprive the troops of bread, and to subsist them on beef, horseflesh and codfish.

The provisions brought by several ships during the year have been immediately forwarded to the armies, but Quebec has always remained in its melancholy situation.

Yet, people have to defend themselves at Carillon against thirty thousand men; against ten thousand at Fort Duquesne and against six thousand towards Chouaguen. The capture of Louisbourg, the settlements pretended to have been made by the English at Gaspé and on the Island of Anticosty, at the entrance of the Gulf of St. Lawrence, have rendered the situation of Canada much more afflicting, but the late misfortune experienced at Fort Frontenac by the Colony, is the most prejudicial of those it has been threatened with, and 'twill run the greatest risks if that fort be not retaken, as it served as an entrepôt for all the King's forts and Indian posts, and as the English will close all the passages. Then, the Indians, who constitute our principal force, finding themselves deprived of all they want, by failure of the succors the French would furnish them, will not fail to go over to the English, and will come and scalp at the very gates of the towns in which the people will be obliged to shut themselves up.

'Twill probably cost a great many men and much money to retake that fort, but it is of such great necessity for the preservation of Canada, that 'tis impossible to dispense with making every effort to retake it.

The harvest is reported very bad, and we must not be surprised at that, if we observe that all the farmers have been obliged to march to oppose the efforts of the enemy.

'Tis therefore to be presumed that this Colony is about to be exposed to much more serious suffering than it has experienced in preceding years, during which people have been under the necessity of consuming all the cattle.

Many persons have died of hunger, and the number would have been much greater had the King not subsisted a greater part of the people.

The land in Canada is in general, very good, and has often supplied in time of peace, provisions to other colonies, and almost always to Isle Royale; but not having had the good fortune to participate in the last peace, and being forced since fifteen years into continual war, which has employed almost all the farmers, the land could not be cultivated, and the failure of the crops which has ensued, has augmented so considerably the price of provisions and rendered them so excessively dear, that the officer can no longer subsist there without running considerably in debt; this is not the case with the soldier to whom too considerable an allowance, and one too expensive to the King has been made.

'Tis certain that Canada will, next year, have to fight more than sixty thousand men, as the English have just sent thither additional troops; no more than fifteen to eighteen thousand men can be employed in its defence, because many will be required for conveyance of provisions and ammunition, in consequence of the difficulty of the roads and the distance of the different posts.

Supposing the English are not yet at Gaspé, we may rest assured that they will seize it in the spring, and then they will be able to impede the navigation so much, that 'tis to be feared they will capture the greater portion of the succors which will be on the way to Quebec.

### 3. Unknown, "Memoir on Canada"

*First Question*: Is it of importance to preserve Canada?

There have been, from all time, people who have thought, and perhaps there are some still who are of opinion, that the preservation of Canada is of little importance to France. Some allege that it costs the King a great deal, and that it will eventually cost more; that it yields nothing, or next to nothing; that, in 1755, 1756, 1757 and 1758, probably more than fifteen millions have been expended yearly, which might have been better employed in the centre of the Kingdom. Others say that the Kingdom, which is itself stripped of people, is being depopulated to settle a country which is extremely rough, full of lakes and forests, frequently subject to the greatest scarcities; that there are within the Kingdom good lands which remain uncultivated; that the Indian trade is little worth; that, so far from increasing, it will always diminish, as the trade in peltries cannot last a century; they add, that the Canadian voyages are long, fatiguing and dangerous.

Finally, the third pretend that, in all the wars we shall have with the English, Canada will be taken, at least in part; that will always be the cause of preventing France, at the peace, preserving European conquests. Besides, that when Canada will be well settled, it will be exposed to many revolutions; is it not natural that Kingdoms and Republics will be formed there, which will separate from France?...

1st. It is certain that if France abandon Canada, heresy will establish itself there; Nations known and unknown, will remain in Paganism or adopt the religion of England. How many souls eternally lost! This reflection may strike a Christian Prince.

2nd. France possesses, in North America, more territory than is contained in the European continent. Its riches are not yet known; the best spots are not yet settled; the King's glory seems to require that so extensive a country be preserved notwithstanding the immense expenditure incurred there; it is always painful to behold the enemy aggrandizing themselves at our expense; besides, these expenses might considerably diminish; and, after all, this object is not so remarkable in times of peace; it would even be easy for those who are acquainted with finance to demonstrate that the trade and consumption of goods which is going on in Canada, produces for the King in time of peace, much more than is expended. This is the place where general reasons might be adduced to prove that it is of importance to a state to possess Colonies. It is wrong to object, that it is depopulating the kingdom. One year of European war causes the loss of more men than would be required to people New France. It might be complained that no care has ever been taken to increase its population; that might be easily done now in a perceptible manner, because the Colony begins to grow in numbers. How many thousands of useless men within the heart of the Kingdom and in other states! Every year the English are transporting into foreign parts a great number of families whom they encourage to settle in New England. Were New France peopled, there is no country so easy of preservation; naval forces essentially necessary to Old France, would guard Acadia, Louisbourg; and it may be asserted that if Canada be lost to France the latter will require a larger naval force than ever, because the English will become absolute masters of the sea....

3rd. Supposing, in fact, that Canada will never be of much use to France; that it will cost even a trifle, must it be reckoned as nothing, the preventing a rival nation aggrandizing itself, establishing, on the seas, a despotic empire and monopolizing all the trade?

The English, once masters of Canada, will necessarily take Louisiana and the Islands, because, being no longer disturbed by the Canadians, they will direct all their weight against the Islands, which are an object of importance for France. For the same reason it may be relied on, that the English will soon wrest New Mexico from Spain, and Portugal may truly be affected by it.

Our immense forests, our vast prairies, once in the hands of the English, will carry abundance everywhere, and facilitate forever the construction of all the ships they will desire.

Were it only the codfishery, this would be an object of infinite importance and which we should lose. Of all commerce, this is the richest, the easiest, the least expensive and the most extensive. As early as 1696, the trade of the Island of Newfoundland alone amounted yearly to 15 millions. Canada once taken, all the fishing ground must be renounced.

Without knowing all the branches of trade which is and can be carried on throughout New France, it may be said that if the King lose that country, the commerce of England will soon be augmented more than 150 millions.

A thousand other reflections present themselves to the mind, but it is unnecessary to abuse the patience of those who will read this Memoir.

*Second Question*: Should the war continue in 1759, will Canada be able to defend herself?

The number of men in that Colony bearing arms has perhaps been exaggerated. I dare assert that there are not fifteen thousand of them, but at least eleven thousand must be deducted from that number for the reasons following:

1. We must strike off 4,000, to wit: the old men, those necessary in the country, the sick, the husbands of sick women, the servants of the parish priests, the sextons, those who hide themselves to avoid being called out, those who find means to be exempted, the pilots for navigating the river, sailors for a great many sloops and bateaux, those at outposts, who watch the signal fires day and night.

It is, in general, doing much to levy more than two-thirds of the men.

2. Of the eleven thousand men to be levied, nearly 1,000 must necessarily be deducted for the Upper and Lower posts, and usually these are the best; it would be easy to enumerate them.

3. 1,500 mechanics of different sorts, carpenters for bateaux, artillery work, blacksmiths, gate-keepers, cartmen in the towns, must also be deducted; again add to these, 1,500 domestics for the officers, the town's people, necessary couriers, clerks, writers.

4. Again, 3,000 men must be employed for the transportation of provisions, utensils and all the necessaries for the camps.

We have 4,000 leagues of country to preserve; we have scarcely 78 settled; the current must be surmounted, the wind is oftenest contrary; sloops are frequently a month going up to Montreal....

Add to this, that we have in Canada scarcely 5 months of the year suitable for transportation.

It follows that, supposing eleven thousand men could be raised in Canada, 4,000 only of them will be fit to fight, the others being occupied elsewhere, and, in fact, they are perhaps never met in the camps.

The 8 battalions of French Regulars, the forty companies of the Marine, hardly form a corps of 6,000 men; 'tis a great deal, still, to add two thousand fighting Indians.

I ask now, if it be possible for twelve thousand men to resist the enemy's army, which certainly amount to sixty thousand men....

I refer to the last question what regards our scarcity of provisions and liquors and presents for the Indians. I will not say that there is every prospect that no ploughing will be done this year, that the enemy will prevent this and the putting in seed the early part of spring.

*Third Question*: Is it easy for France to relieve Canada in 1759?

Troops and provisions are required; all must arrive in May; the examination of this article will point out the difficulty.

It is not too much to demand an augmentation of eight thousand troops. On arriving at Quebec, they will probably be reduced, by death or disease, to 6,000; consequently, we shall have only 18,000 to oppose against 60 thousand. Is this too much? Is it sufficient? The situation of the country must be relied on, and calculations made on the mistakes of the enemy.

Men-of-war or merchantmen are necessary for conveying 8,000 men; if the former be employed, 300 on board each, exclusive of the crew, is a liberal allowance; 27 ships will be required; if merchantmen, they will carry only 200, and 40 of them will be necessary; but will it be possible to dispense with having them convoyed by ships of the Line, Isle Royale and Gaspé being actually in the hands of the English?

The Contractor-General of Canada demands 40 ships for his share alone, but how many of these will be intercepted? 20 at least will be required by the merchants; here are at once 100 ships of 300 tons required, exclusive of those which are to carry the munitions of war; still more are necessary for the conveyance of provisions, for though the harvest be good, it is not sufficient for the Colony and for extra mouths. This has been proved in 1756.

The difficulty of transportation in Canada occasions a great consumption of provisions by pure loss, and it is impossible to remedy it; the necessity of employing Indians is another occasion of wasteful consumption. A party of Indians [is sent] to make prisoners, with 15 days' provisions; it returns at the end of 8 days victorious, or without striking a blow; it has consumed everything and demands provisions. How are they to be refused? Another inevitable abuse: Our domiciliated Indians are unwilling to go to fight unless we feed their women and children, so that if you have 2,000 Indians, it will require provisions at least for 6,000. It is not flour alone that is wanting, the Colony is very bare of oxen and sheep, and at the close of 1759, hardly any will be found for refreshments for the troops or the ships, and 'tis certain, if the war continue, the Colony will be obliged to live on salt meat, which will have to be imported from France, and in that case what a number of ships will be required. Finally, supposing France could furnish all those vessels, will they arrive in sufficient season? ... It is to be feared that they will meet the enemy on quitting France; some they will find about the roadsteads of Halifax; others will be about Louisbourg and Gaspé. Should those succors be sent altogether, a strong convoy will be required, and it will happen that many vessels will be separated by fogs and storms; it will happen that those ships will not be ready soon enough to sail together, and though they should be, their voyage will be a great deal longer. All these succors are necessary; can France furnish them? If an attempt be made to recover Louisbourg or Gaspé, or if any considerable diversion be made on the coasts of New England by a considerable fleet, then the whole of the succors I have enumerated may not be wanting; but has France ships and seamen? Enough for the seas of America and Europe.

*Detached Thoughts*

... It is almost impossible to retake Louisbourg; we possess no port in those seas; the enemy has, or will have, 8,000 men there, and doubtless after our example, will keep some ships of the line in that port.

Acadia is entirely ruined, stripped of all domestic animals; most of the inhabitants dead; 'twill cost immense sums to reestablish the few of them that remain.... Indeed, New England must be very weary of the wars our Indians are waging against it. It sees in its midst nearly 4,000 of its frontier families bewailing their kindred who have been massacred and whose properties have been laid waste. It knows that in taking Canada it will be rid of the cruelty of the Indians and enjoy forever the sweets of peace.

Quebec is not a strong place; all our hope depends on preventing the landing and having outside a flying camp of 4,000 men, to annoy the enemy in their march and during the siege; it is very improbable that the enemy is ignorant of the strength of the fleets which will be sent; 'tis natural that they will oppose stronger ones, especially as they can station them in the most advantageous ports.

To send succors in divisions is to run the risk of losing all in detail; to send them together, is to expose ourselves to a general action and to lose all at once; it is to expose oneself to a very long voyage....

Canada has but one very narrow outlet, that is the gulf. If the English preserve Louisbourg and Acadia, 'twould be difficult to receive any relief by that way.

'Tis to be feared that the English will leave in New England 15 or 18 thousand Regulars, which they will, on declaring war, push suddenly into Canada; what means of resistance are there, if we do not keep up 8 or 10 thousand troops; but unfortunately the Colony will be unable to feed them except in the most abundant years, and supplies of provisions, all the implements and munitions of war necessary for 10,000 men, will be required from time to time from France. It will be necessary to think seriously of establishing granaries or magazines of reserve, on account of the scarcities which frequently overtake us.

The people of Canada must naturally be quite tired of the war, many have perished in it; they are burdened with the most harassing works, have not time to increase their property nor even to repair their houses; a portion of their subsistence has been wrested from them, many have been without bread for 3 months, the troops that incommode them are quartered on them, they have not throughout the year as much food as they think they need; they are told that the English will allow them freedom of religion, furnish them goods at a cheaper rate and pay liberally for the smallest service. These ideas are spreading. Some persons above the populace do not blush to speak in the same style; it is natural for the people to murmur and allow themselves to be seduced; the inhabitants of the cities will be the most easily debauched.

### 4. Marie de la Visitation, *Narrative of the Doings During the Siege of Quebec, and the Conquest of Canada*

*Sister Marie de la Visitation (born before 1736, death unknown) remains a mystery though we know that her father was a highly decorated soldier and seigneur and that her mother was an outstanding businesswoman in the colony. We also know that Marie served as the Mother Superior of the general hospital for nine years and that a published version of her account did not appear until 1826.*

My very reverend Mothers, ... The General Hospital is situated in the outer limits of Quebec, about half a mile from the walls.

The fire, from which our Sisters in Quebec have lately suffered, having rendered it impossible for them to continue their charge of the sick, Mr. Bigot, the Intendant of the country, proposed that we should receive them in our hospital. We readily agreed so to do; being desirous of rendering service and zealously fulfilling the duties of our calling, the Sisters lost no time in entering upon the sacred work. His Majesty, attentive to the wants of his subjects, and being informed of the preparations making by the English, did not fail to forward succour to the country, consisting in numerous vessels, laden with munitions of war and provisions, of which we were entirely destitute; and several regiments, who landed in a deplorable state, unfit for service, a great many men having died soon after. They were suffering from malignant fever. All the sick, officers and privates, were conveyed to our hospital, which was insufficient to contain them; we were therefore compelled to fill most parts of the building, even to the church, having obtained the permission of the late bishop Pontbriand, our illustrious prelate....

Thereupon, the enemy, despairing of vanquishing us, ashamed to retreat, determined to fit out a formidable fleet, armed with all the artillery that the infernal regions could supply for the destruction of human kind. They displayed the

British flag in the harbour of Quebec on the 24th May, 1759. On the receipt of intelligence of their arrival, our troops and militia came down from above. Our Generals left garrisons in the advanced posts, of which there is a great number above Montreal, in order to prevent the junction of their land forces, which it was understood were on the march, from Orange. Our Generals did not fail to occupy most points where the enemy might land; but they could not guard them all. The sickness suffered by our troops, lately from France, and the losses they sustained in two or three recent actions with the enemy, though victorious, weakened us considerably; and it became necessary to abandon Point Levi, directly opposite to and commanding Quebec. The enemy soon occupied it and constructed their batteries; which commenced firing on the 24th July, in a manner to excite the greatest alarm in our unfortunate Communities of religious ladies....

The only rest we partook of, was during prayers, and still it was not without interruption from the noise of shells and shot, dreading every moment that they would be directed towards us. The red-hot shot and carcasses terrified those who attended the sick during the night. They had the affliction of witnessing the destruction of the houses of the citizens, many of our connexions being immediately interested therein. During one night, upwards of fifty of the best houses in the Lower Town were destroyed. The vaults containing merchandise and many precious articles, did not escape the effects of the artillery. During this dreadful conflagration, we could offer nothing but our tears and prayers at the foot of the altar at such moments as could be snatched from the necessary attention to the wounded.

In addition to these misfortunes, we had to contend with more than one enemy; famine, at all times inseparable from war, threatened to reduce us to the last extremity; upwards of six hundred persons in our building and vicinity, partaking of our small means of subsistence, supplied from the government stores, which were likely soon to be short of what was required for the troops. In the midst of this desolation, the Almighty, disposed to humble us, and to deprive us of our substance, which we had probably amassed contrary to his will, and with too great avidity, still mercifully preserved our lives, which were daily periled, from the present state of the country....

The enemy, more cautious in their proceedings, on observing our army, hesitated in landing all their forces. We drove them from our redoubts, of which they had obtained possession. They became overwhelmed, and left the field strewed with killed and wounded. This action alone, had it been properly managed, would have finally relieved us from their invasion. We must not, however, attribute the mismanagement solely to our Generals; the Indian tribes, often essential to our support, became prejudicial to us on this occasion. Their hideous yells of defiance tended to intimidate our foes, who instead of meeting the onset, to which they had exposed themselves, precipitately retreated to their boats, and left us masters of the field. We charitably conveyed their wounded to our hospital, notwithstanding the fury and rage of the Indians, who, according [to] their cruel custom, sought to scalp them. Our army continued constantly ready to oppose the enemy. They dared not attempt a second landing; but ashamed of inaction, they took to burning the country places. Under shelter of darkness, they moved their vessels about seven or eight leagues above Quebec....

After remaining in vain nearly three months at anchor in the Port, they appeared disposed to retire, despairing of success; but the Almighty, whose intentions are beyond our penetration, and always just, having resolved to subdue us, inspired the English Commander with the idea of making another attempt before his departure, which was done by surprise during the night. It was the intention, that night, to send supplies to a body of our troops forming an outpost of the heights near Quebec. A miserable deserter gave the information to the enemy, and persuaded them that it would be easy to surprise us, and pass their boats by using our countersign. They profited by the information, and the treasonable scheme succeeded. They landed on giving the password; our officer detected the deceit, but too late. He defended his post bravely with his small band, and was wounded. By this plan the enemy found themselves on the heights near the city. General de Montcalm, without loss of time, marched at the head of his army; but having to proceed about half a league, the enemy had time to bring up their artillery, and to form for the reception of the French. Our leading battalions did not wait the arrival and formation of the other forces to support them, they rushed with their usual impetuosity on their enemies and killed a great number; but they were soon overcome by the artillery. They lost their General and a great number of officers. Our loss was not equal to that of the enemy; but it was not the less serious. General De Montcalm and his principal officers fell on the occasion.

Several officers of the Canadian Militia, fathers of families, shared the same fate. We witnessed the carnage from our windows. It was in such a scene that charity triumphed, and caused us to forget self-preservation and the danger we were exposed to, in the immediate presence of the enemy. We were in the midst of the dead and the dying, who were brought in to us by hundreds, many of them our close connexions; it was necessary to smother our griefs and exert ourselves to relieve them. Loaded with the inmates of three convents, and all the inhabitants of the neighbouring suburbs, which the approach of the enemy caused to fly in this direction, you may judge of our terror and confusion. The enemy masters of the field, and within a few paces of our house; exposed to the fury of the soldiers, we had reason to dread the worst. It was then that we experienced the truth of the words of holy writ: "he who places his trust in the Lord has nothing to fear."...

The loss we had just sustained, and the departure of that force, determined the Marquis De Vaudreuil, Governor General of the Colony, to abandon Quebec, being no longer able to retain it. The enemy having formed their entrenchments and their Camp, near the principal gate; their fleet commanding the Port, it was impossible to convey succour to the garrison....

The principal inhabitants represented to him that they had readily sacrificed their property; but with regard to their wives and children, they could not make up their minds to witness their massacre, in the event of the place being stormed; it was therefore necessary to determine on capitulation.

The English readily accorded the articles demanded, religious toleration and civil advantages for the inhabitants. Happy in having acquired possession of a country, in which they had on several previous occasions failed, they were the most moderate of conquerors. We could not, without injustice, complain of the manner in which they treated us. However, their good treatment has not yet dried our tears....

The reduction of Quebec, on the 18th September, 1759, produced no tranquillity for us, but rather increased our labours. The English Generals came to our Hospital and assured us of their protection, and at the same time, required us to take charge of their wounded and sick.

Although we were near the seat of war, our establishment had nothing to fear, as the well understood rights of nations protected Hospitals so situated, still they obliged us to lodge a guard of thirty men, and it was necessary to prepare food and bedding for them. On being relieved they carried off many of the blankets, &c. the officer taking no measures to prevent them. Our greatest misfortune was to hear their talking during divine service....

Let us now return to the French. Our Generals not finding their force sufficient to undertake the recovery of their losses, proceeded to the construction of a Fort, about five leagues above Quebec, and left a garrison therein, capable of checking the enemy from penetrating into the country. They did not remain inactive, but were constantly on the alert, harassing the enemy. The English were not safe beyond the gates of Quebec. General Murray the commander of the place, on several occasions was near being made a prisoner; and would not have escaped if our people had been faithful. Prisoners were frequently made, which so irritated the Commander, that he sent out detachments to pillage and burn the habitations of the country people.

The desire to recover the country and to acquire glory, was attended with great loss to our citizens. We heard of nothing but combats throughout the winter; the severity of the season had not the effect of making them lay down their arms. Wherever the enemy was observed, they were pursued without relaxation; which caused them to remark, "they had never known a people more attached and faithful to their sovereign than the Canadians."

The English did not fail to require the oath of allegiance to their King; but, notwithstanding this forced obligation, which our people did not consider themselves bound to observe, they joined the flying camps of the French, whenever an opportunity offered.

The French forces did not spare the inhabitants of the country; they lived freely at the expense of those unfortunate people. We suffered considerable loss in a Seigneurie which we possessed below Quebec. The officer commanding seized on all our cattle, which were numerous, and wheat to subsist his troops. The purveyor rendered us no account of such seizures. Notwithstanding this loss, we were compelled to maintain upwards of three hundred wounded sent to us after the battle of the 13th September....

Reverend Mothers, as I give you this account, merely from memory, of what passed under our eyes, and with a view to afford you the satisfaction of knowing that we sustained with fortitude and in an edifying manner the painful duties, imposed upon us by our vocation; I will not undertake to relate to you all the particulars of the surrender of the country. I could do it but imperfectly, and from hearsay. I will merely say that the majority of the Canadians were disposed to perish rather than surrender; and that the small number of troops remaining were deficient of ammunition and provisions, and only surrendered in order to save the lives of the women and children, who are likely to be exposed to the greatest peril where towns are carried by assault.

Alas! Dear Mothers, it was a great misfortune for us that France could not send, in the spring, some vessels with provisions and munitions; we should still be under her dominion. She has lost a vast country and a faithful people, sincerely attached to their sovereign; a loss we must greatly deplore, on account of our religion, and the difference of the laws to which we must submit. We vainly flatter ourselves that peace may restore us to our rights; and that the Almighty will treat us in a fatherly manner, and soon cease to humble us; we still continue to experience his wrath. Our sins, doubtless, are very great, which leads us to apprehend that we are doomed to suffer long; the spirit of repentance is not general with the people, and God is still offended. We, however, yet entertain the hope of again coming under the dominion of our former masters....

FURTHER READINGS

Anderson, F. *The Crucible of War: The Seven Years War and the Fate of Empire in British North American, 1754-1766*. New York: Vintage, 2000.

Boire, M. "Le Marquis de Montcalm and the Battle for Quebec, September 1759: A Re-Assessment." *Canadian Military Journal* (Summer 2006): 77-84.

Brumwell, S. *The Paths of Glory*. Montreal and Kingston: McGill-Queen's University Press, 2006.

Eccles, W. "The Battle of Quebec: A Reappraisal." In *French Colonial History Society*, ed. A. Heggby. Athens: University of Georgia, 1978.

Eccles, W. "The French Forces in North America during the Seven Years' War." In *Dictionary of Canadian Biography*, Vol. III, ed. Francis Halpenny. Toronto: University of Toronto Press, 1974.

Fowler, W. *Empire at War: The Seven Years War and the Struggle for North America*. Vancouver: Douglas and McIntyre, 2005.

Fregault, G. *Canada: The War of Conquest*. Toronto: Oxford University Press, 1969.

Greer, A. "Mutiny at Louisbourg, December 1744." *Social History* 10 (November 1977): 305-36.

Gwyn, J. "French and British Naval Power at the Two Sieges of Louisbourg, 1745 and 1758." *Nova Scotia Historical Review* 10, 2 (1990): 63-93.

Jennings, F. *Empire of Fortune: Colonies and Tribes in the Seven Year's War in America*. New York: Norton, 1988.

Johnston, A. *Control and Order in French Colonial Louisbourg, 1713-1758*. East Lansing: Michigan State University Press, 2001.

Johnston, A. *Endgame 1758. The Promise, the Glory and the Despair of Louisbourg's Last Decade*. Lincoln: University of Nebraska Press, 2008.

Macleod, P. *The Canadian Iroquois and the Seven Years' War*. Toronto: Dundurn Press, 1996.

Macleod. P. "Microbes and Muskets: Smallpox and the Participation of the Amerindian Allies of New France in the Seven Years War." *Ethnohistory* 39, 1 (Winter 1992): 42-64.

McLennan, J. *Louisbourg: From Its Foundation to its Fall, 1713-1758*. Repr. Halifax: Book Room, 1990.

Nicolai, M. "A Different Kind of Courage: The French Military and the Canadian Irregular Soldier during the Seven Years' War." *Canadian Historical Review* 70, 1 (1989): 53-75.

Pritchard, J. *Anatomy of a Naval Disaster: The 1746 French Expedition to North America*. Montreal and Kingston: McGill-Queen's University Press, 1995.

Stacey, C. *Quebec, 1759: The Siege and the Battle*. Toronto: Macmillan, 1959.

Stanley, G. *New France: The Last Phase, 1744-1760*. Toronto: McClelland and Stewart, 1968.

Steele, I. *Guerillas and Grenadiers: The Struggle for Canada, 1689-1760*. Toronto: Ryerson, 1969.

Steele, I. *Warpaths: Invasions of North America*. New York: Oxford University Press, 1994.

# CHAPTER 5

# "Suffering Much by Toil and Want"

## LOYALISTS IN NOVA SCOTIA

### INTRODUCTION

Those who did not support the American revolt against Britain formed the basis of the Loyalists, though not all anti-republicans were necessarily Loyalists, nor were all Loyalists fond of the British Crown or even unsympathetic to the rebel cause. There were likely as many reasons for not supporting the revolution as there were people who did not. The American revolution did, however, pit those who wanted liberty from Britain against those who did not—which obviously included not only the British colonial administration but also thousands of others for whom treason was simply unacceptable or for whom republicanism was anathema. Thus the American War of Independence was also a war between residents within the Thirteen Colonies.

The struggle was long and bloody, but the rebels prevailed, establishing the United States of America in 1783—the world's first modern republic. Those civilians and soldiers who fought against the revolution now found themselves in a foreign and hostile nation-state. Their properties were confiscated, they were put on trial at kangaroo courts, and their lives were made miserable by being cast as traitors. Many of them had never even visited

Britain, despite their loyalty to it. America was their home—in which they were now unwelcome. For many, remaining in the United States was simply impossible, and a steady stream of such refugees fled for the nearest facsimile—Canada. Most of these Loyalists came from the eastern seaboard and therefore logically sought out an equivalent new home, in Nova Scotia in particular. Though they landed in territory that was theoretically friendly, the situation there was very complex and not as accommodating as they expected.

Britain expelled the Acadian population during the Conquest of the 1750s, and thereafter encouraged New Englanders to settle the vacated lands of Nova Scotia, some quarter of a century before the American War of Independence. Roughly 8,000 "Planters" took up the offer and brought with them notions of participatory democracy and fundamentalist religion, the very creed of the American revolution. Thus it was not surprising that American rebels initially sought to win Planter support for their cause. In this they failed, not necessarily because of a lack of sympathy, but because the Planters did not care about issues of western expansion, had developed excellent trade networks with Britain that would be threatened by revolution, and simply wanted to get on with their lives. Into their midst, and after the revolution, landed the Loyalists, some 35,000 of them.

British administrators wanted to accommodate the Loyalists. After all, their loyalty deserved recognition and having them on the border was of strategic value. Thus, officials helped the newcomers with immediate accommodation, surveying and giving free land to them, and assisting their settlement process. Nova Scotia Governor Parr's administration was, however, severely strained by the task. Discontent soon developed among the Loyalists since the methods of granting land were chaotic, inefficient, complex, and slow. In particular, Parr was accused of discriminating against Black Loyalists. British investigators exonerated him, but most Loyalists felt that he failed to demonstrate the degree of sympathy they deserved. For his part, Parr referred to the Loyalists as pretentious and a "cursed set of dogs." Animosity diminished over time, especially after a partition in 1784 split Nova Scotia. From its former territory Cape Breton and New Brunswick were created as exclusively Loyalist colonies.

For their part, many Loyalist newcomers came from solid middle-class backgrounds with an abiding belief in family, commerce, education, community, and a tempered sense of democracy, all of which they set about infusing into Nova Scotian society. They also developed a subconscious and defensive ethos in which they were determined to show the world, and themselves, that rejecting the American revolution was the right thing to have done. This generated a strong streak of self-righteousness, a tendency toward conspicuous consumption and ostentation, and an irritating sense of elitism. This, plus their strong conservatism, immediately set them on a collision course with local residents who resented and distrusted them.

Many Loyalists came from comfortable lives in the New England colonies, where money and the comforts it bought were relatively plentiful and where well-established and thriving communities and infrastructures were commonplace. Though some arrived with a modicum of their former wealth, more arrived destitute and had to start from nothing, which was difficult, both physically and psychologically. Nor could the Loyalists, unlike the Planters before them, simply parachute into lands already cleared. Instead, they had to open up new regions from scratch, the main area being the St. John River valley in what became New Brunswick. The contrast was stark: lives of relative gentility in the former New England colonies versus their new existence in muddy little hamlets in New Brunswick's back country. The price for loyalty was high.

One group of Loyalists posed a unique problem. Britain promised freedom to any slaves who revolted against their American pro-revolutionary masters, and many accepted the offer. These insurrectionist slaves found themselves on the losing end of the conflict, however, and fled north with the other Loyalists, hunted and terribly vulnerable—but free. While Blacks received land and provisions like others, life in "Nova Scarcity" turned out to be bitterly cold and painful. Canada's first race riot, for example, occurred at Shelburne in 1784, shortly after the Black Loyalists' arrival. Conditions in New Brunswick were even worse, with restrictions on where Blacks could fish and settle and with whom they could consort, along with a myriad of other racially based discriminatory laws. It made life very tough indeed. Many newly freed Loyalist slaves failed to cope and either reverted to quasi-bondage to opportunistic employers or fled. Nearly a third of the Black Loyalists opted for passage back to Africa; at least 20 per cent of all other Loyalists eventually returned to the United States after a relatively short period in Canada.

Nonetheless, Loyalist mythology runs deep in Canadian history. Many historians, for example, argue that the Loyalist migration indelibly stamped both Canada and the United States, the former by their arrival, the latter by their exodus. This interpretation posits Loyalist sentiments as strengthening the already thick sinews of conservatism running through Canadian culture. Meanwhile, the liberal republican individualism of the new United States was purified by the cleansing of this more conservative element that fled northward. Thus, the two nations, so the story goes, would forever be psychologically different, despite superficial similarities and a common ancestry.

### DISCUSSION POINTS

1. What were the major difficulties encountered by the Loyalists? How much of this was related to unrealistic expectations on their part? What reasons would they have to return to the United States?

2. A large number of Loyalists were women who left no accounts of their immigration experience. Would they have had similar experiences to King and Winslow?

3. Did the Loyalists exhibit a unique ideology that still forms part of the Canadian identity? In what respects were Loyalist attitudes similar to those of the French Canadians?

## DOCUMENTS

### 1. Benjamin Marston, *Diary*, 1783-1784

*Benjamin Marston (1730-92) was a prosperous businessman when the revolution erupted. A confirmed Loyalist, he fled after rebel mobs attacked his home, reaching Halifax in 1776. There he became surveyor of the Shelburne area in 1783 and surveyed the new Loyalist townships. Governor Parr fired him in 1784 over unsubstantiated accusations of favouritism, after which he became New Brunswick's forestry surveyor. Marston left for Britain in 1787 to press his claim for Loyalist compensation, in which he only partially succeeded.*

Sunday, May 4, [1783]. Ashore in the morning. About 4 o'clock p.m. some of the fleet from New York hove in sight. Weather fair, wind north westerly, fresh.

Monday, 5. Last night the fleet got in below, upwards of thirty sail in all, in which there are three thousand souls (as an agent tells me). They all came up into the North East Harbour. Set up our Marquee on shore. At night we came up to our old anchoring place at the cove, having been down to the Fleet. Wind westerly, moderate, weather fair.

Wednesday, 14. Ran one line today. People turning very indolent, some parties not at work till 11 o'clock. Many of the people who came in this fleet are of the lower class of great towns. During the war such employment's as would not cost them much labour afforded them a plentiful support. This has made them impatient of labour. They begin to be clamorous, and to have a thousand groundless rumors circulating among them to the prejudice of those to whom they ought to submit.

Saturday, 24. Thursday last the people drew for their town lots. By indulging their cursed republican principles they committed an irregularity which cost them another day's work. Yesterday I was ashore all day apportioning people to their lots—'tis a task trying to humanity, for while those engaged in settling them are justly exasperated at the insolence and impertinence of one sort of people, they can't help they must feel for the distress of the sensible feeling part, who have come from easy situations to encounter all the hardships of a new plantation and who wish to submit cheerfully to the dispensations of Providence. Ashore again all today appointing people to their lots. Some grumble, some are pleased. They are upon the whole a collection of characters very unfit for the business they have undertaken. Barbers, Taylors, Shoemakers and all kinds of mechanics, bred and used to live in great towns, they are inured to habits very unfit for undertakings which require hardiness, resolution, industry and patience....

Thursday, 29. Yesterday at Town all day fixing people upon their lots. Many are pleased. The idea of owning land is somehow or other exceedingly agreeable to the human mind. Some whose lots have fallen to them in not so pleasant places are much out of temper, and some designing ones, who have missed the advantageous situations, are likewise dissatisfied.

Monday, 9. Today lay'd out a half block for a few elect ones. Company to dine with us. Too much dissipation. Sir Guy's commissions have made many men here gentlemen, and of course their wives and daughters ladies, whom neither nature nor education intended for that rank.

Thursday, 19. Yesterday and today engaged in surveying the shore and laying out 50 acre lots for private parties. 'Tis a hard service, and though I make good wages 'tis all earned. The heat in the woods and the black flies are almost insupportable.... Our people much at variance with one another, a bad disposition in a new settlement. Two of the Captains appointed to fight a duel this morning, but were prevented by friends who thought better of the matter.

Saturday, 12. The people yesterday drew for their 50 acre lots. They have left many out of the drawing who are equally entitled to a lot as those who have drawn. They want government, more knowledge and a small portion of generosity. They wish to engross this whole grant into the hands of the few who came in the first fleet, hoping the distresses of their fellow loyalists, who must leave New York, will oblige them to make purchases.

Wednesday, 16. Rainy weather for these 6 or 7 days past has kept us from doing much; we have, however, drawn the town water lots—finished yesterday. As usual many are discontented because their lots are low and wet.

Monday, 26. [July 1784]. Great Riot today. The disbanded soldiers have risen against the Free negroes to drive them out of Town, because they labour cheaper than they—the soldiers.

Tuesday, 27. Riot continues. The soldiers force the Free negroes to quit the Town—pulled down about 20 of their houses. This morning I went over to the

Barracks by advice of my friends, who find I am threatened by the Rioters, and in the afternoon took passage for Halifax. By further advice from Town, find I have been sought after. Arrived in Halifax Thursday, 29th.

Wednesday, August 4.... I find I have been hunted for quite down to Point Carleton, and had I been found should have had a bad time among a set of villainous scoundrels—by some subsequent advice, I find I should have been fairly hung.

Wednesday, 18. A ship from England, by which we learn this Province is to be divided, and a new government erected on the western side of the Bay of Fundy by the name of New Brunswick. If I can get some employment in the new Province, I shall choose my residence there, as most of the New England Refugees will be there and among them my nearest and dearest friends. Shelburne is composed of such a mixed multitude, so very few people of education among them, that it will take me all the rest of my life to get myself well accommodated to their ways of acting and thinking; and unless one can give in to the general mode of thinking and acting of those he lives with he can have but little enjoyment.

Tuesday, 7. Presented a memorial to Governor Parr this day and date, requesting a public inquiry to be made into my conduct while Chief Surveyor at Shelburne. He says only ... that everybody accuses me of the most corrupt partial conduct while in my office of Chief Surveyor. He has ordered me to wait upon him tomorrow at 12 o'clock. He will then tell me if I shall be heard or not. I find he has sent my character home under all these infamous accusations—

### 2. Memoirs of Boston King, 1784

*Boston King (1760–1802) fled his American owner in 1780, fighting for Britain in the revolution. Twice captured, he managed to escape. Along with his wife he accepted British promises of freedom and went to Nova Scotia in 1783. There they settled in "Birchtown," a township for Black Loyalists. A trained carpenter, King supplemented the income from his small plot by working in nearby Shelburne. In 1792, discouraged by racism and unfulfilled promises, he left for the West African nation of Sierra Leone, which had been created for freed slaves. He taught there and became Africa's first Methodist missionary.*

... About which time, (in 1783) the horrors and devastation of war happily terminated and peace was restored between America and Great Britain, which diffused universal joy among all parties; except us, who had escaped from slavery and taken refuge in the English army; for a report prevailed at New York, that all the slaves, in number 2000, were to be delivered up to their masters although some of them had been three or four years among the English. This dreadful rumour filled us all with inexpressible anguish and terror, especially when we saw our old masters coming from Virginia, North Carolina, and other parts, and seizing upon their slaves in the streets of New York, or even dragging them out of their beds. Many of the slaves had very cruel masters, so that the thoughts of returning home with them embittered life to us. For some days we lost our appetite for food, and sleep departed from our eyes. The English had compassion upon us in the day of distress, and issued out a Proclamation, importing, That all slaves should be free, who had taken refuge in the British lines, and claimed the sanction and privileges of the Proclamations respecting the security and protection of Negroes. In consequence of this, each of us received a certificate from the commanding officer at New York, which dispelled all our fears, and filled us with joy and gratitude. Soon after, ships were fitted out, and furnished with every necessary for conveying us to Nova Scotia. We arrived at Birch Town in the month of August, where we all safely landed. Every family had a lot of land, and we exerted all our strength in order to build comfortable huts before the cold weather set in....

About this time the country was visited with a dreadful famine, which not only prevailed at Birchtown, but likewise at Chebucto, Annapolis, Digby, and other places. Many of the poor people were compelled to sell their best gowns for five pounds of flour, in order to support life. When they had parted with all their clothes, even to their blankets, several of them fell down dead in the streets, thro' hunger. Some killed and eat their dogs and cats; and poverty and distress prevailed on every side; so that to my great grief I was obliged to leave Birchtown, because I could get no employment. I traveled from place to place, to procure the necessaries of life, but in vain. At last I came to Shelwin on the 20th of January. After walking from one street to the other, I met with Capt. Selex, and he engaged me to make him a chest. I rejoiced at the offer, and returning home, set about it immediately. I worked all night, and by eight o'clock next morning finished the chest, which I carried to the Captain's house, thro' the snow which was three feet deep. But to my great disappointment he rejected it. However he gave me directions to make another ...

While I was admiring the goodness of God, and praising him for the help he afforded me in the day of trouble, 2 gentlemen sent for me, and engaged me to make three flat-bottomed boats for the salmon-fishery, at 1£ each. The gentleman advanced two baskets of Indian-corn, and found nails and tar for the boats. I was enabled to finish the work by the time appointed, and he paid me honestly. Thus did the kind hand of Providence interpose in my preservation; which appeared still greater, upon viewing the wretched circumstances of many of my black brethren at the time, who were obliged to sell themselves to the merchants, some for two or three years; and others for five or six years. The circumstances of the white inhabitants were likewise very distressing, owing to their great impudence in building large houses, and striving to excel one another in this piece of vanity. When their money was almost expended, they began to build small fishing vessels; but alas, it was too late to repair their error. Had they been wise enough at first to have turned their attention to the fishery, instead of the fine houses, the place would soon have been in a flourishing condition; whereas it was reduced in a short time to a heap of ruins, and its inhabitants were compelled to flee to other parts of the continent for sustenance....

October 24, we left Pope's Harbour, and come to Halifax, where we were paid off, each man receiving 15£ for his wages; and my master gave me two barrels of fish agreeable to his promise. When I returned home, I was enabled to clothe my wife and myself; and my Winter's store consisted of one barrel of flour, three bushels of corn, nine gallons of treacle, 20 bushels of potatoes which my wife had set in my absence, and the two barrels of fish; so that this was the best Winter I ever saw in Birchtown. In 1791, I removed to Preston, where I have the care of the Society.... The Blacks attended the preaching regularly; but when any of the White inhabitants were present, I was greatly embarrassed because I had no learning, and I knew that they had ...

The people regularly attended the means of Grace, and the work of the Lord prospered. When the rains were over, we erected a small chapel, and went on our way comfortably.... When a sufficient quantity of timber was procured, and other business for the Company in this place completed, I was sent to the African town to teach the children to read, but found it difficult to procure scholars, as the parents showed no great inclination to send their children. I therefore said to them, on the Lord's-Day after preaching, "It is a good thing that God has made the White People and that he has inclined their hearts to bring us into this country, to teach you his ways...."

### 3. Edward Winslow, "To Ward Chipman," April 26, 1784

*A descendant of a Mayflower pilgrim, a soldier, and a confirmed Loyalist, Edward Winslow (1746-1815) fought against the American rebels at Lexington in 1775 and retreated with British forces to Halifax in 1776. Afterwards, as a refugee, Winslow moved to Annapolis County, Nova Scotia, where he assisted Loyalist settlement. In frustration he lobbied for a separate Loyalist province, which happened when*

*New Brunswick was created in 1784. There he accepted several government appointments, including to the colony's Supreme Court and the boundary commission.*

... I'll introduce another argument in favour of dividing this province, which ... is of some consequence. You will I think enter into the spirit of it. A large proportion of the old inhabitants of this country are natives of New England, or descendants from New Englanders, they, from their situation, never experienced any of the inconveniences which resulted from the violence of political animosity, they remained quiet during all the persecutions in the other provinces, they retained a natural (perhaps laudable) affection for their country ... by degrees the Nova Scotians became firmly persuaded of the justice of their cause.... On our side the principal people are men who have served in a military line—irritable from a series of mortifications scarcely cooled from the ardor of resentment— jealous to an extreme, some of them illiberally so. Either of these kinds of men may form useful societies among themselves but they can't be mixed—separate them,—and this very difference of opinion will increase the emulation and contribute to the general good; together—wrangles and contests would be unavoidable. Lord Sydney's declaration quoted in your letter, "That he will make Nova Scotia the envy of the American States," has excited a kind of general gratitude, I cannot describe it. Other ministers and Great men have by their patronage of new settlers, relieved individuals from distress, and rendered services to their country, but it is a God-like task that Lord Sydney has undertaken. Such an event as the present, never happened before perhaps never will happen again. There are assembled here an immense multitude (not of dissolute vagrants such as commonly make the first efforts to settle new countries,) but gentlemen of education, Farmers, formerly independent & reputable mechanics, who by the fortune of war have been deprived of their property. They are as firmly attached to the British constitution as if they never had made a sacrifice. Here they stand with their wives and their children looking up for protection, and requesting such regulations as are necessary.... To save these from distress, to soothe and comfort them by extending indulgencies which at the same time are essentially beneficial to the country at large, is truly a noble duty. By Heaven we will be the envy of the American States.... When the people of the neighboring states shall observe our operations, when they see us in the enjoyment of a regular system of Government protected by the mother country, not saddled with enormous taxes, and compare their state with ours—, Will not they envy us? Surely they will. Many of their most respectable Inhabitants will join us immediately....

#### 4. M.S., *A Sketch of Shelburnian Manners, Anno 1787*

*The identity of "M.S." is not definitively known but evidence suggests he was the Hon. James Fraser (Frazer) of Miramichi (1760–1822). Fraser was born in Aberdeen, Scotland, and immigrated in 1780 to what later became New Brunswick. There he established himself in the fishing and wooden mast cutting businesses. Both enterprises were very successful and Fraser became a wealthy man, known and well-respected for his integrity and business acumen. He was appointed a district judge of the Province of New Brunswick in 1788, afterwards became a merchant in Halifax, and represented the County of Northumberland in the House of Assembly from 1795 to 1819.*

The Inhabitants of Shelburne from the highest to the lowest have a pitiable passion for finery, revelling & dancing & every Species of Sensual gratification. They vie with one another in making an external appearance in the public eye, as being persuaded, that the world will judge of them much more by this, than from their internal worth. The modish Sort of Females, ever studious to attract public notice, spare no expense to set off their persons with Shewish vanities. So much are they abject Slaves to Fashion! That charming-bewitching thing.

The higher orders of people have private dancing parties each consisting of a few families who live in a constant habit of intimacy with one another. The Dance takes place in rotation at each Family, where a Suitable repast is provided for the Guests. It is matter of regret, that the Assembly for the Season, though designed for promoting social & friendly Intercourse among neighbors, should yet become the occasion of Censoriousness, Affronts & ill will, thro' the imprudence of Some Forward, pert & Gay young people who assume consequential airs by showing themselves reserved, haughty & distant towards those whom they deem their Inferiors, & by scoffing at proprieties as well as improprieties in dress & behaviour. Their shewish dress bespeaks a frivolous, loose & extravagant turn of mind. If you except their dress, diet & a few articles of furniture, everything else belonging to them indicate that they are of the Dregs of mankind. As further indications of this, might I not add the low kinds of artifice which they practise in order to gratify their inclination towards Gaiety & pleasure. Never were known greater mixtures of privy & meanness than many of the families here exhibit. Those among them who seem passionately fond of all kinds of delicious food & drink are not few in number. To gratify their desire after these, no expense is spared & to support this extravagance, recourse is had I to iniquitous means.... Officers of the army on Half pay & Loyal refugees who have had Compensation for their losses do in the general run give into fashionable extravagancies & follies, & the better to support these, the former in particular monopolize (if I may use the expression) almost every public office which is in the gift of Government.

The liberal Provision made for them allowing them a great deal of idle Time, & enabling them to live well at ease, their manners are loose & Corrupt; the generality of them being luxurious, mean spirited & subservient. The ruinous effects of luxury not limited by fortune have been so felt by some families as to reduce them to very straitened Circumstances, which has obliged them to content themselves with the bulk of mankind, the native consequence of the necessity of Circumstances. It is fortunate for such at least that this necessity has made them temperate & frugal. Deprived of a multitude of animal enjoyments with which they were infatuated in the days of ease & of affluence, they are less exposed to those temptations which might Corrupt & debase the hearts. To an extravagant passion for fine clothes & sensual pleasure, they join an immoderate love of money which tempts many to practice these roguish tricks. Thence it is that they have no Scruple to get gain by illicit trades, to import & to circulate base Coppers, to make use of those gross methods of dishonest Gain, the false balance, deceitful weights, & illegal measures, to adulterate Spirituous liquors, & to make an artificial want of Several articles brought to market. Some few, by keeping a Sort of Grocery Shop, have raised & enriched themselves, while others bred up in the lap of ease & plenty, not having it in their power to add to their fortunes, have exhausted them & fallen to decay.

The bulk of the inhabitants having been accustomed to a trading & rambling way of life during the late war, contracted an aversion to all kinds of work which are laborious. Add to this, that business being dull makes many idle hours in the day, which the inactive spend in hearing something new, in playing at games of hazard & in tippling or what may be termed a sort of sober intemperance. Then it is, that schemes of gainful artifice & commercial speculation are more common methods than hard labour & application for gaining a livelihood. Knavish, fraudulent tricks are so common in this place, that but few seem to blush at standing chargeable with them, because they are not branded with the disgrace they deserve. This trickish, disingenuous turn of mind is accompanied with a proness to harass with duns & vexatious law-suits. So true is this, that the Houses & lands in the settlement round are mostly encumbered with mortgages or attachments. This has been the fertile source of animosities & litigations. It is to be lamented that property is often taken away by Subtilty of law; the law being made an instrument of injury instead of personal Security. A man is too often oppressed where he expected Security, & the Dispenser of Justice becomes more terrible than a Highwayman.

An Insolent, & vagrant Habit so easily noticeable in the Inhabitants is contrasted with a Supine disregard, if not contempt of religion. Habituated to a wandering way of life during the late civil Commotions, & living amid the alarms of war, the hurry of business, & dissipations of pleasure, in a forgetfulness of God & divine things, they became regardless of religious Concerns. Hence they appear to have a greater zeal for anything than religion. Of this the temporary houses of public worship both for Episcopalians & Presbyterians are striking evidences. Those religious edifices being mean & shabby exhibit no fair emblem of the Piety of the Inhabitants. They have suffered their desires, hopes & fears to be so engrossed either by the Cares or pleasures of life as to leave them no disposition for religious regards. This irreligious bias has been strengthened by blemishes in those who make an open & solemn profession of their pious faith & hope, and by the ridiculous extravagancies of Character so palpably glaring in Bigots & Enthusiasts which have thrown a disgrace on true religion. A Spirit of discontent & repining pervades the whole Settlement. When people accustomed to live easily, like many in this place, are obliged to work hard & to feel straits, they become dissatisfied & restless; suffering much by toil & want, breeds discontent & wretchedness, especially where they have no near prospect of bettering their Circumstances. After enduring much fatigue & many hardships, in a Country which does not afford people but very scanty provision, they become impatient for a change of Scene. Happy as they may seem to be under an easy, free Government, the happiness of it is very little perceived or felt, neither Rulers nor ruled having virtue enough to forego immediate petty Gains for the public good. Accordingly we find that not a few who enjoy posts of profits, betray their trusts & embezzle the public money & that almost every public undertaking is made a Job of.

People brought up in the lap of ease & plenty cannot endure the straits & inconveniencies to which the inhabitants of a new settlement are subjected. Having been accustomed to what we call good living in a plentiful Country, they cannot enjoy life out of it. And even numbers who removed from the British dominions in Europe, previous to the late war, have contracted a restless, roving Spirit, the effect of an ardent desire after those pleasures & Conveniences which they once enjoyed there, but which they may now seek in vain. To many those days of ease, of pleasure & of happiness are no more. All they have got by tasting the Sweets of a fertily pleasant Country, is a restless desire after ease & plenty, which disturbs their tranquility & distracts their minds. After living very easily, they cannot be contented with a scanty allowance of the Comforts of life ... Hence it is, that they are tormenting their brains. With some scheme of private utility are immoderately solicitous saying "what shall we eat? what shall we drink? wherewith shall we be clothed?" while they think within themselves "what shall we do to fare sumptuously, to wear fine apparel & to live in grander?" Sure am I that people who are strangers to the enjoyments & advantages of rich Countries, may be accounted happier, as enjoying more of an easy peace of mind.

### 5. Edward Winslow to the *Royal Gazette*, July 1802

... It is an established fact that the Province of New Brunswick has been principally settled by an order of men who call themselves Loyalists, men who fought in the service of the King during a long war, and who, at the unfortunate termination of it, made an election to plunge into a wilderness with their wives and children rather than submit to the humiliating and degrading necessity of soliciting mercy from those whom they were in the habit of considering rebels. Actuated by the same laudable and manly spirit they persevered, and they combated difficulties, fatigues and toils which, in a bad cause, they would have sunk under. Here they soon obtained a constitution or government similar (so far as was practicable) to the British. Lands were assigned to them, ... Huts were erected which at first were hardly sufficient to shelter their families, and little holes were cut in the forest. A few potatoes and a scanty crop of rye were the only rewards for the immense labor of the first and second years. During the 3d, 4th, 5th and 6th, although the prospects brightened a little, the difficulties were great and many discouraging circumstances occurred; but under all this pressure of care and perplexity the voice of murmur could scarcely be heard among them. At the expiration of fifteen or sixteen years the scenes are materially changed. Enter the habitations of the Farmers in almost every part of the Province now and, with very few exceptions you'll find them tight, warm and comfortable, you'll see the man and woman surrounded by a flock of children robust, hearty and useful, clad in homespun, feeding upon their own mutton, with bread, butter and cheese in abundance. In many instances you may discover not only the comforts of life, but luxuries procured by their over-plus produce, which never fails to find an easy and sure market, or by their winter exertons in masting, getting timber, wood, &c, for which they receive the most liberal wages. Their barns and out-houses contain a stock of cattle, horses, sheep, swine, &c, of more value than their ancestors in [New] Jersey or New England ever possessed for three generations before they were born. Enquire among 'em for a Grievance and they'll not be able to point out one: Are you oppressed with taxes? No. Does anybody interrupt you in matters of conscience? No. Do the laws afford you sufficient protection? Why yes. This is the unexaggerated state of the Province now, and this too—at a time when one half the countries in the world have been ruined by a calamitous war. Notwithstanding all which, among the very people I have described, a few giddy, eccentric, and discontented characters have appeared who, forgetting all the favors which they received from our government, have made a voluntary sacrifice of their former honorable principles and professions, have sold the lands that were granted them, and meanly skulked into the United States.... Another class, who are not quite so culpable, but who appear to be influenced by the same extraordinary caprice. I mean those who have lately removed with their families to other parts of the King's dominions, particularly to Niagara. In comparing the two countries I declare that I have no intention of casting a reflection upon the Province of Upper Canada. I have a high respect for the government there, a good opinion of the country, and sincerely wish it prosperity. The final determination of a few changeable people with respect to the place of their residence is a matter of no importance either to them or to us, and the remarks which I shall make will perhaps apply with equal force to those who would wantonly and inconsiderately leave that Province and come to this. The principal object I have in view is to enquire whether there is any sufficient temptation offered to induce a Farmer, who has conquered the great difficulties of making an establishment here, to disturb the peace of his family and to undertake the arduous task of removing to a place so difficult to approach and so remote. It is obvious that there is no essential difference between the constitutions and the laws of the two Provinces. Allow that in Canada the climate is more mild, the winters not so long, the land if you please easier cleared, and the crops (particularly of wheat) more abundant. Possibly these considerations might have afforded good reasons for an original preference, but let us put against these advantages the acknowledged unhealthiness of the climate, the impossibility of selling that part of their produce which they cannot consume, the immense prices of many of the necessaries of life and the total want of winter employment. Would any man in his senses readily barter sound health for fevers, agues and debility? Would he relinquish a Farm, cleared with his own hands, which supplies him with everything he wants and something to spare, for a redundance of wheat, which he can't sell and a surplusage of Pork which he can't find salt to save?

FURTHER READINGS

Allen, R., Ed. *The Loyal Americans: The Military Role of the Loyalist Provincial Corps and Their Settlement in British North America, 1775-1784.* Ottawa: National Museums of Canada, 1983.

Bell, D. *Early Loyalist Saint John: The Origin of New Brunswick Politics, 1783-1786.* Fredericton: New Ireland Press, 1983.

Bell, D. "Sedition Among the Loyalists: The Case of Saint John, 1784-86." *University of New Brunswick Law Journal* 44 (1995): 163-78.

Brown, W., and H. Senior. *Victorious in Defeat: The Loyalists in Canada.* Toronto: Methuen, 1984.

Bumsted, J. "The Loyalist Question on Prince Edward Island, 1783-1861." *The Island Magazine* 25 (Spring/Summer 1989): 20-28.

Bumsted, J. *Understanding the Loyalists.* Sackville, NB: Centre for Canadian Studies, Mount Allison University, 1986.

Buzek, B. "'By Fortune Wounded': Loyalist Women in Nova Scotia." *Nova Scotia Historical Review* 7, 2 (1987): 45-62.

Cahill, B. "The Black Loyalist Myth in Atlantic Canada." *Acadiensis* XXIX, 1 (Autumn 1999): 76-87.

Condon, A. *The Envy of the American States: The Loyalist Dream for New Brunswick.* Fredericton: New Ireland Press, 1984.

Kimber, S. *Loyalists and Layabouts: The Rapid Rise and Faster Fall of Shelburne, Nova Scotia: 1783-1792.* Toronto: Doubleday, 2008.

Knowles, N. *Inventing the Loyalists: The Ontario Loyalist Tradition and the Creation of a Usable Past.* Toronto: University of Toronto Press, 1997.

Leyden, S. *Crimes and Controversies: Law and Society in Loyalist Saint John.* Saint John: Saint John Law Society, 1987.

MacKinnon, N. "A Death of Miracles: Governor John Parr and the Settling of the Loyalists in Nova Scotia." *Nova Scotia Historical Review* 15, 1 (June 1995): 33-44.

MacKinnon, N. *This Unfriendly Soil: The Loyalist Experience in Nova Scotia, 1783-1791.* Montreal and Kingston: McGill-Queen's University Press, 1986.

MacNutt, W. "The Loyalists: A Sympathetic View." *Acadiensis* VI, 1 (Autumn 1976): 3-20.

MacNutt, W. *New Brunswick, A History: 1784-1867.* Toronto: Macmillan, 1963.

Moore, C. *The Loyalists: Revolution, Exile and Settlement.* Toronto: Macmillan, 1984.

Potter-Mackinnon, J. *While the Women Only Wept: Loyalist Refugee Women.* Montreal and Kingston: McGill-Queen's University Press, 1993.

Rogers, P. "The Loyalist Experience in an Anglo-American Atlantic World." In *Planter Links: Community and Culture in Colonial Nova Scotia*, ed. B. Moody and M. Conrad. Series: Planter Studies, No. 4. Fredericton: Acadiensis Press, 2001.

Walker, J.W. St. G. *The Black Loyalists: The Search for a Promised Land in Nova Scotia and Sierra Leone, 1783-1870.* Halifax: Dalhousie University Press, Holmes and Meier, 1976; repr. University of Toronto Press, 1992.

Walker, J.W. St. G. "Myth, History and Revisionism: The Black Loyalists Revisited." *Acadiensis* 29 (Autumn 1999): 88-105.

Weatherell, C., and R. Roetger. "Another Look at the Loyalists of Shelburne, N.S., 1783-1795." *Canadian Historical Review* 70 (March 1989): 76-91.

# CHAPTER 6

# "The Abundant Blessings of British Rule"

## QUEBEC'S NEW ADMINISTRATION

### INTRODUCTION

In 1945 Hugh MacLennan published the quintessentially Canadian *Two Solitudes*, a novel exploring Quebec's canyon-deep schism between the Anglophone and Francophone populations. The societies lived in parallel as "two solitudes" without mixing, comprehending, or even seeing one another. MacLennan's observation, of course, was hardly new, and Canadians still struggle with the great national conundrum: how to get two cultures with a long tradition of mutual animosity and exclusion, with one conquered by the other, to live in harmony.

After the Conquest, many British administrators in Quebec expressed exasperation with the French Canadians whom they perceived as ignorant, lazy, priest-ridden, and possibly disloyal. Their response was, as often as not, a defensive irritation at what they saw as the Habitants' stultifying inertia and ingratitude for the "abundant blessings of British rule," which they believed the Conquest brought. The essence of British policy hinged on both a pragmatic and an altruistic wish to save French Canadians from themselves.

Most French Canadians, however, did not wish to be saved. They interpreted the Conquest as a humiliating defeat that threatened their very cultural existence through an invasion of foreign rules, money, people, language, and mores. That they were a subservient people whose leaders abandoned them after the Conquest exacerbated this situation, they argued, by leaving them foundering rudderless in an incoming tide of Anglos. Later French-Canadian nationalist historians likened their society to a body with its head decapitated, a situation, they say, that left the Québécois vulnerable to easy exploitation and subjugation. With attitudes like that, it is hardly surprising that many French Canadians erected physical and psychological bulwarks against what they feared as cultural genocide—and that they always remembered who they were. It is not by chance that Quebec's provincial motto, still stamped on every licence plate, is *je me souviens* [I remember]. The two peoples, British and French Canadian, could not, and would not, empathize with each other. They invariably dug in their heels, retreated behind their cultural barricades, and periodically lobbed inflammatory rhetoric at one another.

In fairness to both, empathizing with a foreign culture is problematic because it involves an inherent contradiction made particularly troublesome, if not impossible, when the two find themselves involuntarily tossed together as a result of war. Could British residents ever understand a Habitant's world view and vice versa? Is it not asking too much to have them perceive each other objectively and to develop a *modus vivendi* based upon that?

Three profoundly important pieces of legislation dominated the period between the Conquest and the early nineteenth century and anchor an understanding of the social dilemmas of the day: the Royal Proclamation of 1763, the Quebec Act of 1774, and the Constitution Act of 1791. These, plus the American War of Independence, stamped the face of Quebec as it emerged in its new Britannic guise.

The Royal Proclamation of 1763 took no one by surprise, though it confirmed the Québécois' worst fears. Now conquered, they were to be Anglicized as rapidly as possible by eliminating the foundations that structured their society: the Catholic church, their legal code, their system of land tenure, and their administrative formation. The Proclamation essentially swept the French regime asunder, replacing it with institutions consistent with the rest of the British Empire. A small coterie of British civil and military administrators was to implement the changes—which they didn't, fearing it would foment revolt among the Habitant majority. Their concern was well founded: New Englanders to the south increasingly demanded independence from Britain and logically urged the Québécois to join in.

Quebec's governor in the 1770s, Guy Carleton, wooed the remaining French-Canadian leadership as a way of guaranteeing Habitant loyalty in this revolutionary era. Getting the seigneurs and the clergy on side, however, required abrogating the hated Royal

Proclamation, which Carleton did with the Quebec Act of 1774. The Act defined the nature of the colony and still serves, to many French Canadians, as proof of their distinct society. It stipulated that Quebec was, in fact, different from the rest of the Empire: French civil law ruled in a British colony; the Catholic church had official recognition; the seigneurial system lived; and without an elected Assembly, democracy lay in the distant future. And, despite concerted efforts, rebels did indeed fail to win the hearts of the Québécois during the American revolution. A vindicated Carleton believed this was at least partly because of the Quebec Act, though he was disappointed by what he perceived as feeble overt Habitant loyalty to Britain.

The creation of the United States fed a stream of refugees heading north into British Quebec where, much to their chagrin, these so-called Loyalists found themselves living under the Quebec Act and its French orientation. They demanded British institutions for a British colony, particularly after fighting and losing to defend them south of the border. Quebec's British administrators wanted to oblige, but tinkering with the Quebec Act was unacceptable to the ever-vigilant Québécois. The Constitution Act of 1791 resolved this apparent impasse by splitting Quebec into two colonies, Upper and Lower Canada, the former with British rule, the latter under the unique Quebec Act—but with an elected Assembly based upon male representation by population.

Thus the socio-political battle lines emerged in Lower Canada: the Anglos and their supposedly co-opted "friends" the seigneurs and clergy, versus the Habitants now led by a small cohort of up-and-coming young middle-class French-Canadian patriots. If Britain sought a tranquil colony in Quebec, it was sorely disappointed. Canada continues to live with the legacy of this turbulent era, and two referenda on separation at the end of the twentieth century, plus another promised in the twenty-first, surely prove that resolution still eludes the two solitudes.

DISCUSSION POINTS

1. Were French Canadians better off or not under British rule?

2. British visitors such as Lambert and Gray were outsiders commenting upon a culture and people with whom they did not identify. In what respects, if any, did they demonstrate an ethnocentric bias?

3. Why did French-Canadian nationalism emerge in this period?

4. Did members of the Catholic clergy such as Plessis "sell out" to the British?

## 1. Joseph-Octave Plessis, Bishop of Quebec, "Sermon on Nelson's Victory at Aboukir," 1799

*Msgr. Joseph-Octave Plessis (1763–1825) was the Quebec-born, and thoroughly Qué-bécois, Bishop of Quebec from 1806 to 1825. He cemented the alliance between the Catholic Church and its new political masters, preached deference and submission to British authority, and yet maintained a remarkable degree of clerical independence. No British sycophant, Plessis interpreted French Canada's history to its people, explained incidents like the Conquest, and strove to ensure that the Québécois remembered, and celebrated, who they were. His speech was part of the celebrations marking Britain's victory over Napoleon's armies in 1799.*

... What sort of government, Gentlemen, is the best suited for our happiness? Is it not the one marked by moderation, which respects the religion of those it rules, which is full of consideration for its subjects, and gives the people a reasonable part in its administration? Such has always been the British government in Canada. To say this is in no way to practise the flattery that cowards use to bless the powers that be. God forbid, my brothers, that I should profane this holy pulpit by base adulation or interested praise. This testimony is demanded by truth as well as gratitude, and I have no fear of being contradicted by anyone who knows the spirit of the English government. It always proceeds with wise deliberation; there is nothing precipitous in its methodical advance. Do you see in its operations any of the delusive enthusiasm, the thoughtless love of novelty, the liberty without limits or restraints that, before our very eyes, is destroying certain malconstituted states? What care it takes for the property of its subjects! What skillful efforts are made to arrange the public finances so that its subjects are scarcely aware of the burden! Have you heard any complaints, these past forty years under their rule, of the poll-taxes, the tariffs, the head taxes under which so many other nations groan? What of those arbitrary requisitions of immense sums that unjust conquerors arrogantly impose on the unhappy conquered? Have you been reduced, by their lack of foresight, to those famines that formerly afflicted our Colony, which we still recall with horror and shuddering? Have you not seen, on the contrary, that in years of scarcity the government wisely prohibits the export of grain until enough has been put aside for your own needs? Have you been subjected to military service since the Conquest, obliged to leave your wives and children destitute in order to go to some far-off place to attack or repulse some enemy of the State? Have you contributed a penny to the expenses of this costly war that Great Britain has been waging for almost six years? Almost the whole of Europe has been given over to carnage and destruction, the holiest cloisters have been violated, virgins dishonoured, mothers and children slaughtered in several places. Is it not evident, and can it not be said, that at the height of this war you enjoy all the advantages of peace? To whom, my brothers, aside from God, do you owe these favours, if not to the paternal vigilance of an Empire which, in peace as in war, I dare to say, has your interests closer to its heart than its own? In every field I see evidence of this partiality. Your criminal code, for example, was too severe; it provided no sufficiently reliable rule for distinguishing the innocent from the guilty, and it exposed the weak to the oppression of the strong. It has been replaced by the criminal law of England, that masterpiece of human intelligence, which checks calumny ... which convicts only those whose guilt is obvious, which gives the accused every means of legitimate defence, and which, leaving nothing to the discretion of the judge, punishes only in accordance with the precise provisions of the law. Finally, what about the common law? While in France all is in disorder ... , is it not wonderful to see a British Province ruled by the common law of Paris and by the Edicts and declarations of the kings of France? To what are we to attribute this gratifying peculiarity? To the fact that you wanted to maintain these ancient laws; to the fact that they seemed better adapted to the nature of real property in this country. There they are, then, preserved without any alterations except those that provincial Legislation is free to make. And in that Legislation you are represented to an infinitely greater degree than the people of the British Isles are in the Parliaments of England or Ireland.

Do such benefits, Gentlemen, not demand from us some return? A lively feeling of gratitude towards Great Britain; an ardent desire never to be separated from her; a deep conviction that her interests are no different from our own; that our happiness depends upon hers; and that if sometimes it has been necessary to grieve over her losses, we must, by the same principle, rejoice today in the glory she has won and regard her latest victory as an event no less consoling for us than it is glorious for her.

Where do we stand, Christians, if we add to these political considerations another that, above all else, makes this empire worthy of your gratitude and praise? I mean the liberty left our religion and guaranteed by law; the respect shown to those in our monasteries; the unbroken succession of Catholic Bishops, who have so far enjoyed the favour and confidence of the King's Representatives; the unfailing support our curés have enjoyed in the villages and countryside in their efforts to conserve faith and morals. If this faith is growing weaker among us, my brothers, if morality is becoming more lax, it is not because of any change of government; it is to you yourselves that this disorder must be attributed; to your lack of submission to the teaching of the Gospels; to your foolish pursuit of a liberty you already enjoy without knowing it; to the poisonous harangues of those dishonest and unprincipled men, those perpetual grumblers who are offended by order, humiliated by obedience, and outraged by the very existence of religion.

Alas! Where would we be, my brothers, if such men should ever get the upper hand, if their desires should be fulfilled, if this country, by a grievous misfortune, should return to its former masters? This house of God, this august temple, would soon be converted to a den of thieves! Ministers of religion— you would be displaced, banished, and perhaps decapitated! Fervent Christians—you would be deprived of the ineffable consolations you enjoy in the accomplishment of your religious duties! Your land, consecrated by the sweat and tears of so many virtuous missionaries who have planted the faith here, would, to a religious eye, display nothing but a vast, melancholy solitude. Catholic fathers and mothers, under your very eyes, in spite of yourselves, you would see your beloved children nursed on the poisoned milk of barbarism, impiety, and dissoluteness! Tender children, whose innocent hearts still manifest only virtue, your piety would become prey to these vultures, and a savage education would soon obliterate the pleasing sentiments that humanity and religion have engraved on your souls!

*Conclusion.*—But what am I saying? Why dwell on such sad reflections on a day when all ought to be joy? No, no, my brothers. Fear not that God will abandon us if we remain faithful. What he has just done for us should inspire only comforting thoughts for the future. He has struck down our perfidious enemies. Let us rejoice in this glorious event. Everything that weakens France tends to draw us away from it. Everything that separates us from her assures our lives, our liberty, our peace, our property, our religion, and our happiness. Let us give everlasting thanks to the God of victories. Let us pray that He will long preserve the bountiful and august Sovereign who governs us, and that he will continue to lavish on Canada his most abundant blessings.

### 2. Anglo-Canadiensis, "To the Editor of the *Quebec Mercury*," *Le Canadien*, November 29, 1806

*Author unknown, "Le Canadien" first appeared a week earlier on November 22, 1806. Founded in Quebec City by several prominent politicians, this newspaper became the voice of French Canadians. It ceased publishing in March 1810 when Governor James Craig seized the press and jailed its editors because of allegations of conspiracy and treason.*

Sir:

... That the rising flood of French ambition must be opposed, no worthy subject would deny; all those who love freedom must agree with that sentiment; and a truth so widely recognized is universally felt; but to argue that this opposition should be carried out, even in part, through a change of language and way of life in Canada, and therefore, that Canada must be relieved of its Frenchness, is a proposition that, while itself ridiculous....

*The time has come*, says he, *for this Province, after 47 years of possession, to be English*, but might that end not be achieved without leaving behind the way of life and the language of the French? Might a Canadien not be, and is not he, truly English, by reason of his love for English freedoms, his commitment to the English Government, and his aversion to the principles of the French? Does loyalty lie in similarity of language? If not, and if it is only to be found in similarity of principles, then why *de-Frenchify* Canada? On what essential point do Canadien subjects differ from their English counterparts? If such a difference exists, why then did the Americans, whose language, religion, and way of life were those of the English, break free of their governance, and call on the French for assistance? Why have the inhabitants of Guernsey, who are French-speaking, remained loyal to the Crown of England for so long? Why did those of Jersey, French-speaking as well, give asylum to Charles II at a time when no part of the British Empire dared recognize him? Those islands have belonged to the English for more than 47 years, and they are still not English! Still not de-Frenchified! They even now retain their customs, their Norman laws, their feudal system, and their State assemblies! So how foolhardy would Edward I have been to recognize these rights, and how much more so would our minister have been to conserve them. Anglicanus knows all that (if he knows anything), he knows how close those islands are to France, our mortal enemy; he knows that nothing untoward has come of that proximity, of the language, laws, or way of life of those peoples, and he claims that Canada, as far from France, in principle, as the breadth of the sea that separates them, must be *anglicized—that we must raise a rampart against French ambition, by propagating the English language!!*...

Would it not be more apposite to raise *a rampart* (since ramparts must be raised) against the intrigues of our neighbours, rather than facilitating communication with them, by *propagating* their language? For, following his reasoning, if the English language is a *rampart* against French ambition, why should the French language not be the same against American speculations, especially at a time when Congress, which is English-speaking, is dictating laws of commerce to our British merchants?

So why *de-Frenchify* Canada? Why abolish an education that can shape such worthy subjects? No, the Canadiens, if left with their customs and way of life, even though they speak like the French and, like them, eat soup, will never cease to be what they have been until now. The Scots have not proven unworthy subjects for having retained the dress of their forebears; the Welsh for having kept their dialect and primitive way of life, and a Canadien will be no less worthy a subject for speaking in that tongue in which he vowed eternal loyalty to the English, and in which he continues to rejoice in their success.

### 3. John Lambert, *Travels Through Lower Canada and the United States of North America in the Years 1806, 1807, and 1808*, 1810

*Lambert (1775-?) came to Canada in 1806 in order to encourage hemp production after supplies dwindled in Europe. He toured the Montreal and Quebec area for a year, concentrating his efforts on discussions with influential Québécois rather than with Habitants who would actually grow the crop and whom he ignored. Lambert returned to Canada for a second visit in 1809 and over the next six months concluded that Britain did not understand its new colony—a fault he hoped to rectify by publishing a book in 1810 on the Québécois and Quebec. It sold well through several editions.*

The French Canadians, are an inoffensive, quiet people, possessed of little industry, and less ambition. Yet from the love of gain, mere vanity, or that restlessness which indolence frequently occasions, they will undergo the greatest hardships. There cannot be a stronger proof of this, than in those who labour in the spring to collect the sap of the maple tree: their exertions for five or six weeks while the snow is on the ground, are excessive. None also undergo severer trials than those who are employed in the fur trade. They penetrate the immense forests of the north-west for thousands of miles, exposed to all the severities of the climate, and often to famine and disease....

The suppression of the male orders was wise and politic, because, however useful the Jesuits might have been to their own government, it is hardly possible that they could have ever been reconciled to act in favor of one whose religious tenets clashed with theirs. As to the begging friars, no nation could be benefitted by them. The priests or catholic clergy at present so numerous, and who have received the support and protection of the English government, are entitled to particular notice. From the great influence which they possess over the minds of the Canadians, their importance cannot be questioned....

The Habitants content themselves with following the footsteps of their forefathers. They are satisfied with a little, because a little satisfies their wants. They are quiet and obedient subjects, because they feel the value and benefit of the government under which they live. They trouble themselves not with useless arguments concerning its good or bad qualities, because they feel themselves protected, and not oppressed by its laws. They are religious from education and habit, more than from principle. They observe its ceremonies and formalities, not because they are necessary to their salvation, but because it gratifies their vanity and superstition. They live in happy mediocrity, without a wish or endeavour to better their condition, though many of them are amply possessed of the means. Yet they love money, and are seldom on the wrong side of a bargain. From poverty and oppression they have been raised, since the conquest, to independent affluence. They now know, and feel the value of money and freedom, and are not willing to part with either. Their parsimonious frugality is visible in their habitations, their dress, and their meals; and had they been as industrious and enterprizing as they have been frugal and saving, they would have been the richest peasantry in the world....

The Habitants have almost every resource within their own families. They cultivate flax, which they manufacture into linen; and their sheep supply them with the wool of which their garments are formed. They tan the hides of their cattle, and make them into moccasins and boots. From woollen yarn they knit their own stockings and bonnets rouges; and from straw they make their summer hats and bonnets. Besides articles of wearing apparel, they make their own bread, butter, and cheese; their soap, candles, and sugar; all which are supplied from the productions of their farm. They build their own houses, barns, stables, and ovens; make their own carts, wheels, ploughs, harrows, and canoes. In short, their ingenuity, prompted as much by parsimony as the isolated situation in which they live, has provided them with every article of utility and every necessary of life. A Canadian will seldom or never purchase that which he can make himself; and I am of opinion that it is this saving spirit of frugality alone, which has induced them to follow the footsteps of their fathers, and which has prevented them from profiting by the modern improvements in husbandry, and the new implements of agriculture introduced by the English settlers....

The children of the Habitants are generally pretty, when young, but from sitting over the stoves in winter, and laboring in the fields in summer, their complexion becomes swarty, and their features ordinary and coarse. The boys adopt the pernicious habit of smoking, almost as soon as they have strength to hold a pipe in their mouth, this must insensibly injure the constitution.... The girls from manual labour, become strong boned and masculine; and after thirty years of age have every appearance of early decrepitude; yet their constitutions frequently remain robust and healthy, and some live to a considerable age.

The manners of the Habitants are easy and polite. Their behaviour to strangers is never influenced by the cut of a coat, or a fine periwig. It is civil and respectful to all, without distinction of persons. They treat their superiors with that polite deference which neither debases the one nor exalts the other. They are never rude to their inferiors because they are poor, for if they do not relieve poverty they will not insult it. Their carriage and deportment are easy and unrestrained; and they have the air of men who have lived all their days in a town rather than in the country.

They live on good terms with each other; parents and children to the third generation residing frequently in one house. The farm is divided as long as there is an acre to divide; and their desire of living together is a proof that they live happy, otherwise they would be anxious to part.

They are universally modest in their behaviour; the women from natural causes, the men from custom. The latter never bathe in the river without their trousers, or a handkerchief tied round their middle.

They marry young, and are seldom without a numerous family. Hence their passions are kept within proper bounds, and seldom become liable to those excesses which too often stigmatize and degrade the human character.

The men are possessed of strong natural genius and good common sense; both of which are however but seldom improved by education, owing to the paucity of schools in Canada. The women are better instructed, or at least better informed, for they are more attended to by the priests. Hence they generally acquire an influence over their husbands, which those who are gay and coquettish know how to turn to their own advantage.

As agriculture and commerce have increased, the British settlers have risen into consequence, and men of respectability been sent over to govern the country. The French inhabitants have however degenerated in proportion as the British have acquired importance. The noblesse and seigniors have almost dwindled into the common mass of the vulgar; their estates and seigniories have been divided among the children, or have fallen into the hands of the opulent British merchants. The few who still possess an estate or seigniory seldom live upon it, but reside wholly in the towns, equally adverse to agriculture, commerce, and the arts. They visit their estates merely to pick up their rents; and in collecting these, often have many broils with their tenants, whose contributions in kind, are not always of the best quality; and so far do they sometimes carry their contempt of their seignior,...

For a small society like that of Canada, the number of unfaithful wives, kept mistresses, and girls of easy virtue exceed in proportion those of the old country; and it is supposed that in the towns, more children are born illegitimately than in wedlock. The frequent infidelity of wives and husbands, creates much animosity and discord in some of the higher circles of Canadian society....

The general deficiency of education and learning among the great body of the people in Canada has been long a subject of newspaper-complaint in that country. But it is extremely doubtful whether the condition of the people would be ame-liorated or the country benefitted by the distribution of learning and information among them. The means of obtaining instruction, at present, are undoubtedly very limited; but it is occasioned, in a great measure, by their own parsimonious frugality; for if they were willing to spare a sufficient sum for the education of their children, plenty of masters would be found and plenty of schools opened. The British or American settlers in the back townships teach their own children the common rudiments of education; but the Canadians are themselves unedu-cated, and ignorant, even of the smallest degree of learning; therefore they have it not in their power to supply the want of a school in their own family, and thus do they propagate from age to age, the ignorance of their ancestors....

With respect to their obtaining a knowledge of the English language, I agree with those who are of opinion that so desirable an object might, to a certain extent, be attained by the interference of the government, and the establishing of parochial Sunday schools. The number who understand, or speak, English in Lower Canada, does not amount to one fifth of the whole population, including the British subjects. Few of the French clergy understand it, for in the semi-nary at Quebec, where it ought to form an indispensable part of the student's education, it is totally neglected; in consequence of which, a great many French children who are educated there, besides those that are designed for the church, lose a favourable opportunity of becoming acquainted with it; and that which is omitted in youth is neither easily, nor willingly, acquired in manhood. It is possible that the French clergy may look with jealousy upon the diffusion of the English language among their parishioners; they may think that as the inter-course between the British and French Canadians will be facilitated by such a measure, the eyes of the latter would be opened to many of the inconsistencies and defects of their religion; and that, in consequence, they may be induced to change their faith, and throw off the dominion of their priests. These, however, are but groundless fears, for as long as vanity retains its hold in the breasts of the Canadians, and while the clergy continue that indefatigable perseverance in their ministry, and that unblemished character and reputation, which distinguish them at present, it is not probable that their parishioners will depart from the religion of their forefathers. The instruction of the French children in the English language, is, therefore, neither difficult, nor liable to any serious objection. That it is a desirable object, and highly necessary for political as well as private reasons, is without doubt: that it is necessary for the dispatch of business, and for the impartial administration of justice, every man, who has been in a Canadian court of law, must acknowledge without hesitation.

Upon a review of the preceding sketch of the character and manners of the Habitants, who constitute the great body of the Canadian people, it will be found that few peasantry in the world are blest with such a happy mediocrity of property, and such a mild form of government as they universally enjoy. They possess every necessary of life in abundance, and, when inclined, may enjoy many of its luxuries. They have no taxes to pay, but such as their religion demands. The revenues of the province are raised, in an indirect manner, upon those articles which are rather pernicious than beneficial to them; and therefore it is their own fault if they feel the weight of the impost. They are contented and happy among themselves, and protected by a well regulated government. The laws are severe, but tempered in their administration with so much lenity and indulgence for human failings, that it has occasioned a singular proverbial saying among the people, that "it requires great interest for a man to be hung in Canada;" so few in that country ever meet with such an ignominious fate.

They have now enjoyed an almost uninterrupted peace for half a century, for they were so little disturbed in the American war, that that event can hardly be considered as an interruption. This has increased the population, agriculture, commerce, and prosperity of the country; and while it has raised the people to all the comforts of moderate possessions, of freedom, and independence, it has strengthened their attachment to the constitution and government under which they have thus prospered....

The Canadians have no reason to complain of the change of government. Before the conquest they were often unacquainted with that protection which the laws now afford them....

The French lawyers are not possessed of very shining abilities. Their education is narrow and contracted, and they have but few opportunities of becoming acquainted with those intricacies and nice discriminations of the law, that prevail in the English courts. The English advocates are generally better informed, and some of them either study law in England, or under the attorney and solicitor-generals, in Canada, who are generally men of considerable ability, and extensive practice. The Canadian lawyers are not excelled in the art of charging, even by their brethren in England. Their fees are high, though regulated, in some measure, by the court.... Tenacious as the Habitants are of their money, they are often involved in litigation, and the young advocates know how to avail themselves of the ignorance of their clients....

A very small proportion of the British Canadians were born in the colony, and consequently very little difference in person, dress, or manners, is discernible between them and the inhabitants of the mother-country. The French have also assimilated themselves so nearly to the British in dress, manners, and amusements, especially the younger branches, that if it was not for their language, there would be little to distinguish their respective coteries....

The Catholics of Canada, are a living evidence of the beneficial effects of religious toleration, regulated by the prudent measures of a mild and liberal government, though professing a contrary faith, and one too that was formerly viewed by the Papists with as much horror, as we looked upon theirs. But the Canadian Catholics never concern themselves about the religion of those who hold the reins of government. It is sufficient for them that they are allowed every privilege which the Protestants enjoy; that they sit in the executive and legislative councils, in the House of Assembly, and upon the Bench....

For fifty years the Roman Catholics of Canada have lived under a Protestant government.—They have been dutiful and obedient subjects, and when our other colonies shook off the yoke of Great Britain, they remained true and faithful notwithstanding great inducements were held out to them, by their neighbours, to follow their example. This steady adherence of the Canadians to their conquerors, can be attributed only to their due sense of the benefits they had received from them; and to the firm attachment of the clergy to the British government; for had the latter been inimical, either from religious or political causes, they could with the greatest ease have stirred up the whole body of the people to rebellion....

### 4. Hugh Gray, *Letters from Canada Written During a Residence There in the Years 1806, 1807 and 1808*, 1809.

*In 1809 Hugh Gray (dates unknown) published a series of 24 letters about life in Canada. His primary objective was to acquaint the British public with the largely unknown commercial opportunities available in North America. Little is known of him other than that he was British, a businessman, and described himself as a "landlubber." At the height of the War of 1812, he also published a book entitled* The Right and Practice of Impressment, As Concerning Great Britain and America, Considered.

The Canadians are legitimate Frenchmen,—the descendants of the worshippers of Louis the Fourteenth and of Cardinal Richelieu,—the descendants of men who never once formed an idea, themselves, of the nature of civil and religious liberty, and who, of course, would not be likely to impress it on the minds of their children. The authoritative mandates of the French king have never sounded in their ears in vain;—they were issued with all the arrogance of despotism, and received with implicit and passive obedience. Even now, to reason with the great bulk of the Canadians on the measures of government, is what they never look for; they have no idea of questioning their propriety;—command them *au nom du Roi*, and you will be obeyed.

The government of Britain have thought fit to give to Canada a constitution upon the same principles as their own; and have given to the Canadians the right of electing, and being elected members of the legislature.... Is it clear, that the British form of government is fitted for Canada, and that the Canadians are in a state to be benefited by being allowed a share in the government? Does their knowledge, their education, the whole train and direction of their ideas, prejudices, and passions, fit them for being legislators? I suspect that the answer must be in the negative. How can those men attain a knowledge of the principles of government, and of civil and religious liberty, who can neither read nor write, which is the case with the great mass of the people, and however strange it may appear, is the case with many of the members of the House of Assembly. This must seem incredible, but is however strictly true; and is of itself a most convincing proof that it was too soon to give them a share in the government. The state of the country is so low as to arts and letters, that it is impossible to find in the counties, and even sometimes in the towns, men, who in any respect are capable of taking a part in the legislature. Let knowledge be more generally spread through the country; let the people be taught to read and to reason, which Englishmen had long been habituated to before they received their constitution, and then, and not till then, ought they to have a voice in the deliberations of government....

Quebec, March, 1807. There is a great deal of misapprehension in Britain relative to this country. It is naturally concluded that, in a British colony such as Canada, a conquered country, those who govern and who give law to it, would be Englishmen. This, however, is by no means the case; for though the governor and some of the council are English, the French Canadians are the majority in the house of assembly; and no law can pass, if they choose to prevent it. The English (supposing the governor to exert all the influence he possesses) cannot carry one single question; and the Canadians have been in the habit of showing, in the most undisguised manner, the power of a majority, and a determination that no bill should pass contrary to their wishes. They carry things with a high hand; they seem to forget that the constitution under which they domineer over the English, was a free gift from Britain; and that what an act of parliament gave, an act of parliament can take away.

You will naturally imagine also, that in a British colony, the English language would be used in the house of assembly, public offices, and courts of justice. No such thing; the French language is universally used, and the record is kept in French and in English. That Canadians will not speak English; and Englishmen are weak enough to indulge them so far as to speak French too, which is much to their disadvantage; for though they may speak French well enough to explain themselves in the ordinary affairs of life, they cannot, in debate, deliver themselves with that ease, and with the same effect as in their native language.

I really do not see what they have to complain of; and yet they are very much dissatisfied.

Their dissatisfaction has lately had vent through the medium of a newspaper edited at Quebec in the French language. I have taken notice of it in a previous letter. They call it "Le Canadien." It affords to a certain class of the community a mode of expressing their feelings, to which they wish to give as extensive a circulation as possible. If one were really to believe that there are grounds for all that has appeared in this paper against the English, it would be concluded that the Canadians are the most oppressed people in the world.

I have taken pains to find out if they have any real cause of complaints—if they are oppressed or maltreated in any one way; but I have looked for it in vain. I have every wish to do them justice, and would gladly state to you any circumstance to justify their apparent dissatisfaction; but really, I cannot find any. I am afraid I must look for it only in their own tempers and dispositions, influenced by the peculiarity of their situation, as descendants of those who formerly had entire possession of the country, and of its government, civil and military; and who feel sore at being deprived of any part of the inheritance of their fathers....

Government, from the beginning, instead of showing a decided preference to their own language, adopted a temporising system, which left the Canadians without a motive to learn English. Had the knowledge of the English language always been held out as a recommendation to favour, and a preference given on that account, where other qualifications were equal—had English alone prevailed in the courts of justice, and in all departments of state, and public offices; it is highly probable that it would have been the general language of the country at the present moment: at least, it would have become a necessary part of the education of the better sort of people; as they could not have appeared at the governor's without it, nor have had any thing to say, either in the provincial parliament, or courts of justice. Had the leading men of the country been Englified, their influence would have been felt by the lower classes; and you might now, in a great measure, have had a colony of Englishmen, instead of Frenchmen. I may be told that language is only sound, and that a man may have good principles, whatever language he speaks. All that may be very true; but I deny that the descendants of Frenchmen, retaining the French language, manners, and customs, and constantly talking of the French as their progenitors, can ever be good British subjects, or enter heartily into her interests. The French man's *amor patriae* is not easily rooted out; may, nor any other man's *amor patriae*. It can only be done by giving a proper direction to the minds of young people; to accomplish which not the least pains are taken in Canada.

I have no hesitation in saying, that I think it would have been a fortunate thing for the country, if the English civil laws had been also firmly and permanently established; not on account of its own superior excellence, which the Canadians might justly question, but because it would have been understood by the judges, and uniformly and properly interpreted. A proper line of proceeding would, by this time, have been fixed upon; the practice and rules of court would have been ascertained and determined; the decisions would have been uniform; the laws would have been strictly enforced; and the minds of the people kept alive to proper notions of right and wrong....

Previous to the conquest by the English, I am told that the Canadians were an upright, honest people, fulfilling every engagement, and punctual in the performance of their various duties....

After the conquest, the people of greatest respectability both civil and military, retired to France—judges, counsellors, great landholders, governors, and rulers of all sorts; all those who, by example, precept, or authority, were qualified to keep good order in the country, who knew the people, their prejudices, and wants: almost all such left it. In their room came English governors and judges, who, though well meaning and just men, yet knew neither the people, nor their laws, language, nor customs; and (from not being brought up in the country) they were unacquainted with the thousand minute and undescribable impressions and notions acquired in childhood, which have a strong influence on our character and conduct through life. They could not, in the nature of things, preserve that check on the people to which they had been accustomed under the judges of their own nation....

Nothing debases a people so soon or so effectually as bad laws, or a bad administration of laws, in themselves good: the latter more frequently occurs than the former....

Here it is that Canada is defective; the courts are ill arranged; the forms of proceeding, vague and undefined. The French and English laws and forms, though good by themselves, have made a very bad mixture. There is, in short, something so bad in these matters, that the ends of justice are completely defeated. In Quebec, civil justice is really laughed at. A man who pays his debts here, has greater merit than in most other countries; he need not do it unless he thinks proper; he has only to entrench himself behind the forms and quibbles of the law, and laugh at his creditors....

In Canada there are no bankrupt laws; and you cannot arrest your debtor, unless you can swear that he is about to leave the country. You cannot put his property in trust for the benefit of his creditors, or deprive him of the power of disposing of it. You may easily conceive what an opening is thus given to those who are fraudulently inclined....

One of the principal causes of the poverty, not only of the Canadian farmer, but also of all ranks amongst them, is the existence of an old French law, by which the property of either a father or mother is, on the death of either, equally divided amongst their children. Nothing seems more consonant to the clearest principles of justice than such a law; yet it assuredly is prejudicial to society....

This division of property is extremely prejudicial to the interest not only of the landholder but also to that of the merchant, shopkeeper, and mechanic....

One effect of this law, and not only of the least material, is, that the affection between parents and children is likely to be destroyed by it: and, in fact, it is remarked, that in this country the instances of unfeeling conduct between parents and children are extremely frequent, and a spirit of litigation is excited amongst them. One is at a loss to account for such unnatural conduct, until an acquaintance with the laws and customs of the country gives a clue to unravel the mystery.

The law, making marriage a co-partnership, and creating a *communité de bien*, is sanctioned by the code of French law, called *Coutume de Paris*, which indeed is the text book of the Canadian lawyer; the wife being by marriage invested with a right to half the husband's property; and being rendered independent of him, is perhaps the remote cause that the fair sex have such influence in France; and in Canada, it is well known, that a great deal of consequence, and even an air of superiority to the husband, is assumed by them. In general (if you will excuse a vulgar metaphor), the grey mare is the better horse....

However, I believe I can safely say, that nowhere do the Roman Catholics and Protestants live on better terms than here. They go to each other's marriages, baptisms, and burials without scruple; nay, they have even been known to make use of the same church for religious worship, one party using it in the forenoon, and the other in the afternoon. There is something truly Christian in all this; it evinces a meekness of spirit, and degree of charitable forbearance with one another, which greatly promote general happiness....

### FURTHER READINGS

Bernier, G., and D. Salée. *The Shaping of Quebec Politics and Society: Colonialism, Power and the Transition to Capitalism in the 19th Century.* New York: Crane Russak, 1992.

Cook, R. "Some French-Canadian Interpretations of the British Conquest." *Historical Papers.* Canadian Historical Association, (1966): 70-83.

Greenwood, F. *Legacies of Fear: Law and Politics in the Era of the French Revolution.* Toronto: University of Toronto Press, 1993.

Greer, A. *Peasant, Lord and Merchant: Rural Society in Three Quebec Parishes, 1740-1840.* Toronto: University of Toronto Press, 1985.

Igartua, J. "A Change in Climate: The Conquest and the Merchants of Montreal." *Historical Papers.* Canadian Historical Association (1974): 115-34.

Lawson, P. *The Imperial Challenge: Quebec and Britain in the Age of the American Revolution.* Montreal and Kingston: McGill-Queen's University Press, 1989.

Miquelon, D., Ed. *Society and Conquest: The Debate on the Bourgeoisie and Social Change in French Canada 1700-1850.* Toronto: Copp Clark, 1977.

Neatby, H. *Quebec: The Revolutionary Age, 1760-1791.* Toronto: McClelland and Stewart, 1966.

Neatby, H. *The Quebec Act: Protest and Policy.* Toronto: Prentice Hall, 1972.

Nish, C., Ed. *The French Canadians, 1759-1766: Conquered? Half-conquered? Liberated?* Toronto: Copp Clark, 1966.

Ouellet, F. *Economic and Social History of Quebec, 1760-1850: Structures and Conjunctures.* Ottawa: Gage, 1980.

Standen, S. "The Debate on the Social and Economic Consequences of the Conquest: A Summary." In *Proceedings of the Tenth Meeting of the French Colonial Society,* ed. P. Boucher. New York: University Press of America, 1985.

Tousignant, P. "The Integration of the Province of Quebec into the British Empire." In *Dictionary of Canadian Biography*, Vol. IV, ed. F. Halpenny. Toronto: University of Toronto Press, 1978.

# CHAPTER 7

# *"All is gloomy"*

## THE WAR OF 1812

### INTRODUCTION

In a curious historical anomaly, Canada's strongest modern ally was its most feared enemy throughout much of the nineteenth century when its prime military objective was to prevent or resist invasion from the United States. Still more puzzling is the fact that both Canadians and Americans claim to have emerged victorious in the key conflict for domination of North America. In fact, Canada's best known military historian, Charles Stacey, referred to the War of 1812 as one of those rare historical episodes that satisfied everyone. According to Stacey, the Americans believed they had humbled the world's greatest military power, the Canadians thought they had turned back the massed might of the United States, and Britain was happiest of all because its people didn't even know the war had happened. Although somewhat exaggerated, Stacey's conclusions ring especially true when one reads the standard history survey texts. For Canadians, the War of 1812 also created the enduring perspective that part-time militia soldiers, not professionals, would be a sufficient and effective basis upon which to defend the country. Now widely known as the "militia myth," historians have come to believe that Canada's faith in part-time soldiers resulted in unnecessary casualties and serious organization difficulties in the wars that followed.

For their part, the British largely tend to forget the war; if they mention it at all, it appears as a small diversion during their life-and-death struggle against Napoleonic France. In their eyes, this "war" between small bands of professional soldiers, militia, and their Native allies fought in the backwoods of British North America was an inconsequential nuisance. Upper Canadians and French Canadians, on the other hand, perceived the war as a great victory, although in somewhat different terms. Since it was the first time they successfully fought alongside the British in their own units of French-speaking *Voltigeurs* under the command of their fellow countrymen from Lower Canada, French Canadians took pride in their accomplishments. For Upper Canadians, victory was related more directly to defending the British Empire and was more reserved since it overshadowed an ominous sense of foreboding, as Upper Canada remained largely surrounded by American territory and largely inaccessible to the British navy.

What precipitated American President Madison to declare war on Britain in June 1812? There were legitimate grievances. Britain sought to defeat Napoleon by using a naval blockade of continental Europe. The United States, as a neutral power, insisted that it had the right to trade with whomever it wished, including France, and would challenge anyone at gunpoint who threatened that freedom. Britain refused to allow this and regularly boarded American ships on the high seas where they also sought British deserters and regularly pressed former British subjects—even though they might now be American citizens—into the British navy. "Free Trade and Sailor's Rights" became the rallying cry of American war hawks. This precipitated an attack on the nearest British territory.

Why else declare war? There was the issue of Native land rights in the Ohio country and westward. Britain still insisted that part of the agreement for the creation of the United States some 30 years previously included guarantees of western land for Indigenous people, a promise unfulfilled by subsequent American governments. Since one of the central motivations for the revolution was demand for access to those lands in the first place, later British meddling in what was seen as an internal American affair was unacceptable.

Once declared, it was virtually guaranteed that the battlefield would be the weakly defended and underpopulated Upper Canada. The Americans reasonably expected a quick victory and annexation. Not only were Canadian defences inadequate, the local population of Upper Canada was largely of American ancestry so there was an assumption that these people would rally to the Stars and Stripes once American soldiers crossed the frontier. Thus, the American perception was that they came as liberating brethren to be welcomed by all but the British colonial administration. In this they were indeed partially correct— certainly more so than most Canadians comfortably acknowledge.

There was indeed significant reluctance on the part of Upper Canadians to serve in the militia, despite it being law to do so for able-bodied men between ages 16 and 60. First, the rumours of war were so routine by 1812 that no one believed them. The people also had better things to do, such as tend their farms. Finally, many Upper Canadians probably did not care under which flag they lived as long as they could go about their business. Those who did show up for mandatory militia muster often deserted shortly thereafter, often immediately upon receiving their pay. Though they were to supply their own muskets and shot, many showed up empty-handed to receive British army issue weapons, which some promptly sold. Other Canadians even crossed over and joined the Americans, though their number was small. Among even the enthusiastic fighters, training was so inadequate as to be almost non-existent.

The man charged with defending the colony, Sir Isaac Brock, despaired at the lack of enthusiasm and loyalty among his countrymen and arguably spent more time trying to keep his own people in line than he did fighting the enemy. This also applied to many Native people. Natives on both sides of the border did not wish to end up fighting against each other and on behalf of countries they suspected of duplicity based upon a long history of unscrupulous conduct. And the French Canadians? Their priests warned them of "ungodly Americans" who would surely not respect their culture and already threatened them economically. French-Canadian participation wavered at first but became more enthusiastic, particularly after one of their own, Charles De Salaberry, took on a heroic status. Meantime, the Canadian Maritimes remained uninvolved and disinterested throughout the war.

Why did American forces not overrun the Canadian colonies in a matter of days let alone weeks? There are several possible explanations. Much of the American population, especially that from the eastern seaboard, was distinctly unenthusiastic for a war. Ironically, as the war dragged on, some of those eastern states—the ones that originally revolted against Britain—now threatened to revolt against the United States unless it ended. By law, American militiamen were not required to cross into foreign territory. When they reached Canada, these men repeatedly invoked that right. Their training was also no better than the Canadians. Ineptness played a part on the American side, as did great competence and shrewdness on the part of the tiny and beleaguered British garrison. Finally, the British did have a secret weapon of sorts: Native allies. Despite reticence to join the fight and questions about their commitment, the Native presence alongside British and colonial troops created panic among some American commanders. Natives were correctly known as ferocious warriors who broached no quarter and took no prisoners—or at least brutally tortured any they captured. Brock knew this and used it to great effect as a psychological terror weapon. Before marching on Detroit, for example, he let it be known to the American defenders that his Native allies were "beyond control the moment the contest commences"; thus, American General Hull surrendered Detroit without firing a shot, an action for which he was later court-martialed.

The war dragged on through 1812, 1813, and into 1814 without signs of ending. It even extended to naval battles on the Great Lakes, where the Americans tended to have the upper hand. The eventual resolution resulted from secret negotiations between the weary British and American governments at the Dutch town of Ghent at the end of 1814. Canadians were not involved or privy to the talks.

How can Americans claim victory in the War of 1812? One answer can be found in the lines of the American national anthem "bombs bursting in air and our flag was still there," which refer to the British attack on Baltimore in August 1814. American authors focus on the last year of the war when Britain, finally finished fighting France, unleashed its entire navy to blockade American ports and sent invading armies into Maine, Lake Champlain, Washington, and New Orleans. Outnumbered and outgunned, the Americans held off every British attempt to secure American territory. Canadians, meanwhile, tend to focus on the earliest years of the war when they too were outnumbered and outgunned but resisted domination.

The Treaty of Ghent solved few of the contentious issues. A boundary commission was established to clarify the border west of the Great Lakes, and both sides agreed not to maintain warships on inland waters. Despite these apparent gestures of good will, Britain began a serious program to militarize North America by constructing new fortresses and the Rideau Canal. The open door policy that had welcomed American immigrants to Upper Canada as "late loyalists" well after the revolution was now closed. With the Alien Act of 1818 many former Americans realized that it was better to return to the United States. Britain, meanwhile, concluded that if it wanted to secure this territory, it would have to encourage large-scale immigration from the British Isles.

### DISCUSSION POINTS

1. What made General Hull think that most Canadians would not fight?

2. How objective was Michael Smith in his exposé of Canada West and its people? What are the possible strengths and weaknesses of his assessment?

DOCUMENTS

## 1. William Hull, Brigadier-General and Commander of the Northwestern Army of the United States, Proclamation, July 12, 1812

*Connecticut-born William Hull (1753–1825) studied law at Yale. He fought in many campaigns for the American revolutionary army, becoming a lieutenant-colonel and later a judge. President Jefferson made him governor of Michigan, which he set out to populate against the wishes of Native people. He reluctantly became commander of western American forces in 1812 and invaded Canada. After retreating, he later surrendered Fort Detroit without a fight. Court-martialed for cowardice, President Madison commuted Hull's death sentence.*

Inhabitants of Canada! After thirty years of peace and prosperity the United States have been driven to arms. The injuries and aggressions, the insults and indignities of Great Britain have once more left them no alternative but manly resistance or unconditional submission. The army under my command has invaded your country, and the standard of the Union now waves over the territory of Canada. To the peaceable unoffending inhabitant it brings neither danger nor difficulty. I come to find enemies not to make them. I come to protect, not to Injure you.

Separated by an immense ocean and an extensive wilderness from Great Britain, you have no participation in her councils, no interest in her conduct—you have felt her tyranny, you have seen her injustice; but I do not ask you to avenge the one or redress the other. The United States are sufficiently powerful to afford every security consistent with their rights and your expectations. I tender you the invaluable blessings of civil, political, and religious liberty, and their necessary result individual and general prosperity.—That liberty which gave decision to our councils, and energy to our conduct in a struggle for independence, and which conducted us safely and triumphantly through the stormy period of the revolution. That liberty which has raised us to an elevated rank among the nations of the world; and which afforded us a greater measure of peace and security, of wealth and improvement, than ever fell to the lot of any people.

In the name of my country, and by the authority of government, I promise you protection to your persons, property, and rights; remain at your homes, pursue your peaceful and customary avocations; raise not your hands against your brethren. Many of our fathers fought for the freedom and independence we now enjoy. Being children, therefore, of the same family with us, and heirs to the same heritage, the arrival of an army of friends, must be hailed by you with a cordial welcome. You will be emancipated from tyranny and oppression, and restored to the dignified station of freemen. Had I any doubt of eventual success, I might ask your assistance, but I do not. I come prepared for every contingency—I have a force that will look down all opposition, and that force is but the vanguard of a much greater. If, contrary to your own interests and just expectations of my country, you should take part in the approaching contest you will be considered and treated as enemies, and the horrors and calamities of war will stalk before you.

If the barbarous and savage policy of Great Britain be pursued, and the savages are let loose to murder our citizens, and butcher our women and children, this war will be a war of extermination.

The first stroke of the tomahawk—the first attempt with the scalping knife, will be the signal of one indiscriminate scene of desolation. No white man found fighting by the side of any Indian will be taken prisoner; instant destruction will be his lot. If the dictates of reason, duty, justice, and humanity, cannot prevent the employment of a force which respects no rights, and knows no wrong, it will be prevented by a severe and relentless system of retaliation.

I doubt not your courage and firmness—I will not doubt your attachment to liberty. If you tender your services voluntarily, they will be accepted readily.

The United States offer you Peace, Liberty, and Security—your choice lies between these and WAR, slavery, and destruction. Choose then, but choose wisely; and may HE who knows the justice of our cause, and who holds in his hand the fate of nations, guide you to a result the most compatible with your rights and interests, your peace and prosperity.

### 2. Major General Isaac Brock to Sir George Prevost, July 12, 1812

*British soldier Isaac Brock (1769-1812) distinguished himself in the early Napoleonic period and was posted to Canada in 1802. He commanded all forces in Upper Canada in 1810. Though greatly outnumbered in the War of 1812, Brock repeatedly took the initiative, which damaged American confidence. He died leading his men into battle at Queenston Heights in October 1812. Chief Tecumseh said of him: "This is a man." Much of Brock's correspondence was directed to his superior, Lieutenant-General George Prevost, who retained command of all British forces in North America.*

... The Militia which assembled here immediately on the account being received of war being declared by the United States have been improving daily in discipline, but the men evince a degree of impatience under their present restraint that is far from inspiring confidence. So great was the clamour to return and attend to their farms, that I found myself, in some measure, compelled to sanction the departure of a large proportion, and I am not without my apprehensions that the remainder will, in defiance of the law, which can only impose a fine of twenty pounds, leave the service the moment the harvest commences. There can be no doubt that a large portion of the population in this neighbourhood are sincere in their professions to defend the country, but it appears likewise evident to me that the greater part are either indifferent to what is passing, or so completely American as to rejoice in the prospects of a change of Governments. Many who now consider our means inadequate would readily take an active part were the regular troops increased. These cool calculators are numerous in all societies. The alacrity and good temper with which the Militia marched to the frontier have tended to infuse in the mind of the enemy a very different sentiment of the disposition of the inhabitants. He was led to believe that on the first summons they would declare themselves an American State. The display for several days of a large force was made, I have every reason to believe, in that expectation. Nearly the whole of the Arms at my disposal have been issued. They are barely sufficient to Arm the Militia immediately required to guard the frontier. Were I furnished with the means of distributing Arms among the people in whom confidence can be placed they would not only overawe the disaffected but prove of essential use in the event of invasion. The Militia assembled in a wretched state in regard to Clothing—many were without shoes, an article which can scarcely be provided in the Country. After the cannons, which have arrived this morning, are mounted, I shall consider my front perfectly secure. I do not imagine the enemy will hazard a water excursion with a view of turning my flanks. He probably will wait until winter when the ice will enable him to cross with the utmost facility to any port between Fort Erie and Long Point—My situation will then depend upon the force the enemy may bring to invade the Provinces. Should the troops have to move the want of tents will be severely felt— ... The expense of defending this Province will unquestionably be great. Upon a rough calculation, and supposing that 4000 Militia be constantly embodied it cannot be estimated at less than 140,000p: annum. However great the sum it will be applied to very considerable advantage provided Your Excellency be enabled to send reinforcements, for without them it is scarcely possible to expect the United States' Government will be so inactive and supine as to permit the present limited force to remain in possession of the Country. Whatever can be done to preserve it, or delay its fall Your Excellency may rest assured will be exerted.

### 3. Major General Isaac Brock to Lord Liverpool, August 29, 1812

*A former Secretary of War and Colonies, Liverpool became prime minister of the United Kingdom in 1812. Occasionally, he had requested information directly from his commanders in the field. Brock responded with his usual frankness.*

My Lord

The invasion of the Western District by General Hull was productive of very un-favourable sensations among a large portion of the population, and so completely were their minds subdued, that the Norfolk Militia, when ordered to March, peremptorily refused. The state of the country required prompt and vigorous measures. The majority of the House of Assembly was likewise seized with the same apprehensions, and may be justly accused of studying more to avoid, by their proceedings, incurring the indignation of the enemy than the honest fulfillment of their duty ... I cannot hide from Your Lordship, that I considered my situation at that time extremely perilous; not only among the Militia was evinced a disposi-tion to submit tamely, five hundred in the Western district having deserted their Ranks, but likewise the Indians of the six Nations, who are placed in the heart of the Country on the Grand River, positively refused, with the exception of a few individuals taking up arms. They audaciously announced their intention, after the return of some of their chiefs from General Hull, to remain neutral, as if they wished to impose upon the Government the belief that it was possible they could sit quietly in the midst of War. This unexpected conduct of the Indians deterred many good men from leaving their families and joining the Militia. They became more apprehensive of the internal than the external enemy, and would willingly have compromised with the one to secure themselves from the other.

I shall think it my bounden duty at some future day to call your Lordships attention to the absolute necessity of removing this infatuated people from their present situation. The loud voice of self preservation, every consideration of Policy recommends the measure, although they have changed their tone with the late success yet the necessity of guarding against the evil they may still commit, is not less imperious.

The Proclamation which General Hull published ..., tended in a great degree to create the disposition in the inhabitants already noticed, and his emissaries were numerous and active. I caused a Counter Proclamation to be issued which I had the satisfaction to find produced immediate effect among the well disposed who from that day increased in their activity and Vigilance. Having declared my intention of proceeding to the Western District with such of the Militia as might voluntarily offer to accompany me, in a few days five hundred, principally the sons of Veterans, whom His Majesty's munificence settled in this Country cheerfully tendered their service. The threatening attitude however of the enemy on other parts of the frontier obliged me to content myself with half the number, with whom I arrived in safety late on the 13th instant at Amherstburg. In no instance have I witnessed greater cheerfulness and constancy than were displayed by these Troops under the fatigue of a long journey in Boats and during extremely bad weather, and it is but justice to this little band to add that their conduct through excited my admiration.

To my official dispatch to His Excellency the commander of the Forces I beg leave to refer your Lordship for my subsequent proceedings.

Among the Indians whom I found at Amherstburg, and who had arrived from distant parts of the country, I found some extraordinary characters. He who attracted most my attention was a Shawnee chief, Tecumseh, brother to the Prophet, who for the last two years has carried on (contrary to our remonstrances) an Active Warfare against the United States—a more sagacious or a more gallant Warrior does not I believe exist. He was the admiration of everyone who conversed with him: from a life of dissipation he is not only become, in every respect, abstemious but has likewise prevailed on all his nation and many of other Tribes to follow his example. They appear determined to continue the contest until they obtain the Ohio for a boundary. The United States Government is accused, and I believe justly, of having corrupted a few dissolute characters whom they pretended to consider as chiefs and with whom they contracted engagements and concluded Treaties, which they have attempted to impose on the whole Indian race. Their determined opposition to such ficticious and ruinous pretensions, which if admitted would soon oblige the Indians to remove beyond the Mississippi, is the true ground of their enmity against the Americans. The jealousy with which they view the British Merchants continue their commercial intercourse with the Indians has likewise been attended with serious inconvenience. Under the difficulty ... of the first necessity. The consequence has been fatal to many. Deprived of ammunition the poor Indian was unable to provide the necessary quantity of food or even cover his nakedness with the skins of animals. The Armistice concluded between His Excellency Lt. Gen'. Sir George Prevost and General Dearborne, has suspended all active operations. However wise and politic the measure must be admitted to be, the Indians, who cannot enter into our views will naturally feel disheartened and suspicious of our intentions. Should hostilities recommence I much fear the influence the British possess over them will be found diminished: no effort however of mine shall be wanting to keep them attached to our cause—If the condition of this people could be considered in any future negotiation for peace, it would attach them to us forever. The reinforcements lately arrived from the Lower Province places this portion of the country beyond the likelihood of an attack. The enemy must increase his present force considerably before he can hazard an Invasion with a view of keeping possession of the country

### 4. M. Smith, *A Geographical View of the Province of Upper Canada, and Promiscuous Remarks upon the Government,* 1813

*A Baptist minister born in Pennsylvania, Michael Smith (1776–1816) moved to Upper Canada in 1810, apparently attracted by the land prices. He taught school and travelled extensively but by 1812 complained that he and his family were constantly harassed as "Yankees." Although he had taken the oath of allegiance to the British monarchy, he decided to return to the United States in December 1812 where he continued to work as both a minister and teacher. His account was first published in 1813 and enlarged in 1814.*

Population.—One out of twelve of the inhabitants of Upper Canada are natives of England, Ireland, and Scotland; and all the children born of such, born in Canada, make the proportion a little more than two out of ten. There are about an equal number of those who took part with the King in the revolutionary war, who, with their children born in Canada, make about one sixth part of the inhabitants at present;—the rest, with their children, are Americans. Or, in other words, if all the people were divided into ten equal parts, eight parts would be natives of the United States, with their children born in Canada, and two parts of these eight would be what are now called loyalists, (though natives of the United States before the war,) with their children born in Canada. The other six parts would be natives of the United States, and their children born in the province.

Within the term of 12 years, the inhabitants of the upper province have increased beyond all conjecture, as the terms of obtaining land have been extremely easy.

In the year 1811, the number of inhabitants in both provinces was 360,000. In the upper province, there were 136,000, not including Indians in the settled parts of the province.

The number of the militia, or of those who are liable to do duty, from the age of sixteen to sixty, are 22,660, including Indians in the bounds of the province at that time.

It is an idea entertained by the generality of the people of the United States, that the inhabitants of Canada are some of the worst people in the world, made up of rogues, murderers, and the like mean characters.

However, the idea is entirely false. That there has some bad characters escaped from different parts of the United States to Canada, no one will deny; but these cannot be called the inhabitants, but only sojourners. But I must say, whether I am believed or not, that the main body of the people of Canada are peaceable, just, and generous in all their intercourse with each other, and strangers also; they are benevolent, being once poor themselves, they know how to feel for human want and human woe. I have been acquainted with some of the inhabitants of almost every neighbourhood, and have found them to be nearly all alike, except those from England or Ireland. I have also attended a number of the courts of justice and was surprised to see so little business done at them. The most of the inhabitants of the western or upper part of the province are from the states of New Jersey, Pennsylvania, and New York, and yet retain a considerable degree of that rectitude of conduct and conversation observed among the Quakers and Presbyterians in those States. There is hardly ever an instance of a person stealing in this province, not perhaps because all the inhabitants are too good, but partly from this cause, and partly because the penalty annexed to the crime is death; however, no one has been put to death in the province yet.

In writing upon this subject, I feel as if I was treading upon delicate ground. Although I feel as much neutrality in the contest as perhaps it is possible for anyone to feel, except that I have one wish which is that of peace....

I have already noted that six out of ten of the inhabitants, were natives of the United States, or their children born in Canada. These people did not move to the province because they preferred the government of Great Britain to that of the United States, but in order to obtain land upon easy terms, for it must be remembered, that all the land of Canada now inhabited, was given to the people by the King who bought it of the Indians.

In a little time after [the outbreak of war] the flank companies [of militia] raised in different parts of the province some distance from Fort George, were called to it; and at the same time Gen. Hull invaded the province at Sandwich, nearly 300 miles west of Fort George. I then lived on the main road that leads to it, on which all the soldiers passed, and conversed with some hundreds of them, respecting their feelings and views, and found that nearly all of them were of the same mind, and that was, if Hull came down to Fort George, (which was the universal expectation,) and they were ordered to march against him, they would not obey. Such was their dread of war, and partiality to the United States' government. But not a man would have joined him and fought against the King, as was the opinion. But the event was, Hull did not come, but continued at Sandwich, and sent a proclamation among the people, telling them he was coming to deliver them from tyranny, and that he was able to accomplish the task; but, at the same time, he invited them to join him, like true rebels against their King and oaths, or else stay and mind their own work; but if any should come against him, and be found fighting by the side of an Indian, they should be murdered without mercy. I believe almost every one that saw or heard of this proclamation, treated its contents with contempt. People are hardly ever so willing to do wrong from the advice of others, as of their own accord.

Now, to take up arms against their King, whom they had sworn to protect, was too much. They were offended at any man, who could think that they were capable of such conduct; and as to assisting Hull in freeing them from tyranny, it was a mere notion—for if they had been under any, they could at any time have crossed the line to the United States. But they were told that they might stay at home and mind their business;—this proposal they would willingly have acceded to, for they dreaded the war with their whole souls. Some of them indeed took the friendly advice, for which they were sharply rebuked by their rulers, and in consequence of this some fled to the wilderness, and some remain there until this day for aught I know; but all of them were much exasperated against Hull, for threatening not to give any one quarters, who should be found fighting by the side of an Indian....

None of the people in this district [Newcastle district] bear arms, except twelve at Presquile harbour. They are universally in favour of the United States, and if ever another army is landed in Canada, it ought to be here, which would be a hundred miles from any British force, and before one could march there, nearly all the Canada militia would desert, especially if the American army was large. But whenever the Americans attempt to land where there is an army, that army will fight till they are nearly all destroyed, for they dare not rebel, not having now any faith in any offers of protection in a rebellion, as they have been deceived. Indeed many of the militia are considerably exasperated against the invaders, for they think that it is hard that they should feel the misery of war who have no agency in the councils of England, and know that the United States government cannot force any man over the line, of course those that come, they view as coming of their own choice, as void of justice and humanity, and therefore deserve to be killed for their intrusion.

In August, the inhabitants were called together, in order that all who had not taken the oath of allegiance, might take it without exception. However, some refused, some were put in the cells, and others were not dealt so hard with. Many took the oath rather than suffer thus....

The inhabitants at large would be extremely glad to get out of their present miserable situation, at almost any rate; but they dare not venture a rebellion, without being sure of protection. And as they now do not expect that the American government will ever send in a sufficiently large army to afford them a security, should they rebel, they feel it their duty to kill all they can while they are coming over, that they may discourage any more from invading the province, that the government may give up the idea of conquering it, and withdraw their forces, that they may go home also; for they are greatly distressed in leaving their families so long, many of whom are in a suffering condition.

Ever since the commencement of the war, there has been no collection of debts by law, in the upper part of the province, and towards the fall in no part; nor would one pay another. No person can get credit from any one to the amount of one dollar; nor can anyone sell any of their property for any price, except provision or clothing; for those who have money, are determined to keep it for the last resort. No business is carried on by any person, except what is absolutely necessary for the time.

In the upper part of the province, all the schools are broken up, and no preaching is heard in the land. All is gloomy—all is war and misery....

### 5. P-S. Bédard, "Memorandum In Support of the Petition of the Inhabitants of Lower Canada," 1814

*Pierre-Stanislas Bédard (1762-1829), a French-Canadian lawyer elected to Lower Canada's Assembly in 1792, believed that only an elected parliament truly represented the people's will. He therefore demanded responsible government and fought against the Anglo-dominated and appointed Executive and Legislative Councils. He co-founded the newspaper* Le Canadien *and its counterpart, the liberal* Parti Canadien. *Governor Craig sent him to prison for a year in 1810 for "treasonable activities" associated with his newspaper. This article, written in the war when many believed that Canada would fall into the hands of the Americans, suggests that French-Canadian culture would not survive if the United States won the war.*

The ideas that those of the English party are striving to keep alive, namely, that the Canadiens are less suited to filling positions of trust because they are too concerned for their own country and have less interest in and affection for the mother country, are less than sound. A Canadien is more attached to his country than to any other part of the Empire, the way a Scot is more attached to Scotland, or an Englishman is more attached to England, and he is no less capable, for that, of holding positions of trust in his own land. The honour or even the risk of losing his place will have no less influence on him than on any other, assuming the mistaken principle of there being a difference between the mother country's interests and those of his own land. It is true that a former subject is bound to be more attached to the Empire; but he also has less aversion to the people and Government of the United States, and if everything is taken into account, it will be seen that a Canadien is far more strongly attached to the interests of the mother country, in respect to the preservation of this land.

The Canadiens unable to protect themselves have only the mother country to protect them. Once this country is lost, they no longer have a homeland they can turn to; an Englishman still has his homeland.

If the Canadas pass under the authority of the United States, their population will be overwhelmed by that of the United States, and they will become nothing, without influence whatever in their Government; unable to protect their religion, which will only render them offensive to all the other sects that abound in the United States, and which, while tolerant of one another, all agree in their abhorrence of this one.

No fathers attached to their religion could think with anything but horror of dying and leaving their children under such domination. While the country remains under the British Empire, they need not fear the same dangers; they need not dread that a population hostile to their religion will emigrate from the mother country; they have hopes that their population will always be the largest in the country, and that with a constitution such as has been granted by the mother country, they will have the means of keeping their religion and all that is dear to them, provided that the mother country truly wishes to allow them the enjoyment of that constitution without its serving to render them offensive, and provided that the encouragement given to the American population in this country by the English party's administration ceases to bring about the evil they must fear.

Those of the English party are hostile to their concerns, in that, having far more affinity with the Americans in terms of customs, religion, and language, they encourage the American population, as a means of ridding themselves of the Canadiens whom they still regard as an alien population, as a French and Catholic population, with the same prejudice that the general population in the mother country harbours for the French and for Catholics, they cannot keep from seeing themselves in a foreign country, in a province in which the (French) Canadien population is predominant; a colony peopled by Americans seems to them more English, and in it, they would not see themselves as being so much in a foreign land. These effects are further compounded by the fact that perhaps the greater part of the Government's officials have become personally involved in introducing the American population to this country, through Crown land concessions granted to them in proximity to the United States; thus, the English party is at odds with the Canadien party, precisely on the point at which the latter's life and existence as a people is affected.

All that remains to the Canadiens in their present circumstances is their hope that the mother country will ultimately find that their interests converge with her own in terms of the preservation of the country, that the swallowing up of the Canadien population by the American population will be the swallowing up of the mother country's authority over this land, and that the loss of political life of the Canadiens, as an incipient people, will also be the loss of political life of the whole country.... They hope that these things will be perceived by the mother country, and that there, a good enough opinion will be formed of their interest, if not their loyalty, to judge them worthy of enjoying the use of their constitution, in common with His Majesty's other subjects without distinction whatsoever, and failing this good fortune, they see themselves, based on their present situation, destined to become, in the eyes of the mother country, an offensive and endlessly suspect people, preparing to be swallowed up by the abyss that awaits them.

We beseech Your Lordship to believe that His Majesty's Canadien subjects are true and loyal subjects; called up by His Majesty, they have already saved their country at a time when His Majesty's other subjects have shown less loyalty, they are still being called up by His Majesty to defend it; if their small efforts can bear sufficient witness to their loyalty, they hope that His Royal Highness will be so good as to take their situation under consideration, and grant them such remedy as he deems suitable.

### 6. William Dunlop, *"Recollections of the American War 1812-14,"* 1847

*The recollections of William "Tiger" Dunlop (1792-1848) were not published until 1847, long after the events they describe. A Scot, he had enlisted with the British army as an assistant surgeon in 1813 and was immediately dispatched to Upper Canada where he participated in the battles of Crysler's Farm and Lundy's Lane. Army life did not suit him, and he moved to India in 1817. He returned to Canada in 1826 to work as an agent for the Canada Company. Like many others, he published a guide for immigrants intending to settle in Upper Canada, but his fame rested more upon his local reputation as an eccentric storyteller and practical joker.*

Such a force opposed to an equal number of regulars, it may be said, was no very hopeful prospect for defending a country. But there are many things which, when taken into consideration, will show that the balance was not so very much against them as at first sight may appear. Men who are fighting for their homes and friends, and almost in sight of their wives and children, have an additional incentive over those who fight for pay and glory. Again, the enemy to attack them had to land from a rapid [Niagara River], a thing which precludes regularity under any circumstances, and they would not be rendered more cool by a heavy fire of artillery while they were yawning and whirling in the current. They must have landed in confusion, and would be attacked before they could form, and should they get over all this, there was a plateau of land in the rear ascended by high steep bank, which, in tolerable hands, could neither be carried nor turned. Add to all this that the American regulars, if equal, were not superior to our troops in drill and discipline, the great majority of them having been enlisted for a period too short to form a soldier, under the most favourable circumstances. And much even of that short time had been consumed in long harassing marches through an unsettled country that could not supply the commissariat, and exposed to fatigue and privation that was rapidly spreading disease among them; dispirited too by recent defeat, with a constantly increasing force hanging on their rear. If they even had forced us at Lachine, they must have done it at an enormous loss. In their advance also towards Montreal, they must have fought every inch of the way, harassed in front, flank and in rear, and their army so diminished that they could not hold Montreal if they had it.

The enemy then took a position and fortified a camp, where they remained during the winter, and when preparations were made to drive them out of it in the spring, they suddenly abandoned their position, leaving behind them their stores and baggage, and retreated, followed by our forces, as far as the village of Malone, in the State of New York.... The fact is, the Americans were deceived in all their schemes of conquest in Canada; the disaffected then as now were the loudest in their clamour, and a belief obtained among the Americans that they had only to display their colours to have the whole population flock to them. But the reverse of this was the case. They found themselves in a country so decidedly hostile, that their retreating ranks were thinned by the peasantry firing on them from behind fences and stumps; and it was evident that every man they met was an enemy.

At this time the expense of carrying on the war was enormous. Canada, so far from being able to supply an army and navy with the provisions required, was (as a great many of her effective population were employed in the transport of military and naval stores) not fit to supply her own wants, and it was essential to secure supplies from wherever they could be got soonest and cheapest. Troops acting on the Niagara frontier 1,000 miles from the ocean, were fed with flour the produce of England, and pork and beef from Cork, which with the waste inseparable from a state of war, the expense and accidents to which a long voyage expose them, and the enormous cost of internal conveyance, at least doubled the quantity required, and rendered the price of them at least ten times their original cost. Not only provisions, but every kind of Military and Naval Stores, every bolt of canvas, every rope yarn, as well as the heavier articles of guns, shot, cables, anchors ... and all the numerous etceteras for furnishing a large squadron, arming forts, supplying arms for the militia and the line, had to be brought from Montreal to Kingston, a distance of nearly 200 miles, by land in winter, and in summer by flat-bottomed boats, which had to tow up the rapids, and sail up the still parts of the river, (in many places not a mile in breadth, between the British and American shores,) exposed to the shot of the enemy without any protection; for with the small body of troops we had in the country, it was utterly impossible that we could detach a force sufficient to protect the numerous brigades of boats that were daily proceeding up the river, and we must have been utterly undone, had not the ignorance and inertness of the enemy saved us. Had they stationed four field guns, covered by a corps of riflemen, on the banks of the St. Lawrence, they could have cut off our supplies without risking one man. As it was we had only to station a small party at every fifty miles, to be ready to act in case of alarm; but fortunately for us, they rarely or never troubled us. If they had done so with any kind of spirit, we must have abandoned Upper Canada, Kingston and the fleet on Ontario included, and leaving it to its fate, confined ourselves to the defence of such part of the Lower Province as came within the range of our own empire, the sea.

When the soldier leaves his clean comfortable barracks in England and is put into the field, where he has few or none of the accommodations he had at home, he is utterly helpless, and his officer on whom he leant, is just as helpless when a new state of things arises, as he can possibly be. All this was most fully illustrated before Fort Erie.... One of the great drawbacks of the service in Canada was that we got the rubbish of every department in the army. Any man whom The Duke [Wellington] deemed unfit for the Peninsula was considered as quite good enough for the Canadian market, and in nothing was this more conspicuous than in our Engineer Department.... I very much doubt if one shot in ten reached the rampart at all, and the fortunate exceptions that struck the stone building at which they were aimed, rebounded from its sides as innocuous as tennis balls.... Weeks passed at this kind of warfare, that served no purpose to the parties except to harass one another, and mutually to thin our ranks....

When the enemy retired, the Indians who had shown so much wariness in the fight, and had talked to me of the folly of my young men exposing themselves, suddenly seemed to lose all their caution, and bounded forward with a horrible yell, threw themselves on the retreating enemy with their tomahawks, and were soon out of our sight; but as we advanced, we saw they left their trace behind them in sundry cleft skulls. They also, when their opponents were from fifteen to twenty yards in advance of them, threw their tomahawks with unerring aim and great force, burying the head of the hatchet up to the eye in the body of their opponents.

### 7. John Strachan, Report of the Loyal and Patriotic Society of Upper Canada to Thomas Jefferson, January 30, 1815

*Once called "the most dangerous and spiteful man in Upper Canada," the first Anglican Bishop of Toronto, John Strachan (1778-1867), was born in Scotland and spent his early years teaching school in Kingston and Cornwall. Ordained in 1803, he regularly denounced the Americans and feared that Upper Canada was "mixed with doubtful characters and secret Traitors." During the war he raised funds for disabled militiamen and cared for the wounded. By the 1820s he had become one of the most important and influential members of the provincial government.*

Sir ... you are angry with the British for the destruction of the public buildings at Washington, and attempt, with your accustomed candour, to compare that transaction to the devastations committed by the Barbarians in the middle ages. As ... you must have known that it was a small retaliation after ... those acts of the army of the United States in the Canadas ... A stranger to the history of the last three years, on reading this part of your letter, would naturally suppose that Great Britain, in the pride of power, had taken advantage of the weak and defenceless situation of the United States to wreak her vengeance upon them. But what would be his astonishment when told that the nation [the United States] ..., had provoked and first declared the war, and carried it on offensively for two years, with a ferocity unexampled, before the British had the means of making effectual resistance. War was declared against Great Britain by the United States of America in June, 1812,—Washington was taken in August, 1814.... In July, 1812, General Hull invaded the British province of Upper Canada, and took possession of the town of Sandwich. He threatened, (by a proclamation) to exterminate the inhabitants if they made any resistance; he plundered those with whom he had been in habits of intimacy for years before the war—their plate and linen were found in his possession after his surrender to General Brock; he marked out the loyal subjects of the King as objects of peculiar resentment, and consigned their property to pillage and conflagration. In autumn, 1812, some houses and barns were burnt by the American forces near Fort Erie, in Upper Canada. In April, 1813, the public buildings at York, the capital of Upper Canada, were burnt by the troops of the United States, contrary to the articles of capitulation. They consisted of two elegant halls, with convenient offices, for the accommodation of the legislature and of the courts of justice. The library and all the papers and records belonging to these institutions were consumed at the same time. The church was robbed, and the town library totally pillaged. Commodore Chauncey, who has generally behaved honourably, was so ashamed of this last transaction, that he endeavoured to collect the books belonging to the public library, and actually sent back two boxes filled with them, but hardly any were complete. Much private property was plundered, and several houses left in a state of ruin. Can you tell me, Sir, the reason why the public buildings and library at Washington should be held more sacred than those at York ... McClure was actually retreating to his own shore when he caused Newark to be burnt. This officer says that he acted in conformity with the orders of his government;... He not only complies with his instructions, but refines upon them by choosing a day of intense frost, giving the inhabitants almost no warning till the fire began, and commencing the conflagration in the night. In Nov., 1813, the army of your friend General Wilkinson committed great depredations in its progress through the eastern district of Upper Canada, and was proceeding to systematic pillage, when the commander got frightened, and fled to his own shore, on finding the population in that district inveterately hostile. The history of the two first campaigns proves, beyond dispute, that you had reduced fire and pillage to a regular system. It was hoped that the severe retaliation taken for the burning of Newark, would have put a stop to a practice so repugnant to the manners and habits of a civilized age; but so far was this from being the case, that the third campaign exhibits equal enormities. General Brown laid waste the country between Chippewa and Fort Erie, burning mills and private houses, and rendering those not consumed by fire, uninhabitable. The pleasant village of St. David was burnt by his army when about to retreat. On the 15th of May a detachment of the American army, under Colonel

Campbell, landed at Long Point, district of London, Upper Canada, and on that and the following day, pillaged and laid waste as much of the adjacent country as they could reach. They burnt the village of Dover, with the mills, and all the mills, stores, distillery, and dwelling houses in the vicinity, carrying away such property as was portable, and killing the cattle. The property taken and destroyed on this occasion, was estimated at fifty thousand dollars. On the 16th of August some American troops and Indians from Detroit, surprised the settlement of Port Talbot, where they committed the most atrocious acts of violence, leaving upwards of 234 men, women, and children in a state of nakedness and want. On the 20th of September, a second excursion was made by the garrison of Detroit, spreading fire and pillage through the settlements in the western district of Upper Canada. Twenty-seven families, on this occasion, were reduced to the greatest distress. Early in November, General McArthur, with a large body of mounted Kentuckians and Indians, made a rapid march through the western and part of the London districts, burning all the mills, destroying provisions, and living upon the inhabitants. If there was less private plunder than usual, it was because the invaders had no means of carrying it away. On our part, Sir, the war has been carried on in the most forbearing manner. During the two first campaigns, we abstained from any acts of retaliation, notwithstanding the great enormities which we have mentioned. It was not till the horrible destruction of Newark, attended with so many acts of atrocity, that we burnt the villages of Lewiston, Buffalo, and Black Rock....

The farmers were dragged out of their houses, and carried into the States.... It appeared to make no difference whether a man was in arms or not,—he was sure to experience the same treatment. Many people, when prisoners, have been treated in the most infamous manner. Officers, though sick and wounded, have been forced to march on foot through the country;... Our captured troops have been marched, as spectacles, through the towns,... The officers of the 41st Regiment were confined in the penitentiary, at Kentucky, among felons of the most infamous description. They were treated with harshness, often with cruelty; and persons who wished to be kind to them were insulted by the populace. Even the stipulations respecting prisoners, agreed to by the American government, have been most shamefully broken.... To the soldiers of this regiment (as indeed to all others) every temptation had been presented, to induce them to desert and enlist in. Some nations of the natives were at war with the Americans, long before hostilities commenced against England; many others not. When attempts were made to conquer the Canadas, the Indians beyond our territories, part by choice and part by solicitation, came and joined us as allies; while those within the Provinces had as great an interest in defending them, as the other proprietors of the soil. To mitigate as much as possible the horrors of war, it was expressly and repeatedly told the Indians that scalping the dead, and killing prisoners or unresisting enemies, were practices extremely repugnant to our feelings, and no presents would be given them but for prisoners. This, therefore, instead of becoming an article of accusation, ought to have excited their gratitude for the presence and authority of a British force uniformly tended to secure the lives of all who were defenceless, and all who surrendered. It almost without exception saved the lives of our enemies; yet the American government brands us as worse than savages, for fighting by the side of Indians, and at first threatened our extermination if we did so, although they employed all the Indians they could.... It is a fact that the first scalp taken this war was by the Americans, at the river Canard, between Sandwich and Amherstburgh. At this place an Indian was killed, by the advance of General Hull's army, and immediately scalped. At the skirmish of Brownston, several Indians fell, and were scalped by the American troops. The Kentuckians were commonly armed with a tomahawk and long scalping-knife; and burned Indians as a pastime... An Indian never scalps his enemy until after he is dead, and does so to preserve a proof or token of his victory. The American troops, under General Winchester, killed an Indian in a skirmish near the river Au Raisin, on the 18th January, 1813, and tore him literally to pieces, which so exasperated the Indians, that they refused burial to the Americans killed on the 22nd. The Indian hero, Tecumseh, after being killed, was literally flayed in part by the Americans, and his skin carried off as a trophy. Twenty Indian women and children, of the Kiokapoo nation, were inhumanly put to death by the Americans a short time ago, near Prairie, on the Illinois River, after driving their husbands into a morass, where they perished with cold and hunger. Indian towns were burnt as an amusement, or common-place practice. All this, however, is nothing, compared to the recent massacre of the Creeks. General Coffee, in his letter to General Jackson, dated 4th November, 1813, informs him that he surrounded the Indian towns at Tullushatches, in the night, with nine hundred men; that, about an hour after sunrise, he was discovered by the enemy, who endeavoured, though taken by surprise, to make some resistance. In a few minutes the last warrior of them was killed. He mentioned the number of warriors seen dead to be 186, and supposes as many among the weeds as would make them up two hundred. He confesses that some of the women and children were killed, owing to the warriors mixing with their families. He mentions taking only eighty-four prisoners of women and children. Now, it is evident that, in a village containing two hundred warriors, there must have been nearly as many women and men, perhaps more; and, unquestionably, the number of children exceeded the men and women together. What, then, became of all these? Neither does General Coffee mention the old men. Such things speak for themselves. The poor Indians fought, it appears, with bows and arrows, and were able only to kill five Americans. Their situation was too remote, for them to receive assistance from the British. Their lands were wanted, and they must be exterminated. Since this period, the greater part of the nation has been massacred by General Jackson, who destroyed them wantonly, in cold blood. There was no resistance, if we except individual ebullition of despair, when it was found that there was no mercy. Jackson mentions, exultingly, that the morning after he had destroyed a whole village, sixteen Indians were discovered hid under the bank of the river, who were dragged out and murdered.... The cruelties exercised against these wretched nations are without a parallel, except the coldness and apathy with which they are glossed over by the President. Such is the conduct of the humane government of the United States, which is incessantly employed, as they pretend, in civilizing the Indians.... This brief account of the conduct of your government and army, since the commencement of hostilities will fill the world with astonishment at the forbearance of Great Britain, in suffering so many enormities, and such a determined departure from the laws of civilized warfare....

### FURTHER READINGS

Allen, R. *His Majesty's Indian Allies: British Indian Policy and the Defence of Canada, 1774–1815.* Toronto: Dundurn Press, 1992.

Auger, M. "French Canadian Participation in the War of 1812: A Social Study of the Voltigeurs Canadiens." *Canadian Military History* 10, 3 (2001): 23-41.

Benn, C. *The Iroquois and the War of 1812.* Toronto: University of Toronto Press, 1999.

Berton, P. *Flames Across the Border, 1813–1814.* Toronto: McClelland and Stewart, 1981.

Berton, P. *The Invasion of Canada, 1812–1813.* Toronto: McClelland and Stewart, 1980.

Bowler, A. "Propaganda in Upper Canada in the War of 1812." *The American Review of Canadian Studies* 18, 1 (Spring 1988): 11-32.

Bowler, R., Ed. *War along the Niagara: Essays on the War of 1812 and its Legacy.* Youngstown: Old Fort Niagara Association, 1991.

Calloway, C. *Crown and Calumet: British-Indian Relations, 1783–1815.* Norman: University of Oklahoma Press, 1987.

Douglas, W. *Gunfire on the Lakes: The Naval War of 1812–1814 on the Great Lakes and Lake Champlain.* Ottawa: National Museums of Canada, 1972.

Errington, J. *The Lion, the Eagle, and Upper Canada: A Developing Colonial Ideology.* Montreal and Kingston: McGill-Queen's University Press, 1987.

Guitard, M. *The Militia of the Battle of Chateauguay: A Social History.* Ottawa: Parks Canada, 1984.

Hickey, D. *Don't Give Up the Ship: The Myths of the War of 1812.* Toronto: Robin Brass, 2006.

Hickey, D. *The War of 1812: A Forgotten Conflict.* Urbana: University of Illinois Press, 1989.

Hitsman, J. *The Incredible War of 1812.* Toronto: University of Toronto Press, 1965.

Mills, D. *The Idea of Loyalty in Upper Canada 1784–1850.* Montreal and Kingston: McGill-Queen's University Press, 1988.

Sheppard, G. "'Deeds Speak': Militiamen, Medals, and the Invented Traditions of 1812." *Ontario History* 3, 83 (September 1990): 207-32.

Sheppard, G. *Plunder, Profit and Paroles: A Social History of the War of 1812 in Upper Canada.* Montreal and Kingston: McGill-Queen's University Press, 1994.

Sheppard, G. "'Wants and Privations': Women and the War of 1812 in Upper Canada." *Social History* 28, 55 (May 1995): 159-79.

Stacey, C.P. "The War of 1812 in Canadian History." *Ontario History* 50, 3 (Summer 1958): 153-59.

Stanley, G. *The War of 1812: Land Operations.* Toronto: Macmillan, 1983.

Suthren, V. *The War of 1812.* Toronto: McClelland and Stewart, 1999.

Turner, W. *The War of 1812: The War that Both Sides Won.* Toronto: Dundurn Press, 1990.

Weekes, W. "The War of 1812: Civil Authority and Martial Law in Upper Canada." *Ontario History* 48, 4 (Autumn 1956): 147-61.

Wohler, P. *Charles de Salaberry: Soldier of the Empire, Defender of Quebec.* Toronto: Dundurn Press, 1984.

Zaslow, M., Ed. *The Defended Border: Upper Canada and the War of 1812.* Toronto: Macmillan, 1964.

Zuehlke, M. *For Honour's Sake: The War of 1812 and the Brokering of an Uneasy Peace.* Toronto: Knopf Canada, 2006.

# CHAPTER 8

# "A Train of Undisguised Violence"

## NORTH WEST COMPANY VS. HUDSON'S BAY COMPANY

### INTRODUCTION

The firefight was brief but intense that June day in 1816. After the smoke cleared, 21 corpses, some mutilated and stripped, lay where they fell on the prairie, and the despairing Selkirk settlers once again prepared to flee their fledgling colony at Red River. This latest in a series of escalating incidents became known as the "Seven Oaks Massacre" and responsibility for its eruption remains controversial. What is not questioned, however, is the fact that the northwest, in the early part of the nineteenth century, was a powder keg waiting for a spark.

In the late-eighteenth century, many landowners in the Scottish highlands evicted their tenants in favour of more lucrative and less labour-intensive sheepherding. These "highland clearances," as they were called, left thousands of destitute and rootless Scots drifting around Scottish and English cities. Thomas Douglas, the Earl of Selkirk, was one such landowner. He was also, however, one of those rare aristocrats who tempered his egocentric business acumen with a streak of humanitarianism. He planned to obtain land in British North America and to relocate homeless Scottish paupers there. This, he argued, would benefit the dispossessed, eliminate potential rabble-rousers from Britain, strengthen the Britishness of the empire, and make him money through land sales. He orchestrated two such schemes, both with limited success, one on Prince Edward Island and the other in Upper Canada, before planning the third at Red River in what is now Manitoba—and for which he did not have official British government sanction.

Red River formed part of the Hudson's Bay Company's lands according to its 1670 charter. Well-connected and once a major shareholder of the HBC, Selkirk convinced the company to grant him 300,417 square kilometres of that land, stretching along the Red River and into what is today North Dakota and Minnesota. There he proposed to create a colony independent of the HBC, but which would supply it with food and provide land to retired HBC employees. As part of the agreement, Selkirk promised to settle 200 immigrants per year via Hudson Bay, despite the colony's remoteness and the fact that it lay in the heart of land already inhabited by local Métis and the HBC's rival North West Company. The vanguard of first settlers arrived in 1812.

The North West Company was an amalgam of independent Montreal-based fur traders, who realized that their only hope of competing against the giant HBC was by uniting, which they did in 1783. The Company aggressively sought fur-trading areas in the Athabasca country, beyond the HBC's lands, and soon developed a thriving business rivaling their arch foe. The Company's biggest impediment was its lack of proximate access to a deep-water port for exporting furs and importing trade goods, something the HBC had in Hudson Bay, and which it jealously guarded. The North West Company compensated by creating a transcontinental transportation system whereby furs from the Athabasca went to China and in return trade goods arrived from Europe via Montreal, the Great Lakes, and westward by canoe through the Red and Saskatchewan river systems.

And what of Selkirk's new colony? Could the HBC even grant him the land? Not according to the North West Company, which refused to accept the HBC's monopoly over the area and, on the contrary, claimed it *de facto* as its own. Indians and Métis already lived there, many of them making pemmican for the NWC or working as paddlers for its cargo canoes. Furthermore, the area was geographically and strategically vital, serving as the sole conduit through which North West traders must travel on their annual trek.

Natives, Métis, and Montreal traders thus worried about Selkirk's new settlers, suspecting that the Earl's real motivation was less an altruistic desire to create a colony and more a ruthless bid to destroy the NWC by cutting its east-west transportation artery. Selkirk vehemently denied that accusation. Distance further exacerbated tensions. Montreal and London, the respective companies' headquarters, were many months away, and their local agents had to take matters into their own hands, responding to evolving conditions as they saw fit.

Relations between the two groups deteriorated when the Earl's chosen governor, Miles MacDonell, issued the Pemmican Proclamation in January 1814. The Proclamation placed an embargo on exporting any food produced at Red River, the rationale being the very real danger of starvation there, particularly since MacDonell expected the imminent arrival of a new group of settlers whom the tiny colony lacked the resources to feed. This, of course, meant no pemmican for the North West Company, a serious liability to both it and to the local producers who depended on the trade. The arbitrary and perceived capriciousness of the Proclamation fueled the fire of the "pernicious HBC conspiracy" theorists, who hardly needed persuading. The predictable results pitted the tiny group of settlers against the Métis and Montrealers, who apparently managed to divide and conquer Selkirk's people through intimidation and by convincing them of the hopelessness of their settlement venture. They did, however, promise to ship the settlers to Upper Canada where land grants supposedly awaited. The colony disbanded in 1815 when most of Selkirk's small and disheartened band accepted this offer.

Back in Britain, Selkirk fretted and concluded he must personally take the colony's reins if it were to survive. He set out in 1816, arrived at Montreal, and launched an expedition back to Red River where a few of his colonists had re-established his colony and had even captured some North West Company posts. Selkirk believed justice was on his side and that the actions of the North West Company were indefensible and criminal. If the government of Canada refused to uphold the law and arrest the Montrealers, then he would, and he hired a group of disbanded Swiss soldiers to make it happen.

Then the "massacre" occurred. Selkirk heard about it as he neared the North West Company's depot at Fort William on the western edge of Lake Superior. He and his mercenaries arbitrarily captured the fort and arrested the Montreal traders inside, including William McGillivray, the director. Selkirk seized the fort's goods and held them as compensation for the "massacre." He then proceeded west to reclaim his Red River Colony, but not before refusing two Canadian government warrants for his arrest as a result of his unilateral actions at Fort William. What Selkirk failed to realize was the antipathy many powerfully placed eastern Canadians felt toward him and his adventures. He also chose to ignore the shaky legal basis of the Red River Colony's very existence. That legality was in itself a conundrum: which court had the right to establish its legitimacy? By the Canada Jurisdiction Act of 1803, the Colony of Canada, not the HBC, enjoyed jurisdiction over criminal matters in HBC territory. Furthermore, HBC's land claims, particularly its expansion, remained highly contentious and legally untested. Selkirk soon found himself embroiled in a litigious brawl that tarnished his image, virtually bankrupted him, broke his health, and contributed to his early death from tuberculosis in 1820.

The Canadian press and public figures initially vilified Selkirk as, at best, an unrealistic and misguided romantic who stooped to criminal behaviour. At worst, they cast him as a conniving HBC agent gunning for a rival and who used innocent immigrants and broke the law to achieve his ends. Montreal-based North West Company executives and senior colonial staff, who did not like Selkirk, certainly pushed this interpretation, both privately and publicly. The pendulum swung over time, and by the mid-nineteenth century writers increasingly portrayed Selkirk's efforts as an idealistic and altruistic crusade to pacify and Europeanize the Canadian west, which was defeated by "savages" and "uncivilized half-breeds." Seven Oaks, in this interpretation, became a link in the chain of events culminating in the Riel uprisings of 1869 and 1885, and helped justify government suppression of the Natives and Métis. Selkirk was now the tragic hero and the Nor'Westers the villain—especially because of Seven Oaks and despite evidence that the gunmen acted on their own and without NWC sanction. Coltman's analysis of 1818 seems to be the most objective report on the event but was later ignored, buried beneath a mountain of mythology eulogizing Selkirk. Perhaps Coltman's ambiguous conclusions did not sit well with those later nation-builders who wished to justify subsequent exclusion of Natives and Métis from large tracts of prairie land and who revere Selkirk as a founding father of the Canadian west. In the end, no one was found responsible for the deaths at Seven Oaks.

DISCUSSION POINTS

1. Was the North West Company justified in resisting the Selkirk Colony?

2. The Métis celebrate Seven Oaks as a landmark in their evolution as a distinct people and object to the term "massacre." Was this really their victory against unauthorized intruders?

3. How should we commemorate this complex historical event? Can we regard Selkirk as a "founder" of Canada?

DOCUMENTS

## 1. Thomas Douglas, Earl of Selkirk,
### *The Memorial of Thomas Earl of Selkirk*, October 2, 1818

*Scottish Thomas Douglas, the 5th Earl of Selkirk (1771–1820) came unexpectedly into his title upon the death of his six brothers. At university he discovered the desperate plight of the crofters being evicted from their lands in the infamous Highland Clearances and set out to ameliorate their plight. He obtained land first in Prince Edward Island in 1803, then in Upper Canada in 1804, and finally in the Red River area of what is now Manitoba. There he planned to settle the displaced Scottish farmers. Not one of his ventures succeeded and the third cost him his fortune, his reputation, and ultimately led him to an early grave.*

... That in the year 1811, your memorialist obtained from the Hudson's Bay Company for a valuable consideration a conveyance of a tract of land situated on Red River, being a part of the Territory granted to that Company by Royal Charter: your memorialist had previously consulted several of the most eminent Counsel in London, who concurred in opinion, that the title was unquestionably valid; and he had good reason to believe that a similar opinion has been expressed to His Majesty's Government by the Attorney and Solicitor General of England.

By the terms of the conveyance, your memorialist was bound to settle a specified number of families on the tract of land conveyed to him: and your memorialist as well as all persons holding lands under him were debarred from interfering in the fur trade. Notwithstanding this restriction, your memorialist was early apprized that any plan for settling the country in question, would be opposed with the most determined hostility by the North West Company of Montreal; and threats were held out by the principal partners of that association in London, that they would excite the native Indians to destroy the settlement. In order to obviate this danger, your memorialist instructed his agents to use their utmost endeavours to conciliate the good will of the native Indians, to make a purchase from them of the land requisite for the settlement, and also to abstain from all interference with the servants of the North West Company, except in so far as it should be unavoidable in self-defence. But as it was probable that the influence of the North West Company might be sufficient to mislead the native Indians, it was thought necessary to provide the settlers with the most effectual means of defence, which the local situation of the country would admit.

In pursuance of the condition of his grant, your memorialist sent out a small party of men to commence a settlement. They reached the Red River in autumn of the year 1812, and were followed shortly after, by several families of emigrants. These people were under the direction of Miles Macdonell, Esq. who had been appointed Governor of the District under a provision of the Charter of the Hudson's Bay Company. From the circumstances under which the settlement had been undertaken, an intercourse of mutual accommodation naturally arose between the settlers and the traders of the Hudson's Bay Company; but the establishment was in every respect, completely distinct from the trade of that Company. During the first two years after the arrival of the settlers, various clandestine machinations were carried on by the partners and clerks of the North West Company to excite the jealousy of the Indians, to debauch the servants employed on the establishment, to stir up discontent among the settlers, and to prevent them from obtaining supplies of provisions from the natural produce of the country. There can be no doubt that this was done by desire of the partnership, not only from the continued and systematic manner in which the intrigues were carried on, but also from direct evidence of these instructions given by some of the partners, and from a letter of one individual of the greatest influence among them then residing in London, pointing out to his associates in the interior of this Continent, the absolute necessity of preventing the colonization of Red River—The obstructions thus superadded to all the usual difficulties of an infant settlement, would have been sufficient to defeat the undertaking entirely, if the natural advantages of the country had not been very great. But in spite of every obstacle, the establishment was on the point of taking firm root.

Within a few months after the arrival of Mr. Miles Macdonell, the jealousy which had been instilled into the minds of the Indians, was entirely removed, and they became zealously attached to the settlement. In the second year after the arrival of the settlers, their crops (though sown under very unfavorable circumstances) were so abundant as to leave no probability of their being forced to abandon the country from want of provisions—another year of uninterrupted industry would have rendered them independent of any resources except the produce of their own farms. At the same time the favorable reports which they had sent home to their friends as to the fertility and salubrity of the country, the abundance of game, and the facility of cultivation, had operated to attract other settlers, and in the course of the ensuing year, there was reason to expect a considerable increase of numbers, so that the establishment would have become too strong to be attacked by open violence with any prospect of success.

It was in these circumstances that the partners of the North West Company at their annual meeting in the year 1814, determined to adopt more effectual measures for destroying the settlement, before it should be too late to make the attempt. For this purpose they sent instructions to collect from various quarters a set of men whom they judged fit instruments for acts of violence, viz: the sons of their Canadian, and other servants by Indian women, a great number of whom are reared about their trading posts. These men are bred up in the most entire dependence on the Company, and had been always employed in their service in the same manner as their Canadian servants from whom they were never distinguished till the period alluded to. It was then for the first time that they were taught to consider themselves a separate tribe of men, and distinguished by a separate name, with the view of ascribing their violences to the native Indians. These half-breeds (or Bois Brulés as they were now to be called) have been described as a Nation of independent Indians: but they are in fact with very few exceptions in the regular employment and pay of the North West Company, mostly as canoemen, some as interpreters and guides, and a few of better education as clerks. The latter are the progeny of partners of the Company, at whose expense most of them have been brought up, and through whose influence they may look to be themselves partners. These are the chiefs of this "New Nation."

These men being accustomed to live at a distance from the restraints of civilized society, were ignorant of any law but that of the strongest: or, if they had any idea of the punishments denounced by law against robbers and murderers, the mode of life to which they were habituated, led them to feel confident of escaping from the hand of justice. But they were not allowed to entertain any apprehension on this head, as their superiors constantly inculcated on their minds, that the North West Company had sufficient influence with his Majesty's Government, to screen from punishment any persons who might commit crimes by their direction. They have even been led to believe, that the Company had authority for all that they did, and were actually identified with the Government.

A great number of these half-breeds were collected at Red River in the spring of the year 1815, and were led on from one act of violence to another, till they ended in hostile attacks, openly and regularly carried on against the colonists, and repeated until they succeeded in driving them away from the place, and effecting the destruction of the settlement. As a preparatory step to these measures, Mr. Duncan Cameron, the partner of the North West Company in charge of their affairs on Red River, took his station in the immediate vicinity of the settlement, and laboured assiduously through the whole of the winter, to seduce the settlers to desert their engagements and go to Canada, where they were assured that the

North West Company would procure for them gratuitously, not only lands, but also provisions, tools, cattle and every other accommodation they could desire. He gained over some leading individuals by the promise of direct pecuniary rewards, and used every artifice to gain popularity with the others, and to excite discontent against the gentlemen in charge of the settlers. When bribery and flattery would not prevail, intimidation was resorted to. Stories were invented and circulated to terrify the ignorant strangers, with the idea that the Indians had expressed the most vehement hostility, and were determined to assemble in the spring to massacre all those who should not avail themselves of the opportunity of escaping in the canoes of the North West Company.

By the assiduous use of these means of corruption and intimidation, a majority of the settlers were gained over to enter into the views of the North West Company, and their ringleaders were then secretly instructed to avail themselves of a favourable opportunity, to carry off some swivels and other small pieces of artillery. By this robbery the settlement was deprived of the only means of defence by which superior numbers could have been repelled, and the North West Company, being then confident in the indisputable superiority of their force, commenced a train of undisguised violence, which continued without interruption for nearly three months, directed against all the settlers who did not choose to join their party, and which ended in driving them away from Red River, burning their houses, and laying waste their fields.

Among the pretexts for these violences, it had been alleged that they were justifiable on the principle of retaliation, because the Governor of the settlement had, in the preceding year, seized a quantity of provisions belonging to the North West Company. Though it can hardly require any argument to demonstrate the injustice of retaliating upon the innocent settlers, for any act of their Governor, yet, as the seizure in question has been much misrepresented, and great importance has been ascribed to the occurrence, it may be proper to explain the circumstances under which it took place.

In all the British Colonies, Governors have occasionally exercised the power of laying an embargo on the exportation of provisions, in cases of urgent necessity in order to obviate the danger of famine. In the month of January 1814, Mr. Miles Macdonell deemed it necessary to adopt this measure, and to prohibit, for a period of twelve months, the exportation of provisions from the District over which he had been appointed Governor. He had reason to believe that, in addition to the settlers then under his charge, a considerable number of emigrants were to arrive from Europe in the course of the ensuing season, and he had ascertained that the people, then at the place, had not the means of raising a crop sufficiently abundant for the wants of all these additional inhabitants. It was therefore evident that it would be necessary still to have recourse to the natural resources of the country, and of these, the North West Company were endeavouring to deprive the settlers. For the purpose of distressing them and creating an artificial scarcity, the servants of the North West Company, being well supplied with fleet horses, were ordered to drive away the Buffalo from the hunters of the settlers, who not being well mounted were in the habit of hunting these animals on foot, by cautiously approaching them unobserved. These orders were given soon after the canoes of the North West Company arrived from Fort William in autumn, and were acted upon through the whole course of the winter. The settlers had experienced these obstructions continually for several months before Mr. Macdonell resolved upon the embargo....

While the North West Company were congratulating themselves on the idea of having finally destroyed the settlement of Red River, the people, who had been driven away, were joined in their place of refuge by some other settlers, with whose assistance they returned and re-occupied their farms....

The crimes, which had been committed by Duncan Cameron during the preceding season, had been of the most flagrant description: On evidence of these transactions, bills of indictment have been found against him in the Courts of Montreal for three capital felonies, besides other crimes and misdemeanours. These crimes were of sufficient notoriety, to justify any individual, who might think fit to incur the responsibility in arresting and sending him in custody to this Province....

Three days after the date of this letter, his half-breeds attacked the servants of the Hudson's Bay Company by force of arms, took them prisoners, and seized the whole of the property under their charge, and in particular, the provisions on which the subsistence of the settlers depended.

After this blow, Macdonell no longer disguised his intentions to destroy the settlement. He invited the Indians to join his expedition, and declared that if the settlers dared to resist, the ground should be drenched with their blood. He encouraged his men by the prospect of plunder, and even promised to give up the women of the settlement to gratify their brutal lusts. His whole force being assembled, he proceeded in military array from Qu'appelle towards the settlement. The half-breeds on horseback, passed through the plains along the rivers, escorting the boats which conveyed the provisions, and other property of which he had robbed the Hudson's Bay Company, as well as that which he had obtained by trade from the Indians. On the 1st June, he arrived at Brandon House, a post of the Hudson's Bay Company, where he sent a party of his men to force their way into the fort, to seize the property it contained, and carry it to a neighbouring post, occupied by one of his clerks. Of this plunder, some trifles were distributed among his men, but all the most valuable articles were deposited in the stores of the North West Company. From thence Macdonell proceeded on his march to a place called Portage des Prairies, where he remained with most of the Canadians in his service; while he sent forward sixty or seventy half-breeds on horseback to the settlement, under the command of Cuthbert Grant, a clerk of the North West Company who had acted a conspicuous part in all the violences of the preceding year, and who was now brought forward in the character of the "great Chief of the new Nation."...

Grant in the mean time perceiving this small party, collected his men, and dividing them into two bodies, gallopped up with one division directly against Semple; while he ordered the other to make a circuit in the plain, so as to cut off his retreat to the fort. The two parties of horsemen closing in from opposite sides, surrounded him in the form of a semicircle, leaving no opening except towards the river. At this moment Grant sent a Canadian of the name of Boucher to summon the Governor to surrender, Boucher accosted him with the most insulting language and gestures, which even in that perilous situation, Semple could not brook. With an expression of indignation, he took hold of the bridle of Boucher's horse: the latter leaped down, and ran off towards his comrades, who immediately commenced firing, by which Semple himself and a great proportion of his party were wounded, and several killed on the spot. A few straggling shots only were returned, and as the half-breeds still continued to keep up a constant fire, Semple called out to his men to provide for their own safety: three only succeeded in making their escape, some others made the attempt, but were shot in their flight. The wounded men were lying on the field incapable of resistance, and calling out for mercy, when the half-breeds came up, and butchered them with the most horrid imprecations, stripping them of their bloody clothing, and in several instances, mangling the bodies in wanton cruelty. The half-breeds were not the only men engaged in this massacre: a Canadian of the name of Francois Deschamps was among the most active, and collected a large booty from the person of those he had despatched. One gentleman only, of the name of Pritchard, who had formerly been in the service of the North West Company, was saved through the interference of a Canadian, who had great difficulty in protecting him. This was the scene which has been called "a battle," "an affray," "an unfortunate occurrence."

In the course of the same evening, Mr. Pritchard was sent by Grant, to summon the settlers at the fort to surrender. With no small difficulty he had obtained a promise that their lives should be spared, and that they should be allowed to leave the country, provided they would give up all the property belonging to your memorialist, or to the Hudson's Bay Company. The settlers saw that resistance would be unavailing, and on the day following the massacre, Grant, at the head of the murderers, took possession of the fort and the property it contained, in the name of the North West Company. It was not long before his masters arrived to sanction his proceedings, and appropriate the plunder to their own use.

The news of the victory obtained by Grant, with the slaughter of more than twenty of the "English," was speedily communicated to Macdonell, at Portage des Prairies, and was received by him, and the clerks under his command, with shouts of joy and exultation. Having thus "cleared the way," as he termed it, Macdonell proceeded with the remainder of his men, to receive possession of his conquest, and was soon after joined at the fort, lately occupied by the settlers, by an assemblage of partners and clerks of the North West Company, coming from various and distant quarters, with great numbers of armed men. At their head, was Mr. Archibald Norman Macleod, who is not only a partner, but one of the agents....

The conduct of Macleod was imitated by his partners in the other parts of Athabasca, where undisguised acts of robbery and arson were committed, all under pretext of retaliation, a pretext for which the North West Company are never at a loss, when a crime is to be committed. It is an established maxim among them, that they have a right to take redress at their own hands for any act of which they think fit to complain, and this principle is not only acted upon by the subordinate partners, but systematically prescribed as their rule of conduct, by the head of the "concern," a member of the Legislative Council of this Province. It certainly cannot require much comment, to show the consequences which are to be expected, when a body, so powerful as the North West Company, are allowed to determine at their own pleasure, the proper measure of compensation for any injury which they may suppose, or allege to have been committed against them, and to give the name of retaliation to any crime, which they may find it for their interest to perpetrate: to devastation, to robbery, to arson, and to murder.

The outrages which have been detailed, are so extraordinary, that some hesitation may naturally be felt, in supposing them possible. It may seem incredible, that such a tissue of atrocities, should be the work of men professing the Christian religion, and enjoying the respectable character of British merchants. The Indian trade, as it has been hitherto carried on from Canada, though certainly contemptible as a national object, is the whole fortune of those who are engaged in it, and among those who profit the most by the present system, are several individuals of the highest station in this Province. But the impressions which have been diffused, as to the extent and importance of the trade of the North West Company, and their services to the British Government, are extremely mistaken. It is only by a constant use of the arts of deception, and much arrogance of pretension, that they preserve an external appearance, calculated to impose upon strangers.... The motives for the massacre of Red River were precisely the same; to maintain by means of violence and intimidation, a monopoly which is not yet secured by law, yet a monopoly by which the native Indians are held in worse than Turkish slavery, and an extensive and valuable country is condemned to endless sterility. The North West Company, though invested with no right but those common to every British subject, have succeeded for more than thirty years past, in excluding all others from the extensive countries to the North and West of Lake Superior. All the Indian countries, the North West Company arrogate to themselves as their own territories, and consider the entrance of any others of His Majesty's subjects, from whatsoever quarter, as an invasion of their rights. In order to repress such attempts, open violence is systematically employed against every intruder, with no other reserve than the caution necessary to avoid committing the principals of the "concern." From the immense distance of any courts of justice, the subordinate agents in these acts of violence have hitherto been assured of impunity, but it is evident, that as soon as agricultural settlements shall be firmly established in these countries, together with those institutions of religion, law, and police, which must accompany a civilized population, such a system of ferocious violence will no longer be practicable....

The North West Company, though well aware that the settlement at Red River, has always been an undertaking completely separate from the trade of the Hudson's Bay Company, yet in order to give greater scope to their detestable principle of retaliation, have attempted to identify these establishments. Even his Majesty's Government, by lending too ready an ear to these misrepresentations, has been induced to believe, that all the crimes which have been committed in the Indian countries, have only been the result of mutual violence between contending parties of traders. But from the statement which is now submitted to your Grace, it cannot but be evident, that this opinion is completely erroneous. The question now at issue is not whether this or that Company shall engross the fur trade:—But whether the British Government, does or does not afford protection to its subjects: Whether the strong may be permitted to trample upon the weak without restraint, to expel the tillers of the earth from their habitations, to lay waste their fields, to reduce their cottages to ashes, to drive their helpless wives and children into the desert, and to commit every species of enormity, in furtherance of their criminal views: Whether this extensive and valuable Province is to have a system of judicature, calculated only to crush obnoxious men, while those who are in favor, may commit the most atrocious crimes, with impunity: Whether to promote the sordid purposes of individual gain or illegal monopoly, murder may be systematically organized, and the blood of British subjects remain unattoned, because some of those who profit by it, are members of the Executive and Legislative Councils of Lower Canada, and reputed to be under the special protection of His Majesty's Government.

### 2. William McGillivray, "To Sir G. Drummond," June 24, 1815

*William McGillivray (1764-1824) came to Montreal from Scotland in 1784 to work with his uncle in the North West Company, the only real competitor to the Hudson's Bay Company. By 1804 he headed the firm, became a Justice of the Peace for the Indian Territory, and had along the way gained a Métis wife as well as much experience living and working in the northwest. McGillivray was elected into the Lower Canadian Assembly in 1808 and served with British forces against the Americans during the War of 1812. The governor of Lower Canada appointed him to the Legislative Council in 1814.*

My dear Sir,

I cannot but express the feelings of indignation to which this calumny gives rise. I deny, in the most solemn manner, the allegations whereon this shameful accusation is founded: so far from their having any existence in truth, the contrary is the fact; for it can be proved, that the first year of his Lordship's [Selkirk] settlement, the innocent people who had been enticed from their homes by his golden but delusive promises, and misrepresentations, had no other means of avoiding starvation, but the supplies which they derived from the stores of the North West company; therefore had the principles of the body, or of those employed by them, been such as the Earl of Selkirk has been pleased to impute to them, there was no need of hostile Indians to interfere in the destruction of the settlement: hunger alone would speedily have accomplished the work.

... I therefore declare, that I am an utter stranger to any instigation, or any determination of the Indian nations to make any attack on the settlement in question; but I will not take upon me to say, that serious quarrels may not happen between the settlers and the nations, whose hunting grounds they have taken possession of, in the American style of injustice and land pillage, exclusive of the danger they run from the vicinity of the Sioux nation, who from time immemorial have made it a practice to make war on the Indians on the Red River, their permanent enemies, and upon the whites who are found in that country; many instances of which can be adduced, because the Indian nations, when in a state of hostility, consider the whites found in the country of their enemy, as being in his interest, and to be treated accordingly.

The arrogant and violent conduct of Lord Selkirk's agents, cannot well fail to produce such a result as the quarrels above mentioned. The Indians require no instigation to commit violence, where they consider their own interests as concerned, for notwithstanding the influence which it is supposed the North West company has over them, within a few years, a brigade of boats coming down the Red River was attacked without any apparent previous cause or provocation, and several men killed or wounded; lives are occasionally lost in like manner in every part of the North West country.

The influence, whatever it may be, which the North West company possess over the Indians, has been exerted in a manner essentially different from the false and atrocious idea of intending to be instrumental in the massacre of Lord Selkirk's helpless and deluded settlement ... and it is strange that at the time the exertion of this influence ... the agents of his Lordship should, under a pretended, but usurped authority, with force and arms have plundered the company of their property on the banks of the Red River, which actually took place in the Spring of the year 1814, when their depôt of provisions, which had been collected during the preceding winter, and which was the only supply they had for their canoe men in their voyage from the interior to their place of rendezvous on Lake Superior, was forcibly seized, and the greater part feloniously retained.... Consequently this act of robbery was committed with the express intention of either starving the North West canoe men, or putting a total stop to the exit of the company's returns. Insinuations against the North West company, and pretended alarms brought forward by persons capable of such acts, come indeed from them with an ill grace; but the motives are manifest, and meant to anticipate or counteract the feelings which their own conduct, when known, would naturally produce.

The robbery above mentioned might have been prevented, or his lordship's agents made to pay dear for their unjustifiable conduct, had the North West company's people availed themselves of what was in their power, and been as regardless of consequences as their opponents appeared to be; but all aid from the nations was refused, and other means avoided, which in strict justice they had a right to resort to in defence of their property and right, as British subjects. His Excellency has been misinformed in regard to our being the only people who had intercourse with the Indian nations; there are great numbers of hunters, Canadians and others, who are to be found in many parts of the North West country, and particularly on the Red River, who live among the Indians and not being in the company's service are not subject to their control. Besides the Hudson's Bay company as traders (of which company Lord Selkirk is now an associate) have their posts close to those of the North West company, in every part of the country eastward of the rocky mountains, excepting Athabasca, which forms no portion of the alleged Hudson's Bay territory; and as they supply the natives to the extent of their means in like manner as the North West company; therefore it is presumed, that with equal justice and good faith in their dealings they must possess the same influence.

It would indeed be extraordinary if the North West company, who cannot always save their own people from violence, should be held responsible for whatever misfortune may happen to Lord Selkirk's, or to the servants of the Hudson's Bay company; against such doctrines I most solemnly protest. Individuals in the Indian country are personally responsible for their own criminal acts, in like manner as elsewhere; and an act of the British parliament was passed for this express purpose. The British government has not only an influence, but a legal authority over the community; but does this make the members thereof personally responsible for the murders and robberies committed in the United Kingdom? His Excellency may rest assured that the North West company will never instigate, nor authorize any of their servants to instigate, the Indian nations to commit murder, were they even as void of humanity as the Earl of Selkirk seems to consider them; they know too well the consequences to themselves of encouraging disorders of any kind in the Indian country. The Indians, once roused to arms, would hardly distinguish between a Highlander or Canadian from the shores of Hudson's Bay, and people of the same country coming from Canada. I beg leave to enclose some documents which may be considered as referred to in this letter. I wish his Excellency to be possessed of facts, in order to remove from his mind any unfavorable impression which the unfounded and self-interested calumnies, raised and propagated against us by the Earl of Selkirk and his agents and partisans are calculated to produce. That nobleman has thought proper lately to become the rival of the North West company in the trade which they have carried on for upwards of thirty years with credit to themselves, and it is hoped with benefit to their country. Under the guise and cloak of colonization, he is aiming at ... an exterminating blow against their trade. Insinuations of alarm and false accusations form part of the system, and his agents and servants are probably instructed to bring them artfully forward, to raise prejudices against us; surely interested representations from such a quarter should be received with caution, and be better supported than the correspondence of his Lordship's agent sent to Canada, who collects and reports his pretended information as derived from a common Canadian whom he does not name. It is matter of astonishment, that the idea of colonization in the Indian country, at the distance of 2,000 miles from home, should be tolerated by His Majesty's government, and its consequences not seen through. If it fail, as it must and ought, numerous innocent individuals will fall a sacrifice to his Lordship's visionary pursuits; and if it succeeds, it must infallibly destroy the Indian trade in the result: as experience proves, that when colonization advances, Indians and their trade disappear. Thus his Lordship is contributing towards Indian extermination. Besides the planting of colonies so far in the interior, where they are placed out of the reach and control of the mother country, is, as it were, transferring them and their future interests to the United States, in whose territory, by the terms of the late treaty of peace, they will most probably be found; and thus a strength is raising up to be hereafter employed in aid of American ambition against British interests. In a fair commercial competition, we have no objection to enter the lists with his Lordship, but we cannot remain passive spectators of the violence used to plunder or destroy our property, under any pretended or usurped authority as was assumed by Mr. Miles McDonnell, who styles himself governor, ... respecting our depôts or collection of provisions for the trade as above stated. In all such attempts hereafter, the North West company would assuredly be justified in repelling force by force; at all events, I cannot but consider the rights and property of that body as equally entitled to the protection of His Majesty's government as the Earl of Selkirk's....

### 3. W.B. Coltman, "Report," May 14, 1818

*William Bacheler Coltman (?–1826) came to Quebec from England in 1799 and joined a prominent firm of retailers, importers, and land developers. He was appointed Justice of the Peace for Quebec in 1810 and a member of Lower Canada's Executive Council two years later. In 1816 he became Commissioner of Peace for the Indian territory of the northwest and, shortly after, received a special commission, with the rank of lieutenant-colonel, to examine events at Seven Oaks. Coltman's reputation for honesty, integrity, and diligence served him well after his arrival in Red River in the summer of 1817.*

Sir,

... Whilst such appears to me to be the case, established by the evidence against the Hudson's Bay company, that against the North West company is still more strong and clear; as their violations of law have evidently been much greater, and attended with results shocking to the feelings of humanity; at the same time that they have no pretexts of legal rights, by which they may have been misled, nor any claims upon Government, for more than the ordinary protection of law; any pretension they might have made, as a body, for the enterprise and vigor with which they pursued and extended a trade, beneficial to themselves and the empire, being completely destroyed by the vices inherent to the system on which they conducted their affairs, and which have during the late disturbances been brought forward in so conspicuous a light, and produced events so fatal, as to appear imperatively to call for the interference of Government. The foundation of the whole evil, is probably to be traced to that violent spirit, which is nurtured by the species of monopoly that the North West company has established, and continues to maintain, in the Indian territories; still more by physical force than by any fair advantage, derived from capital or connection; the various illegal measures adopted to crush minor adventurers who have attempted to oppose this monopoly, are recorded in the courts of Montreal, and are of public notoriety, whilst the pernicious effects produced on the character of individuals, employed to maintain the same, have been exhibited in strong colours, by the late events.

By the arrangements of the North West company, a strong stimulus is held out to the junior members of this association, in the considerable share of profits reserved to reward their successful exertions in the service of the company; this, whilst it has produced those results, which are so creditable to their character as a trading body, has at the same time given rise to an "esprit de corps," little attentive to the rights and claims of others, and accustomed to consider an exclusive devotion to the interests and honour of the company, as a primary duty, dignified in some of their intercepted letters, by the appellation of "loyalty to the concern;" to this feeling is added a spirit much more disposed to inflict, than submit to acts of injury and insult, formed originally perhaps by the local circumstances of the parties, far removed from the protection and control of civilized society, and where every man must to a certain degree, feel his life to be in his own keeping, and to be best secured by a constant and open preparation for self-defence. These circumstances tending naturally to produce habits of overbearing violence, left unchecked by any salutary regulations, or rather indeed encouraged, as far as they tended to promote the interests of the association, have at length formed the general character of its members, as exhibited in the evidence before me, in their violent and oppressive conduct towards the natives of the country, frequently to their own servants, and still more so to their opponents in trade. To this last point my inquiries have of course been chiefly directed, as being one of the immediate objects of my mission; and it appears to me, that a short review of the conduct of both parties, will be sufficient to show, that although the Hudson's Bay company may have been the first aggressors, the retaliatory measures of the North West company have so much exceeded all lawful or reasonable bounds of self-defence, and been carried to such violent extremes, as to render the proceedings of their party, beyond comparison, the most criminal....

Beginning however from this period, it appears to me that there can be no doubt the Hudson's Bay company's servants must be considered as the first aggressors; the fact indeed, although a good deal of contradictory evidence had previously been collected ...

From this correspondence, your Excellency will perceive, that exclusive of individual offences on each side, the North West company impute to the Earl of Selkirk a criminal conspiracy, in the view of forcibly and illegally driving them out from the Indian territories; whilst it is well known, that a similar charge of conspiracy, "for the purpose of destroying the Red River colony," is the principal offence which his Lordship now attaches to the North West company, as a body. The substance of most of the principal facts that have been established before me, in evidence against the Earl, has already been stated, in speaking of his proceedings in connection with the governors and other agents of the Hudson's Bay company; but although these may involve great moral responsibility, and as it appears to me, make out a case seriously affecting the chartered rights of the company, yet I do not see how they can be deemed sufficient, even with the addition of the very illegal and unjustifiable proceedings of the Earl at Fort William, to support a criminal charge of so serious a nature as conspiracy. With regard to the partners of the North West company also, I am doubtful how far such a charge, if at all made out; can apply to any number of them, as it appears to me, they will be found in general to have acted under a sense of injury and insult, (a submission to which might often be inconsistent, in the Indian territories with personal safety,) and under some pretext of self defence, although pushed by their habitual system of violence, far beyond all grounds of law or reason. From the evidence before me, it appears certainly, that a very great jealousy was expressed against the colony from its first establishment, especially by the partners in London; of this the most striking evidence is afforded by a letter of Mr. Simon McGillivray, dated London, 9th April 1812, to the wintering partners of the North West company, in which, speaking of the Earl of Selkirk's plans of colonization, he says, "it will require some time, and I fear cause much expense to us as well as to himself, before he is *driven to abandon* the project, and yet *he must be driven to abandon* it, for his success would strike at the very existence of our trade;" but these feelings do not appear to have given rise to any violent or illegal proceedings, till after the forcible seizure of the provisions on the Red River, by Miles McDonnell.

On the occurrence of this event, however, alarming as it might be to the North West company, from the state of the war, and at the same time as indicative of a future intention to give practical effect by force, to the exclusive rights of territory, which had been publicly claimed from the first settlement of the colony, measures of retaliation were adopted far beyond what it appears to me the case could be supposed to justify; for independent of the warrants issued against Miles Mc-Donnell and other officers of the colony, and the offer of free passages to Canada, to any of the settlers or servants, who chose to quit the place, measures which are avowed by the North West company, there can scarcely be a doubt, that if actual orders were not given at the general meeting of the partners at Fort William, the summer in question, for the entire expulsion of the colony, (of which there is certainly no proof,) that such sentiments of hostility and desire of revenge, for the injuries and insults supposed to have been inflicted, were loudly expressed, as to satisfy all the junior members of the association, that the complete breaking up of the colony would be a measure most acceptable to their superiors, and to the company at large; and that the means adopted to accomplish the same, would not be very scrupulously examined.

With respect to the charges against the North West company, of having adopted at this meeting measures for the destruction of the colony, by means of the Indians, no proof has been produced of any combined plan, to which the agents or leading partners had given their sanction, and but slight and second-hand evidence, even that any measures of the kind had been discussed amongst individuals; to men indeed of the characters, and actuated by the motives which have been already mentioned, a more direct appeal than that which I have stated, was probably unnecessary. On the return of the partners and servants of the North West company, in the autumn, from Fort William to the neighbourhood of Red River, they induced the natives before mentioned, to quit their different posts, which of course added to the irritation already existing on their minds, and confirmed any hostile views they might previously have entertained; these notices, it appears evident from their intercepted letters, they apprehended would be practically acted upon, and from the same source, it is indisputably established, that in the course of the ensuing winter, most, if not all, the partners of the company, with many of their inferior partisans in the neighbourhood of Red River, had become parties to plans for driving off the colonists, and for employing the aid of the Indians for that purpose, although resolved however, to hazard this measure with all its consequent dangers, it appears to have been done rather with a view of alarming the settlers, and thereby inducing them to leave the country, than for the purpose of direct attacks, with any design of their general destruction;...

Persons who could, however, make up their minds to the employment of Indians in any shape, against their fellow subjects, were not to be expected to hesitate about that of the less savage force of half-breeds; of this class of persons, some few who have received their education in Canada, and are employed by the North West company, as clerks, are nearly as much civilized as the traders themselves, a few others on the contrary, are scarcely removed from the savage state, and the greater bulk fill the various gradations between these two; the connection between this class of people and the North West company, (from the former partners, clerks, or servants, of which company, those now on Red River are chiefly descended,) is naturally very intimate, and is further kept up by the number of them whom the company constantly employ as clerks, exclusive of frequently engaging the remainder as hunters and canoe-men. These men, who form for their number, a formidable force, being habituated to all the arts of Indian warfare, and at the same time possessed of a considerable portion of the energy of the whites, Miles McDonnell had most injudiciously offended, by some restrictions on what they conceived their natural rights, about the same time that he commenced his system of aggression on the North West company.

By the partisans of this latter company, the ill-will thus excited was sedulously kept alive; their proceedings in this and other respects, during the winter and following spring, in the course whereof considerable violence was exhibited on both sides, although beyond comparison the greater on behalf of the North West company, will be found fully detailed in my statement. The result was, that after inducing more than three-fourths of the settlers and servants to abandon the colony, and accept their offers of a passage to Canada, and arresting and taking down Miles McDonnell, and Spencer, the sheriff, as prisoners, the North West company were enabled by secretly instigating the half-breeds, to succeed in driving away the remaining settlers; and by the burning of their houses, to destroy nearly every vestige of the colony, without themselves taking an open part in the more violent proceedings. At the meeting at Fort William, the ensuing summer, when Mr. Simon McGillivray appears to have replaced his brother, as principal agent of the company, the parties from Red River were all received with unqualified approbation; to the half-breeds, in particular, praises and rewards were given, consisting (exclusive of a public feast) of a suit of clothes each, and presents of arms to a few of the leaders; and evidence has been produced, that they were at the same time told by Mr. Simon McGillivray, that they had done well in defending their lands; and that if the colonists attempted to return, they should drive them away again, and should be supported by the North West company.... For the numerous and mutual violences of the ensuing winter and spring, I must again refer to the statement, observing, that in the seizure of Duncan Cameron's person and post at the forks of Red River, and the pertinacious retention of this latter, the Hudson's Bay company's party, so far exceeded any legitimate measures of defence, that they must I think be considered as aggressors, in most of the occurrences previous to the 19th June; although at the same time there can be no doubt that the half-breeds, acting at the instigation of the North West company, (by whom they were collected, and furnished with supplies of food and ammunition,) had early in the year resolved on again attempting to drive off the colonists. On the 19th June, when the unfortunate affray took place in which Governor Semple lost his life, the two parties seem to have met accidentally, and with arms in their hands, and mutually irritated feelings; that the action took place without previous design on either side; the first shot appears, next to a certainty, to have been fired by the Hudson's Bay company's party, at the moment that Governor Semple, enraged by the insolent address of Boucher, attempted to snatch away his gun; the savage massacre of the wounded, and the inhuman plundering and butchering of the dead bodies after the action, appears therefore to form the most aggravated part of the proceeding. This, Grant, their leader, states, he endeavoured in vain to prevent; and the total absence of any accusation against him on this score, and the numerous testimonies to his general humanity, leave little doubt of the truth of this assertion; if admitted, however, it furnishes only an additional proof of the ferocity of a part of the body, and shows in the stronger point of view, the dangerous course adopted by the North West company, in employing so ungovernable and almost savage a force. This indeed forms the great offence of the company as a body, and has, together with the melancholy consequences which have followed therefrom, naturally and justly excited a strong public feeling against them; it is true, that few comparatively of the partners of the company appear to have actually taken part in the assembling of the half-breeds this year, but a similar measure had been universally approved the preceding one, and a large number of the partners who arrived at Red River shortly after the 19th June, with the mixed views of liberating Duncan Cameron, retaking their own post, and revenging these and the other violences they attributed to their opponents, appear to have given an unqualified approbation to all the proceedings of the half-breeds, and many of them to have expressed their triumph and joy on viewing the scene of action; if one witness who speaks to this particular fact could be fully credited, in terms and with circumstances of ferocity scarcely human; at all events, it is clearly established, that about forty suits of clothes which Mr. Archibald Norman McLeod, the principal agent of the company, then present, had brought up, were distributed amongst the half-breeds, including those present on the 19th June, as a recompence for their services to the company, and that further rewards of the same kind were found prepared at Fort William, on the Earl of Selkirk's taking possession of that post, for such as had not received them in the first instance. It is on these proceedings at Red River, that Archibald Norman McLeod and so many other of the partners of the North West company, are indicted as accessories to the murder of Governor Semple; and it is chiefly for the approval of the proceedings of the half-breeds, implied by further rewards prepared at Fort William, at a period when Mr. William McGillivray was residing there as principal agent, that the same charge is expected to be made out against him....

The observations relative to this last occurrence, apply equally or perhaps more strongly to the half-breeds, in respect to the greater part of whom there are also many other circumstances of extenuation; they evidently acted in the first instance under a mistaken sense of right, and an impression that the settlers were invaders of the natural rights of themselves and the North West company; their claim to the soil, jointly with the Indians (in favour of which the evidence before me shows that plausible grounds might be assigned,) was evidently strongly impressed on them by the partners of the North West company, to whose opinions they naturally looked up, and during the contest, many circumstances of mutual irritation had occurred; yet their final plan of attack appears to have been confined to the expulsion of the colonists, without further violence than might be unavoidable in the accomplishment of that object; the affray of the 19th of June, melancholy as it was in its result, seems clearly to have been unpremeditated, and it appears that but few individuals amongst the half-breeds partook of the massacre that succeeded it. Of the sincerity of the half-breeds in the opinions they profess to have acted upon, strong presumptive proof is afforded by the openness with which they generally avowed their intentions, by their address to Government, and in the final voluntary submission of its principal leaders to public authority.

After this long detail of the final impressions remaining upon my mind, on the coolest and most deliberate consideration of the evidence before me, I deem it right to state, that I now feel more strongly convinced than ever of the general correctness of the opinion, which I had the honour of submitting to your Excellency on my return from the Indian country, as the result of my inquiry, as far as it had then gone; namely, "that the moral character of most of the offences, was, that of each party instead of appealing to the laws of their country, endeavouring to enforce the rights to which they conceived themselves entitled, or to redress their supposed injuries by force;"...

FURTHER READINGS

Brown, J. *Strangers in the Blood: Fur Trade Families in Indian Country.* Vancouver: University of British Columbia Press, 1980.

Brown, J., and J. Peterson, Eds. *The New Peoples: Being and Becoming Métis in North America.* Winnipeg: University of Manitoba Press, 1985.

Bumsted, J. "Introduction." In *The Collected Writings of Lord Selkirk 1810-1829*, Vol. 2, ed. .J. Bumsted. Winnipeg: Manitoba Record Society, 1987.

Bumsted, J. "The Quest for a Usable Founder: Lord Selkirk and Manitoba Historians." *Manitoba History* 2 (1981): 2-7.

Burley, E. *Servants of the Honourable Company: Work, Discipline, and Conflict in the Hudson's Bay Company 1770-1879.* Toronto: Oxford University Press, 1997.

Dick, L. "The Seven Oaks Incident and the Construction of a Historical Tradition." *Journal of the Canadian Historical Association* 2 (1991): 91-113.

Foster, J. "The Origins of Mixed Bloods in the Canadian West." In *Essays on Western History*, ed. L. Thomas. Edmonton: University of Alberta Press, 1976.

Gallagher, B. "A Re-examination of Race, Class and Society in Red River." *Native Studies Review* 14 (1988): 25-65.

Gray, J. *Lord Selkirk of Red River.* Toronto: Macmillan, 1963.

Gressley, G. "Lord Selkirk and the Canadian Courts." In *Canadian History Before Confederation*, 2nd ed., ed. J. Bumsted. Toronto: Gage, 1979.

Judd, C. "Native Labour and Social Stratification in the Hudson's Bay Company's Northern Department, 1770-1870." *Canadian Review of Sociology and Anthropology* 17, 4 (November 1980): 305-14.

Mcleod, M., and W. Morton. *Cuthbert Grant of Grantown.* Toronto: McClelland and Stewart, 1974.

Morton, A. *A History of the Canadian West to 1870-71.* 2nd ed. Toronto: University of Toronto Press, 1973.

Pannekoek, F. *The Fur Trade in Western Canadian Society.* Ottawa: Canadian Historical Association, 1989.

Podruchny, C. "Unfair Masters and Rascally Servants? Labor Relations Among Bourgeois Clerks and Voyageurs in the Montreal Fur Trade, 1760-1821." *Labour* 43 (Spring 1999): 43-70.

Ray, A. *Indians in the Fur Trade.* Toronto: University of Toronto Press, 1974.

Rich, E. *The Fur Trade and the North West to 1857.* Toronto: McClelland and Stewart, 1967.

Rich, E. *The History of the Hudson's Bay Company, 1670-1870.* London: Hudson's Bay Record Society, 1959.

# CHAPTER 9

# "For the Sake of Humanity"

## NEWFOUNDLAND AND THE BEOTHUK

### INTRODUCTION

Of the many mysteries in Canada's early history, few generate more controversy and speculation than the tragic extinction of the Beothuk, Newfoundland's Indigenous people. We do know that Shawnadithit, typically referred to as the last Beothuk, died of tuberculosis in 1829. We don't know why. Did her people lose a protracted tribal rivalry with the Micmac and, if so, did the British encourage the Micmac to do their dirty work, as some scholars contend? Did the Beothuk perhaps disappear because they lost the competition for the limited resources of Newfoundland's harsh terrain? Possibly, but, as some contend, since they used different hunting styles the Beothuk would not come into contact, let alone conflict, with either the European or Micmac. Thus, if correct, the explanation lies elsewhere. Some claim they were doomed because they lacked the critical mass for survival—that a population of some 2,000 souls was simply insufficient to sustain a nomadic tribe in an unforgiving land, regardless of outside interference.

Another factor in their demise may have been the unique relationship, or lack thereof, between European and Beothuk. European fishermen and fish processors living in Newfoundland went about their business without needing local Native assistance and, indeed, found the Native presence a nuisance. Such was not the case in areas concentrating on the fur trade, such as New France, where Indigenous people actually provided most of the pelts and were indispensable. Being superfluous to European needs perhaps increased the Beothuk's vulnerability.

We do know that the European-Beothuk relationship was dangerously lopsided. Beothuk developed a dependency for European goods, especially iron items such as fish hooks, knives, and cooking utensils. They had little to barter in exchange, however, and therefore helped themselves to what they needed from temporarily abandoned fishing camps during the winter months. Such incidents inevitably led to reprisals from frustrated settlers and fishermen who owned the stored goods, who depended upon them for survival, and whose legal system dealt severely with thievery. Ironically, the Beothuk may not have perceived their actions as "theft" at all because they possibly shared a common nomadic belief: unused objects are unowned. Regardless of the interpretation, however, clashes possibly accelerated the Beothuks' demise because when the two groups met, which was uncommon, it was rarely amicable, frequently violent, and the Beothuk usually lost. Evidence does suggest that neither side held the monopoly on brutality.

What about the accusation of genocide: that the British government, either through studied indifference or passive collusion, systematically encouraged the Beothuk's extinction? The British government knew fishermen harassed the Beothuk and occasionally hunted them, but Britain had limited resources and a huge empire spanning the globe. Controlling a land as vast and harsh as Newfoundland was well nigh impossible without considerable reallocation of stretched assets, and for what? Most of the rest of the empire was both easier to police and paid far better dividends. There was, realistically, little motivation for expensive enforcement and protection. A plan to forbid harassment existed, and the government did call an inquiry into the fishery in 1793, but it was too little, too late. In the end, British officials offered bounties for Beothuk taken alive in a strange plan intended to make the captives into mediators and translators for future amicable dealings with other Beothuk.

Theories on the Beothuk's disappearance are legion, but objective scrutiny of historical and anthropological evidence paints a picture in subtle shades of grey rather than the black-and-white of popular mythology. One scholar even challenges the Beothuk's very "disappearance," speculating that remnants of the Beothuk may have integrated with other Indigenous people or that they were simply an offshoot of the Labrador Inuit whose culture continues to this day.

1. Were Europeans in Newfoundland solely or chiefly responsible for the extinction of the Beothuk?

2. To what extent, if any, were the Beothuk responsible for their own demise?

3. Newfoundlanders often referred to "stealing" by the Beothuk. What evidence shows that the Europeans were the real thieves who failed to honour Native concepts of property?

4. In the absence of the Beothuck's own perspectives of their situation, can these documents be used to further our knowledge of them? How?

## DOCUMENTS

### 1. *"Report of Committee Appointed to Inquire into the State of the Trade to Newfoundland in March, April and June, 1793"*

#### 1.1 TESTIMONY OF GEORGE CARTWRIGHT

*At age 15, George Cartwright (1739-1819) joined the British army and was a captain by the end of the Seven Years' War. He visited Newfoundland in 1766 and again in 1768, ordered by the governor there to establish friendly relations with the Beothuk. He later quit the army to trade in fish, seals, and furs, voyaging far into Labrador where he befriended the Inuit. He sponsored a British tour for one Inuit family. American privateers pillaged his posts in 1778, and he retired, ruined, to Britain.*

George Cartwright Esq., being examined, informed your Committee, that he was an Officer of Foot in His Majesty's service. And being asked whether he has been in Newfoundland? he said, "Yes; several times."

And being asked in what capacity? he said, "Twice on pleasure, five times on business, on his way backwards and forwards to Labrador; the last time he was there was in 1786; he has been much in that part of Newfoundland inhabited by the native Indians, he has reason to believe that their numbers are considerable, but he cannot state what the numbers are, as they have been so much chased and driven away by the Fishermen and Furriers."

And being asked, How near to any of our settlements do the Indians come? he said, "They frequently come in the night into the harbours to pilfer what they can get, to supply their necessities."

And being asked, What were the articles which they mostly steal? he said, "Sails, hatchets, boats, kettles and such other things as they think will be of use; they use the sails as covering for their wigwams or tents."

And being asked, could he state any particulars respecting the condition of the Indians in Newfoundland? he said, "He thinks their condition is very wretched and forlorn indeed; our fishermen and furriers shooting at the Indians for their amusement." He said, "He has heard many say they had rather have a shot at an Indian than at a deer: A few years ago there two men, one of whom he knew personally, went up the Great River Exploits in the winter, on purpose to murder and plunder such Indians as they could meet with; when they got to the head of the river where it comes out of a great lake, they met with an Indian town, containing above one hundred inhabitants; they immediately fired upon them with long guns loaded with buckshot; they killed and wounded several, the rest made their escape into the woods, some naked, others only half clothed; none of them provided with implements to procure either food or fuel; they then plundered their houses or wigwams of what they thought worth bringing away, and burnt the rest, by which they must necessarily have destroyed the remainder, as they could not exist in the snow."

And being asked, If he meant to state that the conduct of the Fishermen and Furriers towards the Indians was in general of that cruel nature, or that these were only particular instances? he said, "He has reason to believe from the conversations he has had with the fishermen of these parts, that there are very few who would not have done the same thing."

The witness having stated, that the Indians sometimes come down into the ports where our cod-fishery is carried on, and steal various articles, he was asked, Whether he believes that was in consequence of any provocation or molestation that they might have received from the Fishermen and Furriers? he said, "Most certainly, and also from the impossibility of their ever getting anything they want by any other means; he has been well assured, that formerly a very beneficial barter was carried on between our people and the Indians, somewhere near the port of Bonavista, by our people leaving goods at a certain place, and the Indians taking what they wanted and leaving furs in return: but that barter was at length put a stop to by one of our fishermen hiding himself near the place of deposit, and shooting a woman dead upon the spot as she was suiting herself to what she wanted."

And being asked, Whether he believes, from what he has seen of the Indians, that any intercourse could be again established between them and the British Fishermen and Furriers in Newfoundland? he said, "He thinks it very possible and practicable that he gave in a plan several years ago to the administration for that purpose, and then stated generally these circumstances, and he offered to undertake the execution of it himself."

And being asked, from what he has seen of the Indians, did they seem to be of a more sanguinary and savage disposition than people in that state of society generally are? he said, "By no means, for he has heard many instances of their saving the lives of our people, when they might very easily have put them to death; he heard one man tell his master, that a few days before he left the Bay of Exploits, as he was going to land out of his boat to look at a trap that he had set for an otter, he was surprised by the voice of an Indian; and on turning his head, saw an Indian standing on the shore with an arrow in his bow ready to shoot him; the Indian made a motion with his hand for him to retire; he was then not above four or five yards from the Indian; he immediately pulled his boat round and made off as fast as he could; the Indian remained in the same posture until he had got some distance from the shore, and then retired into the woods; the Fisherman then added, that he regretted not having his gun with him, as he would have shot him dead upon the spot."

And being asked, Whether the Indians are large and stout men? he said, "From what few he had seen of them, he believes they are."

And being asked, Did the cruelties which he mentioned to be exercised by the Fishermen and Furriers to the Indians happen in summer as well as in winter? he said, "Yes, in both, but more opportunities happen in summer than in winter."

And being asked, Did the merchants and persons who go out from this country to Newfoundland use their influence and endeavours to prevent such practices? he said, "He did not recollect an instance of it."

And being asked, Had the Magistrates used any exertions to prevent those outrages? he said, "There are no Magistrates within that district, that he knew of, he means the district between Cape St. John and Cape Freels."

And being asked, Whether the Magistrates resident within any of the other districts were capable of preventing these horrors if they exerted themselves for that purpose? he said, "He does not believe they could, because they reside at too great a distance."

And being asked, Did he conceive that those horrors could be prevented without the establishment of a regular Court of Judicature in Newfoundland? he said, "He thinks that if his plan, or something similar to it, was adopted, it would effectually prevent every thing of the kind and the offender might be carried to St John's to be tried by any Court of Judicature established there for the trial of criminal offences."

And being asked, Whether there is not a trade at present carried on with the Indians? he said, "No: he knew not when the intercourse was interrupted; it was twenty-seven years ago that he first heard of it."

And being asked, Whether there is any English merchant that carries on a Fishery North of Cape St. John? he said, "Not now he believes."

And being asked, Whether the people that he states to have committed those enormities were annual Fishermen from England or residents in Newfoundland? he said, "Generally the resident Fishermen."

And being asked, If that residence was prohibited, would not these enormities be in a great measure prevented? he said, "If residency within the district he alludes to was not permitted, it would in a great measure have that effect;" he means the district between Cape Freels and Cape St. John.

And being asked, Whether he thinks that the disposition of the Indians is such as to lead them to live upon good terms with our people, provided there were only a sufficient number left to take care of the fishing materials? he said, "He thinks our people would be in danger, unless some intercourse was first established."

And being asked, In what year did the enormities he represents happen, and who were the Officers of the Navy commanding in those parts at the time? he said, "He could not recollect."

And being asked, if he was conversant with the Coast of Labrador? he said, "Yes."

And being asked Whether there is not an annual Fishery carried on there from Great Britain, without any residence? he said, "No, there are very few who go out for the summer there."

And being asked, How is justice administered in Labrador? he said, "There has been neither law, justice, nor equity there for many years."

And being asked, Whether there is not a more flourishing Fishery carried on there than in Newfoundland? he said, "He could not tell how flourishing it is, but he knew that numbers of people have suffered there for want of justice."

And being desired to state any instances he might have heard while he resided in Newfoundland, which might make a new Court of Judicature necessary, he said, "He could not pretend to say; he knew of none."

And being desired to state the outlines of his plan, he said, "It was to appropriate that part of the Coast from North Head to Dog Creek, including

Chapel Island, and all other islands within that line, to the use of the Indians, and to have some person stationed there with a schooner and a sufficient number of people to protect them; by which means some acquaintance and connection might be formed betwixt the Indians and the English, and beyond all doubt a traffic would be established." There is no intercourse or barter between those native Indians he speaks of and our people. There are parts of the island where some intercourse is maintained with the Mickmack Indians, and in other parts with the Nescopite Indians.

And being asked, If he meant that all the residents should be removed from that part he has described, and that no person should land or go there without permission? he said, "He does."

And being asked, Whether he ever knew more than one man residing upon the River Exploits? he said, "He knew but of one."

And being asked, Whether the same cruelties were exercised against the Indians of the Coast of Labrador, as against the Red Indians? he said, "Not since the year 1770, since he went amongst them, and learned their language, and got upon terms of friendship with them; previous to that period the cruelties were just as numerous as those exercised in Newfoundland. It appears to him that the Indians wish to be on terms of friendship with the English."

And being asked, Whether the inveteracy of the Indians towards the Europeans is not so great that they murder every European they are able? he said, "Yes."

And being asked, Whether he conceives that, if the traders, going in the summer to Newfoundland, use their influence to prevent the horrors that have been described, that they might not in some degree be prevented? he said, "He believes it would have a good effect, but in general they do not trouble their heads about the matter, for fear it should affect their own interests."

And being asked, Whether those Indians are not universally afraid of an Englishman? he said, "They are."

And being asked, Would they venture to come within sight of an European? he said, "They conceal themselves in the woods as much as possible, and very seldom show themselves."

And being asked, Did not the merchants going to Newfoundland receive the furs that are taken from the Indians without making any enquiry? he said, "Yes."

And being asked, Whether our trade and intercourse with Labrador was not very insignificant before the year 1770? he said, "Yes."

## 1.2 TESTIMONY OF JOHN REEVES

*Educated at Eton and Oxford, lawyer and prolific author John Reeves (1752–1829) became a Newfoundland judge in 1791. A maverick, he earned the enmity of the West Country Merchants by vigorously opposing their autocratic rule, which made him a local folk hero. Actively engaged in local politics, Reeves doggedly fought for greater local autonomy and control. He also wrote the first comprehensive history of the colony.*

John Reeves, Esq., Chief Justice of Newfoundland, being examined, said, "Another subject is the state of the Wild Indians in the interior parts of the island.

At a time when the Legislature is manifesting so much anxiety for the protection and welfare of a people who do not belong to us I make no doubt of being heard while I say a few words on behalf of these poor people, who are a part of the King's subjects. These Indians inhabit a country the sovereignty of which is claimed and exercised by His Majesty. Unlike the wandering tribes upon the continent, who roam from place to place, these people are more peculiarly our own people than any other of the savage tribes; they and everything belonging to them is in our power; they can be benefitted by none others; they can be injured by none others: in this situation they are entitled the protection of the King's government, and to the benefit of good neighborhood from his subjects; but they enjoy neither; they are deprived of the free use of the shores and the rivers, which should entitle them to some compensation from us; but they receive none; instead of being traded with, they are plundered, instead of being taught, they are pursued with outrage and murder.

It seems very extraordinary, but it is a fact known to hundreds in the northern part of the island, that there is no intercourse or connection whatsoever between our people and the Indians but plunder, outrage and murder. If a wigwam is found it is plundered of the furs it contains, and is burnt; if an Indian is discovered he is shot at exactly as a fox or bear. This has gone on for years in Newfoundland, while Indians in all other parts of the King's dominions have received benefit from their connection with us, either in the supply of their worldly necessities by traffic, or in being initiated in the principles of morality and religion; but such has been the policy respecting this island, that the residents for many years had little benefit of a regular government for themselves, and when they were so neglected, it is not to be wondered that the condition of the poor Indians was never mended.

When the Indians show themselves, it is in the Bay of Exploits and in Gander Bay, to the northward. They come down to get what the seashore affords for food. This is a lawless part of the island, where there are no Magistrates resident for many miles, nor any control, as in other parts, from the short visit of a man-of-war during a few days in the summer; so that people do as they like, and there is hardly any time of account for their actions. The persons who are best acquainted with the resort of the Indians, and who are deepest in the outrages that have been committed upon them, are the furriers of the bays I have just mentioned, and of the places thereabouts. Some of these men have been conversed with last summer, and I understand, if they were relieved from the danger of enquiry into what is past, they would open upon the subject, and make themselves useful in commencing any new system of treatment and conduct.

What then do I propose to be done for these Indians, and what is the manner in which I propose it should be accomplished? In the first place, it seems they ought to be protected from violence, and that ought to be done by executing the present laws against offenders. I hope something is already begun towards attaining this, by what I said to the Grand Jury, last year, and the apprehension expressed, as I understand by some furriers, who feared they should be brought to justice; but in so distant a part of the island the fear of the law is little security, and if it is really to be executed, I hardly know the means of doing it in the present circumstances of the island and its government.

But supposing this attained, does our bare duty towards these people end here? Separated as they are from all the world but us, is it not incumbent upon us to use the means in our power to impart to them the rights of religion and civil society? Or at least, does not our interest suggest an advantage that might be derived by a free and unrestrained trade with them, in which furs and other produce might be exchanged for British manufactures? Should any or all of these considerations be thought sufficient for endeavouring to conciliate the confidence of these people, and to open a friendly intercourse with them, there seems no difficulty or hazard in the undertaking. It is similar to what has already been done on the Labrador coast with a race of savages said to be more untractable, and under circumstances much less favourable. It is only to choose between holding out encouragement to the Moravians to send a Missionary, as they now do to Labrador, or employing the present furrier under the direction of some person who has a talent for such enterprises. In both cases, there should be some small force; and if one of the sloops of war upon that station were to winter in the Bay of Exploits, or Gander Bay, for protecting such a project in the season that is most favourable to it, it would be as much force as would be needed; but the mode and manner of carrying into execution such a scheme is for the consideration of the Committee."

## 2. John Peyton Jr., "*Narrative,*" St. John's, Newfoundland, May 27, 1819

*An independent trader with a legendary reputation for brutality against the Beothuk, Englishman John Peyton Sr. (1749–1829) lived on a key Beothuk migration route. Though born in Newfoundland his son, John Peyton Jr. (1793–1879) received a British education and became Justice of the Peace upon his return to "The Rock." In 1818 father and son searched for Beothuk who allegedly stole Peyton family property. They captured a woman named Demasduwit.*

Sir,

I beg leave to lay before Your Excellency the following statements by which it will appear to what extent I have been a sufferer by depredation committed on my property by the Native Indians, and which at last drove me to the necessity of following them to endeavour to recover some part of it again.

In April 1814, John Morris, a furrier of mine, came out from one of my furrier's tilts in the country on business to me, leaving in the tilt his provisions, some fur, and his clothes. On his return to the tilt again he found that some persons had been there in his absence, and carried away and destroyed the provisions, and all the fur with many other little things but yet valuable to a furrier; the distance being 20 miles from the tilt to my residence he was obliged to sleep there that night, but the next day Morris came out and told me what had happened, and that he had every reason to suspect that it had been done by the Red Indians. On the following morning I, with Thomas Taylor, another of my furriers, and John Morris, went to Morris's tilt and found what he had told me to be correct, and near the tilt I found part of an Indian's snow racket and a hatchet, which convinced me that the depredation had been committed by them. We, after this followed their tracks to Morris's different beaver houses and found that they had carried away seven of my traps. The damage done and loss I sustained on this occasion cannot be estimated at less than £5 independent of losing the season for catching fur.

In June 1814 Mathew Huster and John Morris were sent by me to put out a new fleet of salmon nets consisting of two nets 60 fathoms long. On going the following morning to haul them, they were cut from the moorings and nothing but a small part of the Head Rope left. From the manner the moorings were cut and hackled, and the marks of Red Ochre on the Buoys, we were satisfied that it was done by the Indians, no other persons being near us at that season. In the following August some of my people had an occasion to land on a point often frequented by the Indians, they saw there had been two wigwams built there that summer, but the Indians had left it some time, there they found the cork and part of the head rope of the nets, which convinced us who it was had cut away the nets in June. The damage done me by the loss of the nets was £20 independent of the fish that might have been caught by them that summer.

In August 1815 the Red Indians came into the harbour of Exploits Burnt Island in the night, and cut adrift from my stage a fishing boat, carried away her sails and fishing tackle; they also the same night cut a boat adrift belonging to Geo. Luff, of the same harbour. The loss I sustained here was full £10. In October 1817 I sent Edward Rogers, an apprentice, to set a number of traps for catching marten cats, they being apparently very plenty at that time. On going to visit his traps he found that fourteen of his best traps were carried away, and an Indian's arrow driven through the roof of the cat-house, at the end of the path were two Indian paddles, the loss here, independent of the fur, was £4. 18s.

In September 1818 the Indians came to my wharf at Sandy Point, and cut adrift a large boat of mine which I had in the day loaded with salmon, &c., for St John's market, and was only waiting for a fair wind to sail. On my missing her at half past one in the morning, I took a small boat, and with a servant went in search of her. About seven O'Clock in the evening I discovered her ashore in a most dangerous situation. With great difficulty I boarded her, and found that the Indians had cut away her sails and part of her rigging, and had plundered her of almost every thing moveable. Her hull being much damaged, it was impossible to get her off without assistance. I proceeded to Exploits Burnt Island for a crew, and brought her into the harbour, the damage done to the boat and some part of her cargo, and the property stolen cannot be replaced under £140 or £150. Having so frequently suffered such heavy losses, on my arrival I waited on Your Excellency requesting permission to follow the property and regain it if possible, I made deposition of the truth of what I had asserted, and obtained Your Excellency's permission to go into the country during the winter.

On the first of March, 1819, I left my house accompanied by my father and eight of my own men with a most anxious desire of being able to take some of the Indians and thus through them open a friendly communication with the rest, everyone was ordered by me not upon any account to commence hostilities without my positive orders. On the 2nd March we came up with a few wig-wams frequented by the Indians during the spring and autumn for the purpose of killing deer. On the 3rd we saw a fireplace by the side of the brook where some Indians had slept a few days before. On the 4th, at 10 O'Clock we came to a storehouse belonging to the Indians. On entering it I found five of my cat traps, set, as I supposed, to protect their venison from the cats, and part of my boat's jib, from the fireplace and tracks on the snow, we were convinced the Indians had left it the day before in the direction SW. We therefore followed their footing with all possible speed and caution. I could not tell at this time whether the Indian I saw was a male or female. I showed myself on the point openly, when the Indian discovered me she for a moment was motionless. She screamed out as soon as she appeared to make me out and ran off. I immediately pursued her, but did not gain on her until I had taken off my rackets and Jacket, when I came up with her fast, she kept looking back at me over her shoulder, I then dropped my gun on the snow and held up my hands to show her I had no gun, and on my pointing to my gun which was then some distance behind me, she stopped. I did the same and endeavoured to convince her I would not hurt her. I then advanced and gave her my hand, she gave hers to me and to all my party as they came up. We then saw seven or eight Indians repeatedly running off and on the pond, and as I imagined from their wigwams. Shortly after three Indians came running towards us—when they came within about 200 or 300 yds. from us they made a halt. I advanced towards them with the woman, and on her calling to the Indians two of their party came down to us, the third halted again about 100 yards distant. I ordered one of the men to examine one of the Indians that did come to us, having observed something under his cassock, which proved to be a hatchet, which the man took from him,—the two Indians came and took hold of me by the arms endeavouring to force me away. I cleared myself as well as I could still having the woman in my hand. The Indian from whom the hatchet was taken attempted to lay hold of three different guns, but without effect, he at last succeeded in getting hold of my father's gun, and tried to force it from him, and in the attempt to get his gun he and my father got off nearly fifty yards from me and in the direction of the woods, at the same time the other Indian was continually endeavouring to get behind our party. The Indian who attacked my father grasped him by the throat. My father drew a bayonet with the hope of intimidating the Indian. It had not the desired effect, for he only made a savage grin at it. I then called for one of the men to strike him, which he did across the hands with his gun; he still held on my father till he was struck on the head, when he let my father go, and either struck at or made a grasp at the man who struck him, which he evaded by falling under the hand, at the same time this encounter was taking place, the third Indian who had halted about 100 yards, kept at no great distance from us, and there were seven or eight more repeatedly running out from the woods on the look out, and no greater distance from us than 100 yards. The Indian turned again

on my father and made a grasp at his throat—my father extricated himself and
on his retreat the Indian still forcing on him, fired. I ordered one of the men to
defend my father, when two guns were fired, but the guns were all fired so close
together that I did not know till some time after that more than one had been
fired. The rest of the Indians fled immediately on the fall of the unfortunate one.
Could we have intimidated or persuaded him to leave us, or even have seen the
others go off, we should have been most happy to have spared using violence, but
when it was remembered that our small party were in the heart of the Indians'
country, one hundred miles from any European settlement, and that there were
in our sight at times as many Indians as our party amounted to, and we could
not ascertain how many were in the woods that we did not see, it could not be
avoided with safety to ourselves. Had destruction been our object we might have
carried it much further. Nor should I have brought this woman to the capital to
Your Excellency, nor should I offer my services for the ensuing summer, had I
wantonly put an end to the unfortunate man's existence, as in the case of success
in taking any more during the summer and opening a friendly intercourse with
them, I must be discovered.

My object was and still is to endeavour to be on good terms with the Indians for the protection of my property, and the rescuing of that tribe of our
fellow-creatures from the misery and persecution they are exposed to in the interior from Micmacs, and on the exterior by the Whites. With this impression
on my mind I offer my services to the Government for the ensuing summer and I
implore Your Excellency to lend me any assistance you may think proper. I cannot
afford to do much at my own expense, having nothing but what I work for, the
expenses of doing anything during the summer would be less than the winter, as
it will not be safe ever to attempt going into their country with so small a crew
as I had with me last winter. Still these expenses are much greater than I can
afford, as nothing effectual can be expected to be done under £400. Unless Your
Excellency should prefer sending an expedition on the service out of the fleet, in
which case I would leave the woman at Your Excellency's disposal, but should I be
appointed to cruise the summer for them, and which I could not do and find men
and necessaries under £400, I have not the least doubt but that I shall, through
the medium of the woman I now have, be enabled to open an intercourse with
them, nor is it all improbable but that she will return with us again if she can to
procure an infant child she left behind her. I beg to assure Your Excellency from
my acquaintance with the bays and the place of resort for the Indians during the
summer, that I am most confident of succeeding in the plan here laid down.

## 3. W. Cormack, *Royal Gazette*, November 13, 1827

*W. Cormack (1796-1863) came from a Newfoundland merchant family but left the island in 1805 to attend the universities of Glasgow and Edinburgh where he studied natural history. Briefly in Prince Edward Island to lead a group of Scottish immigrants, he returned to his home in 1821 determined to explore and colonize the interior regions of Newfoundland. In his mind establishing friendly relations with the Beothuck would be critical to the success of his venture, but his first expedition failed to locate any natives. His concern did, however, result in the creation of the Beothuck Institute in 1827. Expeditions that followed also failed to make contact, but Beothuk artifacts and information concerning their language, beliefs, and movements were collected at the Institute. In the end Cormack advocated a theory that the Beothuk had originated in Scandinavia.*

Every man who has common regard for the welfare of his fellow beings, and who hears of the cause for which we are now met, will assuredly foster any measures that may be devised to bring within the protection of civilization that neglected and persecuted tribe: the Red Indians of Newfoundland. Every man will join us, except he be callous to the misfortunes or regardless of the prosperity of his fellow creatures. Those who by their own merits, or by the instrumentality of others, become invested with power and influence in society, are bound the more to exert themselves to do all the good they can, in promoting the happiness of their fellow men: and if there be such men in Newfoundland, who say there is no good to be gained by reclaiming the aborigines from their present hapless condition, let them not expose their unvirtuous sentiments to the censure of this enlightened age. Is there no honest pride in him who protects man from the shafts of injustice? Nay, is there not an inward monitor approving of all our acts which shall have the tendency to lessen crime and prevent murder?

We now stand on the nearest part of the New World to Europe—of Newfoundland to Britain; and at this day, and on this sacred spot, do we form the first assembly that has ever yet collected together to consider the condition of the invaded and ill-treated first occupiers of the country. Britons have trespassed here, to be a blight and a scourge to a portion of the human race; under their (in other respects) protecting power, a defenceless, and once independent, proud tribe of men, have been nearly extirpated from the face of the earth scarcely causing an enquiry how, or why. Near this spot is known to remain in all his primitive rudeness, clothed in skins, and with a bow and arrow only to gain his subsistence by, and to repel the attacks of his lawless and reckless foes: there on the opposite approximating point, is man improved and powerful: barbarity and civilization are this day called upon to shake hands.

The history of the original inhabitants of Newfoundland, called by themselves Beothuck, and by Europeans, the Red Indians, can only be gleaned from tradition, and that chiefly among the Micmacs. It would appear that about a century and a half ago, this tribe was numerous and powerful like their neighbouring tribe, the Micmacs: both tribes were then on friendly terms, and inhabited the western shores of Newfoundland, in common with the other parts of the island, as well as Labrador. A misunderstanding with the Europeans (French) who then held the sway over those parts, led, in the result, to hostilities between the two tribes; and the sequel of the tale runs as follows.

The European authorities, who we may suppose were not over scrupulous in dealing out equity in those days, offered a reward for the persons or heads of certain Red Indians. Some of the Micmacs were tempted by the reward, and took off the heads of two of them. Before the heads were delivered for the award, they were by accident discovered, concealed in the canoe that was to convey them, and recognized by some of the Red Indians as the heads of their friends. The Red Indians gave no intimation of their discovery to the perpetrators of the unprovoked outrage, but consulted amongst themselves, and determined on having revenge. They invited the Micmacs to a great feast, and arranged their guests in such order that every Beothuck had a Micmac by his side, at a preconcerted signal each Beothuck slew his guest. They then retired quickly from those parts bordering on the Micmac country. War of course ensued. Firearms were little known to the Indians at this time, but they soon came into more general use amongst such tribes as continued to hold intercourse with Europeans. This circumstance gave the Micmacs an undisputed ascendancy over the Beothucks, who were forced to betake themselves to the recesses of the interior, and retired parts of the island, alarmed, as well they might be, at every report of the fire-lock.

Since that day European weapons have been directed, from every quarter, (and in latter times too often) at the open breasts and unstrung bows of the unoffending Beothucks. Sometimes these unsullied people of the chase have been destroyed wantonly, because they have been thought more fleet, and more evasive, than men ought to be. At other times, at the sight of them, the terror of the ignorant European has goaded him on to murder the innocent, at the bare mention of which civilization ought to weep. Incessant and ruthless persecution, continued for many generations, has given these sylvan people an utter disregard and abhorrence of the very signs of civilization. Shawnawdithit, the surviving female of those who were captured four years ago, by some fishermen, will not now return to her tribe, for fear they should put her to death; a proof of the estimation in which we are held by that persecuted people.

The situation of the unfortunate Beothuck carries with it our warmest sympathy and loudly calls on us all to do something for the sake of humanity. For my own satisfaction, I have for a time, released myself from all other avocations, and am here now, on my way to visit that part of the country which the surviving remnant of the tribe have of late years frequented, to endeavour to force a friendly interview with some of them, before they are entirely annihilated: but it will most probably require many such interviews, and some years, to reconcile them to the approaches of civilized man.

FURTHER READINGS

Budgel, R. "The Beothuks and the Newfoundland Mind." *Newfoundland Studies* 8, 1 (1992): 15-33.

Holly Jr., D. "The Beothuk on the Eve of their Destruction." *Arctic Anthropology* 37, 1 (2000): 79-95.

Marshall, I. *A History and Ethnography of the Beothuk.* Montreal and Kingston: McGill-Queen's University Press, 1996.

Martinjn, C. "Review Article: A History and Ethnography of the Beothuk." *Newfoundland Studies* 12, 2 (1996): 105-31.

McLean, L. "Back to the Beaches: New Data Pertaining to the Early Beothuk in Newfoundland." *Northeast Anthropology* 47 (Spring 1994): 71-86.

Mitchell, J. "All Gone Widdun ('asleep'/died): Was Shawnawdithit Right?" *Newfoundland Quarterly* 93, 1 (Fall 1999): 39-41.

Paul, D. *We Were Not Savages. A Micmac Perspective on the Collision of European and Aboriginal Civilization.* Halifax: Nimbus, 1993.

Pastore, R. "Archaeology, History, and the Beothuks." *Newfoundland Studies* 9, 2 (Fall 1993): 260-78.

Pastore, R. "The Collapse of the Beothuk World." *Acadiensis* 19, 1 (Fall 1989): 52-71.

Pastore, R. "Fishermen, Furriers, and Beothuks: The Economy of Extinction." *Man in the Northeast* 33 (Spring 1987): 47-62.

Pastore, R. *The Newfoundland Micmacs: A History of their Traditional Life.* St. John's: Newfoundland Historical Society, 1978.

Pastore, R. *Shanawdithit's People.* St. John's: Atlantic Archaeology, 1992.

Pope, P. "Scavengers and Caretakers: Beothuk/European Settlement Dynamics in Seventeenth-Century Newfoundland." *Newfoundland Studies* 9, 2 (Fall 1993): 279-93.

Prins, H. *The Mi'kmaq: Resistance, Accommodation and Cultural Survival.* New York: Harcourt Brace, 1996.

Rowe, F. *Extinction: The Beothuks of Newfoundland.* Toronto: McGraw Hill Ryerson, 1977.

Rowley-Conwy, P. "Settlement Patterns of the Beothuk Indians of Newfoundland." *Canadian Journal of Archaeology* 14 (1990): 13-29.

Smith, P. "Beothuks and Methodists." *Acadiensis* 16 (Autumn 1986): 118-35.

Upton, L. "The Beothuk: Questions and Answers." *Acadiensis* 7, 2 (Spring 1978): 150-55.

Upton, L. "The Extermination of the Beothuks of Newfoundland." *Canadian Historical Review* 58, 2 (June 1977): 133-53.

Upton, L. *Micmacs and Colonists: Micmac-White Relations in the Maritimes 1713-1867.* Vancouver: University of British Columbia Press, 1979.

Whitehead, R. *The Old Man Told Us.* Halifax: Nimbus, 1991.

Winter, K. *Shananditti: The Last of the Beothuks.* Vancouver: J.J. Douglas, 1975.

# CHAPTER 10

# "Our Robinson Crusoe Sort of Life"

## SISTERS IN UPPER CANADA

### INTRODUCTION

Libraries bulge with histories written by men about themselves. Conversely, at least until recently, women historians remained few, and monographs on the lives of women in history scantier still—and too often limited to subjects of curiosity such as the great courtesans or rare women who rose to the top of a male-dominated world. This situation is, if anything, even more dire with respect to the historical record of pioneer Canada. Was this because women played a less important role in pioneer society? Perhaps.

The more likely explanation for the dearth of primary sources from early Canadian women is the obstacles posed by life in a patriarchal society. According to traditional biblical teaching, women were created from man as his helpmate, which implies subservience. Could women rebel against this stricture and demand equality, especially in a pioneer society lacking the coercive paternalistic infrastructure of Europe? Yes, and they eventually did, but it was easier said than done. If society inculcates the belief that women are inferior, then girls growing up under those pervasive sociological tenets are unlikely to resist. They are, instead, apt to believe in and accept their lot.

Why else might Canadian pioneer women's voices be so muted? Illiteracy was a common manifestation of subservience, which meant that a woman might not be able to leave documentary evidence even if she wished to. And the literate woman? Creating a written record requires both the leisure time to write and the financial freedom to buy pen, ink, and paper, all of which were relatively expensive. Average pioneer women were mostly too busy, too poor, too exhausted, or all of the above, to write.

Still, there is no doubt that wealth afforded women opportunities the typical Canadian immigrant, who was poor, lacked. Money could purchase writing time by affording servants to perform designated female tasks. Money bought education too, with the result that women from wealthier families were far more literate than those from poor ones. Britain, after all, did not offer universal free education until 1870. Evidence also suggests that the degree of equality, or at least of power, increased for women the higher up the social ladder they stood. Cumulatively this means that historians studying Canadian pioneer society have very few primary sources written by very few women from a very narrow social spectrum. This woeful situation is then further exacerbated by potential dangers of interpreting those tantalizing crumbs as general observations. Did a wealthier woman experience pioneer life in the same way as her working-class sister? Were her observations "typical"? There is compelling evidence from the homeland, Britain, that a middle- or upper-class woman knew absolutely nothing about her servants' lives. Thus, evidence from the few female observers who left written records may only pertain to a very rarified strata of life. It means that we have a view of Canadian womanhood that is at best narrow and opaque, or worse—misleading or false.

One intriguing puzzle is the question of the comparative degrees of independence between the lives of pioneer and European women. Statistics prove that there were fewer women than men in pioneer society, implying that women had more freedom to be selective and could presumably choose a mate to their liking, unlike their European sisters. Also, because pioneer life was tough, survival required burden-sharing. This propelled women into positions of equality that they might not enjoy in a European environment sufficiently developed to keep women restrained. And if the pioneer woman had special skills, like literacy, she might vault above many men in both degrees of independence and prestige.

· The counter argument is that a lack of women was not necessarily liberating. It forced the few pioneer women onto a steep chute leading to a quick marriage because society could not afford to tolerate women outside the family. Did liberty perhaps arrive with a husband's death? Widows in New France remarried within an average of 8.8 months after their spouse's demise. Why? Because of intense social pressures. As for special skills, here too her independence might be illusory. A community of highly trained nuns, for example, apparently ran their convent, taught, nursed, and could command attention from local male administrators. Scratch the surface, however, and the nun is subservient to the patriarchal church structure. Lest we forget, Canadian women only became "persons" in the eyes of the law in 1928. Before then they were "chattel."

Some historians argue that degrees of relative independence between pioneer and European women, or between women of different classes, is a moot point. They state that the greatest impediment to independence for women, regardless of where they lived and of their social class, was repeated pregnancy and the demands of motherhood. Not until women could control their family size, a twentieth-century development in the Western world, could they gain a modicum of independence or equality with men.

And what of the specifics of life for women in mid-nineteenth-century Ontario? Upper Canada (Canada West after 1840) was a frontier backwater. Few roads linked the primitive little settlements, and they typically became impassable in spring, fall, and winter. Thus most new settlers lived in deeply isolated "bush farms" hacked from the land and often many kilometres from their nearest neighbour, let alone village. Life was tough, often teetering on untenable, and required enormous reservoirs of stamina, perseverance, and ingenuity. The few towns of any consequence, such as Toronto or Kingston, were outposts with few trappings of European sophistication, despite their citizens' blustering insistence to the contrary. Upper Canada did, however, offer boundless opportunities to emigrants fleeing economic and social trauma in the British Isles. A person could own land and, with some luck and much hard work, make an independent life better than what they left in the "Old Country," and far beyond the harsh judgement of "society."

### DISCUSSION POINTS

1. If a working-class woman, born in Canada, recorded her experiences of early Upper Canada, how would it differ, if at all, from Moodie and Traill's accounts?

2. Is it obvious that women wrote these accounts?

3. One Canadian novelist referred to Moodie as "a snob, a liar ... a self-righteous, egotistical woman who writes self-indulgently to make herself look great." Was he right?

4. Moodie and Traill, sisters with remarkably similar backgrounds who experienced all-but-identical conditions, interpreted Upper Canada very differently. What does this say about historical evidence? Can we resolve blatant contradictions between two sources?

5. What qualities did immigrants need in order to prosper in Upper Canada? Were sustained effort, thrift, and good faith sufficient for success?

## 1. Susanna Moodie, *Roughing It in the Bush*, 1852

*Of the few female voices detailing life in pioneer Ontario, the best known are Susanna Moodie (née Strickland, 1803-85) and her sister Catharine Parr Traill (1802-99). They had little spare money or time, but ink flowed through their veins long before they immigrated to Canada, and once there it compelled them to write for personal satisfaction and profit, as well as to provide cautionary tales to others contemplating immigration to the "backwoods of Canada." Their accounts were directed toward their own kind: upper- and upper-middle-class English families unable to keep up with the Joneses and anxious to avoid social humiliation by emigrating. That was, after all, why Moodie and her husband left Britain. Her brother, who lived in Upper Canada, encouraged them by sending glowing reports of economic prosperity and high social status, and they followed him there in 1832. Susanna's husband was a perfect stock promoter's mark: he invested much of their precious money on dubious stocks that inevitably crashed. That, plus limited farming experience, lost them two farms and made them all but destitute in a land Susanna called her "prison house."*

*She eventually petitioned the Lieutenant Governor of Upper Canada for help, and in 1839 he secured her husband an appointment as sheriff. She probably wrote* Roughing It in the Bush *during the depths of their troubles, but it was not published until 1852, by which time the Moodies enjoyed modest prosperity. They owned a stone house instead of their earlier crude log structures, there were schools for their children, they bought a piano, and they had servants. This was not the genteel Britain for which Susanna always pined, but it was a far cry from the grim days when there was insufficient money for children's shoes, let alone for hiring maids.*

In 1830, the great tide of emigration flowed westward. Canada became the great landmark for the rich in hope and poor in purse. Public newspapers and private letters teemed with the unheard-of advantages to be derived from a settlement in this highly favoured region.

Its salubrious climate, its fertile soil, commercial advantages, great water privileges, its proximity to the mother country, and last, not least, its almost total exemption from taxation ... were the theme of every tongue, and lauded beyond all praise. The general interest, once excited, was industriously kept alive by pamphlets, published by interested parties, which prominently set forth all the good to be derived from a settlement in the Backwoods of Canada; while they carefully concealed the toil and hardship to be endured in order to secure these advantages.

They told of lands yielding forty bushels to the acre, but they said nothing of the years when these lands, with the most careful cultivation, would barely return fifteen; when rust and smut, engendered by the vicinity of damp over-hanging woods, would blast the fruits of the poor emigrant's labour, and almost deprive him of bread. They talked of log houses to be raised in a single day, by the generous exertions of friends and neighbours, but they never ventured upon a picture of the disgusting scenes of riot and low debauchery exhibited during the raising, or upon a description of the dwellings when raised—dens of dirt and misery, which would, in many instances, be shamed by an English pigsty. The necessaries of life were described as inestimably cheap; but they forgot to add that in remote bush settlements, often twenty miles from a market town, and some of them even that distance from the nearest dwelling, the necessaries of life which would be deemed indispensable to the European, could not be procured at all, or, if obtained, could only be so by sending a man and team through a blazed forest road—a process far too expensive for frequent repetition.

Oh, ye dealers in wild lands—ye speculators in the folly and credulity of your fellow-men—what a mass of misery, and of misrepresentation productive of that misery, have ye not to answer for! You had your acres to sell, and what to you were the worn-down frames and broken hearts of the infatuated purchasers? The public believed the plausible statements you made with such earnestness, and men of all grades rushed to hear your hired orators declaim upon the blessings to be obtained by the clearers of the wilderness.

Men who had been hopeless of supporting their families in comfort and independence at home, thought that they had only to come out to Canada to make their fortunes; almost even to realize the story told in the nursery, of the sheep and oxen that ran about the streets, ready roasted, and with knives and forks upon their backs. They were made to believe that if it did not actually rain gold, that precious metal could be obtained, as is now stated of California and Australia, by stooping to pick it up.

The infection became general. A Canada mania pervaded the middle ranks of British society; thousands and tens of thousands, for the space of three or four years, landed upon these shores. A large majority of the higher class were officers of the army and navy, with their families—a class perfectly unfitted by their previous habits and education for contending with the stern realities of emigrant life. The hand that has long held the sword, and been accustomed to receive implicit obedience from those under its control, is seldom adapted to wield the spade and guide the plough, or try its strength against the stubborn trees of the forest. Nor will such persons submit cheerfully to the saucy familiarity of servants, who, republicans in spirit, think themselves as good as their employers. Too many of these brave and honourable men were easy dupes to the designing land-speculators. Not having counted the cost, but only looked upon the bright side of the picture held up to their admiring gaze, they fell easily into the snares of their artful seducers.

To prove their zeal as colonists, they were induced to purchase large tracts of wild land in remote and unfavourable situations. This, while it impoverished and often proved the ruin of the unfortunate immigrant, possessed a double advantage to the seller. He obtained an exorbitant price for the land which he actually sold, while the residence of a respectable settler upon the spot greatly enhanced the value and price of all other lands in the neighbourhood....

Many a hard battle had we to fight with old prejudices, and many proud swellings of the heart to subdue, before we could feel the least interest in the land of our adoption, or look upon it as our home.

All was new, strange, and distasteful to us; we shrank from the rude, coarse familiarity of the uneducated people among whom we were thrown; and they in turn viewed us as innovators, who wished to curtail their independence by expecting from them the kindly civilities and gentle courtesies of a more refined community.... The semi-barbarous Yankee squatters, who had "left their country for their country's good," and by whom we were surrounded in our first settlement, detested us, and with them we could have no feeling in common. We could neither lie nor cheat in our dealings with them; and they despised us for our ignorance in trading and our want of smartness.

The utter want of that common courtesy with which a well-brought-up European addresses the poorest of his brethren, is severely felt at first by settlers in Canada. At the period of which I am now speaking, the titles of "sir," or "madam," were very rarely applied by inferiors....

Why they treated our claims to their respect with marked insult and rudeness, I never could satisfactorily determine, in any way that could reflect honour on the species, or even plead an excuse for its brutality, until I found that this insolence was more generally practised by the low, uneducated emigrants from Britain, who better understood your claims to their civility, than by the natives themselves. Then I discovered the secret.

The unnatural restraint which society imposes upon these people at home forces them to treat their more fortunate brethren with a servile deference which is repugnant to their feelings, and is thrust upon them by the dependent circumstances in which they are placed. This homage to rank and education is not sincere. Hatred and envy lie rankling at their heart, although hidden by outward obsequiousness. Necessity compels their obedience; they fawn, and cringe, and flatter the wealth on which they depend for bread. But let them once emigrate, the clog which fettered them is suddenly removed; they are free; and the dearest privilege of this freedom is to wreak upon their superiors the long-locked-up hatred of their hearts. They think they can debase you to their level by disallowing all your claims to distinction; while they hope to exalt themselves and their fellows into ladies and gentlemen by sinking you back to the only title you received from Nature—plain "man" and "woman.".... But from this folly the native-born Canadian is exempt; it is only practised by the low-born Yankee, or the Yankeefied British peasantry and mechanics. It originates in the enormous reaction springing out of sudden emancipation from a state of utter dependence into one of unrestrained liberty....

And here I would observe, before quitting this subject, that of all follies, that of taking out servants from the old country is one of the greatest, and is sure to end in the loss of the money expended in their passage, and to become the cause of deep disappointment and mortification to yourself.

They no sooner set foot upon the Canadian shores than they become possessed with this ultra-republican spirit. All respect for their employers, all subordination is at an end; the very air of Canada severs the tie of mutual obligation which bound you together. They fancy themselves not only equal to you in rank, but that ignorance and vulgarity give them superior claims to notice. They demand the highest wages, and grumble at doing half the work, in return, which they cheerfully performed at home. They demand to eat at your table, and to sit in your company, and if you refuse to listen to their dishonest and extravagant claims, they tell you that "they are free; that no contract signed in the old country is binding.'...

When we consider the different position in which servants are placed in the old and new world, this conduct, ungrateful as it then appeared to me, ought not to create the least surprise....

The serving class, comparatively speaking, is small, and admits of little competition. Servants that understand the work of the country are not easily procured, and such always can command the highest wages....

The Canadian women, while they retain the bloom and freshness of youth, are exceedingly pretty; but these charms soon fade, owing perhaps, to the fierce extremes of their climate....

The early age at which they marry and are introduced into society takes from them all awkwardness and restraint....

To the benevolent philanthropist, whose heart has bled over the misery and pauperism of the lower classes in Great Britain, the almost entire absence of mendicity from Canada would be highly gratifying. Canada has few, if any, native beggars; her objects of charity are generally imported from the mother country, and these are never suffered to want food or clothing. The Canadians are a truly charitable people; no person in distress is driven with harsh and cruel language from their doors; they not only generously relieve the wants of suffering strangers cast upon their bounty, but they nurse them in sickness, and use every means in their power to procure them employment. The number of orphan children yearly adopted by wealthy Canadians, and treated in every respect as their own, is almost incredible.

It is a glorious country for the labouring classes, for while blessed with health, they are always certain of employment, and certain also to derive from it ample means of support for their families....

It has often been remarked to me by people long resident in the colony, that those who come to the country destitute of means, but able and willing to work, invariably improve their condition and become independent; while the gentleman who brings out with him a small capital is too often tricked and cheated out of his property, and drawn into rash and dangerous speculation which terminate in his ruin. His children, neglected and uneducated, but brought up with ideas far beyond their means, and suffered to waste their time in idleness, seldom take to work, and not infrequently sink down to the lowest class....

The clouds of the preceding night, instead of dissolving in snow, brought on a rapid thaw. A thaw in the middle of winter is the most disagreeable change that can be imagined. After several weeks of clear, bright, bracing, frosty weather, with a serene atmosphere and cloudless sky, you awake one morning surprised at the change in the temperature; and, upon looking out of the window, behold the woods obscured by a murky haze—not so dense as an English November fog, but more black and lowering—and the heavens shrouded in a uniform covering of leaden-coloured clouds, deepening into a livid indigo at the edge of the horizon. The snow, no longer hard and glittering, has become soft and spongy, and the foot slips into a wet and insidiously-yielding mass at every step. From the roof pours down a continuous stream of water, and the branches of the trees, collecting the moisture of the reeking atmosphere, shower it upon the earth from every dripping twig. The cheerless and uncomfortable aspect of things without never fails to produce a corresponding effect upon the minds of those within, and casts such a damp upon the spirits that it appears to destroy for a time all sense of enjoyment. Many persons (and myself among the number) are made aware of the approach of a thunderstorm by an intense pain and weight about the head; and I have heard numbers of Canadians complain that a thaw always made them feel bilious and heavy, and greatly depressed their animal spirits.

I had a great desire to visit our new location, but when I looked out upon the cheerless waste, I gave up the idea, and contented myself with hoping for a better day on the morrow; but many morrows came and went before a frost again hardened the road sufficiently for me to make the attempt.

The prospect from the windows of my sister's log hut was not very prepossessing. The small lake in front, which formed such a pretty object in summer, now looked like an extensive field covered with snow, hemmed in from the rest of the world by a dark belt of sombre pine-woods. The clearing round the house was very small, and only just reclaimed from the wilderness, and the greater part of it was covered with piles of brush-wood, to be burnt the first dry days of spring.

The charred and blackened stumps on the few acres that had been cleared during the preceding year were everything but picturesque; and I concluded, as I turned, disgusted, from the prospect before me, that there was very little beauty to be found in the backwoods....

The first spring we spent in comparative ease and idleness. Our cows had been left upon our old place during the winter. The ground had to be cleared before it could receive a crop of any kind, and I had little to do but to wander by the lake shore, or among the woods, and amuse myself....

These fishing and shooting excursions were delightful. The pure beauty of the Canadian water, the sombre but august grandeur of the vast forest that hemmed us in on every side and shut us out from the rest of the world, soon cast a magic spell upon our spirits, and we began to feel charmed with the freedom and solitude around us. Every object was new to us. We felt as if we were the first discoverers of every beautiful flower and stately tree that attracted our attention, and we gave names to fantastic rocks and fairy isles, and raised imaginary houses and bridges on every picturesque spot which we floated past during our aquatic excursions. I learned the use of the paddle, and became quite a proficient in the gentle craft....

The summer of '35 was very wet; a circumstance so unusual in Canada that I have seen no season like it during my sojourn in the country. Our wheat crop promised to be both excellent and abundant; and the clearing and seeding sixteen acres, one way or another, had cost us more than fifty pounds; still we hoped to realize something handsome by the sale of the produce; and, as far as appearances went, all looked fair. The rain commenced about a week before the crop was fit for the sickle, and from that time until nearly the end of September was a mere succession of thunder showers; days of intense heat, succeeded by floods of rain. Our fine crop shared the fate of all other fine crops in the country; it was totally spoiled; the wheat grew in the sheaf, and we could scarcely save enough to supply us with bad sickly bread; the rest was exchanged at the distillery for whiskey, which was the only produce which could be obtained for it. The storekeepers would not look at it, or give either money or goods for such a damaged article.

My husband and I had worked hard in the field; it was the first time I had ever tried my hand at field-labour, but our ready money was exhausted, ... I had a hard struggle with my pride before I would consent to render the least assistance on the farm, but reflection convinced me that I was wrong—that Providence had placed me in a situation where I was called upon to work—that it was not only my duty to obey that call, but to exert myself to the utmost to assist my husband and help to maintain my family.

Ah, poverty! thou art a hard taskmaster, but in thy soul-ennobling school I have received more god-like lessons, have learned more sublime truths, than ever I acquired in the smooth highways of the world!...

We found that manual toil, however distasteful to those unaccustomed to it, was not after all such a dreadful hardship; that the wilderness was not without its rose, the hard face of poverty without its smile. If we occasionally suffered severe pain, we as often experienced great pleasure, and I have contemplated a well-hoed ridge of potatoes on that bush farm with as much delight as in years long past I had experienced in examining a fine painting in some well-appointed drawing-room.

I can now look back with calm thankfulness on that long period of trial and exertion—with thankfulness that the dark clouds that hung over us, threatening to blot us from existence, when they did burst upon us, were full of blessings. When our situation appeared perfectly desperate, then were we on the threshold of a new state of things, which was born out of that very distress.

In order more fully to illustrate the necessity of a perfect and childlike reliance upon the mercies of God—who, I most firmly believe, never deserts those who have placed their trust in Him—I will give a brief sketch of our lives during the years 1836 and 1837....

Our utter inability to meet these demands weighed very heavily upon my husband's mind. All superfluities in the way of groceries were now given up, and we were compelled to rest satisfied upon the produce of the farm. Milk, bread, and potatoes during the summer became our chief, and often, for months, our only fare. As to tea and sugar, they were luxuries we would not think of, although I missed the tea very much; we rang the changes upon peppermint and sage,

ne herb at our breakfast, the other at our tea, until I found an excel-
te for both in the root of the dandelion....

y has truly been termed the mother of invention, for I contrived to
manufacture a variety of dishes almost out of nothing, while living in her school.
When entirely destitute of animal food, the different varieties of squirrels supplied
us with pies, stews, and roasts. Our barn stood at the top of the hill near the bush,
and in a trap set for such "small deer," we often caught from ten to twelve a day.

The flesh of the black squirrel is equal to that of the rabbit, and the red, and
even the little chipmunk, is palatable when nicely cooked. But from the lake,
during the summer, we derived the larger portion of our food.... Moodie and I
used to rise by daybreak, and fish for an hour after sunrise, when we returned, he
to the field, and I to dress the little ones, clean up the house, assist with the milk,
and prepare the breakfast.

Oh, how I enjoyed these excursions on the lake; the very idea of our dinner
depending upon our success added double zest to our sport!

One morning we started as usual before sunrise; a thick mist still hung like
a fine veil upon the water when we pushed off, and anchored at our accustomed
place. Just as the sun rose, and the haze parted and drew up like a golden sheet
of transparent gauze, through which the dark woods loomed out like giants, a
noble buck dashed into the water....

That winter of '36, how heavily it wore away! The grown flour, frosted potatoes, and scant quantity of animal food rendered us all weak, and the children
suffered much from the ague....

On the 21st of May of this year, my second son, Donald, was born. The poor
fellow came in hard times.... I was rendered so weak by want of proper nourish-
ment that my dear husband, for my sake, overcame his aversion to borrowing,
and procured a quarter of mutton from a friend. This, with kindly presents from
neighbours—often as badly off as ourselves—a loin of a young bear, and a basket
containing a loaf of bread, some tea, some fresh butter, and oatmeal, went far to
save my life.

Shortly after my recovery, Jacob—the faithful, good Jacob—was obliged to
leave us, for we could no longer afford to pay wages. What was owing to him
had to be settled by sacrificing our best cow, and a great many valuable articles of
clothing from my husband's wardrobe. Nothing is more distressing than being
obliged to part with articles of dress which you know that you cannot replace.
Almost all my clothes had been appropriated to the payment of wages, or to
obtain garments for the children, excepting my wedding dress, and the beautiful
baby-linen which had been made by the hands of dear and affectionate friends

for my first-born. These were now exchanged for coarse, warm flannels, to shield him from the cold.

Reader! it is not my intention to trouble you with the sequel of our history. I have given you a faithful picture of a life in the backwoods of Canada, and I leave you to draw from it your own conclusions, To the poor, industrious working man it presents many advantages; to the poor gentleman, none! The former works hard, puts up with coarse, scanty fare, and submits, with a good grace, to hardships that would kill a domesticated animal at home. Thus he becomes independent, inasmuch as the land that he has cleared finds him in the common necessaries of life; but it seldom, if ever, in remote situations, accomplishes more than this. The gentleman can neither work so hard, live so coarsely, nor endure so many privations as his poorer but more fortunate neighbour. Unaccustomed to manual labour, his services in the field are not of a nature to secure for him a profitable return. The task is new to him, he knows not how to perform it well; and, conscious of his deficiency, he expends his little means in hiring labour, which his bush-farm can never repay. Difficulties increase, debts grow upon him, he struggles in vain to extricate himself, and finally sees his family sink into hopeless ruin.

If these sketches should prove the means of deterring one family from sinking their property, and shipwrecking all their hopes, by going to reside in the backwoods of Canada, I shall consider myself amply repaid for revealing the secrets of the prison-house, and feel that I have not toiled and suffered in the wilderness in vain.

### 2. Catharine Parr Traill, *The Backwoods of Canada*, 1836

*Moodie's sister Catharine (1802–99) could have been writing about a different place, which makes comparisons with her sister so intriguing yet problematical. She arrived in Upper Canada in the same year as Susanna and established a bush farm close by. She came from the same upper-middle-class background and had similar financial worries. She too was a writer, with several published children's books to her credit. Her husband, Thomas, also had little practical farming experience. Repeated crop failures brought them, like the Moodies, to the precipice of bankruptcy. Through it all, however, Catharine maintained a sense of wonder at her new world and remained enthusiastic about life in the backwoods, especially the natural beauty of the countryside. It was not easy. Her husband hated the isolation of the backwoods and suffered from acute clinical depression. This left her to sustain the family, which she did with aplomb, living and writing into her nineties and bearing nine children. Though she never made much money from her writing, her many articles established her as a distinguished naturalist. The following account, published in 1836, comes from a series of 18 letters describing her experiences in the backwoods of Upper Canada.*

*November the 20th, 1832*

... We begin to get reconciled to our Robinson Crusoe sort of life, and the consideration that the present evils are but temporary goes a great way towards reconciling us to them.

One of our greatest inconveniences arises from the badness of our roads, and the distance at which we are placed from any village or town where provisions are to be procured.

Till we raise our own grain and fatten our own hogs, sheep, and poultry, we must be dependent upon the stores for food of every kind. These supplies have to be brought up at considerable expense and loss of time, through our beautiful bush-roads; which, to use the words of a poor Irish woman, "can't be no worser."...

This is now the worst season of the year—this, and just after the breaking up of the snow. Nothing hardly but an ox-cart can travel along the roads, and even that with difficulty, occupying two days to perform the journey to and fro, and the worst of the matter is, that there are times when the most necessary articles of provisions are not to be procured at any price. You see, then, that a settler in the bush requires to hold himself pretty independent, not only of the luxuries and delicacies of the table, but not unfrequently even of the very necessaries.

One time no pork is to be procured; another time there is a scarcity of flour, owing to some accident that has happened to the mill, or for the want of proper supplies of wheat for grinding; or perhaps the weather and bad roads at the same time prevent a team coming up, or people from going down. Then you must have recourse to a neighbour, if you have the good fortune to be near one, or fare the best you can on potatoes. The potato is indeed a great blessing here; new settlers would otherwise be often greatly distressed, and the poor man and his family who are without resources, without the potato must starve....

*November the 2nd, 1833*

...We had a glorious burning this summer after the ground was all logged up; that is, all the large timbers chopped into lengths, and drawn together in heaps with oxen. To effect this the more readily we called a logging-bee. We had a number of settlers attend, with yokes of oxen and men to assist us. After that was over, my husband, with the menservants, set the heaps on fire; and a magnificent sight it was to see such a conflagration all around us. I was a little nervous at first on account of the nearness of some of the log-heaps to the house, but care is always taken to fire them with the wind blowing in a direction away from the building. Accidents have sometimes happened, but they are of rarer occurrence than might be expected when we consider the subtlety and destructiveness of the elements employed on the occasion...

Our crops this year are oats, corn, and pumpkins, and potatoes, with some turnips. We shall have wheat, rye, oats, potatoes and corn next harvest, which will enable us to increase our stock. At present we have only a yoke of oxen, two cows, two calves, three small pigs, ten hens, and three ducks, and a pretty brown pony....

On first coming to this country nothing surprised me more than the total absence of trees about the dwelling-houses and cleared lands; the axe of the chopper relentlessly levels all before him. Man appears to contend with the trees of the forest as though they were his most obnoxious enemies; for he spares neither the young sapling in its greenness nor the ancient trunk in its lofty pride; he wages war against the forest with fire and steel...

*Lake Cottage, March 14, 1834*

...You say you fear the rigours of the Canadian winter will kill me. I never enjoyed better health, nor so good, as since it commenced. There is a degree of spirit and vigour infused into one's blood by the purity of the air that is quite exhilarating. The very snow seems whiter and more beautiful than it does in your damp, vapoury climate. During a keen bright winter's day you will often perceive the air filled with minute frozen particles, which are quite dry, and slightly prick your face like needle-points, while the sky is blue and bright above you. There is a decided difference between the first snow-falls and those of midwinter; the first are in large soft flakes, and seldom remain long without thawing, but those that fall after the cold has regularly set in are smaller, drier, and of the most beautiful forms, sometimes pointed like a cluster of rays, or else feathered in the most exquisite manner....

*September 20, 1834*

...Canada is the land of hope; here everything is new; everything going forward; it is scarcely possible for arts, sciences, agriculture, manufactures, to retrograde; they must keep advancing; though in some situations the progress may seem slow, in others they are proportionately rapid.

There is a constant excitement on the minds of emigrants, particularly in the partially settled townships, that greatly assists in keeping them from desponding. The arrival of some enterprising person gives a stimulus to those about him: profitable speculation is started, and lo, the value of the land in the vicinity rises to double and treble what it was thought worth before; so that, without any design of befriending his neighbours, the schemes of one settler being carried into effect shall benefit a great number. We have already felt the beneficial effect of the access of respectable emigrants locating themselves in this township, as it has already increased the value of our own land in a three-fold degree....

Our society is mostly military or naval; so that we meet on equal grounds, and are, of course, well acquainted with the rules of good breeding and polite life; too much so to allow any deviation from those laws that good taste, good sense, and good feeling have established among persons of our class.

Yet here it is considered by no means derogatory to the wife of an officer or gentleman to assist in the work of the house, or to perform its entire duties, if occasion requires it; to understand the mystery of soap, candle, and sugar-making; to make bread, butter, and cheese, or even to milk her own cows, to knit and spin, and prepare the wool for the loom. In these matters we bush-ladies have a wholesome disregard of what Mr and Mrs So-and-so think or say. We pride ourselves on conforming to circumstances; and as a British officer must needs be a gentleman and his wife a lady, perhaps we repose quietly on that incontestable proof of our gentility, and can afford to be useful without injuring it.

Our husbands adopt a similar line of conduct: the officer turns his sword into a ploughshare, and his lance into a sickle; and if he be seen ploughing among the stumps in his own field, or chopping trees on his own land, no one thinks less of his dignity, or considers him less of a gentleman, than when he appeared upon parade in all the pride of military etiquette, with sash, sword, and epaulette. Surely this is as it should be in a country where independence is inseparable from industry; and for this I prize it.

Among many advantages we in this township possess, it is certainly no inconsiderable one that the lower or working-class of settlers are well disposed, and quite free from the annoying Yankee manners that distinguish many of the earlier-settled townships. Our servants are as respectful, or nearly so, as those at home; nor are they admitted to our tables, or placed on an equality with us, excepting at "bees," and such kinds of public meetings; when they usually conduct themselves with a propriety that would afford an example to some that call themselves gentlemen, viz., young men who voluntarily throw aside those restraints that society expects from persons filling a respectable situation.

Intemperance is too prevailing a vice among all ranks of people in this country; but I blush to say it belongs most decidedly to those that consider themselves among the better class of emigrants. Let none such complain of the airs of equality displayed towards them by the labouring class, seeing that they degrade themselves below the honest, sober settler, however poor. If the sons of gentle-men lower themselves, no wonder if the sons of poor men endeavour to exalt themselves above him in a country where they all meet on equal ground and good conduct is the distinguishing mark between the classes....

*November the 28th, 1834*

You will have been surprised, and possibly distressed, by my long silence of several months, but when I tell you it has been occasioned by sickness, you will cease to wonder that I did not write.

My dear husband, my servant, the poor babe, and myself, were all at one time confined to our beds with ague. You know how severe my sufferings always were at home with intermittents, and need not marvel if they were no less great in a country where lake-fevers and all kinds of intermittent fevers abound...

I will not dwell on this uncomfortable period further than to tell you that we considered the complaint to have had its origin in a malaria, arising from a cellar below the kitchen. When the snow melted, this cellar became half full of water, either from the moisture draining through the spongy earth, or from the rising of a spring beneath the house; be it as it may, the heat of the cooking and Franklin stoves in the kitchen and parlour caused a fermentation to take place in the stagnant fluid before it could be emptied; the effluvia arising from this mass of putrefying water affected us all. The female servant, who was the most exposed to its baneful influence, was the first of our household that fell sick, after which we each in turn became unable to assist each other....

I lost the ague in a fortnight's time—thanks to calomel and quinine; so did my babe and his nurse: it has, however, hung on my husband during the whole of the summer, and thrown a damp upon his exertions and gloom upon his spirits. This is the certain effect of ague, it causes the same sort of depression on the spirits as a nervous fever. My dear child has not been well ever since he had the ague, and looks very pale and spiritless....

In spite of its length and extreme severity, I do like the Canadian winter: it is decidedly the healthiest season of the year; and it is no small enjoyment to be exempted from the torments of the insect tribes, that are certainly great draw-backs to your comfort in the warmer months....

Not to regret my absence from my native land, and one so fair and lovely withal, would argue a heart of insensibility: yet I must say, for all its roughness, I love Canada, and am as happy in my humble log-house as if it were courtly hall or bower; habit reconciles us to many things that at first were distasteful. It has ever been my way to extract the sweet rather than the bitter in the cup of life, and surely it is best and wisest so to do. In a country where constant exertion is called for from all ages and degrees of settlers, it would be foolish to a degree to damp our energies by complaints, and cast a gloom over our homes by sitting dejectedly down to lament for all that was so dear to us in the old country. Since we are here, let us make the best of it, and bear with cheerfulness the lot we have chosen. I believe that one of the chief ingredients in human happiness is a capacity for enjoying the blessings we possess.

Though at our first outset we experienced many disappointments, many unlooked-for expenses, and many annoying delays, with some wants that to us seemed great privations, on the whole we have been fortunate, especially in the situation of our land, which has increased in value very considerably; our chief difficulties are now over, at least we hope so, and we trust soon to enjoy the comforts of a cleared farm.

My husband is becoming more reconciled to the country, and I daily feel my attachment to it strengthening. The very stumps that appeared so odious, through long custom seem to lose some of their hideousness; the eye becomes familiarized even with objects the most displeasing till they cease to be observed. Some century hence how different will this spot appear! I can picture it to my imagination with fertile fields and groves of trees planted by the hand of taste. All will be different; our present rude dwellings will have given place to others of a more elegant style of architecture, and comfort and grace will rule the scene which is now a forest wild....

### FURTHER READINGS

Atwood, M. "Introduction." In S. Moodie, *Roughing It in the Bush*. London: Virago, 1986.

Ballstadt, C. *Catharine Parr Traill and Her Works*. Downsview: ECW Press, 1983.

Ballstadt, C. "Secure in Conscious Worth: Susanna Moodie and the Rebellion of 1837." *Canadian Poetry* 18 (1986): 88-98.

Ballstadt, C., E. Hopkins, and M. Peterman. "'A Glorious Madness': Susanna Moodie and the Spiritualist Movement." *Journal of Canadian Studies* 17, 4 (Winter 1982-83): 88-100.

Ballstadt, C., E. Hopkins, and M. Peterman, Eds. *I Bless You in My Heart: Selected Correspondence of Catharine Parr Traill*. Toronto: University of Toronto Press, 1995.

Ballstadt, C., E. Hopkins, and M. Peterman, Eds. *Letters of Love and Duty: The Correspondence of Susanna and John Moodie.* Toronto: University of Toronto Press, 1993.

Ballstadt, C., E. Hopkins, and M. Peterman, Eds. *Susanna Moodie: Letters of a Lifetime.* Toronto: University of Toronto Press, 1985.

Bentley, D. "Breaking the 'Cake of Custom': The Atlantic Crossing as a Rubicon for Female Emigrants to Canada?" In *Re(Dis)covering Our Foremothers: Nineteenth-Century Canadian Women Writers*, ed. L. McMullin. Ottawa: University of Ottawa Press, 1990.

Buss, H. *Mapping Ourselves: Canadian Women's Autobiography.* Montreal and Kingston: McGill-Queen's University Press, 1993.

Dean, M. *Practising Femininity: Domestic Realism and Performance of Gender in Early Canadian Fiction.* Toronto: University of Toronto Press, 1998.

Eaton, S. *Lady of the Backwoods: A Biography of Catharine Parr Traill.* Toronto: McClelland and Stewart, 1969.

Errington, J. *Wives and Mothers, Schoolmistresses and Scullery Maids: Working Women in Upper Canada, 1790-1840.* Montreal and Kingston: McGill-Queen's University Press, 1995.

Errington, J. "A Woman is a Very Interesting Creature: Some Women's Experiences in Upper Canada." *Historic Kingston* 38 (1990): 16-35.

Fowler, M. *The Embroidered Tent: Five Gentlewomen in Early Canada.* Toronto: Anansi, 1982.

Freiwald, Bina. "The Tongue of Woman: The Language of the Self in Moodie's *Roughing It in the Bush*." In *Re(dis)covering Our Foremothers: Nineteenth-Century Canadian Women Writers*, ed. L. McMullen. Ottawa: University of Ottawa Press, 1990.

Gairdner, W. "Traill and Moodie: The Two Realities." *Journal of Canadian Fiction* 2 (1973): 75-81.

Gerson, C. "Nobler Savages: Representations of Native Women in the Writings of Susanna Moodie and Catharine Parr Traill." *Journal of Canadian Studies* 32, 2 (Summer 1997): 5-21.

Gray, C. *Sisters in the Wilderness: The Lives of Susanna Moodie and Catharine Parr Traill.* Toronto: Viking, 1999.

Hopkins, E. "A Prison-House for Prosperity: The Immigrant Experience of the Nineteenth-Century Upper Class British Woman." In *Looking into My Sisters Eyes: An Exploration in Women's History*, ed. J. Burnet. Toronto: Multicultural History Society of Ontario, 1986.

Light, B., and A. Prentice, Eds. *Pioneers and Gentlewomen of British North America.* Toronto: New Hogtown Press, 1980.

Mathews, R. "Susanna Moodie, Pink Toryism, and the Nineteenth Century Ideas of Canadian Identity." *Journal of Canadian Studies* 10, 3 (August 1975): 3-15.

McKenna, K. "Options for Elite Women in Early Upper Canada Society: The Case of the Powell Family." In *Historical Essays on Upper Canada: New Perspectives*, ed. J. Johnson and B. Wilson. Ottawa: Carleton University Press, 1989.

Morgan, C. *Public Men and Virtuous Women: The Gendered Languages of Religion and Politics in Upper Canada, 1791-1850.* Toronto: University of Toronto Press, 1996.

Peterman, M. *This Great Epoch in Our Lives: Susanna Moodie's Roughing It in the Bush.* Toronto: ECW Press, 1996.

Potter-MacKinnon, J. *While the Women Only Wept: Loyalist Refugee Women in Eastern Ontario.* Montreal and Kingston: McGill-Queen's University Press, 1993.

Raglon, R. "Little Miss Goody Two Shoes: Reassessing the Work of Catherine Parr Traill." In *This Elusive Land*, ed. M. Hessing, R. Raglon, and C. Sandilands. Vancouver: University of British Columbia Press, 2004.

Shields, C. *Susanna Moodie: Voice and Vision.* Ottawa: Borealis, 1977.

Thurston, J. *The Work of Words: The Writing of Susanna Strickland Moodie.* Montreal and Kingston: McGill-Queen's University Press, 1996.

# CHAPTER II

# "The Long and Heavy Chain of Abuse"

## POLITICAL CRISIS IN LOWER CANADA

### INTRODUCTION

C anadians often exhibit a smug self-righteousness about living in a country without the political and social turmoil endemic to the United States. That conceit may, however, be misplaced. 1837, after all, saw both Upper and Lower Canada erupt into violence as bands of American-style republican rebels sought to overthrow their British colonial governments. Though support was far from unanimous and their attempts ultimately failed, there was widespread dissatisfaction with colonial rule. The crux of the issue was over the right to legislate. In Britain considerable power remained with the elected members of the House of Commons. British colonies, however, retained a system where popularly elected representatives sitting in their legislative assemblies were virtually powerless. Instead, appointed governors and their equally appointed councillors implemented policies set by the British Colonial Office in London, often dismissing the demands of local citizens. Increasingly frustrated local democrats took their inspiration from the United States, arguing that people in positions of legislative power should be responsible to the local electorate through election and should not be aristocratic appointees serving at the monarch's pleasure. Nor were the Canadas alone in this rebelliousness. Movements dedicated to political reform arose in the Maritimes as well, but no other British North American colony exploded like Lower Canada.

Lower Canada sank into recession in the mid-1830s, and an already impoverished Habitant population feared for its future as impecunious seigneurs squeezed them for ever higher rents. Fiercely autonomous rural French-Canadian communities also felt threatened by English and urban meddling in their affairs. Greater local democracy, they believed, would prevent their subjugation by such "foreign" vested interests. Many French-Canadian urbanites, especially the politically astute professional classes, saw themselves becoming assimilated and controlled by an Anglo-dominated colonial socio-political elite, derisively named the *Chateau Clique*. Increasingly the *Parti Canadien* became convinced that only full democratic citizenship rights through a system of responsible government, or independence, could check this growing British economic and cultural hegemony.

Demographic trends also caused concern for many French Canadians on at least two fronts. Francophone population numbers soared as a result of a birthrate of epic proportions, but their percentage, as a total, dropped with the annual arrival of thousands of British immigrants. Second, there was a steady flow of young French Canadians from the countryside, the bastion of French-Canadian culture, to cities like Montreal. From there trickled a further exodus to the United States to the point where some towns in Vermont had larger French-Canadian populations than American. This overpowering combination of push-and-pull was a worrisome spectre. Employment opportunities on the increasingly overcrowded seigneuries evaporated, leaving the more ambitious of the next generation without choice but to move. Though hardly Britain's fault, this emigration exacerbated French-Canadian concerns over the perceived threats to their cultural survival. Without decisive action, said the nationalists, French-Canadian culture would disappear to emigration or drown in a sea of Anglo-domination.

The Catholic Church, that protective bastion of French-Canadian life, found itself on the horns of a dilemma as tensions mounted in the colony. Like the political reformers, it sought to preserve French-Canadian culture, but it was also a staunchly conservative and anti-democratic institution with no tolerance for republicanism. It prevaricated but in the end sided with the British government, and by threatening to excommunicate all rebels, it thus forced French Canadians to choose between their church and their independence.

The *Patriotes* could not defeat a deeply entrenched British political structure that believed colonies primarily existed to serve the mother country, not local interests. After years of petitions, resolutions, and attempts at persuasion, the crisis came to a head in October 1837. Flushed with political passion, *Patriotes* prepared for battle. Their leader Louis-Joseph Papineau, however, fled to the United States just as the fighting began. British authorities quickly crushed the rebellion, arrested thousands of participants, and put much of the pro-*Patriote* countryside of Lower Canada to the torch. There would be no second American War of Independence in British North America. The rebellion made it clear, though, that serious problems existed with colonial administration. It became Lord Durham's task to discover what exactly was wrong and to recommend a permanent solution. Meanwhile, refugee rebels set about reinvigorating the rebellion from their sanctuary in the United States. Their efforts lasted for another year, then died.

### DISCUSSION POINTS

1. Did Lower Canada's situation justify rebellion?

2. It was mostly articulate *Canadiens*—newspaper editors, doctors, lawyers, and other professional men knocking at the doors of power—who expressed discontent. Did they express the grievances of the society at large, including those of women and men from other occupations such as farmers, artisans, lumberjacks, and fishermen?

3. Compare the Six Counties Address with Nelson's Declaration. How did these two key documents differ with respect to French-Canadian culture?

4. If Durham was right and the rebellion was indeed a war between races, how does that explain the presence of rebel leaders such as Wolfred and Robert Nelson?

5. The 1830s was a time of political upheaval in much of Europe. Canadians also looked over their shoulders to conditions in the United States. Were British North American reform ideas locally or internationally based?

DOCUMENTS

## 1. "The Six Counties Address," Montreal, *The Vindicator*, October 31, 1837

*Often called "Canada's Declaration of Independence," the Six Counties Address won mass support at a meeting in St. Charles, a farming community outside Montreal, on October 24, 1837 and was Lower Canada's equivalent to the American Declaration of Independence. Afterwards the* Patriotes *of Lower Canada prepared for open resistance; although their leader, Louis Joseph Papineau, expressed serious misgivings about resorting to force, others at the meeting had no such qualms. The document itself was a collaborative effort, but the primary writer was Dr. Wolfred Nelson (1791–1861), one of the few Anglophone* Patriotes*. Nelson came from Loyalist and London stock. His background hardly matched his position as one of the most outspoken advocates of French-Canadian civil rights. After service as a surgeon in the British army in the War of 1812, he established a private medical practice and in 1827 entered politics. He became more incensed about the abuses of the local government, especially after one of his friends died in an altercation with British troops. Following the Six Counties Address, Nelson joined other* Patriotes *in resisting arrest and procuring arms. Undeterred by the arrival of British regular troops, this country doctor led a successful initial defence at St. Denis, which made him a hero among French Canadians. As the rebellion disintegrated, Nelson was captured and tried for treason. After pleading guilty, he spent seven months in prison and then was banished to Bermuda. He returned to Montreal in 1842 and once again served as a Member of the Legislative Assembly, continuing in the struggle for French-Canadian rights. In 1854 he became the first popularly elected mayor of Montreal.*

*Amury Girod, on the other hand, did not survive the rebellion but at its conclusion committed suicide. Arriving in Lower Canada in 1831, he was apparently born in Switzerland and had supposedly served in Simon Bolivar's army of independence in South America as well as in the Mexican cavalry. In Lower Canada he attempted both farming and writing on agricultural projects but ending up as a more successful intellectual than farmer. Involved with political reform throughout the Montreal region, he helped found the* Fils de la Liberté*. In the confused events that followed the outbreak of fighting, he took charge of some* Patriote *farmers but had difficulty asserting his authority. Critics claimed that he lost his nerve and disappeared during the Battle of St. Eustache, while Girod maintained that he had left to locate reinforcements. In any event, fearing capture, he shot himself on December 18, 1837.*

*Another signatory of the Address for whom information is available, Jean-Philippe Boucher-Belleville (1800–74), was a teacher, newspaper owner, and editor who survived the uprising to become a civil servant and linguist. Before the rebellion he had written extensively on farming and education within the colony. Surprisingly, he placed the blame for the agricultural slump of 1836-37 on the unenterprising methods of the French Canadians. Captured in the early phases of the rebellion and released penniless in 1838, Boucher-Belleville emerged as a leading Montreal editor who promoted reconciliation between British and French Canadians.*

Fellow Citizens:

When a systematic course of oppression has been invariably harassing a People, in despite of their wishes expressed in every manner recognized by constitutional usage; by popular assemblies, and by their Representatives, in Parliament, after grave deliberation; when their rulers, instead of redressing the various evils produced by their own misgovernment, have solemnly proclaimed their guilty determination to sap and subvert the very foundations of civil liberty, it becomes the imperative duty of the People to betake themselves to the serious consideration of their unfortunate position—of the dangers by which they are surrounded—and by well-concerted organization, to make such arrangements as may be necessary to protect, unimpaired, their rights as Citizens and their dignity as Freemen.

The wise and immortal framers of the AMERICAN DECLARATION OF INDEPENDENCE, embodied in that document the principles on which alone are based the RIGHTS OF MAN and successfully vindicated and established the only institutions and form of government which can permanently secure the prosperity and social happiness of the inhabitants of this Continent, whose education and habits, derived from the circumstances of their colonization, demand a system of government entirely dependent upon, and directly responsible to, the People.

In common with the various nations of North and South America who have adopted the principles contained in that Declaration, we hold the same holy and self-evident doctrines: that GOD created no artificial distinctions between man and man; that government is but a mere human institution formed by those who are to be subject to its good or evil action, intended for the benefit of all who may consent to come, or remain under, its protection and control; and therefore, that its form may be changed whenever it ceases to accomplish the ends for which such government was established; that public authorities and men in office are but the executors of the lawfully-expressed will of the community, honoured because they possess public confidence, respected only so long as they command public esteem, and to be removed from office the moment they cease to give satisfaction to the People, the sole legitimate source of all power.

In conformity with these principles, and on the faith of treaties and capitulations entered into with our ancestors, and guaranteed by the Imperial Parliament, the People of this Province have for a long series of years complained by respectful petitions, of the intolerable abuses which poison their existence and paralyse their industry. Far from conceding our humble prayers, aggression has followed aggression, until at length we seem no longer to belong to the British Empire for our own happiness or prosperity, our freedom or the honour of the British Crown or people, but solely for the purpose of fattening a horde of useless officials, who not content with enjoying salaries enormously disproportioned to the duties of their offices, and to the resources of the country, have combined as a faction, united by private interest alone, to oppose all reforms in the Province, and to uphold the iniquities of a Government inimical to the rights and liberties of this colony.

Notwithstanding the universally admitted justice of our demands, and the wisdom and prudence of remedying our complaints, we still endure the misery of an irresponsible Executive, directed by an ignorant and hypocritical Chief; our Judges, dependent for the tenure of their office on the mere will and pleasure of the Crown, for the most part the violent partisans of a corrupt administration, have become more completely the tools and mercenaries of the Executive, by accepting the wages of their servility, in gross violation of every principle of Judicial independence, from foreign authority, without the intervention of the people to whom, through their Representatives, belongs the sole right of voting the salaries of their public servants; the office-holders of the Province devour our revenues, in salaries so extravagant as to deprive us of the funds requisite for the general improvement of the Country, whereby our public works are arrested, and the navigation of our rivers obstructed; a Legislative Council appointed by men resident three thousand miles from this country, and systematically composed so as to thwart and oppose the efforts of our freely-chosen Representatives in all measures for the promotion of the public good, after continuing unchanged during the present administration, thereby depriving the country of the advantages of domestic legislation, has at length been modified in a manner insulting to all classes of society, disgraceful to public morality, and to the annihilation of the respect and confidence of all parties in that branch of the Legislature, by the introduction of men for the most part notorious only for their incapacity, and remarkable alone for their political insignificance, thus making evident, even to demonstration, to all, whatever may be their preconceived ideas, the propriety and urgent necessity of introducing the principle of election into that body, as the only method of enabling the Provincial Legislature to proceed beneficially to the despatch of public business.

Our municipalities are utterly destroyed; the country parts of the Province, as a disgraceful exception to the other parts of this Continent, are totally deprived of all power of regulating, in a corporate capacity, their local affairs, through freely elected Parish and Township Officers; the rising generation is deprived of the blessings of education, the primary schools, which provided for the instruction of 40,000 children, having been shut up by the Legislative Council, a body hostile to the progress of useful knowledge, and instigated to this act by an Executive inimical to the spread of general information among the people—the Jesuits' College founded and endowed by the provident government which colonized this Province for the encouragement and dissemination of learning and the sciences therein, has, with a barbarism unworthy the rulers of a civilized state, disgraceful to the enlightened age in which we live ..., been converted into, and is still retained, as a barrack for soldiery, whilst the funds and property devoted to the support of this and similar institutions have been, and continue to be, squandered and maladministered for the advantage of the favourites, creatures and tools of the Government; our citizens are deprived of the benefits of impartially chosen juries, and are arbitrarily persecuted by Crown officers, who to suit the purposes of the vindictive Government of which they are the creatures, have revived proceedings of an obsolete character, precedents for which are to be found only in the darkest pages of British history. Thus our Judiciary being sullied by combined conspiracies of a wicked Executive, slavish Judges, partisan Law Officers, and political Sheriffs, the innocent and patriotic are exposed to be sacrificed, whilst the enemies of the country, and the violators of all law, are protected and patronized, according as it may please the administration to crush and destroy; to save and protect. Our commerce and domestic industry are paralysed; our public lands alienated, at a nominal price, to a company of speculators, strangers to the country, or bestowed upon insolent favorites, as a reward for their sycophancy; our money is extorted from us without our consent, by taxes unconstitutionally imposed by a foreign Parliament, to be afterwards converted into an instrument of our degradation by being distributed among a howling herd of officials, against our will, without our participation, and in violation of all principles of constitutional law ... and as an index of further intended aggression, armed troops are being scattered in time of profound peace throughout the country, with the presumptuous and wicked design of restraining by physical force the expression of public opinion, and of completing by violence and bloodshed our slavery and ruin, already determined upon beyond the seas....

The long and heavy chain of abuses and oppressions under which we suffer, and to which every year has only added a more galling link, proves that our history is but a recapitulation of what other Colonies have endured before us. Our grievances are but a second edition of their grievances. Our petitions for relief are the same. Like theirs, they have been treated with scorn and contempt, and have brought down upon the petitioners but additional outrage and persecution. Thus the experience of the past demonstrates the folly of expecting justice from European authorities.

Dark, however, and unpromising as may be the present prospects of this our beloved country, we are encouraged by the public virtues of our fellow citizens to hope that the day of our regeneration is not far distant. Domestic manufactures are springing up amongst us, with a rapidity to cheer us in the contest. The impulse given but a few short months ago by the example of generous and patriotic minds, of wearing domestic cloths, has been generally followed, and will shortly be universally adopted. The determination not to consume duty-paying merchandise, and to encourage Free Trade with our neighbours, matters of vital importance, is daily becoming more general, resolute and effective. The people are everywhere being duly impressed with the conviction that the sacrifices to be made must bear some proportion to the glorious object to be achieved, and that personal inconvenience for the good cause must therefore be not only freely, but readily, endured.

Fellow-countrymen! Brothers in afflication! Ye, whatsoever be your origin, language or religion, to whom Equal Laws and the Rights of Man are dear; whose hearts have throbbed with indignation whilst witnessing the innumerable insults to which your common country has been exposed, and who have often been justly alarmed whilst pondering over the sombre futurity by misgovernment and corruption for this Province and for your posterity; in the name of that country, and of the rising generation, now having no hope but in you, we call upon you to assume, by systematic organization in your several Townships and Parishes, that position which can alone procure respect for yourselves and your demands. Let Committees of Vigilance be at once put in active operation throughout your respective neighbourhoods. Withdrawing all confidence from the present administration, and from such as will be so base as to accept office under it, forthwith assemble in your Parishes and elect Pacificator Magistrates, after the example of your brother Reformers of the County of Two Mountains, in order to protect the people at once from useless and improvident expense, and from the vengeance of their enemies. Our Young Men, the hope of the country, should everywhere organize themselves, after the plan of their brothers, 'The Sons of Liberty' in Montreal, in order that they may be prepared to act with promptitude and effect as circumstances may require; and the brave Militiamen, who by their blood and valour have twice preserved this country for ungrateful rulers, should at once associate together, under officers of their own choice, for the security of good order and the protection of life and property in their respective localities. Thus prepared, Colonial Liberty may haply be yet preserved.

In this hope, and depending, for a disenthralment from the misrule under which we now groan, on the Providence of GOD, whose blessing on our disinterested labours we humbly implore; relying on the love of liberty which the free air and impregnable fastnesses of AMERICA should inspire in the hearts of the People at large, and upon the sympathy of our Democratic neighbours who in the establishment of arbitrary rule on their borders, wisely and clearly [will foresee] the uprearing of a system which might be made a precedent and instrument for the introduction of the same arbitrary rule into other parts of the American Continent, and who can never consent that the principles for which they successfully struggled in the Eighteenth, shall, in our persons, be trampled in the dust in the Nineteenth century, WE, the DELEGATES of the Confederated Counties of Richelieu, St Hyacinthe, Rouville, L'Acadie, Chambly and Vercheres, hereby publicly register the solemn and determined resolution of the People whom we represent, to carry into effect, with the least delay possible, the preceding recommendations, and never to cease their patriotic exertions until the various grievances of which they now complain shall have been redressed; and We hereby invite our fellow-citizens throughout the Province to unite their efforts to ours to procure a good, cheap and responsible system of government for their common country.

Signed for, and on behalf of, the Confederation of the Six Counties, this 24th day of October, 1837.

### 2. Robert Nelson, "Declaration of Independence," February 22, 1838

*Surgeon Robert Nelson (1794-1873) was a republican reformer and Wolfred's brother. Elected to Lower Canada's Assembly in 1827, he quit in 1830, then returned in 1834. Though not a participant in the initial 1837 rebellions, he was arrested on suspicion, released, and then fled to Vermont. Named general of the rebel "army," and President of the future Canadian republic, he tried to rekindle the rebellion, but the "invasion" of Canada in February 1838 was a fiasco and led to his arrest for violating American neutrality laws. Acquitted, he organized the Hunters Lodges as conduits for another insurrectionist attempt. According to legend, his own men caught him deserting the disastrous invasion of November 1838. He escaped to California where he made and lost a fortune during the gold rush. Upon returning to Canada, he was eventually pardoned for his role in the rebellion.*

DECLARATION ... in view of the fact that we no longer wish to suffer the repeated infringements of our most cherished rights or to patiently endure the numerous and recent insults and acts of cruelty perpetrated by the government of Lower Canada, we, in the name of the people of Lower Canada, worshipping the decree of divine providence that entitles us to overthrow a government that has ignored the purpose and intent of its creation, and to choose the most suitable form of government to establish justice ... and guarantee to us and our descendants the benefits of civil and religious Freedom,

SOLEMNLY DECLARE:

1. That as of today, the People of Lower Canada are ABSOLVED from any allegiance to Great Britain, and that any political link between that power and Lower Canada CEASES from this day forward.

2. That Lower Canada must take the form of a REPUBLICAN government and now declare itself, de facto, a REPUBLIC.

3. That under the free Government of Lower Canada, all citizens will have the same rights; the natives will cease to be subject to any civil disqualification whatsoever, and will enjoy the same rights as those of other citizens of the State of Lower Canada.

4. That the union of Church and State is declared abolished in its entirety, and each person has the right to practise freely the religion and faith dictated by his conscience.

5. That Feudal or Seigneurial Tenure is, de facto, abolished, as if it had never existed in this country.

6. That all persons bearing or who will bear arms, or will provide assistance to the Canadien People in their fight for emancipation are released from all debts and obligations real or assumed, to the seigneurs, for arrears by virtue of the formerly existing Seigneurial Rights.

7. That the "Customary Jointure" is henceforth wholly abolished and banned.

8. That imprisonment for debts will no longer exist, except in the case of obvious fraud as will be specified in an Act of the Legislature of Lower Canada for that purpose.

9. That the death penalty will be pronounced in cases of murder only, and not otherwise.

10. That every Mortgage on Real Estate shall be specific, and to be valid, shall be registered with the Offices set up for that purpose by an Act of the Legislature of Lower Canada.

11. That there will be full and complete freedom of the Press on all public matters and affairs.

12. That trial by JURY is guaranteed to the People of the State, to the most liberal extent in criminal trials, and in civil affairs to a total sum to be established by the Legislature of the State of Lower Canada.

13. That as a necessity and a duty of the Government to the People, universal public education will be put in place and particularly encouraged, as soon as circumstances will allow.

14. That to ensure elective frankness and freedom, all elections will be conducted by means of a BALLOT.

15. That as soon as circumstances will allow, the People will choose Delegates according to the current division of the country into Cities, Towns, and Counties, who will constitute a Convention, or Legislative Body, to found and establish a Constitution, according to the country's needs, and in conformance with the clauses of this Declaration, subject to modification in accordance with the People's will.

16. That every male person over the age of twenty will have the right to vote under the conditions as set out above, for the election of the aforementioned Delegates.

17. That all the Lands known as Crown Lands, as well as those called clergy reserves, and those that are nominally in the possession of a certain company of speculators in England, called the "British American Land Company," become by right, the property of the State of Canada, save for such portions of the said lands as may be in the possession of farmers, who hold them in good faith, for whom we guarantee title in virtue of a law that will be passed to legalize the possession of such plots of land, located in the "Townships" which are now under cultivation.

18. That the French and English languages will be used in all public matters.

AND to support THIS DECLARATION, and the success of the Patriotic cause, which we uphold, WE, confident of the Almighty's protection and of the justice of our actions, hereby mutually and solemnly pledge, one to the other, our life, our fortunes and our most sacred honour. By Order of the Provisional Government....

### 3. Lord Durham, "Report on the Affairs of British North America," 1840

*An odd mix of senior aristocrat and radical reformer, John George Lambton, 1st Earl of Durham (1792–1840), helped create the crucial British reform bills of 1832. He shifted from politics to become ambassador to Russia in 1835, after which Prime Minister Melbourne appointed him Governor-in-Chief of British North America. His mandate was to discover what precipitated the rebellions of 1837 and to recommend a solution. The crux of his solution was threefold: mass emigration of indigents from Britain to British North America, union of the Canadas, and responsible government for that new colony. Always in fragile health, Durham was ill and in chronic pain while in Canada. He left in anger when Britain failed to endorse his Bermuda Ordinance, which provided relatively light punishments and circumvented judicial procedures for some of the captured rebel leaders.*

... A plan by which it is proposed to ensure the tranquil government of Lower Canada, must include in itself the means of putting an end to the agitation of national disputes in the legislature, by settling, at once and for ever, the national character of the Province. I entertain no doubts as to the national character which must be given to Lower Canada; it must be that of the British Empire; that of the majority of the population of British America; that of the great race which must, in the lapse of no long period of time, be predominant over the whole North American Continent. Without effecting the change so rapidly or so roughly as to shock the feelings and trample on the welfare of the existing generation, it must henceforth be the first and steady purpose of the British Government to establish an English population, with English laws and language, in this Province, and to trust its government to none but a decidedly English Legislature.

It may be said that this is a hard measure to a conquered people; that the French were originally the whole, and still are the bulk of the population of Lower Canada; that the English are new comers, who have no right to demand the extinction of the nationality of a people, among whom commercial enterprise has drawn them. It may be said, that, if the French are not so civilized, so energetic, or so money-making a race as that by which they are surrounded, they are an amiable, a virtuous, and a contented people, possessing all the essentials of material comfort, and not to be despised or ill-used, because they seek to enjoy what they have, without emulating the spirit of accumulation, which influences their neighbours. Their nationality is, after all, an inheritance; and they must be not too severely punished, because they have dreamed of maintaining on the distant banks of the St. Lawrence, and transmitting to their posterity, the language, the manners, and the institutions of that great nation, that for two centuries gave the tone of thought to the European Continent. If the disputes of the two races are irreconcileable, it may be urged that justice demands that the minority should be compelled to acquiesce in the supremacy of the ancient and most numerous occupants of the Province, and not pretend to force their own institutions and customs on the majority.

But before deciding which of the two races is now to be placed in the ascendant, it is but prudent to inquire which of them must ultimately prevail; for it is not wise to establish to-day that which must, after a hard struggle, be reversed to-morrow. The pretensions of the French Canadians to the exclusive possession of Lower Canada, would debar the yet larger English population of Upper Canada and the Townships from access to the great natural channel of that trade which they alone have created, and now carry on. The possession of the mouth of the St. Lawrence concerns not only those who happen to have made their settlements along the narrow line which borders it, but all who now dwell or will hereafter dwell, in the great basin of that river. For we must not look to the present alone. The question is, by what race is it likely that the wilderness which now covers the rich and ample regions surrounding the comparatively small and contracted districts in which the French Canadians are located, is eventually to be converted into a settled and flourishing country? If this is to be done in the British dominions, as in the rest of North America, by some speedier process than the ordinary growth of population, it must be by immigration from the English Isles, or from the United States,—the countries which supply the only settlers that have entered, or will enter, the Canadas in any large numbers. This immigration can neither be debarred from a passage through Lower Canada, nor even be prevented from settling in that Province. The whole interior of the British dominions must ere long, be filled with an English population, every year rapidly increasing its numerical superiority over the French. Is it just that the prosperity of this great majority, and of this vast tract of country, should be for ever, or even for a while, impeded by the artificial bar which the backward laws and civilization of a part, and a part only, of Lower Canada, would place between them and the ocean? Is it to be supposed that such an English population will ever submit to such a sacrifice of its interests?

I must not, however, assume it to be possible that the English Government shall adopt the course of placing or allowing any check to the influx of English immigration into Lower Canada, or any impediment to the profitable employment of that English capital which is already vested therein. The English have already in their hands the majority of the larger masses of property in the country;

they have the decided superiority of intelligence on their side; they have the certainty that colonization must swell their numbers to a majority; and they belong to the race which wields the Imperial Government, and predominates on the American Continent. If we now leave them in a minority, they will never abandon the assurance of being a majority hereafter, and never cease to continue the present contest with all the fierceness with which it now rages. In such a contest they will rely on the sympathy of their countrymen at home; and if that is denied them, they feel very confident of being able to awaken the sympathy of their neighbours of kindred origin. They feel that if the British Government intends to maintain its hold of the Canadas, it can rely on the English population alone; that if it abandons its colonial possessions, they must become a portion of that great Union which will speedily send forth its swarms of settlers, and, by force of numbers and activity, quickly master every other race. The French Canadians, on the other hand, are but the remains of an ancient colonization, and are and ever must be isolated in the midst of an Anglo-Saxon world. Whatever may happen, whatever government shall be established over them, British or American, they can see no hope for their nationality. They can only sever themselves from the British Empire by waiting till some general cause of dissatisfaction alienates them, together with the surrounding colonies, and leaves them part of an English confederacy; or, if they are able, by effecting a separation singly, and so either merging in the American Union, or keeping up for a few years a wretched semblance of feeble independence, which would expose them more than ever to the intrusion of the surrounding population. I am far from wishing to encourage indiscriminately these pretensions to superiority on the part of any particular race; but while the greater part of every portion of the American Continent is still uncleared and unoccupied, and while the English exhibit such constant and marked activity in colonization, so long will it be idle to imagine that there is any portion of that Continent into which that race will not penetrate, or in which, when it has penetrated, it will not predominate. It is but a question of time and mode; it is but to determine whether the small number of French who now inhabit Lower Canada shall be made English under a Government which can protect them, or whether the process shall be delayed until a much larger number shall have to undergo, at the rude hands of its uncontrolled rivals, the extinction of a nationality strengthened and embittered by continuance.

And is this French Canadian nationality one which, for the good merely of that people, we ought to strive to perpetuate, even if it were possible? I know of no national distinctions marking and continuing a more hopeless inferiority. The language, the laws, the character of the North American Continent are English;

and every race but the English (I apply this to all who speak the English language) appears there in a condition of inferiority. It is to elevate them from that inferiority that I desire to give to the Canadians our English character. I desire it for the sake of the educated classes, whom the distinction of language and manners keeps apart from the great Empire to which they belong. At the best, the fate of the educated and aspiring colonist is, at present, one of little hope, and little activity; but the French Canadian is cast still further into the shade, by a language and habits foreign to those of the Imperial Government. A spirit of exclusion has closed the higher professions on the educated classes of the French Canadians, more, perhaps, than was absolutely necessary; but it is impossible for the utmost liberality on the part of the British Government to give an equal position in the general competition of its vast population to those who speak a foreign language. I desire the amalgamation still more for the sake of the humbler classes. Their present state of rude and equal plenty is fast deteriorating under the pressure of population in the narrow limits to which they are confined. If they attempt to better their condition, by extending themselves over the neighbouring country, they will necessarily get more and more mingled with an English population: if they prefer remaining stationary, the greater part of them must be labourers in the employ of English capitalists. In either case it would appear, that the great mass of the French Canadians are doomed, in some measure, to occupy an inferior position, and to be dependent on the English for employment. The evils of poverty and dependence would merely be aggravated in a ten-fold degree, by a spirit of jealous and resentful nationality, which should separate the working class of the community from the possessors of wealth and the employers of labour....

There can hardly be conceived a nationality more destitute of all that can invigorate and elevate a people, than that which is exhibited by the descendants of the French in Lower Canada, owing to their retaining their peculiar language and manners. They are a people with no history, and no literature. The literature of England is written in a language which is not theirs; and the only literature which their language renders familiar to them, is that of a nation from which they have been separated by eighty years of a foreign rule, and still more by those changes which the Revolution and its consequences have wrought in the whole political, moral and social state of France. Yet it is on a people whom recent history, manners and modes of thought, so entirely separate from them, that the French Canadians are wholly dependent for almost all the instruction and amusement derived from books: it is on this essentially foreign literature, which is conversant about events, opinions and habits of life, perfectly strange and unintelligible to them, that they are compelled to be dependent. Their newspapers are mostly written by natives of France, who have either come to try their fortunes in the Province, or been brought into it by the party leaders, in order to supply the dearth of literary talent available for the political press. In the same way their nationality operates to deprive them of the enjoyments and civilizing influence of the arts. Though descended from the people in the world that most generally love, and have most successfully cultivated the drama—though living on a continent, in which almost every town, great or small, has an English theatre, the French population of Lower Canada, cut off from every people that speaks its own language, can support no national stage.

In these circumstances, I should be indeed surprised if the more reflecting part of the French Canadians entertained at present any hope of continuing to preserve their nationality. Much as they struggle against it, it is obvious that the process of assimilation to English habits is already commencing. The English language is gaining ground, as the language of the rich and of the employers of labour naturally will. It appeared by some of the few returns, which had been received by the Commissioner of the Inquiry into the state of Education, that there are about ten times the number of French children in Quebec learning English, as compared with the English children who learn French. A considerable time must, of course, elapse before the change of a language can spread over a whole people; and justice and policy alike require, that while the people continue to use the French language, their Government should take no such means to force the English language upon them as would, in fact, deprive the great mass of the community of the protection of the laws. But, I repeat that the alteration of the character of the Province ought to be immediately entered on, and firmly, though cautiously, followed up; that in any plan, which may be adopted for the future management of Lower Canada, the first object ought to be that of making it an English Province; and that, with this end in view, the ascendancy should never again be placed in any hands but those of an English population. Indeed, at the present moment this is obviously necessary: in the state of mind in which I have described the French Canadian population, as not only now being, but as likely for a long while to remain, the trusting them with an entire control over this Province, would be, in fact, only facilitating a rebellion. Lower Canada must be governed now, as it must be hereafter, by an English population: and thus the policy, which the necessities of the moment force on us, is in accordance with that suggested by a comprehensive view of the future and permanent improvement of the Province....

But the period of gradual transition is past in Lower Canada. In the present state of feeling among the French population, I cannot doubt that any power which they might possess would be used against the policy and the very existence of any form of British government. I cannot doubt that any French Assembly that shall again meet in Lower Canada will use whatever power, be it more or less limited, it may have, to obstruct the Government, and undo whatever has been done by it ... nor co-operation to be expected from a legislature, of which the majority shall represent its French inhabitants. I believe that tranquillity can only be restored by subjecting the Province to the vigorous rule of an English majority; and that the only efficacious government would be that formed by a legislative union.

If the population of Upper Canada is rightly estimated at 400,000, the English inhabitants of Lower Canada at 150,000, and the French at 450,000, the union of the two Provinces would not only give a clear English majority, but one which would be increased every year by the influence of English emigration; and I have little doubt that the French, when once placed, by the legitimate course of events and the working of natural causes, in a minority, would abandon their vain hopes of nationality. I do not mean that they would immediately give up their present animosities, or instantly renounce the hope of attaining their end by violent means. But the experience of the two Unions in the British Isles may teach us how effectually the strong arm of a popular legislature would compel the obedience of the refractory population; and the hopelessness of success would gradually subdue the existing animosities, and incline the French Canadian population to acquiesce in their new state of political existence.

FURTHER READINGS

Azjenstat, J. *The Political Thought of Lord Durham*. Montreal and Kingston: McGill-Queen's University Press, 1988.

Bernard, J-P. *The Rebellions of 1837 and 1838 in Lower Canada*. Ottawa: Canadian Historical Association, 1996.

Bernier, G., and D. Salée. *The Shaping of Quebec Politics and Society: Colonialism, Power and the Transition to Capitalism in the 19th Century*. Washington: Crane Russak, 1992.

Buckner, P. *Transition to Responsible Government: British Policy in British North America, 1815 to 1850*. Westport: Greenwood Press, 1985.

Burroughs, P. *The Canadian Crisis and British Colonial Policy, 1828-1841*. Toronto: Macmillan, 1972.

Burroughs, P., Ed. *The Colonial Reformers and Canada, 1830-1849*. Toronto: McClelland and Stewart, 1969.

Greenwood, M., and B. Wright, Eds. *Canadian State Trials. Vol. II: Rebellion and Invasion in the Canada, 1837-1839*. Toronto: University of Toronto Press, 2002.

Greer, A. *The Patriots and the People: The Rebellion of 1837 in Rural Lower Canada*. Toronto: University of Toronto Press, 1993.

Greer, A. "Rebellion Reconsidered." *Canadian Historical Review* 76, 1 (March 1995): 1-18.

Kenny, S. "The Canadian Rebellions and the Limits of Historical Perspective." *Vermont History* 58, 23 (Summer 1990): 179-98.

Manning, H. *The Revolt of French Canada, 1800-1835*. Toronto: Macmillan, 1962.

Martin, G. *The Durham Report and British Policy: A Critical Essay*. Cambridge: Cambridge University Press, 1972.

Monet, J. *The Last Canon Shot: A Study of French Canadian Nationalism 1837-1850*. Toronto: University of Toronto Press, 1969.

Ouellet, F. *Lower Canada 1791-1840: Social Change and Nationalism.* Trans. P. Claxton. Toronto: McClelland and Stewart, 1980.

Schull, J. *Rebellion: The Rising in French Canada.* Toronto: Macmillan, 1971.

Senior, E. *Redcoats and Patriotes: The Rebellions in Lower Canada 1873-38.* Ottawa: Canada's Wings, 1985.

Verney, J. *O'Callaghan, The Making and Unmaking of a Rebel.* Ottawa: Carleton University Press, 1994.

# CHAPTER 12

# "Most Horrible and Heartless"

## IRISH IMMIGRATION

### INTRODUCTION

When Canada became part of the Empire in the mid-eighteenth century, Britain preferred to populate its new colonies with citizens from the British Isles. This policy held distinct advantages: it made British North America more British, less French, and therefore presumably more loyal; it strengthened the connection between the mother country and its new imperial possessions; and colonies like British North America, by acting as dumping grounds for the dispossessed, addressed the problem of a large and troubling poor population back home. Most newcomers therefore came from the poorest classes, those most susceptible to the pitfalls of industrialization, urbanization, intolerance, and starvation. These economic refugees shared the pain of losing familiar surroundings, friends, and family, plus the shock of integrating into a new and often strange society at the other end—a process inevitably exacerbated by their landing in Canada at the bottom of the social ladder. Many faced downright hostility and suspicion as they stepped onto Canadian quaysides after an often miserable two months at sea.

Politics, religion, a population explosion, and famine conspired to make the situation in Ireland particularly volatile in the mid-nineteenth century. Protestant England originally conquered Catholic Ireland in the sixteenth century and established it as a colony to supply agricultural produce for its burgeoning population. To facilitate this, and to ensure Ireland's future loyalty, London imported Protestant Scottish farmers into the northeastern counties of Ulster and divided much of the rest of the island into large estates for loyal English noblemen. The local Irish became a population of repressed and subjugated tenant farmers with few rights and onerous obligations. England strengthened its hold over Ireland by annexing it in the early nineteenth century, making it an actual part of Great Britain rather than a mere colony. The new English-owned agricultural estates produced food for English tables, but a population explosion in Ireland made agriculture inefficient, both in spatial and production terms. Part of the solution was to wean the peasantry from its traditional grain diet to the highly nutritious potato, which took up little space, and thus the New World tuber became the staple for millions of poor Irish.

This functioned until a deadly blight, an airborne fungus, all but destroyed the crop for several years running during the 1840s. Millions of farmers faced one of two choices: stay and die or take a chance by struggling to a coastal port such as Cork, Limerick, Dublin, or even Liverpool in England, find passage on a ship, and leave that living hell. Landlords and the British government used the potato famine as a pretext to encourage mass migration of tenant farmers, thereby freeing up land and lessening long-term financial obligations. Ironically, these starving souls fled amid plenty: grain production in Ireland increased during the famine, but it belonged to the landlords and was for export, not to support an indigent Irish population. The catastrophe was so great that Ireland's population fell from 8 to 4 million, either from death or emigration. Most who fled were Catholics from what is today the Republic of Ireland, and a disproportionate number were young children, widows, the aged, and other less independent individuals. There were, however, Protestant emigrants too, largely from Ulster. The two groups generally did not mix, feared each other, and periodically clashed violently.

Many migrants died long before sighting the New World, and many more who survived the trek to the emigration ports and the voyage to North America never made it farther than the quarantine island of Grosse-Île in the St. Lawrence River. There thousands died, packed cheek by jowl in the unspeakable squalor of the quarantine sheds, tents, and makeshift shelters, at least partly because the sudden influx of immigrants overwhelmed ill-prepared Canadian authorities. The Canadian public was not particularly sympathetic to the Irish plight. Disease, after all, soon wafted from immigrant ships to land, striking without warning, often with deadly results in an age without effective medicinal remedies. Locals came to fear and hate the disease-ridden Irish, shunning them, and forcing them out of range. This was not a new attitude. The stereotypical Irishman was a drunken, brawling, lazy, stupid, papist "Paddy." Thus, new Irish immigrants, usually destitute and weak, survived as best they could, picking up tough labouring jobs on the canals, getting marginal work doing what others refused, or by breaking the law. For most of these people, the land of opportunity was, at best, a sick joke.

## DISCUSSION POINTS

1. What factor was chiefly responsible for mortality among Irish immigrants travelling to Canada? To what extent were the Irish immigrants responsible for their own plight?

2. Was Canada negligent in its treatment of the Irish? Should more government assistance have been forthcoming?

3. Since the bulk of these immigrants were women and children, one could argue that Ireland was actually taking advantage of Canada by shipping out its most dependent and unwanted people. Was it really in the interest of the inhabitants of British North America to receive Irish immigrants during this period?

DOCUMENTS

## 1. Stephen De Vere, "To the Select Committee on Colonization from Ireland," November 30, 1847

*Poet and classicist, Anglo-Irish Sir Stephen Edward De Vere (1812-1904) used his considerable fortune to assist Irish immigrants bound for the new world. In 1847 he tested the horror-stories of the "coffin ships" by taking steerage passage on an immigrant ship bound for British North America, sharing the privations of the other immigrants. The appalling shipboard conditions led to his withering report to Secretary for Colonies Earl Grey which, in turn, encouraged an amendment to the Passenger's Act. Thomas Frederick Elliot (1808-80), to whom De Vere wrote, became Britain's agent-general for emigration in 1837 and, in 1840, a member of the Colonial Land and Immigration Commission, the body charged with creating regulations for settlement throughout the Empire. He then became assistant-under-secretary for the colonies in 1847 and worked tirelessly to strengthen the Passenger's Act, which eventually happened in 1855.*

London, Canada West,

My dear sir

... The fearful state of disease and debility in which the Irish emigrants have reached Canada, must undoubtedly be attributed in a great degree to the destitution and consequent sickness prevailing in Ireland; but has been much aggravated by the neglect of cleanliness, ventilation, and a generally good state of social economy during the passage, and has been afterwards increased, and disseminated throughout the whole country by the mal-arrangements of the Government system of emigrant relief. Having myself submitted to the privations of a steerage passage in an emigrant ship for nearly two months, in order to make myself acquainted with the condition of the emigrant from the beginning, I can state from experience that the present regulations for ensuring health and comparative comfort to passengers are wholly insufficient, and that they are not, and cannot be enforced, notwithstanding the great zeal and high abilities of the Government agents.

Before the emigrant has been a week at sea he is an altered man. How can it be otherwise? Hundreds of poor people, men, women, and children, of all ages from the drivelling idiot of 90 to the babe just born; huddled together, without light, without air, wallowing in filth, and breathing a fetid atmosphere, sick in body, dispirited in heart; the fevered patients lying between the sound, in sleeping places so narrow as almost to deny them the power of indulging, by a change of position, the natural restlessness of the disease; by their agonized ravings disturbing those around and pre-disposing them, through the effects of the imagination, to imbibe the contagion; living without food or medicine except as administered by the hand of casual charity; dying without the voice of spiritual consolation, and buried in the deep without the rites of the Church. The food is generally ill-selected, and seldom *sufficiently cooked*, in consequence of the insufficiency and bad construction of the cooking places. The supply of water, hardly enough for cooking and drinking, does not allow washing. In many ships the filthy beds, teeming with all abominations, are never required to be brought on deck and aired; the narrow space between the sleeping berths and the piles of boxes is never washed or scraped, but breathes up a damp and fetid stench, until the day before arrival at quarantine, when all hands are required to "scrub up," and put on a fair face for the doctor and Government inspector. No moral restraint is attempted; the voice of prayer is never heard; drunkenness, with its consequent train of ruffianly debasement, is not discouraged, because it is profitable to the captain who traffics in the grog.

In the ship which brought me out from London last April, ... The meat was of the worst quality. The supply of water shipped on board was abundant, but the quantity served out to the passengers was so scanty that they were frequently obliged to throw overboard their salt provisions and rice (a most important article of their food), because they had not water enough both for the necessary cooking, and the satisfying of their raging thirst afterwards.

They could only afford water for washing by withdrawing it from the cooking of their food. I have known persons to remain for days together in their dark close berths, because they thus suffered less from hunger, though compelled, at the same time, by want of water to heave over-board their salt provisions and rice. No cleanliness was enforced; the beds never aired; the master during the whole voyage never entered the steerage, and would listen to no complaints; the dietary contracted for was, with some exceptions, nominally supplied, though at irregular periods; but false measures were used (in which the water and several articles of dry food were served), the gallon measure containing but three quarts, which fact I proved in Quebec, and had the captain fined for; once or twice a week ardent spirits were sold indiscriminately to the passengers, producing scenes of unchecked blackguardism beyond description; and lights were prohibited, because the ship, with her open fire-grates upon deck ... was freighted with Government powder for the garrison of Quebec.

The case of this ship was not one of peculiar misconduct, on the contrary, I have the strongest reason to know from information which I have received from very many emigrants well-known to me who came over this year in different vessels, that this ship was better regulated and more comfortable than many that reached Canada.

Some of these evils might be prevented by a more careful inspection of the ship and her stores, before leaving port; but the provisions of the Passenger's Act are insufficient to procure cleanliness and ventilation, and the machinery of the emigration agencies at the landing ports is insufficient to enforce those provisions, and to detect frauds. It is true that a clerk sometimes comes on board at the ship's arrival in port; questions the captain or mate, and ends by asking whether any passenger means to make a complaint; but this is a mere farce, for the captain takes care to "keep away the crowd from the gentleman." Even were all to hear the question, few would venture to commence a prosecution; ignorant, friendless, pennyless, disheartened, and anxious to proceed to the place of their ultimate destination.

Disease and death among the emigrants; nay, the propagation of infection throughout Canada, are not the worst consequences of this atrocious system of neglect and ill-usage. A result far worse is to be found in the utter demoralization of the passengers, both male and female, by the filth, debasement, and disease of two or three months so passed. The emigrant, enfeebled in body, and degraded in mind, even though he should have the physical power, has not the *heart*, has not the *will* to exert himself. He has lost his self-respect, his elasticity of spirit—he no longer stands erect—he throws himself listlessly upon the daily dole of Government, and, in order to earn it, carelessly lies for weeks upon the contaminated straw of a fever lazaretto.

I am aware that the Passenger's Act has been amended during the last Session, ... I would earnestly suggest the arrangement of every passenger ship into separate divisions for the married, for single men, and for single women; and the appointment, from amongst themselves, of "monitors" for each ward; the appropriation of an hospital ward for the sick; the providing of commodious cooking stoves and utensils, and the erection of decent privies; and the appointment, to each ship carrying more than 50 passengers, of a surgeon paid by Government, who should be invested during the voyage with the authority of a Government emigration agent, with power to investigate all complaints at sea on the spot, and at the time of their occurrence to direct and enforce temporary redress, and to institute proceedings on arrival in port, in concert with the resident emigration agent. He ought, for this purpose to have authority to detain witnesses, and to support them during the prosecution at Government expense. I would also suggest the payment of a chaplain of the religion professed by the majority of the passengers.

The sale of spirituous liquors should be prohibited except for medicinal purposes, &c., the minimum supply of water enlarged from three to four quarts.

I believe that if these precautions were adopted, the human cargoes would be landed in a moral and physical condition far superior to what they now exhibit, and that the additional expense incurred would be more than compensated by the saving effected in hospital expenses and emigrant relief.

The arrangements adopted by the Government during the past season, for the assistance of pauper emigrants after their arrival in Canada, were of three sorts, hospitals, temporary sheds, and transmission. These measures were undertaken in a spirit of liberality deserving our best gratitude; and much allowance ought to be made for imperfections of detail, which it was not easy to avoid under the peculiar and unexpected exigencies of the case; but I think I can demonstrate that much of the mortality which has desolated as well the old residents as the emigrants, may be attributed to the errors of those arrangements.

In the quarantine establishment at Grosse Isle, when I was there in June, the medical attendance and hospital accommodations were quite inadequate. The medical inspections on board were slight and hasty; hardly any questions were asked; but as the doctor walked down the file on deck, he selected those for hospital who did not look well, and, after a very slight examination, ordered them on shore. The ill-effect of this haste was two-fold:—some were detained in danger who were not ill, and many were allowed to proceed who were actually in fever. Of the management of the hospitals in general I do not feel myself qualified to speak; and I have no doubt that you are in possession of reports which will enable you to draw your own conclusions.

The sheds were very miserable; so slightly built as to exclude neither the heat nor the cold. No sufficient care was taken to remove the sick from the sound, or to disinfect and clean the building after the removal of the sick to hospital. The very straw upon which they had lain was often allowed to become a bed for their successors; and I have known many poor families prefer to burrow under heaps of loose stones which happened to be piled up near the shore, rather than accept the shelter of the infected sheds.

It would, I am aware, have been difficult to have provided a more substantial shelter for the amount of destitution produced by the peculiar circumstances of the past year; but I hope that, in future, even though the number or emigrants should greatly exceed that of last year, so large an extent of pauper temporary accommodation may not be necessary, and that a better built, and better regulated house or refuge, may be provided.

Of the administration of temporary relief by food to the inmates of the sheds, I must speak in terms of the highest praise. It was a harassing and dangerous duty, and one requiring much judgment on the part of the agent, and it was performed with zeal, humanity, and good sense....

## 2. Dr. G. Douglas, "To Hon. D. Daly," December 27, 1847

*Dr. George Mellis Douglas (1809-64) began his practice in Quebec in 1827, becoming medical superintendent of the quarantine station at Grosse-Île in 1836 after serving in that capacity at the Gaspé station. He was highly respected and published several medical and natural history studies based upon his experiences. One, written in 1847, erroneously hypothesized that cholera was non-contagious, a theory that survived until the discovery of the cholera vibrio in 1885. Twice widowed, Dr. Douglas was known for his integrity and dedication to duty. Dominick Daly was a member of Parliament and a long-time colonial administrator. As provincial secretary he received many of the reports issued by civil servants such as Dr. Douglas.*

Sir,

... I am persuaded that next season the number of sick will exceed that of any previous year. The partial failure of the potato crop last season (1845) caused much sickness; its almost total failure in that country and the north of Scotland this season (1846) will have the effect of pouring upon our shores thousands of debilitated and sickly emigrants. The result of the past season's emigration has more than fulfilled my prediction. Two causes, which could not have been foreseen, have conspired to augment beyond all calculation the number of destitute and diseased emigrants.

The first of these was the enactment of a law by the general government of the United States, which, by limiting the number which each passenger vessel could carry, made the cost of a passage so high as virtually to exclude all but those having a certain amount of means of their own. A law previously in existence in the State of New York, which obliged the master or owner of a vessel bringing passengers to give bonds, that no emigrant brought out by them became chargeable to the commonwealth for a period of two years after their arrival, was more strictly enforced.

The effect of these laws was to turn the stream of pauper emigration to the British provinces. I estimate the accession to our emigration this year through the operation of this cause at from 30,000 to 40,000.

Another cause of the increase this season has been the application to Ireland of a poor-law. To avoid the enormous expense which will attend its execution in some parts of the country where destitution abounds, many landlords have given free passages to those having claims on the land. In selecting these, they have, naturally enough, abstained from choosing the young, strong able-bodied labourer, but have sought to rid their estates of helpless widows with large families, cripples unable to work, aged persons, the confirmed idle and lazy, and those whose constitutions had been enfeebled by previous sickness and destitution. Such was the character and description of many of the settlers sent out from the ports of Liverpool, Dublin, Cork, and Limerick, as more particularly described in my official reports at different times during the past season.

I will enter upon a detailed statement of the operations of the season.

On the 4th of May, the usual hospital staff left for the island, with the addition to the establishment of an hospital steward, one orderly, and one nurse, the duty of the apothecary and steward having previously been performed by the same person, 50 new iron beds were ordered, and double the quantity of straw used in former years for bedding was purchased before leaving town. An additional building was ordered and commenced immediately. These preparations were deemed sufficient for the commencement, as the greatest number of sick had in former years arrived in the months of July and August. The hospital accommodation, as it then existed, was amply sufficient for 200 sick, the average of former years never having attained half that number requiring admission at one time.

On the 14th of May, the barque "Syria" arrived from Liverpool, which port she left on the 28th of March, with 243 passengers. On mustering them for inspection at Grosse Isle, I found that nine had died on the voyage, and 52 were lying ill with fever and dysentery. The sick were landed at once and placed in hospital, and the seemingly healthy were landed with the baggage at the sheds. The day after they were landed it was found necessary to send 21 of these to hospital, and each day others fell ill until the 28th, on which day 125 were patients in hospital.

On the 19th of May, five days after the arrival of the "Syria," the barque "Perseverance" and ship "Wandsworth," both from Dublin, arrived, the former having 62 and the latter 78 cases of fever and dysentery out of 310 and 527 respectively; these were all landed, the sick placed in hospital, and the healthy in the sheds to wash and purify. The passengers of both these vessels were principally tenants from the estates of William Wandesford in Kilkenny. In the "Perseverance" nine had died on the passage, and in the "Wandsworth" 45; being in one vessel about 3 per cent, and in the other 10 per cent. The passengers of both ships were from the same estates, equally provisioned, and I can only account for the greater mortality in the "Wandsworth" from the circumstance of the master of this vessel being unused to the conveyance of passengers, and unacquainted with the necessity of enforcing cleanliness and regularity, he was in all respects a steady, careful seaman. The sickness in both these ships was said by the masters to have been caused by their passengers ravenously devouring the bread-stuffs supplied by the vessel, having previous to their embarkation suffered from starvation. The sick from these two vessels, with those admitted from the "Syria," and a few from the "Jane Black" from Limerick, filled our hospitals at once to overflowing, and afforded just grounds for apprehending that sickness would prevail to an alarming extent in every vessel with Irish passengers....

On the 27th I received by steamer a large number of tents and hospital marquees, with an additional supply of hospital bedding. I received at the same time instructions to detain all passengers where fever had prevailed for a period of ten days. With some difficulty the marquees and tents were pitched, as few men could be found to engage in any work which brought them near the hospitals, and the regular hospital attendants were overworked in their attendance on the sick and in burying the dead.

On the 30th of the month four large hospital marquees were pitched and fitted with 64 beds each, and a large number of bell-tents were also fitted with beds, and that evening 400 more sick were landed, increasing our number to 1200. But there still remained 35 vessels in quarantine, having on board 12,175 souls, and great numbers of these were falling ill and dying daily. It was with much difficulty that people could be found to make coffins, dig graves, and bury the dead, as already observed, all our regular hospital servants were either ill or exhausted by fatigue. Dr. Benson, the gentleman engaged to assist, took fever and died after a short illness. On the 1st of June, I received the aid of two other medical assistants, in addition to Drs. Jacques and M'Grath; and the Superintendent of the Board of Works was employed to erect new hospitals, and to build cook-houses for the passengers' sheds used as temporary hospitals, and now crowded in every part ...

On the 8th of this month another of the medical gentlemen was attacked with fever, and three days previous the Rev. Mr. Gauvran, the Roman Catholic chaplain, who had been unwearied in his attendance upon the sick and dying, was down with the same disease. On the 10th of June, our number of sick had reached to 1800, who were crowded into every place that could afford shelter, hospitals, sheds, tents, and churches; these last, through the kindness of the Lord Bishop of Montreal, and his Grace the Roman Catholic archbishop, were given up for the use of the sick. In the mean time the greatest exertions were being made to put up new buildings; contracts were entered into by the Board of Works for the creation of two, capable of accommodating 120 sick each. Two others of equal size were building, under the immediate direction of the active superintendent of the Board, and a fifth was contracted for in Quebec by the Chief Agent for Emigrants, to be sent down in frame ready to be put up....

In the hospitals, the number of sick continued to increase, being limited only by the amount of accommodation.

The accumulation of so vast a multitude of fever cases in one place generated a miasma so virulent and concentrated, that few who came within its poisonous atmosphere escaped. The clergy, medical men, hospital attendants, servants, and police, fell ill one after another. With respect to the clergymen, a judicious plan was adopted of retaining them for a week only, by this means many escaped; but, with medical men and attendants, this could not be done. The average period of time which a medical man withstood the disease was from 18 to 21 days; out of 26 employed during the season in the hospitals and visiting the vessels, two and myself alone escaped the fever, though otherwise severely affected in general health from breathing the foul air of the vessels and tents.... I experienced much difficulty at one time in retaining any nurses or attendants, and on those days of the week, when an opportunity of leaving the island offered by the arrival of the steamer, great numbers of servants came forward and insisted upon their discharge. I found myself obliged firmly to refuse all such applications, unless the applicant could produce a substitute. It is needless to observe, that many so retained against their will neglected their duty to the sick, and sought by every means to provoke their dismissal. Those sent down to be engaged were, in many cases, the vilest and most profligate of both sexes, and were influenced by the most sordid motives.

On the 12th of June a new hospital, capable of accommodating 120 sick was completed and occupied; two others of the same size and dimensions were finished by the end of the month. From the 19th to 26th of this month, much rain fell, with a high temperature and fog; this had a most pernicious effect upon the sick under canvas, though the tents were, in the first instance, floored with boards, after which iron bedsteads were substituted as soon as a supply of the same, was obtained from the barrack department, yet they afforded but insufficient protection from the weather when wet, and the mortality was, in consequence, much greater among the sick in tents than in the hospitals.

During the prevalence of this rain it was found impossible to wash or dry the vast quantities of hospital bedding....

Throughout the following months of July and August passenger vessels continued to arrive in great numbers, each more sickly than the other. The calm, sultry weather of these two months increased the mortality and sickness on board to an appalling extent, some vessels having lost one-fourth, and others one-third of their passengers, before arriving at the quarantine station. Of these I may cite the ship "Virginius," from Liverpool; this vessel left with 476 passengers, of whom 158 died before arrival at Grosse Isle, including the master, mate, and nine of the crew. It was with difficulty the few remaining hands could, with the aid of the passengers, moor the ship and furl the sails. Three days after her arrival there remained of the ship's company only the second mate, one seaman, and a boy, able to do duty; all others were either dead or ill in hospital. Two days after the arrival of this ill-fated ship, the barque "Naomi" arrived, having left Liverpool with 334 passengers, of whom 110 died on the passage, together with several of the crew. The master was just recovering from fever, on his arrival. The barque "Sir Henry Pottinger" arrived about this time from Cork, which port she had left with one cabin and 399 steerage passengers, of whom 106 died, including the master's son and several of the crew. The passengers of the two first of these vessels were sent out at the expense and from the estates of the late Major Mahon, in county Tyrone, and the survivors were, without exception, the most wretched, sickly, miserable beings I ever witnessed....

Those who were landed at the tents in comparative good health, fell ill from the exciting causes of change of air and diet, and many died suddenly before they could be transferred to the hospitals.

By the end of August, however, long ranges of sheds had been erected, with berth-places, capable of lodging 3500 people, at the east end of the island. These buildings enabled us to dispense with all the tents....

I have had occasion to observe in former reports, that emigrants who come from distant country places to large sea-ports, there to await the sailing of a vessel, living in the meantime in crowded cellars and lodging-houses, invariably suffer more from illness during the voyage, and arrive in a more unhealthy condition than those who have but a short distance to come, and little delay at the port of their embarkation....

The disease which proved so fatal was, in most cases, brought on board, and many masters of vessels would, on going into the hold, point out to me the particular berth, place, or places, where the disease originated, and the direction in which it spread; in all such cases it was ascertained that the family occupying this berth had come on board diseased or convalescent from fever with foul and unwashed clothes.

The total number of passenger vessels inspected at the station this year has been 400, being about double the number of any previous year, the number of passengers being also double that of any former season. Of these vessels, the large number of 129 have had fever and dysentery among their passengers; 20 have had small-pox, and nine have had both fever and small-pox. 5293 passengers have died on ship board ... upon the whole number of passengers; of these, 11 were women in child-birth....

I regret that it is not in my power to suggest any means by which the great sickness and mortality among emigrants on their voyage out may be avoided. Much may be done by strict attention to cleanliness and ventilation as far as this is practicable, in the hold of a ship, by having the berth places and new wood-work of the between-decks, whitewashed with quick lime at least once a-week during the voyage, and by obliging the bedding and clothes of passengers to be taken on deck whenever the weather will permit. And, in the fitting up of the sleeping berths, the accumulation of much filth might be prevented if the lower boards were carried down flush to the main deck. It is customary, to leave the few inches of space which they are obliged by the Passenger's Act to have from the deck, open, this enables the passengers to keep their pots and vessels under the berths, which, in the rolling of the ship, get capsized, and the place becomes a receptacle of filth and dirt, which remains undisturbed as it is not seen, and cannot be readily got at to clean out. As I have already observed, the health of passengers would be better if a small quantity of animal food was issued three times a week in addition to the usual allowance of bread stuffs.

All the remedial means that may be adopted, however, will not prevent the occurrence of sickness and death to a fearful extent on ship-board so long as fever and destitution prevail in Ireland as it now does. Some one of the many passengers is sure to embark either just recovering from fever, with foul clothes and bedding, or with the seeds of the disease latent in his system, which the change of life and the discomforts of a sea voyage rapidly develop in so favourable a locale as the hold of a vessel.

Medical men are generally agreed, that the three grand measures to be taken to prevent the spread of fever are *separation*, *ventilation*, and *cleanliness*, from the nature of things the two first of these are rendered impracticable in a crowded passenger-ship, and the last, of difficult attainment. Sea-sickness and the mental depression which usually attends it render it a matter of extreme difficulty to induce people to practice a virtue which they have never been accustomed to. Hence there is much reason to apprehend that next season will bring with it a recurrence of the sickness and mortality of this year, limited only in extent by the numbers who may emigrate....

### 3. Mayor W. Boulton, "To Earl of Elgin and Kincardine, Governor General of British North America," 1847

*William Henry Boulton (1812–74) was a scion of the Family Compact of Upper Canada. Despite such elite and prestigious roots, he befriended the colony's working people upon whom he depended for political support. Boulton was a staunch member of the Orange Order, a virulently anti-Catholic organization, and rose to be Deputy Grandmaster of the Orange Lodges of British North America. He served as Toronto's mayor from 1845–47.*

May it please your excellency,

We, the inhabitants of the city of Toronto, in public meeting assembled, respectfully invite the attention of your Excellency to the consideration of a subject, the urgency and importance of which will warrant our pressing it most earnestly on your Excellency's earliest notice.

During the past season the city of Toronto, in common with several other parts of Canada, has been the recipient of a very large body of emigrants from the British Isles, landed on our shores in a state, beyond all description, of lamentable and almost hopeless destitution, and bearing with them a pestilence of the most virulent and destructive character.

Out of the 100,000 emigrants landed in Quebec, nearly 40,000 were forwarded to this city; and from the month of June to the present time, the city has exhibited an amount of pauperism, suffering and disease unparalleled in her annals, and tolerable only from the belief of its having been utterly unforeseen, and from a trust in the mercy of Providence that it will not be suffered again to occur.

During the same period the hospitals appropriated to the suffering emigrants have, including the sick and convalescent divisions, been generally filled to overflowing with a number of patients often nearly reaching 1000 souls.

In addition to this mass of sickness and wretchedness, the number of persons, men, women, and children, begging from street to street for relief, has been fearfully on the increase; and a large mendicant population, once unknown to our Canadian towns, has rapidly sprung into existence....

If the wide-spread suffering of the past year were a dispensation from the chastening hand of Providence, unaffected and uncaused by human agency, the city of Toronto would willingly or at least silently bear their portion of the general loss and misery.

Sincerely believing it to have arisen in a very serious degree from neglect, indifference, and mismanagement, we respectfully venture to press on your Excellency the absolute necessity that exists for the adoption of prompt remedial measures.

The dreadful sufferings from want of wholesome food, ventilation room, and decent clothing on board the emigrant vessels—the startling fact of many thousands having found a grave in the ocean, that they thought was to bear them to a land of peace and plenty—the apparently total disregard of any inspection of the vessels, at the British ports—the neglect of salutary regulations as to the number of passengers proportioned to the size of the vessels, or the providing of a sufficient supply of food—the manner in which the healthy and the sick were shipped up the river and the lakes, and the catalogue of deaths at the numerous hospitals from Grosse Isle to Sandwich—all these are now matters of history, and are, doubtless, fresh in your Excellency's recollection.

We now most earnestly request your Excellency, without waiting for any action on the part of the Provincial Legislature, to aid the inhabitants of Canada in procuring from Her Majesty's Home Government such a vigorous interposition in the conduct of the anticipated emigration of 1848 as may ensure, so far as human precautions may extend, the nonrecurrence of the melancholy and revolting sufferings of the past season. A watchful and complete system of inspection of every emigrant vessel previous to its being allowed to leave port—due attention to the clothing and provisions of the passengers—strict rules as to the number allowed to be carried—all these can avail much to diminish the risk of pestilence. Above all, the fact cannot be too widely promulgated in Great Britain and Ireland, that the throwing of a half-clad and penniless emigrant on the shores of the St. Lawrence, may be the means of ridding an estate of a burdensome tenant; but it is an almost hopeless method of providing for a fellow-Christian.

This city has already lost some of her best and most valued citizens by the malignant fever introduced by the emigrants last season. Universal alarm has pervaded the community, and considerable interruption to business and travelling has been caused by the general state of the great thoroughfares of the province, from the prevalence of disease.

Most respectfully, but firmly, do the citizens of Toronto protest, through your Excellency, against their hitherto healthy and prosperous country being made the receptacle for the cast-off pauperism and disease of another hemisphere. To those already among us, without reference to national origin or other distinction, we trust we shall ever be ready to extend a helping hand and an active charity; but we look upon it as unjust and intolerable that the neglect and misconduct of others are to be the means of impoverishing and infecting our young country.

A well regulated emigration from the British Isles will confer inestimable advantages on the North American provinces, and on this city and its environs in particular. An emigration, such as has made memorable the season of 1847, must ever prove the opposite of a blessing to all concerned in it.

We feel persuaded that Her Majesty's Government will take such necessary precautions as to relieve the province at large, and its municipalities in particular, from the most painful, but most imperative duty of adopting such stringent measures as the exigency of the crisis may require for their own preservation....

### 4. H. Perley, "To Sir William Colebrooke, Lieutenant-Governor of the Province of New Brunswick," December 31, 1847

*Moses Henry Perley (1804–62) was a lawyer who became New Brunswick's emigrant agent in 1843 and then Britain's agent to New Brunswick in 1847. Thus, while wearing two hats, he supervised the immigration/emigration process and enforced both quarantine regulations and the Passenger's Acts that theoretically guaranteed passengers a modicum of space, food, security, and service. He earned the wrath of many ship owners by prosecuting those who broke the law.*

May It Please Your Excellency,

I have the honour to submit, for the information of Her Majesty's Government, the annual report from this office, together with the returns (in duplicate) for the quarter, and for the year, ending 31st December, 1847.

The return for the year shows the total number of emigrants landed in New Brunswick, during the past season, to have been 16,251, being an increase on the previous year's emigration of 6486, equal to 66 per cent. Of the whole number of vessels with emigrants, 99 came direct from Ireland; and although the other seven vessels sailed from Liverpool, yet the passengers were very nearly, without exception, all from Ireland also. The immigration of the season was confined almost solely to the humblest class of Irish peasantry, chiefly from the south and west of Ireland, who, long prior to embarkation, had suffered from every species of privation, and had become enfeebled by disease. Some thousands consisted of those who had been tenants holding less than five acres of land, and of mere cottiers, who had never held land at all, sent out at the expense of the landlords, or proprietors of the soil, on which they had lived, to relieve the estates from the expense of their support. They landed in New Brunswick in the greatest misery and destitution; so broken down and emaciated by starvation, disease, and the fatigues of the voyage, as to be, in a great measure, incapable of performing sufficient labour to earn a subsistence, and they became a heavy burthen upon private charity, as well as upon the public funds.

Of 17,074 who embarked this season for New Brunswick, 823 died on shipboard, 96 in the lazaretto at Miramichi, 601 in the lazaretto at St. John, and 595 in the hospital at the same place, making a total of 2115 deaths officially reported. The whole number of deaths for the season, up to the present date, may be safely estimated at 2400, or one-seventh of those who embarked.

Of the survivors, very nearly one half have found their way into the United States, notwithstanding the exertions used to prevent their entrance there. Of the residue, some were forwarded to the interior of this province at the public expense, and others made their way into the rural districts; but these were too feeble, and so little accustomed to work of any kind, that they were almost useless to the farmer; and I regret to say, that their course through the country was almost invariably marked by disease and death. They introduced fever into the farm-houses where they were employed, and a very general disinclination was soon manifested to receiving them as inmates on any terms.

There are at present 560 in the hospital attached to the almshouse at this place. To provide for the orphan children of deceased emigrants, an establishment has been opened in this city, into which nearly 200 children have already been received and clothed, and those of sufficient age are being instructed in schools of industry within the building. This establishment bids fair to be of a most useful character; it is to be hoped that it will be permanently sustained, and its means of usefulness increased. The sympathy of benevolent individuals has already been excited on behalf of the undertaking, and contributions have been made, to render the establishment more comfortable and beneficial for these helpless orphans. As the institution advances, charitable assistance will, no doubt, be afforded on an enlarged scale; still a very considerable sum will be required from the public funds for this asylum, which it is trusted will be forthcoming for an object so necessary and so laudable.

Among the emigrants of this season there was an unusual proportion of aged and infirm people of both sexes, and of widows, and deserted wives, with large families of children. Several instances came under my notice, where aged grandfathers and grandmothers arrived with a swarm of young and helpless grandchildren, the intermediate generation having remained in Ireland.

The expenses connected with the emigration of this year have already far exceeded the grant of £3000., made in anticipation by the provincial legislature at its last session, and the head money collected during the season; and as expenses are now being incurred in various parts of the province for the care and support of emigrants, which must be continued for some time, it becomes matter of grave consideration how the amount is to be met....

The number of able-bodied labourers, such as were able and willing to work, was this year unusually small; in fact, far less than the business of the country required. While this city was literally crowded with emigrants, and others were daily arriving, the rate of wages for good labourers steadily advanced, and the average for the season was as high as it ever was before. But few employers could be found who would incur the trouble of teaching men who were willing to work, but who were wholly unaccustomed to continuous labour, whose strength was unequal to any but light work; whose diet and management required great attention, or they fell ill directly, and with whom there was the constant risk of infectious fever, the seeds of which appeared to lurk in the constitutions of all, without exception....

The corporation return which is enclosed shows that, in the year 1844, only 2,500 emigrants landed at this port, and that the number has steadily advanced since then, until in the past season it reached 15,000. In former years, also, there was a very small amount of sickness, and the hospital accommodations at the quarantine station on Partridge Island were considered quite sufficient. But they were altogether inadequate to the emergency of the past season, when cargo after cargo of sick, filthy, and miserable wretches, had to be landed in rapid succession, infecting the medical men, the nurses and attendants, and nearly all who in any way had communication with them....

As great numbers have been buried on the island during the past season, in trenches imperfectly covered with soil, some expense must be incurred in covering these trenches with lime, sea-sand, and soil, to prevent the unpleasantness and injurious effects of the cadaverous exhalations.

No time should be lost in making these preparations, as the brief space until the arrival of emigrants in the spring, will barely admit of the necessary buildings being erected, and other arrangements made in due season.

The following prosecutions were instituted during the past season for violations of the Passenger's Act, in every one of which a conviction was obtained:— Austin Yorke, master of the "Lindon," from Galway, for insufficient issues of provisions and water to passengers, convicted in the penalty of 20l. sterling, and costs, which have been paid.

Samuel Fox, master of the Brigantine "Susan Anne," from Beerhaven, for carrying passengers without beams for a lower deck, convicted in the penalty of 20l. sterling, and costs, which have been paid.

The same Samuel Fox, master of the "Susan Anne," for an excess of passengers, convicted in the penalty of £5 sterling, and costs, which were paid.

Michael Brown, master of the schooner "Lady Dombrain," from Killybegs, for carrying passengers without permanent beams for a lower deck, convicted in the penalty of 20l. sterling, and costs, which were paid.

Patrick Beegan, master of the schooner "Bloomfield," from Galway, for insufficient issues of provisions and water, convicted in the full penalty of 50l. sterling, and costs, not yet paid....

The issues of the "Eliza Liddell," at Shippegan, and of that unfortunate vessel, the "Looshtank," at Miramichi, having been thoroughly investigated, I have only now to refer to my special reports on those cases, dated 18th and 19th October last.

I observed, during the season, that in those ships which had ample height between decks, and sufficient means of ventilation, there was less sickness and a smaller number of deaths than in others not possessing those advantages. In all cases, cleanliness, regular issues of provisions at short intervals, and the encouragement of active exercise on deck were most beneficial. The good effects of air and exercise were always evident in inspecting the emigrants upon their arrival. The use of Sir William Burnett's disinfecting fluid (chloride of zinc) was also highly advantageous. In the case of the brig "St. Lawrence," from Cork to St. Andrews, the passengers embarked with several cases of fever, yet from good management on the voyage, and the free use of this chloride, they landed at St. Andrews in better health than when they embarked.

The provision of the Passenger's Act, in reference to good sound boats, of suitable size, is in many cases shamefully evaded, and more attention to their inspection is absolutely requisite. Some of the boats attached to passenger ships this season were mere baskets, an incumbrance to the ship and nothing more. Anything boat-shaped is deemed sufficient by some masters and owners, if the necessary certificates for clearance can be obtained. After such certificate and safe voyage across the Atlantic, it would be difficult to procure a conviction here for this violation of the Act, more especially as it is easy to allow boats to be stove by a sea....

The use of biscuit in the Irish passenger trade should be limited as much as possible, as also the issue of "whole meal" made from wheat without any sifting, which is passed as wheat flour. In some cases, biscuit only was furnished to the passengers, to which they were wholly unaccustomed, and they nearly starved in consequence. It is difficult to make the whole meal into palatable bread, even when of the best quality; and with the imperfect means of working on board a passenger vessel at sea, it is quite out of the question. In the absence of potatoes, oatmeal should be strictly insisted upon, as a species of food to which the Irish peasantry are accustomed, and which they can prepare in any weather, and under all circumstances. The destitute emigrants of this season relied almost wholly upon the supply of provisions furnished by the ship, and many suffered greatly in consequence of the food not being such as they could prepare or use.

During the past season no money whatsoever has been remitted to this office by landholders or others in Ireland, to be paid to passengers on their arrival here; and although various noblemen and gentlemen have sent out pauper emigrants this year, no money, to my knowledge, has been paid to them, on or after arrival here. All were left to shift for themselves, or become a burthen upon the revenues of the colony, or else to subsist upon charitable institutions, or the assistance of the benevolent.

The character of the emigration during the past year having been altogether different from any that has preceded it, no comparison can be drawn between it and that of any former year. Heretofore sturdy labourers and farmers have arrived, very often possessed of some means, however small, and all looking forward to becoming settlers and proprietors of the soil by their energy and industry; but a large proportion of the emigrants of this season will require time and training to become even useful labourers....

FURTHER READINGS

Akenson, D. *Being Had: Historians, Evidence and the Irish in North America.* Port Credit: P.D. Meany, 1985.

Akenson, D. *The Irish in Ontario: A Study in Rural History.* Montreal and Kingston: McGill-Queen's University Press, 1984.

Cowan, H. *British Emigration to British North America: The First Hundred Years.* Rev. ed. Toronto: University of Toronto Press, 1961.

Duncan, K. "Irish Famine Immigration and the Social Structure of Canada West." *Canadian Review of Anthropology and Sociology* 2, 1 (February 1965): 19-40.

Elliot, B. *Irish Migrants in the Canadas: A New Approach.* Montreal and Kingston: McGill-Queen's University Press, 1988.

Grace, R. *The Irish in Quebec: An Introduction to the Historiography.* Quebec: Institute Québécois de Recherche sur la Culture, 1993.

Houston, C., and W. Smyth. *Irish Emigration and Canadian Settlement: Patterns, Links and Letters.* Toronto: University of Toronto Press, 1990.

Houston, C., and W. Smyth. *The Sash Canada Wore: A Historical Geography of the Orange Order in Canada.* Toronto: University of Toronto Press, 1980.

Lockwood, G. "Irish Immigrants in the 'Critical Years' in Eastern Ontario: The Case of Montague Township, 1821-1881." In *Historical Essays on Upper Canada: New Perspectives*, ed. J. Johnson and B. Wilson. Ottawa: Carleton University Press, 1989.

Mackay, D. *Flight from Famine: The Coming of the Irish to Canada.* Toronto: McClelland and Stewart, 1990.

Mannion, J. *Irish Settlement in Eastern Canada: A Study of Cultural Transfer and Adaptation.* Toronto: University of Toronto Press, 1974.

O'Driscoll, R., and C. Reynolds, Eds. *The Untold Story: The Irish in Canada.* Toronto: Celtic Arts of Canada, 1988.

Parr, J. "The Welcome and the Wake: Attitudes in Canada West Toward the Irish Famine Migration." *Ontario History* 66, 2 (1974): 101-13.

Power, T., Ed. *The Irish in Atlantic Canada, 1780-1900*. Fredericton: New Ireland Press, 1991.

Quigley, M. "Grosse Isle: Canada's Irish Famine Memorial." *Labour* 39 (Spring 1997): 195-214.

See, S. *Riots in New Brunswick: Orange Nativism and Social Violence in the 1840s*. Toronto: University of Toronto Press, 1990.

Senior, H. *Orangism: The Canadian Phase*. Toronto: McGraw-Hill Ryerson, 1972.

Shea, D. "The Irish Immigrant Adjustment to Toronto, 1840-1860." *Canadian Catholic Historical Association*, Study Sessions 39 (1972): 53-60.

Stewart, W. *Life on the Line: Commander Pierre-Etienne Fortin and his Times*. Ottawa: Carleton University Press, 1997.

Toner, P., Ed. *New Ireland Remembered: Historical Essays on the Irish in New Brunswick*. Fredericton: New Ireland Press, 1988.

# CHAPTER 13

# "A Great Humbug"

## BRITISH COLUMBIA'S GOLD RUSHES

### INTRODUCTION

British Columbia remained largely untouched by Europe until the latter part of the nineteenth century. Geography played the single greatest role in this: the area was simply too far removed from eastern Canada, let alone Europe, to be accessible. Topography did not help either. A fog-shrouded craggy coastline, riptides, impenetrable vegetation, impassable mountain ranges, treacherous river gorges, and sheer distance all conspired to thwart development. Much of the interior was too arid for crops, and trees too enormous to hew covered the tiny fertile belt along the coast. Why bother settling, especially since there was plenty of arable land, thriving communities, and far better communications in eastern British North America? British Columbia indeed offered too few rewards for too much effort. This changed in the late 1700s when Russian, American, and British ships ventured along the coast to reap the bountiful sea otter for its valuable pelt. Then traders from the North West Company, which merged with the Hudson's Bay Company in 1821, sought routes from their trading grounds in the Athabasca country to the Pacific. The British government sent expeditions led first by Captain Cook and later by his garrulous successor, George Vancouver, to map the coast and to assert claim over the land. By the mid-nineteenth century, the European presence in the area remained minuscule; Victoria was by far the largest centre with its population of some 300. The gold rush in the late 1850s changed this.

Gold fever could drive the most reticent and sombre individual to give up everything for Lady Luck. The earlier California Gold Rush attracted every sort: naïve city boys, hardened criminals, prostitutes, people down on their luck, shrewd businessmen and women, new immigrants without better prospects, genuine miners, and a myriad of others. The boom, of course, inevitably went bust, leaving dreamers high and dry, often in debt, and casting about for a new Eldorado. By the mid-nineteenth century, San Francisco teemed with luckless miners looking for new prospects.

Vague reports of gold on the Fraser River filtered south to California as early as 1855, and rumours became reality by the fall of 1857. Frantic fortune hunters packed onto ships or came overland via Whatcom Trail through the Washington territory. Fort Victoria, the somnolent HBC post, groaned under the strain of a transient and enthusiastic throng of some 30,000 miners who descended upon the unprepared village in 1858. Most miners remained just long enough to buy provisions at grossly inflated prices before heading for the sandbars along the Fraser or, later, to instant towns like Barkerville in the Cariboo. What they lacked in experience, they made up for in tenacity and enthusiasm—and they needed both. Mining the bars along the Fraser was either relatively easy or impossible. At low water in the summer and autumn, anyone with a gold pan and lots of patience could strike it rich—so legend said. Gold-seekers, the story went, required neither skills nor capital. Theoretically, one simply registered a claim for a sandbar, scooped up pans full of gravel and water, and gently sloshing the debris over the edge until nothing remained but the heavy gold. Wintertime and spring runoff, however, covered the sandbars with turbulent and frigid water that made panning untenable or at least desperately dangerous. Frustrated miners camped along the banks and prayed for river levels to drop faster than their money and supplies. Many, if not most, found their prayers unanswered.

British colonial officials fretted about the American multitude in the interior of British Columbia, fearing it would encourage the land's annexation to the United States by sheer weight of numbers. Only Vancouver Island, after all, had colonial status. Thus, James Douglas, the Island's governor, proceeded without official consent and asserted direct British authority over the mainland in 1858. This, however, was more theory than practice, particularly after many miners moved from the Fraser and Thompson rivers further north into the distant and isolated Cariboo.

Why did miners follow upriver once sandbar yields declined? Logic dictated that the gold dust on the river originated upstream where floodwaters scoured it from solid rock. Thus, a miner could theoretically follow the trail of dust to the "mother lode."

North they went into the Cariboo, where gold strikes occurred at Keithly, Antler, Williams, and Lightning Creek. Mining towns popped up like mushrooms. Barkerville, for example, briefly became the biggest town west of Chicago and north of San Francisco. Unlike panning sandbars, however, this latest iteration of the gold rush required capital to cover the costs of boring deep shafts and refining the ore. Unless miners had money, and few did, they had to create partnerships, work for wages, or give up and drift to the next discovery. Shaft mining also required skill and at least rudimentary geological knowledge, which few possessed. And the chances? A handful, usually those staking early claims, made famous fortunes. Billy Barker, who gave his name to Barkerville, was one. John Cameron, who successfully bragged of digging his and his dog's weight in gold, another. The vast majority, however, eked out bare subsistences or drifted back to Victoria, broke and broken. Many never lived to tell their tales.

Communities in the mining areas often disappeared as quickly as they emerged. Ten years on, Barkerville was all but abandoned. Lack of civic institutions, a single economic basis, and gender imbalance, plus the transient nature of the rush, all conspired against stable community development. Life in the little towns was also seasonal, with frenzied summer activity tapering off to somnolent and frigid winter boredom.

## DISCUSSION POINTS

1. Why was British Columbia not a land of opportunity?

2. How were the colonies of Vancouver Island and British Columbia different from their counterparts in eastern British North America?

3. Anti-Asian discrimination became common in late-nineteenth-century British Columbia. In what respects is this reflected in MacFie's account?

4. If you were a would-be miner desperate to beat the crowds and make a lucky strike, how would you describe British Columbia to those with whom you corresponded back home? Is there any indication that some of the negative images could have been deliberately designed to discourage competition?

DOCUMENTS

## 1. C. Gardiner, "To the Editor of *The Islander*," November 17, 1858

*Gardiner's history remains opaque, though evidence suggests he lived in Prince Edward Island, was a Methodist, and married Lucy Narraway. Archival material further indicates that Gardiner became a general merchant in the Bedeque area of Prince Edward Island after his gold rush adventures.*

... No doubt you are aware that about the 1st of May last a great excitement arose, and spread quickly over the lands of California, Oregon and Washington Territories, proving equally infectious to men of all vocations—the merchant, the farmer, the mechanic and miner—that gold in abundance was found on the Fraser and Thompson Rivers. I being, perhaps, like many others, of somewhat an excitable disposition, left, on the 20th May [1858], a mining town in the interior of California, and proceeded to San Francisco, where I found the excitement even more intense than in the mountains—the greatest credence being given to the stability of the reports, they going unanimously to prove the country could not be surpassed in richness with gold.

... Some thousands men were waiting there at that time in the greatest dilemma not knowing which way to proceed to the new mines. Fraser River being so high could not be ascended for two months, a sufficient distance to reach the main diggings, on account of the current running so swiftly through the Big Canyon, forming rapids, which would be impossible to navigate at that stage of water. Nevertheless, many would form in companies, buy a canoe, lay in from three to six months' provisions, and start, working their way as far as possible, until the river fell. Others would assert they would wait for the trail, which was then in operation of being cut through the country, across the Cascade Mountains to Thompson River, at the expense of some Land and Town Lot speculators, who were determined to have the great depot and centre of trade, effected by the new mines, on American soil. The balance of the men were divided in opinion, the weaker, or perhaps I may now justly allow, the wiser, being disgusted with the chances of getting to the New Eldorado, resolved to return to California.

... The upsetting of our canoe was nothing more than an accident, which most every company experienced, many not only losing their grub, but their lives. We very nearly lost two of our men, but were providentially saved by catching hold of the branches of a leaning tree, as the current was taking them swiftly down.

... Every day of the 23 [days to get up the river] we were in the cold water most of the time, with our heads out, but very frequently with them under, an unpleasantness which could not be avoided, in passing the line outside the trees and brush which grew on the banks of the river, when the water was low, but were now submerged half way to their tops. Those nights we passed in sleeping in our wet clothes, or part of them only, as each in his turn had to keep watch, with revolver in hand, that the Indians did not steal our provisions, as well as Mamaloose [kill] us while asleep. Notwithstanding our guard, every few mornings one or the other of the companies would have something missing that the Red Skin had stolen at night. Indeed it is considered as impossible to keep them from or detect them stealing....

We found quite a number of men camped on the river banks, the most of whom had come by trail from the Colville Mines in Washington Territory, and who were forced to kill their horses and mules, the flesh of which they had been subsisting on for the last 4 weeks. Flour we soon ascertained (if there was any for sale) was worth $125 per 100 lb., meat of all kinds $1.75, beans $1.00, and everything else in proportion.

Fraser River was still very high, and the miners informed us they could only make from two to five dollars per day, that not being sufficient to grub them the way provisions sold, and there was not a probability of it getting much cheaper for some time.

Five of us in Company pitched our tent, fixed up our mining tools, and went to work. We prospected up and down the river a distance of 40 miles each way, and could find gold in small quantities most anywhere on the surface of the bars, which were then getting bare, as the river fell. The gold is much finer than any found in California, and found in a different deposit. On Fraser River what has been dug has been found within three to eighteen inches of the surface, in a kind of sand being underneath a very pretty gravel, but no gold in it. In this country it is just the reverse, in sand like on Fraser, we can find nothing in California, but in the gravel, and the nearer we approach the bed rock, the coarser the gold, and the richer it pays. We found a bar which prospected better than any other in that section, and set in to try our luck. We worked early and late, averaging from $3 to $5 per day. We washed out dirt in rockers, using quick silver, not then being able to save all the gold, it being so fine, much would float off, and some rusty that would not amalgamate. After working there about six weeks our stock of provisions was getting nearly exhausted, and we concluded to pack up and start down stream. I for one was getting tired of living on bread and water alone, for long since the Indians had stolen the coffee. Not any of the miners within fifty miles of us at this time were making grub, at the price of provisions; indeed it was hard to get it at any price, as few had it to spare. The river had fallen quite low, and where we expected, as in California, to find it rich, we could make nothing. Men began to think it a great humbug, and the glowing accounts of Fraser River became gradually pronounced a fiction. The natives there were all so very troublesome, stealing and pointing guns at men was a prominent feature of their character....

I am afraid, Mr. Editor, I have taken up too much space in your columns, and shall conclude by saying I should not advise anyone from P. E. Island to come to Fraser River, with the intention of making his fortune; and I'm quite sure, speaking from experience, nothing will be gained by going for anything else, as the trip is a very expensive and laborious one.

Michigan Bluffs, Placer County, California.

### 2. Charles Major, "News from British Columbia," *The Daily Globe*, January 2, 1860

*Major's life remains unknown. He possibly came from Toronto, location of the* Globe *newspaper, since this article mentions his friends there.*

Fort Hope, Frazer River
Sept. 20th, 1859

Dear Sir: I am afraid you will think I had forgot my promise,—but I wanted to know something about the country before writing to you. In the first place, do not think that I have taken a dislike to the country because I am not making money; the dislike is general all over the country. To give you anything like a correct idea of it would take more paper than I have small change to purchase, and more time than I could spare, and then it would only be commenced.

The country is not what it was represented to be. There is no farming land in British Columbia, as far as I can learn, except a very small portion joining Washington Territory, and on Vancouver's Island, where there is one valley of 20,000 acres; but that cannot be sold until Col. Moody's friends come out from the old country, and get what they want.

It never can be a place, because there is nothing to support it, except the mines, and just as soon as they are done the place goes down completely, for there is absolutely nothing to keep it up; and I tell you the truth the mines are falling off very fast. There is nothing in this country but mines—and very small pay for that; they are you may say, used up. We have been making two, three and four dollars per day, but it would not last more than two or three days; and so you would spend that before you would find more. There has been great excitement about Fort Alexander, three hundred miles above this, and also about Queen Charlotte's Island. They have both turned out another humbug like this place. A party arrived here yesterday from Alexander, and they are a pitiful looking lot. They are what the Yankees call dead broke. They have been six hundred miles up the river. When they got down here they had no shoes to their feet. Some had pieces of shirt and trowsers, but even these were pinned together with small sharp sticks; and some had the rim of an old hat, and some the crown. They had nothing to eat for one week, and not one cent in money. This is gold mining for you!

I expect the Frazer River fever has cooled down by this time, at least I hope so; for I do pity the poor wretches that come out here to beg. They can do that at home; as for making money, that is out of the question. Since we came here (to use the miners' term) we have been making grub; and those who can do that, think they are doing well. If there are any making arrangements to come to this place, let them take a fool's advice and stay at home. I would just about as soon hear that anyone belonging to me was dead, as to hear they had started to come here. They say it wants a man with capital to make money here; but a man with money in Canada will double it quicker than he will here. And if I, or any other, was to work as hard and live as meanly, I could make more money in Canada than I can here. Since we have been on the River we have worked from half-past two and three o'clock in the morning till nine and ten o'clock at night (you can see the sun twenty hours out of the twenty-four in the summer season) and lived on beans! If that is not working, I don't know what it is. Besides this you go home to your shanty at night, tired and wet, and have to cook your beans before you can eat them. And what is this all for? For gold of course; but when you wash up at night, you may realize 50 cents, perhaps $1.

There have been some rich spots struck on this river, but they were very scarce, and they are all worked out; and the miners are leaving the river every day, satisfied there is nothing to be made. But now that I am in the country I will remain for a year or so, and if nothing better turns up by that time, I think I will be perfectly satisfied. I have met with some that I was acquainted with, and it is amusing to see those who felt themselves a little better than their neighbors at home, come here and get out of money, and have to take the pick and shovel, perhaps to drag firewood out of the woods and sell it, or make pack-mules of themselves to get a living. I do not mean to say that it is so all over the Colony, but it is from one end of Frazer River to the other. I dare anyone to contradict what I say; and I have good reason to believe it is as bad all over the country.

I saw a patch of oats here the other day. They were out in head, only four inches in height, yellow as ochre, and not thick enough on the ground to be neighbours. Vegetables and other things are as poor in the proportion; and as for the climate, it is just as changeable as in Canada, if not more so. I can't say much about the climate on Vancouver's Island, but I think it is rather better.

I met T.G., the carpenter, from Sarnia, who left there about a year ago. He went round the Horn, and he was ten months and fifteen days in coming here. He is cutting saw logs making a little over grub. He says he is going to write to the Sarnia Observer, and give this place a cutting up! There are a great many Canadians here, and they would be glad to work for their board. A man could not hire out to work a day if he was starving. I have seen some parties from California; they say times are very hard there. There are just three in our party now, H.H., J.R., and myself. There were two of the H's; one was taken sick and had to leave the river; he is in Victoria, and is quite recovered again; has been there two months, and has not got a day's work yet. I was very sick myself when I just came here, but am quite healthy now, and so fat I can hardly see to write. The rest are quite well.

The Indians are not very troublesome at the mines; they are kept down pretty well. They are very numerous here and on the Island, the lowest degraded set of creatures I ever saw.

It is estimated that the number of miners who make over wages, is one in five hundred; and the number that do well in the mines is one in a thousand. So you see it is a very small proportion. If you know anyone that wants to spend money, why, this is just the place. Anyone bringing a family here would require a small fortune to support them in this horrible place, hemmed in by mountains on all sides, and these covered with snow all the year.

I have lived in a tent since I came up the river, and I have to lie on the ground before the fire and write; it gives a very poor light, so excuse the writing. It has been raining here steady one week, and the mountains are all covered with snow; for when it rains here it is snowing upon the mountains. It is a wild looking place. You will please tell our folks you hear from me, and that we are all well. I will write to some of them in about two weeks or so. I have wrote five letters already, but I have not heard from any of them; so many letters go astray in coming here and going from this place, that perhaps they do not get them at all. Give my respects to old friends, and tell them to be contented and stay at home.

### 3. Matthew MacFie, *Vancouver Island and British Columbia*, 1865

*Matthew MacFie (dates unknown) had sufficient sense to stay out of the gold fields. He offered a broader, less jaundiced, and more nuanced perspective of British Columbia's frontier in his 1865 book. A Congregationalist minister who arrived in Victoria in 1859 and preached there until he was recalled to Britain in 1864 to assist Congregationalist fundraising, MacFie generated considerable controversy by supporting the segregation of Black and White worshippers.*

... Between March and June, in 1858, ocean steamers from California, crowded with gold-seekers, arrived every two or three days at Victoria. This place, previously a quiet hamlet, containing two or three hundred inhabitants, whose shipping had been chiefly confined to Indian canoes and the annual visit of the company's trading ship from England, was suddenly converted into a scene of bustle and excitement. In the brief space of four months 20,000 souls poured into the harbour. The easy-going primitive settlers were naturally confounded by this inundation of adventurers.

Individuals of every trade and profession in San Francisco and several parts of Oregon, urged by the insatiable *auri sacra fames*, threw up their employments, in many cases sold their property at an immense sacrifice, and repaired to the new Dorado. This motley throng included, too, gamblers, "loafers," thieves, and ruffians, with not a few of a higher moral grade. The rich came to speculate, and the poor in the hope of quickly becoming rich. Every sort of property in California fell to a degree that threatened the ruin of the State. The limited stock of provisions in Victoria was speedily exhausted. Flour, which on the American side sold at £2 8s. per barrel, fetched in Vancouver Island £6 per barrel. Twice the bakers were short of bread, which had to be replaced with ship biscuit and soda crackers. Innumerable tents covered the ground in and around Victoria far as the eye could reach. The sound of hammer and axe was heard in every direction. Shops, stores, and "shanties," to the number of 225, arose in six weeks.

Speculation in town lots attained a pitch of unparalleled extravagance. The land-office was besieged, often before four o'clock in the morning, by the multitude eager to buy town property. The purchaser, on depositing the price, had his name put on a list, and his application was attended to in the order of priority, no one being allowed to purchase more than six lots. The demand so increased, however, that sales were obliged to be suspended in order to allow the surveyor time to measure the appointed divisions of land beforehand....

The bulk of the heterogeneous immigration consisting of American citizens, it was not wonderful that they should attempt to found commercial depots for the mining locality in their own territory. Consequently, they congregated in large numbers at Port Townsend, near the entrance to Puget Sound and at Whatcom in succession. Streets were laid out, houses built, and lots sold in those places. But inconveniences of various kinds hindered their success. Semiahmo, near the mouth of Fraser River, was next tried as the site of a port; but this rival city never had existence except on paper. These foreign inventors of cities obstinately refused to acknowledge the superior natural advantages of Victoria compared with the experimental ports they had projected. It is not speculators in new towns, however, but merchants and shippers that determine the points at which trade shall centre; and it is only that harbour which combines the greatest facilities for commerce, with the fewest risks to vessels, which is patronised by them. Victoria, judged by these tests, was found most eligible of all the competing places of anchorage in the neighbourhood....

While the majority—comprising Jews, French cooks, brokers, and hangers-on at auctions—stayed in Victoria for the purpose of ingloriously improving their fortunes, by watching the rise and fall of the real-estate market, several thousands, undismayed by dangers and hardships incident to crossing the gulf and ascending the river, proceeded to the source of the gold. When steamers or sailing-vessels could not be had, canoes were equipped by miners to convey them to British Columbia; but this frail means of transit, unequal to the risks of the passage, sometimes occasioned loss of life.

A monthly licence had to be taken out by all bound for the mines, and this gave them the right to take whatever provisions were required for individual use. At the outset steamers on the river allowed miners 200 lbs. and subsequently 100 lbs. free of charge; but they preferred in general to join in the purchase of canoes for sailing up the river as well as across the gulf.

The country drained by the Fraser resembles mountainous European countries in the same latitude, where streams begin to swell in June and do not reach their lowest ebb till winter. Those, therefore, who happened to enter the mining region in March or April, when the water was very low, succeeded in extracting large quantities of gold from the "bars" or "benches" not covered with water. The mass of immigrants not having arrived till a month or two later, found the auriferous parts under water. Ignorant of the periodic increase and fall of the stream to which I have adverted, their patience was soon exhausted waiting for the uncovering of the banks. Not a few, crestfallen and disappointed, returned to Victoria.

A gloomy impression began to prevail among the less venturesome spirits that tarried in this scene of morbid speculation. Gold not coming down fast enough to satisfy their wishes, thousands of them lost heart and went back to San Francisco, heaping execrations upon the country and everything else that was English; and lacing the reported existence of gold in the same category with the South Sea bubble. The rumour took wing that the river never did fall; and as placer-mining could only be carried on rivers, the state of the river became the barometer of public hopes, and the pivot on which everybody's expectations turned. This preposterous idea spread, was readily caught up by the press of California, and proved the first check to immigration. Another impediment was the commercial restrictions imposed by the Hudson's Bay Company in virtue of the term of their charter for exclusive trade in the interior not having yet expired.

A few hundred indomitable men, calmly reviewing the unfavourable season in which they had commenced mining operations, and the difficulties unavoidable to locomotion in a country previously untrodden for the most part by white men, resolved to push their way forward, animated by the assurance that they must sooner or later meet the object of their search and labour. Some settled on the bars between Hope and Yale, at the head of navigation; others advanced still higher, running hair-breadth escape, balancing themselves in passing the brink of some dangerous ledge or gaping precipice encumbered with provisions packed on their backs.

A new route was proposed via Douglas, at the head of Harrison Lake and Lilloet, that should avoid the dangers and obstructions of the river trial. But this did not at first mend matters; for the intended road lay through a rugged and densely-wooded country, and much time and money required to be consumed before it could be rendered practicable. Before the line for the Lilloet route was generally known, parties of intrepid miners, anxious to be the first to reap its benefits, tried to force their way through all the difficulties opposed to them. The misery and fatigue endured by them was indescribable. They crept through underwood and thicket for many miles, sometimes on hands and knees, with a bag of flour on the back of each; alternately under and over fallen trees, scrambling up precipices, or sliding down over masses of sharp projecting rock, or wading up to the waist through bogs and swamps. Every day added to their exhaustion; and, worn out with privation and sufferings, one knot of adventurers after another became smaller and smaller, some lagging behind to rest, or turning back in despair. The only thought seemed to be to reach the river ere their provisions should give out. One large party was reduced to three, and when they came to an Indian camp where salmon was to be had, one of these hardy fellows made up his mind to return....

Nor was this case an uncommon one. Gold there was in abundance, but want of access prevented the country from being "prospected"; and reckless men, without stopping to take this into account, condemned the mines and everything connected with them without distinction.

If the commerce of the interior had been thrown open, and private enterprise allowed to compete with the natural difficulties of the country, these would have soon been overcome. Forests would have been opened, provisory bridges thrown over precipices, hollows levelled, and the rush of population following behind, the country would have been rapidly settled, and the trader have brought his provisions to the miner's door.

Affairs in Victoria, meanwhile, grew yet more dismal. The "rowdy" element that had assembled in the city, finding no legitimate occupation to employ their idle hands, were under strong temptation to create such disturbances as they had been accustomed to get up in California. Losing, for the moment, that wholesome dread of British rule which that class usually feel, a party of them rescued a prisoner from the hands of the police, and actually proposed to hoist the American flag over the old Hudson's Bay Company's fort. But the news that a gunboat was on her way from Esquimalt to quell the riot, soon calmed alarm and restored peace.

Large sums of money, sent up from San Francisco for investment, were shipped back again; and whole cargoes of goods, ordered during the heat of the excitement, were thrown upon the hands of merchants. Jobbers had nothing to do but smoke their cigars or play at whist. Some accused the company; others complained of the Government; others sneered at "English fogyism;" and others deplored the want of "American enterprise." "Croaking" was the order of the day.

The Governor, seeing the tide of immigration receding, managed to control his prejudice against the "foreigners" from a neighbouring state, so far as to moderate the severe restrictions he had put upon goods imported to British Columbia, and adopted more active measures in opening trails to the mines. But his tardy decision came too late to be attended with immediate benefit.

At length, however, the river did fall, and the arrival of gold-dust foreshadowed a brighter future. But sailing vessels left daily, crowded with repentant and dejected adventurers, whose opposition to the country had become so inveterate, that they could not now be made to believe in the existence of gold from Fraser River, though proved by the clearest ocular demonstration. The old inhabitants imagined that Victoria was about to return to its former state of insignificance.

Yet it is asserted, on reliable authority, that in proportion to the number of hands engaged upon the mines—notwithstanding the unequalled drawbacks in the way of reaching them—the yield during the first six months was much larger than it had been in the same period and at the same stage of development in California or Australia....

For a few intelligent and persevering men these facts and figures had weight. But amateur miners, romantic speculators, and "whiskey bummers," could not, by the most attractive representations, be detained in the country.... For such scouts of civilisation—had the "castles in the air" which they built not been demolished—would have reenacted in our colonies such scenes of riot and bloodshed as disgraced California nine years previously. It was well that we should get rid of all who wanted impossibilities and indulged exaggerated hopes. The few hardy and enterprising settlers who remained ceased to pursue Will-o'-the-wisps, and composed themselves to the sober realities of life.

In September '59, when I first set foot in Victoria, the process of depopulation was still going on, though it soon after reached its lowest point. A healthy relation between supply and demand in every department was being effected. The tens of thousands that had pressed into the city in '58 were diminished to not more than 1,500, embracing "the waifs and strays" of every nationality, not excepting a good many whose antecedents were not above suspicion.

Apart from the Government buildings, two hotels, and one shop, all the dwellings and houses of business were at that time built of wood. Many stores were closed and shanties empty. There was little business doing, and no great prospect ahead. This stagnant condition continued with but little abatement till the close of 1860, when intimations came of eminently productive mines being discovered at the forks of Quesnelle, which at that time seemed as difficult of access as the Arctic regions. A few scores of miners, arguing from the fineness of the gold dust found near Hope, Yale and the forks of the Thompson, that it was washed down from some quartz formation in the north, penetrated to the spot just referred to. Language fails to describe the trials these men endured from the utter absence of paths of any kind, the severity of winter climate, and often the scant supply of provisions. The theory by which the daring pioneers were guided was remarkably verified, and the toils of many of them were abundantly rewarded.

Their return to Victoria with bags of dust and nuggets rallied the fainting hopes of the community, and they were regarded as walking advertisements that the country was safe. Business immediately improved, the value of town property advanced; some who had been hesitating about erecting permanent buildings caught inspiration and at once plunged into brick-and-mortar investments.

The few scores that had worked on Antler Creek in '60 increased, in the spring of '61, to 1,500. Some addition to our population in the latter year came from California, and every man who could possibly make it convenient to leave Victoria for the season went to the new diggings. Of those who went, one-third made independent fortunes, one-third netted several hundreds of pounds, and one-third, from a variety of causes were unsuccessful....

The chief misfortune connected with the influx of population at this period was that it comprised an excessive proportion of clerks, retired army officers, prodigal sons, and a host of other romantic nondescripts, who indulged visions of sudden wealth obtainable with scarcely more exertion than is usually put forth in a pleasure excursion to the continent of Europe. These trim young fellows exhibited a profusion of leather coats and leggings, assuming a sort of defiant air, the interpretation of which was, "We are the men to show you 'Colonials' how to brave danger and fatigue!" But their pretensions generally evaporated with the breath by which they were expressed, and many that set out with this dare-all aspect were soon thankful to be permitted to break stones, chop wood, serve as stable-boys, or root out tree-stumps. The vague imaginations with which they left home were soon dissipated, when, on the termination of the voyage, they discovered that 500 miles lay between them and Cariboo—a distance which must be passed over muddy roads and frowning precipices, with whatever necessaries might be required for the trip strapped to their shoulders. Hundreds went half way to the mines, and returned in despondency; hundreds more remained in Victoria, and were only saved from starvation by the liberality of more prosperous citizens. A much larger number came than the country, with a deficient supply of roads, was prepared to receive. Still a considerable number made large amounts of money, and the majority of those who have possessed sufficient fortitude to bear inconveniences and battle against discouragements are in a fair way for speedily acquiring a competency....

It was remarked by an intelligent shipmaster, whom I met in Victoria, that he had not found in any of the numerous ports he had visited during a long sea-faring career, so mixed a population as existed in that city. Though containing at present an average of only 5,000 or 6,000 inhabitants, one cannot pass along the principal thoroughfares without meeting representatives of almost every tribe and nationality under heaven. Within a limited space may be seen—of Europeans, Russians, Austrians, Poles, Hungarians, Italians, Danes, Swedes, French, Germans, Spaniards, Swiss, Scotch, English and Irish; of Africans, Negroes from the United States and the West Indies; of Asiatics, Lascars and Chinamen; of Americans, Indians, Mexicans, Chilanos, and citizens of the North American Republic; and of Polynesians, Malays from the Sandwich Islands....

*"A Great Humbug": British Columbia's Gold Rushes*

In description of resources Vancouver Island may resemble the parent country, and thus merit the proud title of "the England of the Pacific." But the peculiar elements composing the nucleus of the population render it physically impossible for that exact form of national character we have been accustomed to ascribe to Great Britain to be perpetuated in the island of the Far West. Does the presence, so largely, of inferior races forbode the fatal tainting of the young nation's blood and signal its premature decay, or will the vitality of the governing race triumph over the contamination with which more primitive types threaten to impregnate it? This is the important enquiry that engrosses the attention of ethnological speculators in the nascent communities of the North Pacific....

It is maintained also, that while by intermarrying with descendants of Europeans we are but reproducing our own Caucasian type, by commingling with eastern Asiatics we are creating debased hybrids; that the primary law of nature teaches self-preservation; and that such protective enactments as have been referred to are essential to the perpetuation and advancement of the nation.

Happily both these coloured races are admitted to the enjoyment of civil privileges in these colonies upon terms of perfect equality with white foreigners, and are alike eligible for naturalisation. Yet even on the British side of the boundary there is a disposition to look coldly upon the immigration of Celestials. It is alleged that so large an amount of Chinese labour must have the effect of reducing the price of white labour. But such an opinion is without foundation; for those Chinamen, who arrive without capital, are only capable of engaging in menial employments, such as cooking, hawking tea, and keeping laundries. It is but few skilled labourers, I presume, that would desire to compete with them in these callings. Nor can their presence at the mines at all interfere with the enterprises of the superior race; for it is well known that they are unable to resort to those mechanical appliances requisite in the working of rich diggings; that they always keep at a respectful distance from the whites, and are content with such small returns as may be yielded by abandoned "claims," from which the whites have already taken the cream.

As to the fear that, if access to the country were not made strait for them, they might ultimately overrun and devastate it like a plague of locusts, nothing could be more groundless. No people have a more intelligent acquaintance with "the law of supply and demand." They are generally under the direction of shrewd merchants among their own countrymen, who never encourage the poorer classes to leave China without being certain that a fair prospect of occupation exists for them in the parts to which they are imported; and in this respect the judgment of those leading Chinamen is rarely at fault. It must be acknowledged to their credit that in California, British Columbia, and Vancouver Island, an unemployed Chinaman is seldom to be met with, and a more industrious and law-abiding class does not reside in these dependencies. In their social and domestic habits, however, I frankly admit there is room for much improvement as far as cleanliness is concerned.

It is natural that a race so exclusive and so much avoided by their white fellow-citizens on the coast, should give preference to the manufactures of their own country. Much of the clothing they wear and many of their articles of food come from China. They contrive, it is true, to spend as little of their earnings as possible on their adopted soil—most of the money made by the humbler classes among them being remitted home for the laudable object of contributing to the support of needy relatives. But it is a mistake to regard the trade done and the capital acquired by them as so much wealth diverted from the channels of white industry, since but for their presence in the country the greater part of that trade would not have been created; nor would that capital have been accumulated. They cannot prevent commercial advantage accruing to the colonies from their influence, if they would. It is often British bottoms that convey them from China, and they are obliged to buy hardware, waterproof boots, and pork from us. Poultry, too, being esteemed a great luxury, is in great demand among them. When they have lived among the civilised for a time, it not unfrequently happens that they adopt the European and American costume entire....

The Chinese of Vancouver Island and British Columbia, only numbering at present about 2,000, have not yet attempted the erection of any places of devotion. But when attracted in greater force, the pious among them, according to the Buddhist standard, may be expected to erect fanes in which to celebrate traditional rites....

Whether, therefore, we consider the antiquity of these Mongols, their natural ingenuity, or the encouragement afforded by their national institutions to talent, integrity, and industry, the most cogent reasons exist for our extending to them a cordial welcome. Let the colonists show the fruits of a superior civilisation and religion, not in ridiculing and despising these Pagan strangers, but in treating them with the gentle forbearance due to a less favoured portion of the family of mankind, and they will continue to be useful and inoffensive members of society. The prejudice which characterises race or colour as a disqualification for the exercise of civil rights reflects dishonour upon the civilised community that indulges it.

The descendants of the African race resident in the colonies are entitled to some notice. About 300 of them inhabit Victoria, and upwards of 100 are scattered throughout the farming settlements of the island and British Columbia.

The chief part came to the country some time previous to the immigration of '58, driven from California by social taboo and civil disabilities. They invested the sums they brought with them in land, and by the sudden advance in the value of real estate which followed the influx of gold seekers, most of them immediately found themselves possessed of a competency. It was not surprising, under these circumstances, that some, formerly habituated to servitude or reproached as representatives of a barbarous race, should, on being delivered from the yoke of social oppression, fail to show much consideration for the indurated prejudices of the whites, most of whom at that period were either Americans or British subjects, who sympathised with the ideas prevailing in the United States respecting the social status of the coloured people.

Whereas they had been restricted in California to worship Almighty God in their own churches or in a part of those frequented by whites, designed for the exclusive accommodation of persons of colour, they were permitted on coming to Vancouver Island free range of unoccupied pews, in the only church then erected in the colony. The church-going immigrants in the mass wafted to our shores in '58 were at once brought into a proximity with coloured worshippers which was repugnant to past associations. It is difficult to analyse this social prejudice between the races, and impossible to defend it. But I have been astonished to observe its manifestations in Christian gentlemen whose intelligence and general consistency were exemplary. The negro supporters of the church, regarding themselves as the "old families" of the country and the monied aristocracy, and wincing under the recollection of social wrongs endured by them under the American flag, were not disposed to give way in the slightest to the whims and scruples of the whites. Many of the latter remonstrated with the clergyman against allowing the congregation to assume a speckled appearance—a spectacle deemed by them novel and inconvenient. They insisted that they were prepared to treat the "blacks" with the utmost humanity and respect, in their own place; but that the Creator had made a distinction which it was sinful to ignore, that the promiscuous arrangement might lead to the sexes in both races falling in love with each other, entering into marriage, and thus occasioning the deterioration of the whites without the elevation of the negroes being effected. The worthy parson, being direct from the parent country, and till then wholly inexperienced in the social relations of the conflicting races, felt at liberty to take only philanthropic and religious ground in dealing with the question. He maintained that the stains of men's sin, in common, were so dark, that mere difference in colour was an affair of supreme insignificance before the Almighty, in comparison, and that the separation desired by the whites was of carnal suggestion, which Christianity demanded should be repressed. He is said even to have gone so deeply into the subject in a particular sermon as to assert that the disposition of nerves, tendons, and arteries, and the essential faculties of the soul were alike in white and black—the sole distinction between them consisting of colouring matter under the skin, the projection of the lower jaw, and the wool by which the scalp was covered....

The same prejudice of race continues, unfortunately, to interfere with harmony in social gatherings for the purposes of amusement. More than once has the presence of coloured persons in the pit of the theatre occasioned scenes of violence and bloodshed, followed by litigation. When, a few years since, a literary institute was attempted to be formed, and the signatures of one or two respectable negroes appeared in the list of subscribers, the movement came to an untimely close. A white member of a temperance society, which was eminently useful in the community, proposed the name of a coloured man for admission, intentionally avoiding to disclose at the time any information as to his race, and when it was discovered that the society had been beguiled, ignorantly, into accepting a negro as a brother teetotaller, it broke up.

There is nothing in the constitution of the colony to exclude a British born negro from the municipal council or the legislature, and yet, however well qualified he might be by talent and education for the honour, his election could not be carried in the present state of public feeling. The negroes are perfectly justified in claiming those civil rights which British law confers upon them, and they are resolved not to desist struggling till these are fully achieved.

Having by commendable zeal succeeded in organising a rifle corps and a brass band, they expressed a wish to appear in uniform, on occasion of a public procession formed to escort the present Governor to his residence on landing in the colony. But the prejudice of the whites ruled it otherwise. When they sought an opportunity of showing esteem for the retiring Governor at a banquet given to that gentleman, admission was refused them. When the "common-school" system is introduced, in which the families of both races are equally entitled to participate, I foresee that storms will arise.

Many of this people in the country are necessarily endowed with very limited intelligence, while some are well-informed, and eloquent in speech. But, as a race, they compare favourably with whites of corresponding social position, in industry and uprightness....

Let it not be supposed, however, that our female society is entirely composed of this or of any other class that is doubtful. It must be confessed, that there are too many females in both colonies as everywhere else, that reflect as little credit upon the land of their adoption as they did on the land of their birth. Still, we have among us ladies of birth and education, and, what is yet more important, of moral qualities that would render them an ornament to their sex in any part of the world.

Refugees from bankruptcy, disgrace, or family strife, suffered in some other part of the world, are to be met with in Victoria every few yards. But among the unfortunate are some of the most estimable men I have ever seen.

The tone of society has become decidedly more British since 1859; but still, as then, the American element prevails. Citizens of the United States may easily be known by their spare, erect, and manly figure. The business men among them are, for the most part, attired in superfine cloth, most frequently of a dark colour, and highheeled, broad-toed boots, of admirable fit. The coloured shooting-jacket, so frequently worn by Englishmen in the colony during the week, has no attraction for Americans.

For ethereal beauty, handsomeness, liveliness, and general intelligence, American ladies must be allowed to be eminently distinguished. That high refinement, which can only result from breeding and education, and is to be found in the foremost rank of British society, is without parallel among Americans. But it is my impression that the average of educated American ladies cannot be equalled, in interesting expression of countenance and brightness of intellect, by English ladies of the middle-class generally. The charming sweetness of the American beauty, however, fades prematurely, and at the age of 30, when a well-developed English lady is but in her prime, the smooth visage and transparent complexion of our fair cousin have been for years invaded by wrinkles.

Americans appear to me defective in conversational power. However rapid and distinct their speech may be, the diction employed by them is so stilted, and their forms of expression are so elaborate, as to contrast unfavourably with the terse idiomatic phraseology used by those Englishmen who are competent to wield their own language....

The intense pitch to which the feelings of people are strung in a gold-producing country is a frequent cause of insanity. Whether that malady exist in a greater degree in this community than in one of a more settled description, I am not sufficiently versed in the statistics of the subject to aver. But certainly a much larger proportion of cases have been personally known to me here than in the same period I ever saw in the much denser populations of England. I can reckon up eight persons—all of whom I have been on speaking terms with, and most of whom I knew intimately, who, in four years and a half, have become lunatics, and as such are either living or dead....

Society in the interior is very depraved. In Yale, Douglas, Lytton, Lilloet, Forks of Quesnelle, and the mining towns, little trace of Sunday is at present visible, except in the resort of miners on that day to market for provisions, washing of dirty clothes, repairing machinery, gambling, and dissipation. Out of the 5,000 souls in Victoria, a few may be found who respect the ordinances of religion. But at the mines, adherents of religious bodies have hitherto been numbered by scores and units.

Up to the present there have been but two places of worship in Cariboo—one connected with the Church of England, and the other with the Wesleyan Methodists. Till the fall of 1863, when these were built, the services of public worship were conducted in a bar-room and billiard-saloon. At one end of the apartment was the clergyman, with his small congregation, and at the other were desperadoes, collected unblushingly around the faro or pokah table, staking the earnings of the preceding week.

Profane language is almost universal, and is employed with diabolical ingenuity. The names of "Jesus Christ" and the "Almighty" are introduced in most blasphemous connections. Going to church is known among many as "the religious dodge," which is said to be "played out," or, in other words, a superstition which has ceased to have any interest for enlightened members of society....

In a country where so many are governed by impulse, and rendered desperate by losses sustained in speculation, it is not surprising that instances of highway robbery and murder should occasionally happen. The commission of these crimes, however, as in California and Australia, has been hitherto confined to solitary intervals, between the towns of British Columbia, on the way to the mines. The proportion of crime, at present, is decidedly small, considering the character and number of the population....

#### FURTHER READINGS

Bescoby, I. "Society in Cariboo During the Gold Rush." In *Sa Ts'E: Historical Perspectives on Northern British Columbia*, ed. T. Thorner. Prince George: College of New Caledonia Press, 1989.

Careless, J. "The Business Community in the Early Development of Victoria, British Columbia." In *Canadian Business History: Selected Studies, 1497–1971*, ed. D. Macmillan. Toronto: McClelland and Stewart, 1972.

Careless, J. "The Lowe Brothers, 1852-70: A Study in Business Relations on the North Pacific Coast." In *British Columbia: Historical Readings*, ed. W. Ward and R. McDonald. Vancouver: Douglas and McIntyre, 1981.

Clark, S. "Mining Society in British Columbia and the Yukon." In *British Columbia: Historical Readings*, ed. W. Ward and R. McDonald. Vancouver: Douglas and McIntyre, 1981.

Fetherling, D. *The Gold Crusades: A Social History of Gold Rushes, 1849-1929.* Toronto: Macmillan, 1988.

Fisher, R. *Contact and Conflict: Indian European Relations in British Columbia, 1774-1890.* 2nd ed. Vancouver: University of British Columbia Press, 1992.

Gough, B. "The Character of the British Columbia Frontier." *BC Studies* 32 (1976-77): 28-40.

Gough, B. *Gunboat Frontier: British Maritime Authority and the Northwest Coast Indians, 1846-1890.* Vancouver: University of British Columbia Press, 1984.

Gresko, J. "'Roughing It in the Bush' in British Columbia: Mary Moody's Pioneer Life in New Westminster, 1859-1863." In *British Columbia Reconsidered: Essays on Women*, ed. G. Creese and V. Strong-Boag. Vancouver: Press Gang, 1992.

Harris, R. *The Resettlement of British Columbia: Essays on Colonialism and Geographical Change.* Vancouver: University of British Columbia Press, 1997.

Karr, C. "James Douglas: The Gold Governor in the Context of His Times." In *The Company on the Coast*, ed. B. Norcross. Nanaimo: Nanaimo Historical Society, 1983.

Loo, T. *Making Law, Order and Authority in British Columbia 1821-1871.* Toronto: University of Toronto Press, 1994.

Mackie, R. "The Colonization of Vancouver Island, 1849-1858." *BC Studies* 96 (1992-93): 3-40.

Marshall, D. "Rickard Revisited: Native 'Participation' in the Gold Discoveries of British Columbia." *Native Studies Review* 11, 1 (1996): 91-108.

Perry, A. *On the Edge of Empire: Gender, Race and the Making of British Columbia, 1849-1871.* Toronto: University of Toronto Press, 2001.

Roy, P. *A White Man's Province: British Columbia Politicians and Chinese and Japanese Immigrants 1858-1914.* Vancouver: University of British Columbia Press, 1989.

Sterne, N. Fraser. *Gold 1858! The Founding of British Columbia.* Pullman: Washington State University Press, 1998.

Ward, P. *White Canada Forever: Popular Attitudes and Public Policy Toward Orientals in British Columbia.* 2nd ed. Montreal and Kingston: McGill-Queen's University Press, 1990.

Williams, D. "The Administration of Criminal and Civil Justice in the Mining Camps and Frontier Communities of British Columbia." In *Law and Justice in a New Land: Essays in Western Canadian Legal History*, ed. L. Knafla. Toronto: Carswell, 1986.

Williams, D. *"The Man for a New Country": Sir Matthew Baillie Begbie.* Sidney: Gray Publisher, 1977.

Woodward, F. "The Influence of the Royal Engineers on the Development of British Columbia." *BC Studies* 24 (Winter 1974-1975): 3-51.

Van Kirk, S. "A Vital Presence: Women in the Cariboo Gold Rush, 1862-1875." In *British Columbia Reconsidered: Essays on Women*, ed. G. Creese and V. Strong-Boag. Vancouver: Press Gang, 1992.

# CHAPTER 14

# "The Sweet Zephyrs of British Land"

## THE BLACK EXPERIENCE

### INTRODUCTION

Canadians typically pride themselves with being more tolerant and inclusive of visible minorities and cultures than most anyone else, particularly Americans. How often, for example, do we smugly compare our cultural "mosaic" to their "melting pot." Today, government-sanctioned multiculturalism encourages the celebration of diversity and we worry about any suggestions of racism within the social fabric. Canadians indeed have much to be proud of. The historical record, however, suggests that our patronizing sense of superiority may be a bit optimistic, that our perception is perhaps more mythological than real, or at least that reality is more nuanced than we like to admit. The Black experience in British North America in the pre-Confederation era ably illustrates this point.

Many people considered slavery both natural and vital, and abolitionist sentiments only slowly gained momentum in Britain toward the end of the eighteenth century, and not without considerable controversy. Pro-slavery advocates contended that Blacks were inherently inferior and incapable of either handling freedom or of integrating into society. Anti-abolitionists scoffed at this, arguing that a slave's shortcomings sprang from bondage.

Interestingly, Canada was remarkably progressive about slavery and became the vanguard for abolition. Not surprisingly, therefore, racial-based prejudice was muted there compared to the situation in the United States. Going a step further in 1793, John Graves Simcoe, the governor of the new colony of Upper Canada, convinced the Assembly to outlaw importation of slaves and provide for the gradual emancipation of those already in bondage. This was not abolition, but it was a significant step towards it.

There was a Black presence in Canada almost from the beginning of European settlement, though their number amounted to a small number of domestic slaves owned by wealthy French Canadians. This was very different from the New England colonies to the south where thousands of slaves constituted a large percentage of the population and formed an integral part of the agricultural economy.

The first significant group of Blacks arrived in the British North American Maritimes, primarily in Nova Scotia, in the late 1770s and early 1780s as Loyalists fleeing the American War of Independence. In a bid to curtail the revolution, Britain promised freedom to any slave who revolted against his American pro-revolutionary master. Many accepted the offer and not only ran but assisted British military forces during the conflict. They backed the losing side, however, and had to flee north to Canada.

The second major influx of Blacks arrived in Upper Canada as a result of the War of 1812 and changing conditions in the northern United States. Free Blacks and runaway slaves settled in northern American states in relatively large numbers after independence, particularly in urban centres. Integration proceeded reasonably peaceably. In the 1820s the United States experienced economic setbacks, waves of new European immigrants, and a commensurate scramble for diminishing jobs. Blacks lost the contest due to a series of new regulations that increasingly marginalized and persecuted them. Anti-Black riots, violence, and harassment became common in many northern American cities. This new reality culminated in the federal Fugitive Slave Law of 1850, which allowed southern slave owners to track down runaway slaves living in northern slave-free states. Slave hunting became a lucrative business, and many ex-slaves, some with years of liberty, found themselves kidnapped back to southern slavery.

Slavery remained legal in Britain, and thus in British North America, until the 1833 Emancipation Bill formally abolished it and codified the notion that "every man is free who reaches British soil." This bill, plus the implications of the Fugitive Slave Law in the United States, encouraged many Blacks to flee to Canada, which guaranteed their freedom. Southern American slave owners obviously resented this, particularly in the face of a steady flow of slaves escaping via the "underground railway" to safety in Canada. They pressured the American federal government to create an extradition treaty with Canada, but British administrators concluded that slavery was inconsistent with British law and demurred. Virtually no slave who reached Canada faced deportation.

Canada, and particularly Upper Canada, gained mythological status among slaves, as exemplified by abolitionist George W. Clark's song "The Free Slave":

*I'm on my way to Canada*
*That cold and distant land*
*The dire effects of slavery*
*I can no longer stand—*
*Farewell, old master,*
*Don't come after me.*
*I'm on my way to Canada*
*Where coloured men are free.*

And the myth was at least partially true. Runaway slaves and free Blacks arriving in Upper Canada indeed received generous support from a network of Black and White abolitionists, including material assistance and welcome into the community. Courts in most instances acted impartially, even prosecuting those harassing the newcomers. Many Blacks found themselves invited to local churches and their children attended publicly funded schools without colour bars.

All was not well, however. Though Upper Canadian law was colourblind, local citizens often were not. This was insidious. Racism tended to be covert, not overt, and thus beyond the impartiality of the legal system. Many Upper Canadian Whites feared the Black presence and reacted by ostracizing Black newcomers—which was perfectly legal and considered normal behaviour. Many did not wish their children educated with Blacks, arguing that proximity begged trouble, especially considering salacious rumours of Black sexual promiscuity and allure. In some regions parents successfully lobbied for legislation to create separate schools for Black children. Churchgoers in other areas called for distinct churches for Blacks or at least segregated pews. Public snubbing remained a visible indicator that, the law aside, many Whites in Canada did not consider the newcomers as equal at all. The hundreds of minor racial slurs cumulatively made life unpleasant and difficult, and gave rise to the notion of Canadians as "politely racist"—a far cry from the myth.

The Black community was itself divided on how best to cope in the new land or at least what to do next. Integrationists believed that Blacks must abandon their distinct cultural attributes and weave completely into mainstream society if they were to become real partners in the Canadian fabric. Black segregationists, on the other hand, contended that Black salvation lay in distancing the community from White society by creating separate settlement lands, churches, schools, and other social institutions. They, as a group, supported White bids for separate schools. A third Black group argued that Canada should be a mere transit point *en route* to Sierra Leone or Liberia, two new states bought in West

Africa with philanthropic abolitionist money. Haiti, the first independent Black nation in the Americas, beckoned, as did Jamaica. All four destinations, but particularly the two in Africa, attracted considerable numbers of disillusioned immigrants.

Blacks in Canada never amounted to more than one per cent of the population, but there were areas where concentrations rose to as high as one-third. In all, some 62,000 Blacks called British North America home, two-thirds of whom settled in what is today southern Ontario. Approximately two-thirds of the Black population arrived in the decades after the 1830s, but many newcomers saw Canada as a temporary sanctuary rather than "home" and pined for the day they could safely return to the United States. This occurred after the Emancipation Proclamation in 1863, by which the United States made slavery illegal. Canada experienced a large exodus of Blacks who returned to their native land. Canada West (Ontario), for example, saw its Black population decline from a peak of 40,000 in 1859 to some 15,000 by 1871.

### DISCUSSION POINTS

1. To what degree, if any, can Canada boast about its tolerance for ethnic diversity? Were Canadians actually less racist than Americans?

2. What were the greatest obstacles that Blacks faced within Canada?

3. What was worse, covert or overt racism?

DOCUMENTS

## 1. Jehu Jones, "To Charles Ray," August 8, 1839

*Jehu Jones Jr. (1786–1852) was born to free parents in South Carolina. He moved to New York in the 1820s and studied theology. Ordained in 1832 as the first Black Lutheran pastor in the United States, he sought missionary work in the African ex-slave country Liberia but failed to obtain the necessary funding. Unable to obtain a pastorate and dogged by financial troubles and racial prejudice, he left for Canada. Jones arrived in Toronto in 1839 and stayed three years before returning to the United States where he spent his remaining years as a cobbler and missionary.*

Toronto, U[pper] C[anada]

My dear sir:

... I returned to my lodgings to contemplate on the magnanimity of the British nation, who under God, have given liberty to all her slaves. So, sir, you can readily perceive, that since first I inhaled the sweet zephyrs of British land, that it has made deep Impressions upon my heart, not easily to be forgotten—having been introduced to his honor the Mayor, who received and welcomed me in the most cordial, and friendly manner; I visited the city, public buildings, barracks, and the soldiers....

There is a regiment composed entirely of colored men—the commissioned officers are white. I have seen several of the members in this city—the corps are stationed on the Frontier. Great confidence is reposed in this regiment, and they have the most important post, in consequence of their acknowledged loyalty to the British Crown. When I reflect upon the known and acknowledged advantages to be derived by colored men, emigrating into the British provinces, where all distinction of caste is despised, and man known by his merits and loyalty to the Queen and country, I cannot but enquire how is it, that my brethren of the Northern States, who have the advantages of coming over, to examine the province for themselves, and to scrutinize the state of society, and report the result of their investigation in this matter have neglected to do so, it appears that our attention has never been properly directed or we have failed to accomplish any good end, can we always remain in a country, where prejudice against our complexion— which God and nature gave us—operates with violent and unholy hands upon us, to frown—wither and crush us for ever—even the prospects of comfortable living in security of the person and property of colored men are doubtful, and although there are no positive legislative enactments in the professedly free States, to deny us the privileges of advancing in knowledge and understanding of mechanical business and trades; still the blighting influence of prejudice, is so extraordinarily great, that it triumphs over every attempt as yet that has been made to give correct instructions to colored youths, in various & useful branches of mechanicism. I must confess and acknowledge it is passing strange, that there should be so many intelligent and some learned men, residing in the Northern States, that are in possession of ample wealth for any good purpose—still as if infatuated, remain there deprived of every political and of many moral and religious liberties; whilst the kingdom of Great Britain is open to all men where life, liberty, and the pursuits of happiness, without dissimulation, is distributed with an equal hand, to all men, regardless of the country or condition of any. This province especially, seems to invite colored men to settle down among the people, and enjoy equal laws. Here you need not separate into disgusting sect of caste. But once your elastic feet presses the provincial soil of her Britannic Majesty, Queen Victoria, God bless her, you become a man, every American disability falls at your feet—society— the prospects of society, holds out many inducements to men of capital; here we can mingle in the mass of society, without feeling of inferiority; here every social and domestic comforts can be enjoyed irrespective of complexion. Tell my young countrymen this subject requires their most profound consideration—the subject of being in reality free men....

### 2. Mary Ann Shadd Cary, *A Plea for Emigration*, 1852

*Mary Ann Shadd (1823-93) was a staunch integrationist born in Delaware to prosperous free parents active in the abolitionist movement. After receiving an excellent education, she spent 12 years teaching and began a life-long examination of the economics of racism. Shadd moved to Canada in 1851 to assist slaves fleeing the Fugitive Slave Laws. There she joined the weekly* Provincial Freeman, *a Black-oriented magazine, and rose to become the first Black editor in North America. She moved to the United States after the Civil War where she taught and worked for the suffrage movement and for Black self-sufficiency.*

In Canada, as in other recently settled countries, there is much to do, and comparatively few for the work. The numerous towns and villages springing up, and the great demand for timber and agricultural products, make labour of every kind plentiful. All trades that are practised in the United States are there patronized by whomsoever carries on: no man's complexion affecting his business.

If a coloured man understands his business, he receives the public patronage the same as a white man. He is not obliged to work a little better, and at a lower rate. There is no degraded class to identify him with, therefore every man's work stands or falls according to merit, not as is his colour. Builders and other tradesmen of different complexions work together on the same building and in the same shop, with perfect harmony, and often the proprietor of an establishment is coloured, and the majority of all of the men employed are white....

In the large towns and cities, as in similar communities in other Christian countries, the means for religious instruction are ample. There are costly churches in which all classes and complexions worship, and no "negro pew," or other seat for coloured persons, especially. I was forcibly struck, when at Toronto, with the contrast the religious community there presented, to our own large body of American Christians. In the churches, originally built by the white Canadians, the presence of coloured persons, promiscuously seated, elicited no comment whatever. They are members, and visitors, and as such have their pews according to their inclination, near the door, or remote, or central, as best suits them. The number of coloured persons attending the churches with whites constitutes a minority, I think. They have their "own churches."

That that is the feature in their policy, which is productive of mischief to the entire body, is evident enough; and the opinion of the best informed and most influential among them, in Toronto and the large towns, is decided and universal. I have heard men of many years residence, and who have, in a measure, been moulded by the better sentiment of society, express deep sorrow at the course of coloured persons, in pertinaciously refusing overtures of religious fellowship from the whites; and in the face of all experience to the contrary, erecting Coloured Methodist, and Baptist, and other Churches. This opinion obtains amongst many who, when in the United States, were connected with coloured churches. Aside from their caste character, their influence on the coloured people is fatal. The character of the exclusive church in Canada tends to perpetuate ignorance, both of their true position as British subjects, and of the Christian religion in its purity....

The refugees express a strong desire for intellectual culture, and persons often begin their education at a time of life when many in other countries think they are too old. There are no separate schools. At Toronto and in many other places, as in the churches, the coloured people avail themselves of existing schools; but in the western country, in some sections, there is a tendency to "exclusiveness." The coloured people of that section petitioned, when the School Law was under revision, that they might have separate schools. There were counter-petitions by those opposed, and to satisfy all parties, twelve freeholders among them, can, by following a prescribed form, demand a school for their children; but if other schools, under patronage of Government, exist, (as Catholic or Protestant), they can demand admission into them, if they have not one. They are not compelled to have a coloured school....

Much has been said of the Canadian coloured settlements, and fears have been expressed by many that by encouraging exclusive settlements, the attempt to identify coloured men with degraded men of like colour in the States would result, and as a consequence, estrangement, suspicion, and distrust would be induced. Such would inevitably be the result, and will be, shall they determine to have entirely proscriptive settlements. Those in existence, so far as I have been able to get at facts, do not exclude whites from their vicinity; but that settlements may not be established of that character, is not so certain.

Dawn, on the Sydenham River, Elgin, or King's Settlement, as it is called, situated about ten miles from Chatham, are settlements in which there are regulations in regard to morals and the purchase of lands bearing only on the coloured people; but whites are not excluded because of dislike. When purchase was made of the lands, many white families were residents; at least, locations were not selected in which none resided. At first, a few sold out, fearing that such neighbours might not be agreeable; others, and they the majority, concluded to remain, and the result attests their superior judgement. Instead of an increase of vice, prejudice, improvidence, laziness, or a lack of energy, that many feared would characterize them, the infrequency of violations of law among so many, is unprecedented. Due attention to moral and intellectual culture has been given; the former prejudices on the part of the whites have given place to a perfect reciprocity of religious and social intercommunication. Schools are patronized equally; the gospel is common, and hospitality is shared alike by all....

The coloured subjects of Her Majesty in the Canadas are, in the general, in good circumstances, that is, there are few cases of positive destitution to be found among those permanently settled. They are settled promiscuously in cities, towns, villages, and the farming districts; and no equal number of coloured men in the States, north or south, can produce more freeholders. They are settled on, and own portions of the best farming lands in the Province, and own much valuable property in the several cities. There is, of course, a difference in the relative prosperity and deportment in different sections, but a respect for, and observance of the laws, is conceded to them by all. Indeed, much indifference on the part of whites has given place to genuine sympathy, and the active abolitionists and liberal men of the country look upon that element in their character as affording ground for hope of a bright future for them, and as evidence that their sympathy for the free man is not misplaced, as more than compensation for their own exertions for those yet in bonds....

### 3. Samuel Ward, "To Messrs. Bibb and Holly," October 1852

*Born to slaves who fled to New Jersey and freedom in 1820, Samuel Ringgold Ward (1817-ca. 1866) was a teacher, New York Congregational Association minister, and anti-slavery activist. He edited several publications in the 1840s and fought hypocrisy among some White abolitionists whom he accused of "best [loving] the colored man at a distance." Ward moved to Canada in 1851, served as agent for the Anti-Slavery Society there, and co-founded the weekly* **Provincial Freeman,** *targeted at the Black community. He left Canada permanently in 1853 for a successful two-year speaking tour and finally settled in Jamaica.*

Messrs. Bibb & Holly

Gentlemen:
... I now proceed to my second point, the comparing of Canada, with Yankee negro hate.
1. Canadian Negro Hate, is incomparably meaner than the Yankee article. The parties who exhibit most of this feeling, are as poor, as ignorant, as immoral, as low, in every respect as the most degraded class of negroes. In numerous instances, are they very far below them. No one can visit Canada, or any part of Canada, without seeing this, if his eyes be open. Our recently arriving slaves, are, in all respects quite equal to our newly arrived emigrants from Europe, and the free blacks coming from the United States are quite comparable to any class of whites, coming from the same country. The meanness of negro hate, therefore, is greater and lower, than that of the United States, as it is the setting up of one class of poor ignorant people, against another, by themselves, with just nothing under the moon, to boast of. In the United States, we are slaves, and but demi-freemen, if not all slaves. Here we all stand on a legal and political equality. The blacks [are] as free as the whites, and in law and in fact quite equal to them. Hence the greater meanness of Canadian than American Negro Hate.

Again Canadian Negro Hate is not original. Copied aped deviltry is always meaner than the original diabolism. But the negrophobia of Canada, is a poor pitiable, brainless, long eared imitation of Yankeeism, certain parties, go to Yankeedom to work. They return with Yankee cash, and Yankee ideas, and deal out both, in small quantities around their respective neighborhoods. In other cases, Yankees come here to reside. They bring their negrophobia with them. Canadians of the smaller sort catch the infection, straight way, go to aping their Yankee neighbors in this thing, in an awkward manner, and upon a very small scale. All they know is what they have heard, all they feel is second-handed. A meaner set of negro haters, God in his inexplicable mercy, does not suffer to live, than these poor fools of Canadian second-handed imitations.

But the greater meanness of this feeling, here, is also, in the fact that it is *gratuitous*. The whole world despise[s] gratuitous deviltry. A Yankee, commends himself to his richer more aristocratic neighbors, by his negrophobia. He puts himself on the side of Yankee fashion, by it. He sells more of his wares, in this way: he gets trade with men-stealers, and women-whippers, and human flesh mongers by it. If he be a priest he renders himself more acceptable to the occupants of the *front pews*, by it. If a politician he gets more votes, because he better pleases his slave-holding masters, by it. It is to him, therefore, a fair matter about which to *"calculate."* But not one word of this, applies to the Canadian. All he does, in this matter, is gratuitous: a devil serving without reward, in any possible shape. Bad and mean as is Yankee Negro Hate, it cannot be called as the Canadian article can *disinterested deviltry*. Be sure, as Hiram Wilson says, "it came from Hell by way of the United States," but it was *damaged* terribly in the passage hitherwards....

2. Unlike the Yankee product of the same name, Canadian Negro Hate, here has neither the current religion, nor the civil law, to uphold it. Steam-boat Captains, and Hotel keepers referred to above would be fined if brought before our courts, for their maltreatment of black persons. The British law knows no man by the color of his skin. In Yankeedom, negroes have no legal protection against such outrages. I never knew of but one instance, of a colored person receiving damages against a Steam-boat, for maltreatment in the United States. Instances here are numerous. A Hotel in Canada, forfeits its licence by treating a man as Mr. O'Banyan was treated. Trustees, who deny a black child the right of attending school, forfeit £5, each, and lose the Government money for their school. In Boston, no such punishment can be brought upon the white trustees, who exclude black children from the school.

Not a single denomination, have we in Canada, where ministers uphold or sanction this illegal and unchristian treatment of black persons. I have travelled much, and mingled freely with all sects, and I find it invariably true that in their places of worship and in their religious devotions whites and blacks, are on a common footing. The Holy Trinity, is the richest Episcopal church in Canada, equality—prevails there. Knox's church is the largest Free Presbyterian church in Canada, the same is true there. So in the Congregational church, so in the Methodist, so also in the Roman Catholic. Individuals belonging to each of these communions, ministers and laymen, may and do *enjoy* this beautiful brotherly negro hate. But the thing is far from being general. Indeed on this part of all denominations I have received uniformly, the treatment of a Christian gentleman. There are not one dozen places in the United States, where so much can be said.

You will readily judge from the last point, that Canadian Negro Hate can not be eternal. The labors of the anti-slavery society, the improvement, progress, and good demeanor of the black people will, in a very short time, undermine and destroy this abomination, unless, certain things, to which I shall presently refer, exert an unhappy influence. Having law, religion, and British example at headquarters against it, Canadian negrophobia, cannot long abide. When publicly attacked, it hides its head from the indignant gaze of a condemning community. The pulpit, in ninety-nine cases of an hundred could be marshalled against it, at any time. The Press (which in too many instances is far from being what it should be) condemns it, through the most influential papers in our Province. It is therefore, quite destitute of the influences which keeps it alive in our native land, let a hundredth part, of as much be done, here, against it as in the United States, in the shape of direct attack and it would disappear altogether.

There is this to be said, however, touching this feeling here. Ours is an aristocratic country. We make here, no pretentions to "social equality," "Republicanism," "Democracy" all that. Many blacks come here, and finding that they are not treated as equals by the better classes, attribute the treatment they receive, to the prejudice. The mistake, is [i]n not looking at society as it really is. A black gentleman of good education, polite manners, and courtly address, would be received as a gentleman, while a white man destitute of these would not be so received. Then too, as wealth enters largely into a man's position, here, it is not to be wondered at, that our people should be treated, in Canada as are other poor people....

The only thing to be feared, is, that some of the black people will act in such a manner as to increase, rather than diminish the prejudice against us. We have separate and distinct black churches, schools and preachers, whose existence and influence are much against us. Some of our preachers of the Methodist and Baptist denomination, are really too ignorant to instruct any body. The noisy behaviour of some women among whom was a female preacher in one of the Toronto churches not long since, was any thing but creditable or elevating. But if we act rightly, all will be well.

#### 4. William Brown, "The Colored People of Canada," *Pine and Palm*, September–December 1861

*William Wells Brown (ca. 1814–84) fled slavery in 1834 and worked on a Lake Erie steamboat assisting slaves to escape to Canada, then moved to New York in 1836 and there immersed himself in the abolitionist movement. He left in 1849 for a speaking engagement in Britain but stayed to avoid capture by his American owner. British abolitionists secured his freedom in 1854 and he returned to America. During this sojourn he wrote the first novel by an African-American,* Clotel, *and established himself as the continent's most prolific Black writer.*

No section of the American Continent has been watched with so much interest, both by the oppressor, the oppressed, and the friends of freedom and civilization, as the Canadas. The only spot in America, where every child of God could stand and enjoy freedom, and the only place of refuge for the poor whip-scarred slave of the Southern plantation, it has excited the malignant hate of all slaveholding Americans, while it shared the sympathy and approving interest of the friends of the African race everywhere. The colored population of the Canadas have been largely overrated. There are probably not more than 25,000 in both Provinces, and by far the greater number of these are in Canada West, and in a section of country lying west of Toronto, and near Chatham....

Prejudice against color. Canada has so long been eulogized as the only spot in North America where the Southern bondsman could stand a freeman, and the poetical connection of its soil with the fugitive, the "North Star," and liberty, had created such an enthusiastic love in my heart for the people here, that I was not prepared to meet the prejudice against colored persons which manifests itself wherever a member of that injured race makes his appearance.

That old, negro hating cry of "Crow, crow," which used to greet the well dressed colored person on the other side of the line twenty years ago, and which I had not heard for a long time, sounded harshly upon my sensitive ears as I passed through the streets of this city. Indeed, in none of the States, not even in Pennsylvania, is the partition wall between the blacks so high as in Canada. Amongst the colored men here, are some first class mechanics, yet none of these can get employment in shops where white men are at work. I have been informed by the best authority, in every place through which I have passed, that the introduction of a colored mechanic in any establishment here, would be taken as an insult by the white men, who would instantly leave their work. A splendid carpenter has just gone by with his whitewash bucket and brush; unable to get employment at his trade, he resorts to the latter for a livelihood. The equality meted out to colored persons in the hotels of New England, are unknown in Canada. No where here, are our people treated with any kind of respect in the hotels; they are usually put off into inferior rooms by themselves, fed at separate tables from the whites, and not permitted to enter the common sitting rooms of the inn. Most of the towns have excluded the colored children from the common schools....

I think that the prejudice against the colored people in Canada, arises mainly from the following causes: First, the colored inhabitants withdrawing themselves from the whites, forming separate churches, taking back seats in public meetings, and performing the menial offices of labor, and thereby giving the whites an opportunity to regard them with a degree of inferiority.

Second, the main body of the population of Canada appears to be made up of the lower class of the people of England, Scotland, and Ireland. As I walk the streets here, I look in vain for that intelligent portion of the middle classes that I used to meet in London, Edinburgh, and Dublin. This lower stratum, coming from the old world, and feeling keenly their inferiority in education and refinement, and being vulgar and rude themselves, try ... to draw attention from their own uncouthness, by directing the public eye to the other degraded class. It would, however, be doing injustice to the cause of Reform, to say that the entire population of Canada is of the class above mentioned....

Notwithstanding there is so much prejudice, and the colored people are shut out from the more profitable employments, they are nevertheless thrifty, and doing well. Although bad beer and poor whiskey appear to be in good demand in this city, and I have met several persons who seemed to have an over stock on hand, I have not yet seen a colored inhabitant intoxicated. In the vicinity of London there are many of our race who own good farms and carry them on in the best manner. A man I once knew at the South as a slave, now resides upon a beautiful place of sixty acres in a high state of cultivation, fine grafted fruit on it, a well finished house, and large, comfortable barns, all of which he owns himself, without a single debt. Although there seems to be such hatred of the negro here if one is known to be wealthy, the whites vie with each other to see which shall do him the most honor....

The past history and present condition of the colored population of Canada, differ widely from that of any other race in the world. Brought up under the strong arm of oppression, bought, sold, made to toil without compensation, from early dawn till late at night; the tenderest ties of nature torn asunder, deprived of all the rights of humanity, by both law and public opinion, at the South, they escape to Canada with all the hope and enthusiasm that such a long-dreamed of change can bring. On arriving here they are met by two classes; the mongrel whites, half French, Indian and Spanish on the one side, and Irish, Scotch, German and English, on the other. These natives, employ the fugitive, work him late and early, and pay him off in old clothes and provisions, at an exorbitant price, or cheat him entirely out of his wages. If he is so fortunate as to slip through the fingers of these, he then falls into the hands of another class, a set of land speculators, under the guise of philanthropy, owning large tracts of wild, heavy timbered, and low, wet land, which has been purchased for a shilling an acre, or thereabouts, and is importuned to "come and buy yourself a home; you can have ten years to pay for it in. Come now, get you a farm and be independent." The land is bought, the contract duly signed, and the poor man with his family settles in a log hut, surrounded by water a foot deep, in the spring of the year. By hard work, and almost starvation, they succeed in making their annual payments, together with the interest. The "Benevolent Land Association" has its Constitution and By-Laws, with any number of loop-holes for itself to get out at, but none for the purchaser. The fugitive is soon informed that he must fulfil certain obligations, or he will forfeit his claim. Unable to read, he takes his paper, goes to a lawyer, pays a fee, and is told that it is all right, he is bound by the contract. This unexpected stipulation is scarcely settled, ere he is again informed that if he does not comply with another oppressive act, he will forfeit his claim. Away he starts to the lawyer; another fee, and he returns with a flea in his ear. The last requirement is fulfilled with a sigh and a heavy heart. After years of toil, he has paid all that he agreed to, and demands his deed, when he is met with the reply that the "Association" has passed an act that every settler shall erect a frame house, twenty-four by thirty feet, must put a post and paling fence in front, and must ditch his land, or he cannot get his deed. Once more he goes to the lawyer, pays a fee, and then begins to think that "all that glitters is not gold," and gets upon his knees and prays to the Lord to give him patience to bear up under his multitude of misfortunes, or damns the "Benevolent Land Society," and swears that philanthropy in Canada is a humbug. Should he have health, strength, religion, and physical courage enough to pass safely through the meshes of the "Land Society," he then falls into the hands of the political jugglers. In Canada, one must possess a certain amount of property, or pay rent in a given sum, to entitle him to a vote for a member of Parliament. On the "Refugee Home" lands the colored residents voted for the candidates, at the election preceding the last, when it was found that they held the balance of power in their district, and at once it was resolved to disfranchise them. Consequently, at the last election, these people were assessed so low, that they fell under the required sum, and lost the right to vote. Still their taxes are just the same as they were when exercising the franchise. Thus, the names of more than fifty persons in one town were struck from the voters' list, on account of color.

The more I see of Canada, the more I am convinced of the deep-rooted hatred to the negro, here. In no hotel, can a colored person receive the respect given to the same class in New England. In every place except Toronto and Hamilton, they are excluded from the public schools, and in one district, where there were not enough colored children to entitle them to a separate school, the district school was abolished entirely rather than permit the colored children to attend it. One of the wealthiest and most influential colored farmers, and almost white, too, was lately refused a membership to a county agricultural society. Whenever a colored man is employed by a white man, the former is invariably put to a side table to take his meal; in the farming districts it is the same; and even when a white man works for a colored person, he demands a side-table, for he feels himself above eating with his master....

### 5. S. Howe, *The Refugees from Slavery in Canada West: Report to the Freedman's Inquiry Commission*, 1864

*Bostonian Samuel Gridley Howe (1801–76) was an idealistic doctor who followed Byron's steps by participating in the Greek, French, and Polish revolutions of the early nineteenth century. Once back in the United States, he created the first school for the blind and engaged in other philanthropic work. He also ran unsuccessfully for Congress as an abolitionist in 1846 and founded the abolitionist newspaper* The Daily Commonwealth *in 1851. Howe secretly funded both John Brown's proposed efforts to end slavery through armed insurrection and the Underground Railroad. He fled to Canada after Brown's arrest.*

... So the colored people of Canada say the climate suits them; that they are very well; that they bear as many children as whites do, and rear them as well. But the opinion of the most intelligent white persons is different.

Many intelligent physicians who have practised among both classes, say that the colored people are feebly organized; that the scrofulous temperament prevails among them; that the climate tends to development of tuberculous diseases; that they are unprolific and short-lived....

Dr. Fisher, physician at the Provincial Lunatic Asylum, says:—"I think the colored people stand the climate very badly. In a very short time lung disease is developed, and they go by phthisis. The majority do not pass forty years. Of course, there are exceptions. They die off fast. I suppose I have had thirty colored people here with little children, with scrofulous disease, extending as far as ulceration of the temporal bone. Then they are a good deal subject to rheumatism. They bear a great many children, but raise only about one-half of them, I think. The children are generally weakly and puny; not so strong as our white children. A great many of them die in childhood. The principal disease is tubercular deposition of the stomach and intestines."

However, let the rationale of prejudice against the negroes be what it may, it surely does not become the English to reproach the Americans, as a people, with the sin of it; for they themselves have quite as much of it; and their people show it whenever the negroes come among them in sufficient numbers to compete for the means of living, and for civil rights. Whenever circumstances call it forth among the coarse and brutal, they manifest it just as brutally as Americans do. They have done so in Canada; and would doubtless do so in England....

If the French people are, as they boast to be, above this prejudice, (which is improbable,) it must be because they have greater moral culture, (which is more improbable;) or else that the Celtic element in their blood has closer affinity with the African than ours has.

The English Canadians try to persuade themselves that when this malady of prejudice does occasionally appear among them, they do not have it in the natural way, but catch it from the Americans; and that it breaks out in its worst form in towns where Americans most abound.

The colored people, however, say, that this theory of contagion is not sustained by facts; and the bulk of the evidence shows that they are right.

The truth of the matter seems to be that, as long as the colored people form a very small proportion of the population, and are dependent, they receive protection and favors; but when they increase, and compete with the laboring class for a living, and especially when they begin to aspire to social equality, they cease to be "interesting negroes," and become "niggers."...

For instance, the head-clerk in the—hotel at—in answer to our inquiries about the condition of the colored people, broke out as follows:—"Niggers are a damned nuisance. They keep men of means away from the place. This town has got the name of 'Nigger Town,' and men of wealth won't come here. I never knew one of them that would not steal, though they never steal any thing of any great amount. Chickens have to roost high about here, I tell you. The Grand Jury of this county has just indicted seven persons, and every one of them was black. They will steal a little sugar, or a pound of butter, and put it in their pockets. But perhaps they are not to blame for it, for they have been trained to steal in slavery."...

*"The Sweet Zephyrs of British Land": The Black Experience*

It is not, however, hotel clerks alone, but grave officials, Mayors and others, who, when first addressed, are apt to speak contemptuously of the colored people; though they usually do them more justice upon reflection; especially in those cities where the negro vote is large enough to turn an election....

The Hon. Isaac Buchanan, M.P., of Hamilton, said to us:—"I think we see the effects of slavery here very plainly. The children of the colored people go to the public schools, but a great many of the white parents object to it, though their children do not, that I know of. I suppose, if the question was put to vote, the people would vote against having the negroes remain here."

Hon. George Brown, M.P., of Toronto, said:—"I think the prejudice against the colored people is stronger here than in the States. To show you the prejudice that exists against them, I will mention one fact. When I was a candidate for Parliament in Upper Canada, 150 people signed a paper, saying that if I would agree to urge the passage of a law that the negro should be excluded from the common schools, and putting a head-tax upon those coming into the country, they would all vote for me; otherwise they would vote for my opponent. There were 150 men degraded enough to sign such a paper and send it to me."

Mr. McCullum, principal teacher of the Hamilton High School, says:—"Up at the oil springs, the colored people have quite a little town. The white people were there, and they had all the work. They charged six shillings for sawing a cord of wood. The colored people went up there from Chatham, and, in order to get constant employment, they charged only fifty cents a cord. What did the white people do? They raised a mob, went one night and burned every shanty that belonged to a colored person, and drove them off entirely. Well, it was a mob; it was not society at all; it was but the dregs of society who did this. They took a quantity of the oil, and while some of their number were parleying with the colored people in front of their doors, they went behind, threw the oil over their shanties, set it on fire, and the buildings were in flames in a moment. The parties were arrested, and two of them sent to the penitentiary for seven years."

Rev. James Proudfoot, of London, says:—"You will find a great many colored people about Chatham—too many. It has produced a certain reaction among the white people there. The white people do not associate much with them; and even in the courts of justice, a place is allotted to the colored people— they are not allowed to mix with the whites. A number of gentlemen have told me that."

Mayor Cross, of Chatham, says:—"The colored people generally live apart. There has been, hitherto, a very strong prejudice against them, and the result is that they are, generally speaking, confined to a particular locality of the town."

Rev. Mr. Geddes, of Toronto, says:—"The great mass of the colored population will be found in the West; and where they go in any great numbers, the people acquire a strong prejudice against them."

Mr. Sinclair, of Chatham, says:—"Our laws know nothing about creed, color, or nationality. If foreign-born, when they take the oath of allegiance, they are the same as natives. But in regard to social prejudice, that is something we cannot help. The colored people are considered inferior, and must remain so for many years, perhaps forever, because their color distinguishes them. One or two colored men are constables here, but that is all.

"Many of the colored people, even in this town, say that if they could have the same privileges in the States that they have here, they would not remain a moment. The prejudice is not so strong in this town, where they have been so long known, and where the people see they can be improved and elevated; but even in this county, there is one township where no colored man is allowed to settle. One man has tried to build a house there, but as fast as he built it in the day time, the white people would pull it down at night. No personal violence was done to him. That was in the township of Oxford. In the township of Howard, I think there are only four colored families, and they are a very respectable class of people. In that township, there was as much prejudice as anywhere, fourteen years ago; but two colored families, very respectable and intelligent people, settled there—they were rather superior in those respects to the neighborhood generally—and they did a vast amount towards doing away with the prejudice. They were intelligent, cleanly, moral, and even religious; so that ministers of the gospel would actually call and take dinner with these people, as they found every thing so nice, tidy and comfortable, and the poor colored people so kind, and so ready to welcome any decent person who came. So that a good deal depends upon the first samples that go into a town."

The testimony of the colored people is still more striking. Mrs. ____ Brown (colored), of St. Catherines, says:—"I find more prejudice here than I did in York State. When I was at home, I could go anywhere; but here, my goodness, you get an insult on every side. But the colored people have their rights before the law; that is the only thing that has kept me here."

Dr. A.T. Jones (colored), of London, says:—"There is a mean prejudice here that is not to be found in the States, though the Northern States are pretty bad."

Rev. L.C. Chambers (colored), of St. Catherines, says: "The prejudice here against the colored people is stronger, a great deal, than it is in Massachusetts. Since I have been in the country, I went to a church one Sabbath, and the sexton asked me, 'What do you want here to-day?' I said, 'Is there not to be service here to-day?' He said, 'Yes, but we don't want any niggers here.' I said, 'You are mistaken in the man. I am not a "nigger," but a negro.'"

Mrs. Susan Boggs (colored), of St. Catherines, says:—"If it was not for the Queen's law, we would be mobbed here, and we could not stay in this house. The prejudice is a great deal worse here than it is in the States."

G.E. Simpson (colored), of Toronto, says:—"I must say that, leaving the law out of the question, I find that prejudice here is equally strong as on the other side. The law is the only thing that sustains us in this country."

John Shipton (colored), of London, says:—"I never experienced near the prejudice down there, (in the States,) that I have here. The prejudice here would be a heap worse than in the States, if it was not that the law keeps it down.".…

Mr. McCullum, principal of the well-appointed High School in Hamilton, says:—"I had charge of the Provincial Model School at Toronto for over ten years, and I have had charge of this school over four years, and have had colored children under my charge all that time. They conduct themselves with the strictest propriety, and I have never known an occasion where the white children have had any difficulty with them on account of color. At first, when any new ones came, *I used to go out with them in the playground myself, and play with them specially,* just to show that I made no distinction whatever; and then the children made none. I found this plan most healthy in its operation.

"Little white children do not show the slightest repugnance to playing with the colored children, or coming in contact with them. I never knew of a case. But sometimes parents will not let their children sit at the same desk with a colored child. The origin of the difficulty is not being treated like other children. We have no difficulty here. We give the children their seats according to their credit-marks in the preceding month, and I never have had the slightest difficulty. The moral conduct of the colored children is just as good as that of the others."

In London, the head-master of the High School manifested a different spirit: he said—"It does not work well with us to have colored children in school with the white. In our community, there is more prejudice against the colored people, and the children receive it from their parents. The colored children must feel it, for the white children refuse to play with them in the playground. Whether it is a natural feeling or not I cannot tell, but it shows itself in the playground and in the class-room."

One of the teachers said:—"I think that the colored children would be better educated, and that it would be more conducive to the happiness both of colored and white children if they were in separate schools. The colored children would not be subjected to so much annoyance. Some white children of the *lower orders* don't mind sitting by them in school; but there are others who are very particular, and don't like it at all." ...

*Public Schools*

The Canadian law makes no distinction of color. It proposes that common schools shall be beneficial to all classes alike. Practically, however, there is a distinction of color, and negroes do not have equal advantage from public instruction with whites. The law allows colored people to send their children to the common schools, or to have separate schools of their own. They have asked for and obtained such separate schools in Chatham, Malden, and Windsor. Now, there is a growing feeling among the whites that they made a mistake in giving the blacks their choice; and a strong disposition is manifested in many places to retract it, and to confine colored children to separate or caste schools.

On the other hand, there is a growing feeling on the part of the colored people that they made a mistake in asking for separate schools; and a strong disposition is manifested to give them up; but the whites will not allow them to do so.

This again shows how surely the natural sympathy for the refugee is converted into antipathy or prejudice whenever, by increase in number, they come into antagonism with the dominant class. By such antagonism, the natural affinities between the whites become intensified, and they desire to keep the blacks in a separate caste, because they feel that it must be a lower one. Many colored people see this also, and they desire to prevent the establishment of such caste. Each party begins to see that the democratic tendency of the common school is to prevent or weaken castes, while the inevitable tendency of the separate schools is to create and to strengthen them.

The struggle has already commenced in several places. The school committee of London has shown its purpose of removing the colored children from the common school to a separate school; and the colored people have declared their purpose of resisting it....

*Disposition to Work*

No sensible people in Canada charge the refugees with slothfulness. The only charge worth notice is that they "shirk hard work."...

But mulattoes dislike hard manual labor, not only because it is held less respectable than light work or no work, but because by their very organization,—by their lymphatic temperament, and lack of animal vigor, they are less adapted to prolonged muscular effort than full breeds. That they do not lack industry and thrift, the condition of those in Canada proves clearly, for thousands and tens of thousands of colored people have there worked hard for a living, and have earned it....

Hon. George Brown, M.P., of Toronto, says:—"One thing about the colored people here is quite remarkable; they never beg. They only ask for work; and when they get work, if they have borrowed any money, they will come back and pay it—a thing I never knew white men to do...."

Mr. Park, a merchant of Malden, says:—"Part of them (the colored population) are disposed to be industrious, and part of them are pretty indolent. They don't take care of their own poor. We have no poor-house. The poor are relieved either by the government of the municipality, or by the people. The colored people get about the same assistance, in proportion to their numbers, that the whites do. I think they beg more than the whites do."...

### FURTHER READINGS

Bearden, J., and L. Butler. *Shadd: The Life and Times of Mary Shadd Cary.* Toronto: NC Press, 1977.

Brode, P. *The Odyssey of John Anderson.* Toronto: Osgoode Society, 1989.

Cooper, A. "Black Women and Work in Nineteenth-Century Canada West: Black Woman Teacher Mary Bibb." In *"We're Rooted Here and They Can't Pull Us Up": Essays in African Canadian Women's History*, ed. P. Bristow. Toronto: University of Toronto Press, 1994.

Gillie, D., and J. Silverman. "The Pursuit of Knowledge Under Difficulties: Education and the Fugitive Slave in Canada." *Ontario History* 74 (June 1982): 91-105.

Hill, D. *The Freedom Seekers: Blacks in Early Canada.* Agincourt: Irwin, 1981.

Kilian, C. *Go Do Some Great Thing: The Black Pioneers of British Columbia.* Vancouver: Douglas and McIntyre, 1978.

Knight, C. "Black Parents Speak: Education in Mid-Nineteenth Century Canada West." *Ontario History* 4 (December 1997): 269-84.

Martin, G. "British Officials and Their Attitude to the Negro Community in Canada." *Ontario History* 66, 2 (June 1974): 79-88.

Pachai, B. *Beneath the Clouds of the Promised Land: The Survival of Nova Scotia's Blacks.* Halifax: Black Educators Association of Nova Scotia, 1987-90.

Reinders, R. "The John Anderson Case 1860-61: A Study in Anglo-Canadian Imperial Relations." *Canadian Historical Review* 56, 4 (December 1975): 393-415.

Silverman, J. *Unwelcome Guests: American Fugitive Slaves in Canada, 1830-1860.* Port Washington: Associated Faculty Press, 1985.

Spray, W. *The Blacks of New Brunswick.* Fredericton: Brunswick Press, 1972.

Stouffer, A. *The Light of Nature and the Law of God: Antislavery in Ontario 1833-1877.* Montreal and Kingston: McGill-Queen's University Press, 1992.

Walker, J. *The Black Loyalists: The Search for a Promised Land in Nova Scotia and Sierre Leone, 1783-1870.* Repr. Toronto: University of Toronto Press, 1992.

Walker, J. *A History of Blacks in Canada: A Study Guide for Teachers and Students.* Hull: Queen's Printer, 1980.

Wayne, M. "The Black Population of Canada West on the Eve of the American Civil War: A Reassessment Based on the Manuscript Census of 1861." *Social History* 28 (November 1995): 461-86.

Winks, R. *Blacks in Canada.* Montreal and Kingston: McGill-Queen's University Press, 1971.

Winks, R. "Negro School Segregation in Ontario and Nova Scotia." *Canadian Historical Review* 50, 2 (June 1969): 164-91.

Yee, S. "Gender Ideology and Black Women as Community-Builders in Ontario, 1850-1870." *Canadian Historical Review* 75, 1 (March 1994): 53-73.

# CHAPTER 15

# "Like Snow Beneath an April Sun"

## MID-NINETEENTH CENTURY NATIVE DISSENT

### INTRODUCTION

Although confrontations between Native people and governments have become more common in the contemporary world, with the crises at Oka, Gustafsen Lake, Ipperwash, Burnt Church, and elsewhere, it is tempting to assume that, with some notable exceptions, Native people in early British North America did little to resist European settlement and westward expansion. This was not the case and these people were not silent victims. On the contrary, by the nineteenth century many Native leaders set about addressing some of the wrongs they perceived as having been perpetrated against their people. Their voices indeed remained relatively few and muted, but they did cause a stir at the time, and arguably emerged as the precursors to modern Canadian Native militancy. Perhaps more importantly, at least in the pragmatic sense, their words not only inspired their own people, but also affected an increasing number of non-Native Canadians, Americans, and Europeans who felt troubled by what they heard.

The central complaint inevitably revolved around the profound differences between British promises and what they delivered, particularly with respect to Native land ownership. The Royal Proclamation of 1763, signed by George III after Britain's victory in the Seven Years' War, recognized Natives as the original land owners and set aside a large amount of land, in perpetuity, as "Indian Territory." This area encompassed much of present-day central Quebec and Ontario, and an enormous sickle-shaped wedge encircling the 13 New England colonies. The king decreed that non-Natives could not settle within this area unless Natives first voluntarily agreed to sell it to the Crown. The overall implication was that unless Natives relinquished the land, it remained theirs. This agreement changed almost immediately. In 1774 British officials arbitrarily redrew the Indian Territory, essentially excluding it from what is today Quebec and Ontario. The American War of Independence exacerbated this when victorious rebels rejected former British land promises to their west and flooded it with settlers, a situation which Britain, in fairness, did try to prevent, both during and after the revolution.

Native people found themselves pushed from their lands in British North America, either physically or as a result of unfriendly encroachment in the form of unscrupulous land speculators, afflictions of hunger and disease, or the unwelcome presence of farms, villages, and towns. Colonial governments remained unsympathetic to the Native plight, despite the Proclamation, and tended to turn a blind eye to transgressions. Bit by bit, many Native bands gave up and sold out in favour of specific reserves set aside and guaranteed by colonial administrators. Thus, by the nineteenth century, a huge gulf existed between the promises of the Royal Proclamation and what it meant in reality. This inconsistency roused Native ire.

Few Native authors managed to publish their views before the mid-nineteenth century, and their literature usually took the form of local histories, journals, travelogues, religious pamphlets, autobiographies, and letters. By the 1820s, however, a handful of Native ordained ministers shifted their focus to political protest, usually in the form of letters to British, British North American, and American officials, as well as in politicized sermons, tracts, petitions, and analytical reports on the appalling living conditions among their people. Some chiefs also joined the fight, usually concentrating on rallying their fellow chiefs rather than on admonishing non-Natives. A few Native preachers gained international fame and spent years spreading their message throughout eastern North America and northern Europe. Men such as Peter Jones—who eventually married into British society—became popular on the British social circuit, particularly when they showed up in full Native regalia.

Their message remained similar and constant: breech of trust, loss of land and wealth, loss of culture, loss of direction, and perhaps worst of all, loss of hope. It was not that these Christian Natives necessarily rejected European civilization or nostalgically pined for the past. On the contrary, people like Peter Jones endorsed European culture, from its political systems to its table manners, and looked forward to his own people's assimilation into it.

Jones and his people wanted real assistance, not just empty promises, as their people lost their traditional ways and struggled to replace them with something new.

DISCUSSION POINTS

1. These documents are organized regionally. What differences, if any, existed between the Native situations in the Maritimes, central Canada, and Red River?

2. What remedies did Native people propose? Were they realistic and, if so, to what degree?

3. Did non-Native people have an obligation to Native people?

DOCUMENTS

## 1. Pelancea Paul (François Paul) *et al.*, "To His Excellency John Harvey, Lieut. Governor of Nova Scotia," February 8, 1849

*Biographical information on Pelancea Paul (also known as François Paul) (dates unknown) remains elusive though it is known that he was a Micmac chief or "captain."*

To His Excellency John Harvey, K.C.R. and
K.H.H., Lieut. Governor of Nova Scotia:
The Petition of the undersigned Chiefs and Captains of the Micmac Indians of Nova Scotia, for and on behalf of themselves and their tribe humbly showeth:

That a long time ago our fathers owned and occupied all the lands now called Nova Scotia, our people lived upon the sides of the rivers and were a great many. We were strong but you were stronger, and we were conquered.

Tired of a war that destroyed many of our people, almost ninety years ago our Chief made peace and buried the hatchet forever. When that peace was made, the English Governor promised us protection, as much land as we wanted, and the preservation of our fisheries and game. These we now very much want.

Before the white people came, we had plenty of wild roots, plenty of fish, and plenty of corn. The skins of the Moose and Carriboo were warm to our bodies, we had plenty of good land, we worshipped *"Kesoult"* the Great Spirit, we were free and we were happy.

Good and Honorable Governor, be not offended at what we say, for we wish to please you. But your people had not land enough, they came and killed many of our tribe and took from us our country. You have taken from us our lands and trees and have destroyed our game. The Moose yards of our fathers, where are they. Whitemen kill the moose and leave the meat in the woods. You have put ships and steamboats upon the waters and they scare away the fish. You have made dams across the rivers so that the Salmon cannot go up, and your laws will not permit us to spear them.

In old times our wigwams stood in the pleasant places along the sides of the rivers. These places are now taken from us, and we are told to go away. Upon our camping grounds you have built towns, and the graves of our fathers are broken by the plow and harrow. Even the ash and maple are growing scarce. We are told to cut no trees upon the farmer's ground, and the land you have given us is taken away every year.

Before you came we had no sickness, our old men were wise, and our young men were strong, now small pox, measles and fevers destroy our tribe. The rum sold them makes them drunk, and they perish, and they learn wickedness our old people never heard of.

Surely we obey your laws, your cattle are safe upon the hills and in the woods. When your children are lost do we not go to look for them?

The whole of our people in Nova Scotia is about 1500. Of that number 106 died in 1846, and the number of deaths in 1848 was, we believe, 94. We have never been in a worse condition than now. We suffer for clothes and for victuals. We cannot sell our baskets and other work, the times are so hard. Our old people and young children cannot live. The potatoes and wheat do not grow, and good people have nothing to give us. Where shall we go, what shall we do? Our nation is like a withering leaf in a summer's sun.

Some people say we are lazy, still we work. If you say we must go and hunt, we tell you again that to hunt is one thing and to find meat is another. They say catch fish, and we try. They say make baskets, we do but we cannot sell them. They say make farms, this is very good, but will you help us till we cut away the trees, and raise the crop? We cannot work without food. The potatoes and wheat we raised last year were killed by the poison wind. Help us and we will try again.

All your people say they wish to do us good, and they sometimes give, but give a beggar a dinner and he is a beggar still. We do not like to beg. As our game and fish are nearly gone and we cannot sell our articles, we have resolved to make farms, yet we cannot make farms without help.

We will get our people to make farms, build houses and barns, raise grain, feed cattle and get knowledge. Some have begun already. What more can we say? We will ask our Mother the Queen to help us. We beg your Excellency to help us in our distress, and help us that we may at last be able to help ourselves. And your petitioners as in duty bound will ever pray.

### 2. Chief Kahkewaquonaby (Peter Jones), "Answers to the Queries proposed by the Commissioners appointed to enquire into Indian Affairs in this Province," February 6, 1843

*Peter Jones (1802-56), whose Native name was Kahkewaquonaby, or "Sacred Waving Feathers," was an Ojibwa adopted by the Iroquois. Considering that his mother was Native while his father was of Welsh descent, it was not surprising that Jones attended a White school where he learned English and was determined to succeed in the European world he admired. He converted to Methodism in 1823 and became Chief in 1829 because only he among his Mississauga people knew how to negotiate with the Indian Department and missionaries. The Methodist church ordained him in 1833, and he remained a tireless missionary in both the White and Native worlds. Jones was, throughout adulthood, a leader and champion of his people and their rights.*

*Query* No. 1.—How long have you had an acquaintance with any body of Indians?

*Answer* No. 1.—Being an Indian on my mother's side, I am well acquainted with the habits, customs, and manners, of the Chippeway nation of Indians to whom I belong. The tribe or clan with whom I have been brought up is called *Messissauga*, which signifies the eagle tribe, their *ensign* or *toodaim* being that of the eagle. I also lived for several years among the Mohawk Indians on the Grand River, by whom I was adopted. Since my entering upon the work of a missionary, I have travelled very extensively among all the Indian tribes in this country, and am therefore well acquainted with their former and present state; but, as I belong to the River Credit Indians, I intend to confine my remarks principally to them.

*Query* No. 2.—What has been their improvement during that time in their moral and religious character, and in habits of industry?

*Answer* No. 2.—Previous to the year 1823, at which time I was converted to Christianity, the Chippeway and indeed all the tribes were in a most degraded state; they were pagans, idolaters, superstitious, drunken, filthy, and indolent; they wandered about from place, living in wigwams, and subsisted by hunting and fishing. Since their conversion, paganism, idolatry, and superstition, have been removed, and the true God acknowledged and worshipped. The Christians are sober, and comparatively clean and industrious; they have formed themselves into settlements, where they have places of worship and schools, and cultivate the earth.

*Query* No. 3.—Do you find them improved in their mode of agriculture to any extent, since you first became acquainted with them?

*Answer* No. 3.—Many of them have made considerable progress in farming, but not to the extent they would have done if they had been settled on their own farm lots. The Credit Indians live in a village, and some of them have necessarily to go a mile or two to their farms, which has been a great hindrance to their improvement. Before their conversion very few of them raised even Indian corn, but now many of them grow wheat, oats, peas, Indian corn, potatoes, and other vegetables, several cut hay and have small orchards. I find the Indians at Muncey Town far behind their brethren at the Credit in agricultural industry.

*Query* No. 4.—What progress have they made in Christianity?

*Answer* No. 4.—Considerable; many of them can repeat the Lord's prayer, the ten commandments, and the Apostle's creed. They also understand the leading articles of our holy religion. I have translated the Book of Genesis, the gospels of Matthew and John, with other portions of Scripture, which they have now in their possession. They have made some proficiency in singing, are tolerably well acquainted with the rules of sacred harmony, and have a hymn-book translated into their own language, which is in constant use.

*Query* No. 5.—Since their conversion to Christianity are their moral habits improved? What effect has it had upon their social habits?

*Answer* No. 5.—Christianity has done much to improve their moral, social, and domestic habits. Previous to their conversion the women were considered as mere slaves; the drudgery and hard work was done by them; now the men treat their wives as equals, bearing the heavy burdens themselves, while the women attend to the children and household concerns.

*Query* No. 6.—Do they appear sensible of any improvement in their condition, and desirous of advancing?

*Answer* No. 6.—Very much so, and feel grateful to those who instruct them. They are still desirous of advancing in knowledge, seeing their white neighbours enjoy many comforts and privileges which they do not possess.

*Query* No. 7.—Are any of the Indians still heathens? What efforts have been made to convert them? And what obstacles have prevented their conversion?

*Answer* No. 7.—There are no heathens at the Credit, Alnwick, Rice Lake, Mud Lake, Snake Island, Balsom Lake, narrows of Lake Simcoe, Cold Water, St. Clair, and Moravian Town; but there are a number at Muncey Town, some at Sahgeeng, Big Bay, and the Grand River. I believe all the Indians at Walpool Island are pagans. There are a few among the Oneidas settled on the Thames at Muncey, and a number of Pattawatimees wandering about in these western parts who are in a most deplorable state of poverty and degradation. Efforts have been made to introduce Christianity to most of the pagans by missionaries of various denominations, but principally by native teachers. The obstacles to their conversion arise from their strong partiality to the ways of their forefathers, and their prejudices to the white man's religion. I am happy to state that the Wesleyan Missionaries, aided by native teachers, have never yet failed to introduce Christianity among a body of Indians.

*Query* No. 8.—What, in your opinion, is the best mode of promoting their religious improvement?

*Answer* No. 8.—To combine manual labour with religious instruction; to educate some of the Indian youths with a view to their becoming missionaries and school teachers, as it is a well known fact that the good already effected has been principally through the labours of native missionaries.

*Query* No. 9.—Do the children in the Indian schools shew any aptitude in acquiring knowledge?

*Answer* No. 9.—Considering they are taught in a strange language, they show as much aptitude as white children.

*Query* No. 10.—What, in your opinion, is the best mode of promoting the moral, intellectual, and social improvement of the Indians?

*Answer* No. 10.—The establishment of well-regulated schools of industry, and the congregating of the several scattered tribes into three or four settlements, which would be a great saving of expense to the Government and to missionary societies, at the same time it would afford greater facilities for their instruction in everything calculated to advance their general improvement.

*Query* No. 11.—Can you offer any suggestions on the expediency and best means of establishing schools of industry for the Indian youth, and the best system of instruction to be adopted in them?

*Answer* No. 11.—I would respectfully refer the commissioners to my letter on this subject, addressed to them, dated November 21st, 1842. In addition to what is there stated, I am happy to add that most of the Indian youths who have been educated at the academies have become respectable, and are now usefully employed in instructing their countrymen.

*Query* No. 12.—Do the Indians show any aptness for mechanical arts? And if so, to what arts?

*Answer* No. 12.—I know several Indians who have become pretty good mechanics with little or no instruction. At the Credit Mission there are two or three carpenters and a shoemaker. At Muncey we have one blacksmith, and some carpenters and tailors. By a little more instruction they would soon become good workmen in any mechanical art. The only drawback which I have observed is a want of steady application to their respective trades.

*Query* No. 13.—Is the health of the Indians generally good, or otherwise, as contrasted with the white population in their neighbourhood?

*Answer* No. 13.—From observation I am led to conclude that in general they are not as healthy as the white population. I apprehend this arises from their former mode of living, when they were frequently exposed to excessive fatigue and fasting, to carrying heavy burdens, drunkenness, and injuries inflicted on each other when in this state. These things have laid the foundation of many pulmonary complaints from which the present generation are suffering.

*Query* No. 14.—Do you find the Indians on the increase or decrease in numbers, irrespectively of migration? If the latter, what, in your opinion, is the cause?

*Answer* No. 14.—Previously to their conversion to Christianity they were rapidly decreasing. Before the white man came to this country the old Indians say that their forefathers lived long and reared large families, and that their diseases were few in number. In my opinion the principal causes of their decrease have been the introduction of contagious diseases, which hurried thousands off the stage of action; their excessive fondness for the *fire-waters*, and want of proper care and food for the children and mothers. I am happy however to state that this mortality has been greatly checked since they have abandoned their former mode of life.

I have kept a register of the number of births and deaths of the Credit Indians for several years past. After their conversion they remained stationary for some years; but, latterly, there has been a small increase from actual births. I have also observed, in other tribes, that the longer they have enjoyed the blessings of civilisation, the more healthy they have become, and the larger families they have reared.

*Query* No. 15.—Is there in your opinion any means of checking the excessive mortality among the Indians, if such prevails?

*Answer* No. 15.—In my opinion the best means is to promote industry and regular habits amongst them, and to have a good medical man stationed at or near each Indian settlement. I have known many of them suffer much, and die for the want of medical aid. It is also my opinion that intermarriages with other tribes of people would tend greatly to improve their health. Many of the small tribes are degenerating on account of their having continued for ages to marry into the same body of Indians hence the necessity of concentrating the scattered tribes.

*Query* No. 16.—Do the Indian men or women frequently intermarry with the whites?

*Answer* No. 16.—When this country was first visited by the whites it was a common practice for white men to take Indian wives, but at present it seldom occurs. As far as my knowledge extends, there are only three or four white men married to Indian women, and about the same number of Indian men married to white women.

*Query* No. 17.—Is there any marked difference in the habits and general conduct between the half-breeds and the native Indians? If so, state it.

*Answer* No. 17.—The half-breeds are in general more inclined to social and domestic habits. I have always found them more ready to embrace Christianity and civilization than the pure Indian, who, in his untutored state, looks upon manual labour as far too degrading to engage his attention.

*Query* No. 18.—In cases where intermarriages with whites have taken place, do you find the condition of the children of the marriage improved?

*Answer* No. 18.—I think they are, especially as regards their health and constitution.

*Query* No. 19.—Do the Indian women frequently live with white men, without being married?

*Answer* No. 19.—I know of no instances in all the tribes with which I am acquainted.

*Query* No. 20.—Does the birth of illegitimate children among the unmarried women occur frequently? And in what light is the circumstance viewed by the Indians?

*Answer* No. 20.—Such occurrences are not so frequent as when the Indians were in their drunken state; and when they do occur it is regarded as a great sin, and the mother loses her reputation as a virtuous woman.

*Query* No. 21.—Do any of the Indians enjoy all, or any, of the civil and political rights possessed by other subjects of Her Majesty?

*Answer* No. 21.—Not any to my knowledge; except the protection of law which I believe every alien enjoys who may visit or reside in any part of her Majesty's dominions. I am fully persuaded that, in order to improve the condition of the Indians, all the civil and political rights of British subjects ought to be extended to them so soon as they are capable of understanding and exercising such rights.

*Query* No. 22.—Are there any instances of Indians possessing such rights, besides those of the children of educated white men married to Indian women?

*Answer* No. 22.—I know of none.

*Query* No. 23.—In your opinion have the Indians the knowledge and ability to exercise any of those rights?

*Answer* No. 23.—In my opinion, some of the Credit Indians, and a few at other settlements are so far advanced in knowledge as to be able to exercise some of those rights, such as voting for Members of Parliament, township officers, &c., and to sit as jurors.

*Query* No. 24.—Can you offer any suggestions for the improvement of the condition of the Indians?—For the application of their presents, the expenditure of their annuities, and the proceeds of the sales of their lands?

*Answer* No. 24.—I would most respectfully suggest—

1st—The importance of establishing schools of industry as soon as possible, that there may be no further delay in bringing forward the present rising generation.

2nd—In order to promote industry among the Indians, agricultural societies ought to be formed at each settlement, and rewards offered to such as might excel in any branch of farming. This would excite a spirit of emulation, and be productive of good results.

3rd—In forming an Indian settlement, I consider that each family ought to be located on his own farm lot, containing 50 or 100 acres of land, with the boundaries of each lot marked out and established.

4th—I am of opinion that it would have a beneficial tendency were titles given to the Indians by the Government, securing their reserved lands to them and their posterity for ever. In offering these suggestions I do not mean to say that it would be prudent to confer titles individually on the Indians, but on the whole tribe. At present they hold no written documents from Government, and they frequently express fears that they will, at some future period, lose their lands. This fear acts as a check upon their industry and enterprise. In suggesting the impropriety of giving individual titles, I consider at the same time it would be well to hold out the promise to the sober and industrious, that when they shall have attained to a good knowledge of the value of property, and have established a good character, they shall have titles given them.

5th—The power of the chiefs is very different from what it was in former times, when their advice was listened to, and their commands implicitly obeyed. Immoral acts were then punished, and the offenders submitted without a murmur. But I am sorry to say, at present, many of the young people ridicule the attempts of the chiefs to suppress vice. I would humbly suggest that the Legislature, in its wisdom, take this subject into consideration, and pass an Act incorporating the chiefs to act as councillors, and the Superintendents of the Indian department as wardens. Bye-laws [sic] could be passed for the regulation and improvement of the several communities of Indians, such as the enactment of a moral code of laws, performance of statute labour, the regulation of fences, &c.

6th—I think it very desirable that something should be done for the Pottawatimees who wander about in these parts. They are in a state of great poverty and degradation, and an annoyance to the white inhabitants wherever they go. They have no lands in this province, having recently come over from the United States. I would, therefore, suggest the propriety of locating them, and thus bring them under the influence of civilization and Christianity.

7th—Feeling a deep interest for the welfare of the Muncey Indians residing at Muncey Town, I beg to call the attention of the Commissioners to their state. They are an interesting people, strongly attached to the British Government; and during the last American war rendered essential service in the defence of this province. If the Government could do something in the way of assisting them in their farming, it would afford great satisfaction, and be the means of facilitating their civilization. They receive no annuity from Government, and consequently have no means at their command to help forward their improvements.

8th—With regard to their presents, I would respectfully suggest the propriety of issuing them at their respective settlements. This would prevent some of the tribes being obliged to leave home, very often to the great damage of their crops, in order to travel to a distant post to receive the Queen's bounty.

9th—It is my opinion that the annuities payable to the Indians for lands ceded to the Crown ought to be applied in promoting agriculture and education among them.

10th—The proceeds of the sales of their lands ought to be invested in good securities, and the interest paid annually, and applied to such purposes as may improve their condition.

11th—I would suggest the propriety of rendering annually detailed accounts of the receipts and expenditures of the annuities, and the proceeds of the sales of their lands, and that the same be laid before the Indians in council for their satisfaction and information.

All which is respectfully submitted.

### 3. Chiefs Brant Brant, Joseph Penn, and Joseph Smart, "To the Chiefs and People of the Several Tribes Assembled in General Council at Orillia," July 21, 1846

*There is no biographical information available about Joseph Brant Brant (dates unknown), the son of Mohawk chief Joseph Brant, "Thayendanegea"; Joseph Penn (dates unknown); or Joseph Smart (dates unknown).*

Brothers—

We have too long been children; the time has come for us to stand up and be men. We must all join hands like one family, and help one another in the great cause of Indian improvement: this is our only hope to prevent our race from perishing, and to enable us to stand on the same ground as the white man.

Let us then sound the shell, and summon every red man from the woods; let us give up the chase of the deer and the beaver; it is unprofitable: the white man's labour is fast eating away the forest, whilst the sound of his axe and his bells is driving the game far away from their old haunts; it will soon be all gone. Let us then leave the bush to the wolves and the bears, and come forth and build our wigwams in the open fields: let us exchange the gun and the spear for the axe and the plow, and learn to get our living out of the ground, like our white brethren.

Brothers—

Many summers have passed away since our forefathers forsook a wandering life, and built settled homes in cleared places; we may therefore, as elder brothers, testify to you how great are the advantages of changing your mode of life. We confess, with sorrow, that we have not improved, as we ought, the advantages we have enjoyed; we are desirous, therefore, that you should profit by our faults and not neglect your opportunities.

Brothers—

There is no reason why we should not become an intelligent, industrious, and religious people. Experience has proved that the Great Spirit has given us powers of mind and body, not inferior to those of our white neighbours; then, why should we be inferior to them? Besides, Government has given us sufficient land to cultivate which is carefully protected from encroachment; we are supplied with clothing as presents from our Good Mother the Queen, whilst our other wants are relieved by the sale of such of our lands as we do not want to use. Good and careful Fathers are appointed to watch over our interests and attend to all our wants; they are anxious to do everything in their power to improve our people, and it is for this purpose they have called this Council.

Brothers—

Let us listen to all they have to say, with attention, and thankfulness. In all their dealings with us, though they are strong and we are weak, they never command us, they always use us like equals and brethren. In all they propose they have our good at heart; let us then meet their suggestions with generous confidence.

Brothers—

We understand one of the chief objects they have in view at present, is to improve our young people by means of Boarding Schools, at which they will not only be taught book and head knowledge, but also learn to work with their hands; in fact, to make our boys useful and industrious farmers and mechanics, and our girls good housekeepers. This seems to us very necessary, for most of our young people are both ignorant and indolent, and they must be taught and accustomed to work when young, or they will never learn it, nor like it, after they have been taught.

Brothers—

In conclusion, we congratulate you all (we hope all) that you, like ourselves, have been led by the good Spirit of God, out of the darkness of heathenism into the light and knowledge of the true religion, and that, in addition to the ties of blood and colour, we are still more closely bound together by one Faith and one Hope, as believers in our Lord, Jesus Christ. We must not forget that we are yet babes in Christ, and have tasted but slightly of the benefits of Christianity; greater blessings are in store for our race, if we only diligently seek them.

Religion and civilization must go hand in hand, and then they will greatly assist each other in raising our respective Tribes to a safe and honourable position in the scale of society. If we are only faithful to our responsibilities and to ourselves, our Tribes will soon be raised from their present degraded and helpless condition, and be alike useful and respected, both as Members of society and as Christians.

## 4. Chief Peau de Chat, "Address to T.G. Anderson, vice-superintendent of Indian Affairs," Sault Ste. Marie, August 18, 1848

*Chief Joseph Peau de Chat (dates unknown) was chief of the Fort William band. Very little biographical information exists about him, though it is known that his family rose to prominence in Grand Portage in the 1820s and that he acted as spokesman for all of the bands below the Lake Superior watershed.*

Father,

You ask how we possess this land. Now it is well known that 4000 Years ago when we first were created all spoke one language. Since that a change has taken place, and we speak different languages. You white people well know, and we Red Skins know how we came in possession of this land—it was the Great Spirit who gave it to us—from the time my ancestors came upon this earth it has been considered ours—after a time the Whites living on the other side of the Great Salt Lake, found this part of the world inhabited by the Red Skins—the Whites asked us Indians, when there were many animals here—would you not sell the Skins of these various animals for the goods I bring—our old ancestors said Yes. I will bring your goods, they the whites did not say any thing more, nor did the Indian say any thing. I did not know that he said come I will buy your land, every thing that is on it under it &c &c he the White said nothing about that to me—and this is the reason why I believe that we possess this land up to this day. When at last the Whites came to this Country where now they are numerous—He the English did not say I will after a time get your land, or give me your land, he said indeed to our forefathers, when he fought with the French and conquered them come on our Side and fight them, and be our children, they did so, and every time you wanted to fight the Big knives you said to the Indians wont you assist me, Yes! we will help you this Man (pointing to Shinguaconse) was there and he was in much misery—the English were very strong when we gave our assistance. When the war was over the English did not say I will have Your land, nor did we say you may have it—and this father You know, this is how we are in possession of this Land—It will be known every where if the Whites get it from us.

Father,

You ask in what instances the Whites prevent our Farming, there are bad people among us who are continually saying to us don't Farm, live as Indians always did, You will be unhappy if you cultivate the Land, take your Gun go and hunt, bring the Skins to me, and leave off tilling the Soil—and the Queen says to me become Christian my children. Yes I say we will become Christians but when this bad man (the Trader) sees me he says leave it alone do as you formerly did, and this is the way he destroys my religion and farming this is the way I explain the question you have now asked me.

Father,

The miners bum the land and drive away the animals destroying the land Game &c much timber is destroyed—and I am very sorry for it—When they find mineral they cover it once with Clay so that the Indians may not see it and I now begin to think that the White man wishes to take away and to steal my land, I will let it go, and perhaps I will accomplish it. I wish to let the Governor have both land and Mineral, I expect him to ask me for it, and this is what would be for our good. I do not wish to pass any reflections on the conduct of the whites—ask me then, send some one to ask for my land my Mineral &c. I wont be unwilling to let it go to the Government shall have it if they give us good pay. I do not regret a word I have said—You Father You are a White Man make Yourself an Indian, take an Indians heart come assist me to root out the evil that has been among us and I will be glad answer me is there any thing that requires explanation.

Father,

The Indians are uneasy seeing their lands occupied by the Whites, taking away the mineral and they wish that our Great Father would at once settle the matter. Come and ask me for my land and mineral that there be no bad feelings left, I am Sorry, my heart is troubled. I don't know what would be good for us, it will not do for me an Indian to say to the Governor come buy my land, yet this is what I think would be very good, Yes very good for my people, then the White man the miner and trader could do what he liked with the land and so could the Indian on that part which we would like to reserve, when we give our land up we will reserve a piece for ourselves and we, with our families will live happily on it we will do as we please with it. There (pointing to Fort William) I will find out a place for my self. Perhaps you will come and arrange Matters it would be well if you could, and if an officer cannot come this autumn to settle our affairs I will look out for one in the Spring to do it for me and this is nearly all I have to say, tell the Governor at Montreal to send a letter and let us know what he will do and what our land is worth in the mean time I will converse with my tribe on the subject. When I am going to sell my land I will speak again and Settle Matters.

A great deal of our Mineral has been taken away I must have something for it. I reflect upon it, as well as upon that which still remains.

### 5. Chief Peguis (William King), "To the Aboriginal Protection Society," Red River, 1857

*Saulteaux Chief Peguis (ca. 1774-1864) came from the Great Lakes but migrated westward, settling south of Lake Winnipeg in the 1790s. His people helped and protected the Selkirk settlers and the Hudson's Bay Company in their fight with the rival North West Company in the 1810s. In 1817 Peguis finalized western Canada's first treaty, with Lord Selkirk, ceding land along the Red River. He became a Christian in 1840 and was baptized "William King." Well-respected in the White community, the HBC paid him an annuity of £5 for loyal service. Disenchantment with European settlement set in by the 1850s after Peguis watched newcomers illegally push onto Native land.*

... Those who have since held our lands not only pay us only the same small quantity of ammunition and tobacco, which was first paid to us as a preliminary to a final bargain, but they now claim all the lands between the Assiniboine and Lake Winnipeg, a quantity of land nearly double of what was first asked from us. We hope our Great Mother will not allow us to be treated so unjustly as to allow our lands to be taken from us in this way.

We are not only willing, but very anxious after being paid for our lands, that the whites would come and settle among us, for we have already derived great benefits from their having done so, that is, not the traders but the farmers. The traders have never done anything but rob and keep us poor, but the farmers have taught us how to farm and raise cattle. To the missionaries especially we are indebted, for they tell us every praying day (Sabbath) to be sober. honest, industrious and truthful. They have told us the good news that Jesus Christ so loved the world that he gave himself for it, and that this was one of the first messages to us, "Peace on earth and good will to man." We wish to practice these good rules of the whites, and hope the Great Mother will do the same to us, and not only protect us from oppression and injustice, but grant us all the privileges of the whites.

We have many things to complain of against the Hudson's Bay Company. They pay us little for our furs, and when we are old are left to shift for ourselves. We could name many old men who have starved to death in sight of many of the Company's principal forts.

When the Home Government has sent out questions to be answered in this country about the treatment of the Indians by the Company, the Indians have been told if they said anything against the Company they would be driven away from their homes. In the same way when Indians have wished to attach them-selves to missions, they have been both threatened and used badly. When a new mission has been established, the Company has at once planted a post there, so as to prevent Indians from attaching themselves to it. They have been told they are fools to listen to missionaries, and can only starve and become lazy under them. We could name many Indians who have been prevented by the Company from leaving their trading posts and Indian habits when they have wished to attach themselves to missions.

When it is decided that this country is to be more extensively settled by the whites, and before whites will be again permitted to take possession of our lands, we wish that a fair and mutually advantageous treaty be entered into with my tribe for their lands, and we ask, whenever this treaty is to be entered into, a wise, discreet, and honourable man, who is known to have the interests of the Indian at heart, may be selected on the side of the Indian to see that he is fairly and justly dealt with for his land, and that from the first it be borne in mind, that in securing our own advantage, we wish also to secure those of our children and their children's children.

I commit these my requests to you as a body now well known by us to have the welfare of the poor Indian at heart, and in committing this to you on behalf of myself do so also on behalf of my tribe, who are as one man in feeling and desires on these matters. Will you, then, use the proper means of bringing these our complaints and desires in a becoming and respectful manner both before the Great Council of the nation (Parliament and through it to our Great Mother the Queen), who will show herself more truly great and good by protecting the helpless from injustice and oppression than by making great conquests.

Wishing that the Great Spirit may give you every good thing, and warmest thanks for your friendship.

### FURTHER READINGS

Den Otter, A. "The 1857 Parliamentary Inquiry, the Hudson's Bay Company, and Rupert's Land's Aboriginal People." *Prairie Forum* (2000): 143-69.

Getty, A., and A. Lussier. *As Long as the Sun Shines and the Water Flows: A Reader in Canadian Native Studies.* Vancouver: University of British Columbia Press, 1983.

Fisher, R. *Contact and Conflict: Indian-European Relations in British Columbia, 1774-1890.* Vancouver: University of British Columbia Press, 1977.

Francis, D. *A History of the Native Peoples of Quebec, 1760-1867.* Ottawa: Department of Indian and Northern Affairs, 1983.

Hall, T. "Native Limited Identities and Newcomer Metropolitanism in Upper Canada, 1814-1867." In *Old Ontario: Essays in Honour of J.M.S. Careless,* ed. D. Keane and C. Reid. Toronto: Dundurn Press, 1990.

Harring, S. *White Man's Law. Native People in Nineteenth Century Jurisprudence.* Toronto: University of Toronto Press, 1998.

Leslie, J. "The Bagot Commission: Developing a Corporate Memory for the Indian Department." *Canadian Historical Association Papers.* Ottawa: Canadian Historical Association, 1982: 31-52.

Miller, J. *Shingwauk's Vision: A History of Native Residential Schools.* Toronto: University of Toronto Press, 1996.

Miller, J. *Skyscrapers Hide the Heavens: A History of Indian-White Relations in Canada.* Toronto: University of Toronto Press, 1989.

Milloy, J. *The Plains Cree: Trade Diplomacy and War, 1790-1870.* Winnipeg: University of Manitoba Press, 1988.

Petrone, P. *First People, First Voices,* Toronto: University of Toronto Press, 1983.

Petrone, P. *Native Literature in Canada: From the Oral Tradition to the Present.* Toronto: Oxford University Press, 1990.

Rogers, E., and D. Smith. *Aboriginal Ontario: Historical Perspectives on the First Nations.* Toronto: Dundurn Press, 1994.

Schmalz, P. *The Ojibwa of Southern Ontario.* Toronto: University of Toronto Press, 1991.

Smith, D. *Sacred Feathers: The Reverend Peter Jones (Kahkewaquinaby) and the Mississauga Indians.* Toronto: University of Toronto Press, 1987.

Smith, S. "The Dispossession of the Mississauga Indians: A Missing Chapter in the Early History of Upper Canada." *Ontario History* 73, 2 (June 1981): 67-87.

Upton, F. *Micmacs and Colonists: Indian-White Relations in the Maritimes, 1713-1867.* Vancouver: University of British Columbia Press, 1979.

# CHAPTER 16

# *"The Bold Scheme"*

## CONFEDERATION

### INTRODUCTION

Was it wise to create the Dominion of Canada in 1867? Was it even possible to fuse disparate and fiercely autonomous British colonies into one huge nation with a tiny population sprinkled along its southern perimeter? Yes, Canada is a nation-state today, but does that make it good, viable, or natural? Quebec remains ambivalent about the national marriage, and western Canadian alienation simmers on. Newfoundlanders are hardly enthusiastic. Perhaps René Lévesque, the former separatist leader, was right: let's admit that Confederation was a shotgun wedding, get on with the divorce, and become platonic friends and good neighbours. If we don't, we'll spend an eternity squabbling. And yet what about the unity rally in Montreal in 1995 when polls indicated that the independence referendum might go to the "yes" side? What about the thousands of Canadians who converged on Quebec from across the country and wept at the thought of Canada torn asunder? Our present debate on national unity rolls on, as it did from the very day the Fathers of Confederation signed on the dotted line in 1867.

To many residents in the nineteenth century, uniting Britain's North American colonies was unnatural, impractical, and unpopular—but necessary. The colonies shared few things in common other than their British status. They had divergent agendas and religions, differing world views, and even unique cultures, dialects, and languages: Maritimers looked seaward and to Europe, Upper Canadians west to the new frontier, and Québécois inward. Their one commonality was a defensive suspicion of the United States—and even that was not universal. Some Canadians, for example, argued that British North America had so much in common with the United States that our destiny lay with joining its union. This, they argued, made eminent sense from economic, defensive, cultural, and historical perspectives.

The Colony of Canada, created in 1841 from a melding of the former Lower and Upper Canadas, provided stark evidence that colonial mergers were hopeless. The colony indeed proved to be as dysfunctional as naysayers predicted. Canada East and West, the two halves, eyed each other suspiciously, thwarted each other's agendas, and their cobbled political system perpetually teetered on deadlock at a time when decisive action was needed.

French-Canadian nationalists faced only unpalatable alternatives. Their primary objective was to retain French-Canadian cultural identity, which was awkward for a conquered people incorporated into the British Empire. Ironically, their best chance for cultural *survivance* after the catastrophe of the Conquest was as a distinct British colony, which they were between 1791 and 1840. Then, and under the auspices of the 1774 Quebec Act, French Canadians had the constitutional right to be distinct, which did not, however, prevent them from attempting to revolt against Britain in 1837. Nationalists rightly perceived the subsequent forced merger with Upper Canada in 1841 as another assimilationist move, tolerable only as long as Canada East had equal numbers of seats in the new legislature. But that proved untenable because of the ensuing deadlock. How about reverting to being the British colony of Lower Canada again? Unacceptable to Britain, and it still meant being British. And the *status quo*? If Macdonald was right, the autonomous British North American colonies would be picked off by the United States and Quebec culture would drown in an ocean of Americana. The only alternative seemed to be some sort of joint merger with the rest of British North America, which might forestall American annexation but would again leave Quebec struggling in a sea of Anglo culture, British rather than American—which to Quebec nationalists amounted to the same thing anyway.

The Maritime colonies, meanwhile, remained deeply skeptical about lessening ties to Britain and merging with the Canadas. Many Maritimers believed they had little to gain and much to lose in a federation wherein they would be a tiny minority, especially if representation by population ruled the day, as it presumably would. Their trade lay with the eastern American states and with Europe, not with the areas around the St. Lawrence and the Great Lakes, and their colonies wanted nothing to do with the English-French problem. And what did Maritimers care about settling the west? What, after all, would it even mean to become a Canadian province? It was like stepping over an abyss with Macdonald promising to hold a safety net. Meanwhile, the *status quo* as a British colony meant belonging to the world's largest empire, if Britain allowed it. Who would willingly forego that—or would they have to? Ambivalence, suspicion, and scant enthusiasm for federation ruled the day on the eastern seaboard.

Some people, perhaps in a fit of pique, wanted to follow the lead of the United States by creating an independent, transcontinental North American nation shorn from Britain. Their arguments ranged from defence to cultural nationalism, but economic considerations took the spotlight. Britain abandoned much of its traditional Imperial Preference in the 1840s and began buying resources from the cheapest sources, which tended to make Canadian staple exports like wheat uncompetitive. Exports dropped. Matters got worse. In response to British actions during the American Civil War in the early 1860s, the United States abrogated the ten-year-old Reciprocity Agreement it had with Canada's eastern colonies. British North America thus lost its second major market. Could purely intercolonial trade, with each colony retaining its autonomy, perhaps replace them? No. There were too many physical, legal, and political barriers. A united British North American nation, however, might revive dwindling trade by creating an effective internal market and make possible the acquisition of the prairies. Farmland had become expensive and scarce in most colonies, compelling thousands of Canadians intent on agricultural careers to migrate to the American mid-west. How to stem that tide? No single colony had the economic resources to purchase the Hudson's Bay Company's interest in the prairies, but collectively a united Canada might and could offer those emigrants an alternative.

Finally, some cynics also suggested that egocentrics like Macdonald, Brown, and Cartier knew full well the significance of becoming founders of a new nation. Americans like Washington, Jefferson, and Adams, after all, achieved legendary status in the American mythological pantheon, so why couldn't they? Ironically today few Canadians can name the country's first prime minister, let alone any other Father of Confederation.

### DISCUSSION POINTS

1. List the reasons for and against Confederation based upon these documents. Did financial matters take precedence?

2. Were the arguments for Confederation a sufficient basis upon which to build a country?

3. Today people distrust promises or claims made by politicians. How much credibility should we give to the speeches in this chapter?

4. Do any of the objections to Confederation in the 1860s still ring true? What promises, if any, has Confederation not fulfilled?

### DOCUMENTS

### 1. Hon. George Etienne Cartier, Speech, February 7, 1865

*George Cartier (1814-73) came from a well-to-do French-Canadian family and graduated from a Montreal college. As a member of the militant* Fils de la Liberté *organization he fought for the* Patriote *cause in the rebellion of 1837, but he always maintained that he had opposed the oppressive local British government and had not rebelled against the British Crown. Nonetheless, he was charged with treason and had to flee to the United States. Returning in 1839, he dared the British to prove the charges against him. Without any solid proof, they could not prevent him from returning to his legal practice. Elected first in 1848, Cartier was instrumental in lobbying for the Grand Trunk Railway, a corporation for which he also acted as legal advisor. Such blatant conflict of interest brought forth charges of collusion. Nevertheless, he quickly rose to the position of Attorney-General and eventually became joint premier of the Colony of Canada with John A. Macdonald in 1857. His major legislative accomplishments included the codification of Canada East's civil law. Much of his attitude to Confederation stemmed from his morbid fear of the United States. Although active in organizing the 1864 coalition and a principal speaker at the Charlottetown Conference, he remained silent during the Quebec City meetings. As leader of the largest French-Canadian political party, he supported provincial control over education, civil law, and local institutions in opposition to Macdonald's vision of central government. Seen by some as Macdonld's equal, by others as his principal lieutenant, Cartier served Canada's first federal cabinet as Minister of Militia and Defence. Much of Canada's expansion into the west came about due to his efforts.*

… The question for us to ask ourselves was this: Shall we be content to remain separate—shall we be content to maintain a mere provincial existence, when, by combining together, we could become a great nation? It had never yet been the good fortune of any group of communities to secure national greatness with such facility. In past ages, warriors had struggled for years for the addition to their country of a single province.... Here, in British North America, we had five different communities inhabiting five separate colonies. We had the same sympathies, and we all desired to live under the British Crown. We had our commercial interests besides. It was of no use whatever that New Brunswick, Nova Scotia and Newfoundland should have their several custom houses against our trade, or that we should have custom houses against the trade of those provinces. In ancient times, the manner in which a nation grew up was different from that of the present day. Then the first weak settlement increased into a village, which, by turns, became a town and a city, and the nucleus of a nation. It was not so in modern times. Nations were now formed by the agglomeration of communities having kindred interests and sympathies. Such was our case at the present moment. Objection had been taken to the scheme now under consideration, because of the words "new nationality." Now, when we were united together, if union were attained, we would form a political nationality with which neither the national origin, nor the religion of any individual, would interfere. It was lamented by some that we had this diversity of races, and hopes were expressed that this distinctive feature would cease. The idea of unity of races was utopian—it was impossible. Distinctions of this kind would always exist. Dissimilarity, in fact, appeared to be the order of the physical world and of the moral world, as well as of the political world. But with regard to the objection based on this fact, to the effect that a great nation could not be formed because Lower Canada was in great part French and Catholic, and Upper Canada was British and Protestant, and the Lower Provinces were mixed, it was futile and worthless in the extreme. Look, for instance, at the United Kingdom, inhabited as it was by three great races. Had the diversity of race impeded the glory, the progress, the wealth of England? Had they not rather each contributed their share to the greatness of the Empire? Of the glories ... how much was contributed by the combined talents, energy and courage of the three races together? In our own Federation we should have Catholic and Protestant, English, French, Irish and Scotch, and each by his efforts and his success would increase the prosperity and glory of the new Confederacy...: we were of different races, not for the purpose of warring against each other, but in order to compete and emulate for the general welfare. We could not do away with the distinctions of race. We could not legislate for the disappearance of the French Canadians from American soil, but British and French Canadians alike could appreciate and understand their position relative to each other. They were placed like great families beside each other, and their contact produced a healthy spirit of emulation. It was a benefit rather than otherwise that we had a diversity of races....

*"The Bold Scheme": Confederation*

## 2. Hon. George Brown, Speech, February 8, 1865

*George Brown (1818–80) came from a wealthy Edinburgh commercial family. When his father lost municipal funds through a mix-up in his own personal accounts and faced ruin, he decided to start life anew in the United States. Operating a small dry goods shop and publishing his own newspaper, Brown's father drew the attention of Canadian Scots who encouraged the family to move north in 1843. Like his father, George Brown moved into the newspaper business with the establishment of the To-ronto* **Globe**, *which soon had the largest circulation of any paper in British North America. He also emerged as the formidable champion of reform politics in Canada West and one of Toronto's leading businessmen. In particular his advocacy of the secu-larization of clergy reserves and the complete separation of church and state fostered his reputation as both anti-Catholic and anti-French Canadian. First elected in 1852, he quickly launched a campaign to acquire the Hudson's Bay Company lands for Canada. Under his leadership, a reorganized reform party became the Clear Grits. Determined to solve the political deadlock in the Canadas, Brown initiated the 1864 coalition with his political rivals and played a significant role at both the Charlottetown and Quebec Conferences. Disagreements over Canada's relationship with the United States caused his departure from active politics, but he remained influential throughout the 1870s and accepted a Senate appointment in 1874. A lifelong opponent of organized labour, he died from complications after being shot by one of his own disgruntled employees.*

… Well, sir, the bold scheme in your hands is nothing less than to gather all these countries [Newfoundland, Nova Scotia, New Brunswick, Lower Canada, Upper Canada, and British Columbia] into one—to organize them all under one government, with the protection of the British flag, and in heartiest sympathy and affection with our fellow-subjects in the land that gave us birth. Our scheme is to establish a government that will seek to turn the tide of European emigration into this northern half of the American continent—that will strive to develop its great natural resources—and that will endeavor to maintain liberty, and justice, and Christianity throughout the land....

… We imagine not that such a structure can be built in a month or in a year. What we propose now is but to lay the foundations of the structure—to set in motion the governmental machinery that will one day, we trust, extend from the Atlantic to the Pacific. And we take especial credit to ourselves that the system we have devised, while admirably adapted to our present situation, is capable of gradual and efficient expansion in future years to meet all the great purposes contemplated by our scheme. But if the honorable gentleman will only recall to mind that when the United States seceded from the Mother Country, and for many years afterwards their population was not nearly equal to ours at this moment; that their internal improvements did not then approach to what we have already attained; and that their trade and commerce was not then a third of what ours has already reached; I think he will see that the fulfilment of our hopes may not be so very remote as at first sight might be imagined—...

There is one consideration, Mr. Speaker, that cannot be banished from this discussion, and that ought, I think, to be remembered in every word we utter; it is that the constitutional system of Canada cannot remain as it is now. Something must be done. We cannot stand still. We cannot go back to chronic, sectional hostility and discord—to a state of perpetual Ministerial crises. The events of the last eight months cannot be obliterated; the solemn admissions of men of all parties can never be erased. The claims of Upper Canada for justice must be met, and met now. I say, then, that every one who raises his voice in hostility to this measure is bound to keep before him, when he speaks, all the perilous consequences of its rejection,—I say that no man who has a true regard for the well-being of Canada, can give a vote against this scheme, unless he is prepared to offer, in amendment, some better remedy for the evils and injustice that have so long threatened the peace of our country....

I am persuaded that this union will inspire new confidence in our stability, and exercise the most beneficial influence on all our affairs. I believe it will raise the value of our public securities, that it will draw capital to our shores, and secure the prosecution of all legitimate enterprises; and what I saw, while in England, a few weeks ago, would alone have convinced me of this. Wherever you went you encountered the most marked evidence of the gratification with which the Confederation scheme was received by all classes of the people, and the deep interest taken in its success....

But secondly, Mr. Speaker, I go heartily for the union, because it will throw down the barriers of trade and give us the control of a market of four millions of people. What one thing has contributed so much to the wondrous material progress of the United States as the free passage of their products from one State to another? What has tended so much to the rapid advance of all branches of their industry, as the vast extent of their home market, creating an unlimited demand for all the commodities of daily use, and stimulating the energy and ingenuity of producers? Sir, I confess to you that in my mind this one view of the union—the addition of nearly a million of people to our home consumers—sweeps aside all the petty objections that are averred against the scheme. What, in comparison with this great gain to our farmers and manufacturers, are even the fallacious money objections which the imaginations of honorable gentlemen opposite have summoned up? All over the world we find nations eagerly longing to extend their domains, spending large sums and waging protracted wars to possess themselves of more territory, untilled and uninhabited. Other countries offer large inducements to foreigners to emigrate to their shores—free passages, free lands, and free food and implements to start them in the world. We, ourselves, support costly establishments to attract immigrants to our country, and are satisfied when our annual outlay brings us fifteen or twenty thousand souls. But here, sir, is a proposal which is to add, in one day, near a million of souls to our population—to add valuable territories to our domain, and secure to us all the advantages of a large and profitable commerce, now existing.... [H]ere is a people owning the same allegiance as ourselves, loving the same old sod, enjoying the same laws and institutions, actuated by the same impulses and social customs,—and yet when it is proposed that they shall unite with us for purposes of commerce, for the defence of our common country, and to develop the vast natural resources of our united domains, we hesitate to adopt it! If a Canadian goes now to Nova Scotia or New Brunswick, or if a citizen of these provinces comes here, it is like going to a foreign country. The customs officer meets you at the frontier, arrests your progress, and levies his imposts on your effects. But the proposal now before us is to throw down all barriers between the provinces—to make a citizen of one, citizen of the whole; the proposal is, that our farmers and manufacturers and mechanics shall carry their wares unquestioned into every village of the Maritime Provinces; and that they shall with equal freedom bring their fish, and their coal, and their West India produce to our three millions of inhabitants. The proposal is, that the law courts, and the schools, and the professional and industrial walks of life, throughout all the provinces, shall be thrown equally open to us all.

But, thirdly, Mr. Speaker, I am in favor of a union of the provinces because—and I call the attention of honorable gentlemen opposite to it—because it will make us the third maritime state of the world. When this union is accomplished, but two countries in the world will be superior in maritime influence to British America—and those are Great Britain and the United States.... Well may [the French-Canadian people] look forward with anxiety to the realization of this part of our scheme, in confident hope that the great north-western traffic shall be once more opened up to the hardy French-Canadian traders and voyageurs. (Hear, hear.) Last year furs to the value of £280,000 ($1,400,000) were carried from that territory by the Hudson's Bay Company—smuggled off through the ice-bound regions of James' Bay, that the pretence of the barrenness of the country and the difficulty of conveying merchandise by the natural route of the St. Lawrence may be kept up a little longer. Sir, the carrying of merchandise into that country, and bringing down the bales of pelts ought to be ours, and must ere long be ours, as in the days of yore—and when the fertile plains of that great Saskatchewan territory are opened up for settlement and cultivation, I am confident that it will not only add immensely to our annual agricultural products, but bring us sources of mineral and other wealth on which at present we do not reckon....

But, sixthly, Mr. Speaker, I am in favor of the union of the provinces, because, in the event of war, it will enable all the colonies to defend themselves better, and give more efficient aid to the Empire, than they could do separately. I am not one of those who ever had the war-fever; I have not believed in getting up large armaments in this country; I have never doubted that a military spirit, to a certain extent, did necessarily form part of the character of a great people; but I felt that Canada had not yet reached that stage in her progress when she could safely assume the duty of defence; and that, so long as peace continued and the Mother Country threw her shield around us, it was well for us to cultivate our fields and grow in numbers and material strength, until we could look our enemies fearlessly in the face.... But, Mr. Speaker, there is no better mode of warding off war when it is threatened, than to be prepared for it if it comes. The Americans are now a warlike people. They have large armies, a powerful navy, an unlimited supply of warlike munitions, and the carnage of war has to them been stript of its horrors. The American side of our lines already bristles with works of defence, and unless we are willing to live at the mercy of our neighbors, we, too, must put our country in a state of efficient preparation. War or no war—the necessity of placing these provinces in a thorough state of defence can no longer be postponed. Our country is coming to be regarded as undefended and indefensible....

### 3. Legislative Council and House of Assembly of Prince Edward Island, "To The Queen's Most Excellent Majesty," March 6, 1865

To the Queen's Most Excellent Majesty
Most Gracious Sovereign,
We, Your Majesty's loyal and faithful servants, ... humbly beg leave to approach Your Majesty's throne, for the purpose of conveying to Your august Majesty the expression of our desire and determination, as the constitutional representatives of the people of Prince Edward Island, in regard to the great question involved in the said report; and having after most mature deliberation arrived at the conclusion that the proposed Confederation, in so far as it is contemplated to embrace

Prince Edward Island, would prove disastrous to the best interests and future prosperity of this Colony, we would humbly crave leave to state the grounds upon which that conclusion is based.

First.—Prince Edward Island, being entirely dependent on its agriculture and fisheries, has no staple commodity to export for which Canada can furnish a market (Canada being also essentially an agricultural country, and possessing valuable and extensive fisheries in the Gulf of St. Lawrence). That while such is, and ever must be, the relative commercial position of this Island and Canada, the products of our soil and fisheries, find in the extensive markets of our parent country, the United States, and the West Indies ready and profitable customers. That the proposed Union, while admitting the produce and manufactures of Canada into this Island free, would, by assimilation of taxes, enormously increase the duty to which those of Great Britain and the United States are at present subject in this Island, thereby compelling this Colony to take a large portion of its imports from Canada, making payment therefore in money, instead of procuring them from countries which would receive our produce in exchange, an arrangement so inconsistent with the fundamental principles of commerce that it would not only greatly curtail our commercial intercourse with Great Britain and the United States, but materially diminish our exports to those countries, and prove most injurious to the agricultural and commercial interests of this Island.

Second.—That if the relative circumstances of Canada and this Island rendered a Union practicable, the evident injustice of the terms agreed to by the Quebec Conference would prevent their being ratified by this Island. Without entering into full detail on this branch of the subject, or adverting to the fact that by the proposed terms of the Confederation we are called upon to transfer to the Confederate exchequer a steadily increasing revenue, and that too under our comparatively low tariff, for a fixed and settled annual subsidy of a greatly diminished amount, we would briefly notice some of the objectionable features of the said report.

And first in reference to the fundamental principle upon which the Confederation is proposed to rest, namely, representation according to population. Without admitting this principle under all circumstances to be sound or just, we consider it to be particularly objectionable as applied to this Island in connection with Canada, from the fact that the number of our inhabitants is and must continue comparatively small, in consequence of this Island possessing no Crown lands, mines, or minerals, or other extraneous resources, and that we never can expect to become, to any great extent, a manufacturing people, by reason of our navigation being closed for nearly half the year, and all trade, and even communication with other countries (except by telegraph and the medium of a fragile ice-boat) stopped. And when we consider the provision of the said report which is intended to regulate the mode of re-adjusting the relative representation of the various Provinces at each decennial census, and reflect upon the rapid rate of increase in the population of Upper and Lower Canada, particularly the former, heretofore, and the certainty of a still greater increase therein in the future over that of the population of this Island, it follows, as a certain and inevitable consequence, if a Federation of the Provinces were consummated upon the basis of the said report, that the number of our representatives in the Federal Parliament would, in the course of a comparatively short number of years, be diminished to a still smaller number than that proposed to be allotted to us at the commencement of the Union.

Third.—In further noticing the injustice of the terms of the said report, as applicable to us, we would advert to the old imperial policy, so pregnant with ill consequences to us, by which all the lands in this Colony were granted in large tracts to absentees, and which deprives this Island of the revenue drawn by the sister colonies from these sources,—to our insular position and numerous harbours, furnishing cheap and convenient water communication, which render expensive public works here unnecessary,—to the revenue to be drawn by the proposed Federal Government from this Island and expended among the people of Canada and the other Provinces in constructing railways, canals, and other great public works, thereby creating a trade which would build up cities and enhance the value of property in various parts of those Provinces, advantages in which this Island could enjoy a very small participation;—and to our complete isolation during five months of the year, when ice interrupts our trade and communication with the mainland, and during which period this Island could derive no possible benefit from the railroads and other public works which they would equally with the people of those Provinces be taxed to construct. These and many other circumstances placing Prince Edward Island in an exceptional position in regard to the other Provinces, but which seem to have been entirely ignored, ought, in our opinion, to have produced an offer of a financial arrangement for this Island very different in its terms from that contained in the report of the said Conference.

Fourth.—That while we fully recognize it to be the duty of this Colony to use every means, to the extent of its limited resources, to aid in defending its inhabitants from foreign invasion, we cannot recognize the necessity of uniting in a Confederation with Canada for the purpose of defence upon terms, which, in other respects, are so unfair to the people of Prince Edward Island, and thereby sacrificing our commercial and financial interests for the sake of securing the cooperation of Canada in a military point of view, it being our abiding hope and conviction, that so long as we remain a loyal and attached Colony of Great Britain, under whose protecting sway and benign influence we have so long had the happiness to live, and endeavour to aid, by a reasonable contribution towards the defence of our Colony, by placing our militia service upon a sounder and safer footing that it has hitherto attained, the powerful aid of our mother country will continue, as theretofore, to be extended to us in common with the other North American dependencies of the British Crown. For the foregoing reasons, and many other which we could urge, we beg most humbly and respectfully to state to Your Majesty that we, the representatives of Your faithful subjects, the people of Prince Edward Island, in Colonial Parliament now assembled, do disagree to the recommendations contained in the said report of the Quebec Conference, and on the part of Prince Edward Island do emphatically decline a Union, which after the most serious and careful consideration, we believe would prove politically, commercially, and financially disastrous to the rights and best interests of its people....

### 4. Joseph Howe, Speech, 1866

*A newspaperman and politician, in his later years Joseph Howe (1804–73) turned his attention to promoting railways and public works in Nova Scotia. Defeated at the polls in 1855 over his conflict with Catholics, he returned to the premiership of Nova Scotia in 1860. His party fell to defeat again in 1863. Howe then campaigned for a more integrated British Empire while opposing intercolonial union. He declined to attend the Confederation conferences and published his famous "Botheration Letters" in 1865 in order to rally opposition against the idea. Heading a local delegation to London, he failed to change the British government's support for the amalgamation of the Canadian colonies. However, Nova Scotia voters returned only a single pro-Confederation candidate in the 1867 election. As his supporters began to shift toward advocating the more extreme alternatives of insurrection or annexation to the United States, Howe's sense of British loyalty took over, and he agreed to accept a revised set of terms for Nova Scotia in 1869. In the same year he joined the federal cabinet as Secretary of State. His last political appointment took him back to Nova Scotia as its Lieutenant Governor.*

Let us see what these Canadians desire to do. They are not, as we have shown, a very harmonious or homogeneous community. Two-fifths of the population are

French and three-fifths English. They are therefore perplexed with an internal antagonism which was fatal to the unity of Belgium and Holland, and which, unless the fusion of races becomes rapid and complete, must ever be a source of weakness. They are shut in by frost from the outer world for five months of the year. They are at the mercy of a powerful neighbour whose population already outnumbers them by more than eight to one, and who a quarter of a century hence will probably present sixty eight millions to six millions on the opposite side of a naturally defenceless frontier. Surely such conditions as these ought to repress inordinate ambition or lust of territory on the part of the public men of Canada.... While they discharge their duties as unobtrusive good neighbours to the surrounding populations, and of loyal subjects of the empire, Great Britain will protect them by her energy in other fields should the Province become untenable but it is evident that a more unpromising nucleus of a new nation can hardly be found on the face of the earth, and that any organized communities, having a reasonable chance to do anything better would be politically insane to give up their distinct formations and subject themselves to the domination of Canada.

Thus situated, and borne down by a public debt of $75,000,000, or about $25 in gold per head of their population, the public men of Canada propose to purchase the territories of the Hudson's Bay Company, larger than half of Europe. They propose to assume the government of British Oregon and Vancouver's Island, provinces divided from them by an interminable wilderness, and by the natural barrier of the Rocky Mountains; and they propose to govern Nova Scotia, New Brunswick, Prince Edward Island and Newfoundland—countries severally as large as Switzerland, Sardinia, Greece, and Great Britain, appointing their governors, senators and judges, and exercising over them unlimited powers of internal and external taxation....

Anybody who looks at the map of British America, and intelligently searches its geographical features in connection with its past record and present political condition, will perceive that it naturally divides itself into four great centres of political power and radiating intelligence. The Maritime Provinces, surrounded by the sea: three of them insular, with unchangeable boundaries, with open harbours, rich fisheries, abundance of coal, a homogeneous population, and within a week's sail of the British Islands, form the first division; and the Ashburton Treaty, which nearly severed them from Canada, defines its outlines and proportions. These Provinces now govern themselves, and do it well, and Canada has no more right to control or interfere with them than she has to control the Windward Islands or Jamaica. These Provinces have developed commercial enterprise and maritime capabilities with marvellous rapidity. Three of them can be held while Great Britain keeps the sea. Newfoundland and Prince Edward Island are surrounded by it, and the narrow isthmus of fourteen miles which connects Nova Scotia with the mainland can be easily fortified and can be enfiladed by gunboats on either side. But what is more these Provinces can help Great Britain to preserve her ascendency on the ocean. While far-seeing members of the House of Commons are inquiring into the causes which diminish the number of her sailors and increase the difficulty of manning her fleet, is it not strange that the great nursery for seamen which our Maritime Provinces present should be entirely overlooked, and that flippant writers should desire to teach 60,000 hardy seafaring people to turn their backs upon England and fix their thoughts upon Ottawa; and should deliberately propose to disgust them by breaking down their institutions and subjecting them to the arbitrary control of an inland population, frozen up nearly half the year, and who are incapable of protecting them by land or sea.

Referring to the statistics of trade and commerce, it will be found that Nova Scotia employs 19,637 mariners and fishermen; Newfoundland, 38,578; and Prince Edward Island, 2,113. Nova Scotia alone owns 400,000 tons of shipping.

Here are colonies within seven days' steaming of these shores, floating the flag of England over a noble mercantile marine, and training 60,000 seamen and fishermen to defend it, and yet the House of Commons is to be asked to allow some gentlemen in Ottawa to draw these people away from the ocean, which for their own and the general security of the empire they are required to protect, that their hearts may be broken and their lives wasted on interminable frontiers incapable of defence. Parliament, it is hoped, will think twice about this proposition, and of the scheme for launching a prince of the blood into a sea of troubles for the glorification of the Canadians.

Canada forms the second division of British America, in order of sequence as we ascend from the Atlantic. It is a fine country with great natural resources, and may develop into some such nation as Poland or Hungary. Hemmed in by icy barriers at the north, and by a powerful nation on the south, shut out from deep sea navigation for nearly half the year, with two nationalities to reconcile, and no coal, who will predict for her a very brilliant destiny at least for many years to come? The best she can do is to be quiet, unobtrusive, thrifty, provoking no enmities, and not making herself disagreeable to her neighbours, or increasing the hazards which her defence involves, by any premature aspirations to become a nation, for which status at present she is totally unprepared....

### 5. Petition of the Inhabitants of Nova Scotia, "To The Commons of Great Britain and Ireland in Parliament Assembled," August 16, 1866

Humbly Showeth,—

... That the people of this Province, from their maritime position, have developed the pursuits of ship building, navigation, commerce, and fishing into prosperous activity. Their agricultural resources are rich and varied, whilst the vast mineral wealth which underlies the whole area of the country is a special guarantee of its future prosperity under favourable political conditions. The gold mines of Nova Scotia, without rising to the character of dazzling lotteries to attract a promiscuous or disorderly population from abroad, have proved steadily remunerative as a regular department of native industry, and a profitable investment for foreign capital. The great iron mines already discovered give earnest, in connection with its coal fields, of manufacturing capabilities not inferior to those of any country of similar extent. It has the thickest coal seams in the world, and their area is extensive, affording fair ground for the presumption that, for the purposes of peace or war, Nova Scotia's continued connection with Great Britain would prove of mutual advantage. Possessed of these resources, the people desire closer relations with the Mother Country in order to be able to enjoy more largely the benefits, as well as share more fully the responsibilities, of the Empire; and already the Province has enrolled 60,000 efficient militia and volunteers to assist in the maintenance of British power on this Continent, and sends to sea 440,000 tons of shipping, built and owned within the Province, bearing the flag of England, and manned by more than 20,000 seamen.

That Nova Scotia has no controversies with the mother-country, the other Provinces, or with the population of the neighbouring United States; and highly prizes the privileges so long enjoyed of regulating her own tariffs, and conducting trade, but lightly burdened, with the British Islands and Colonies in all parts of the world and with foreign countries.

That the people of Nova Scotia are prepared to entertain any propositions by which greater facilities for commercial and social intercourse with other States and Provinces may be secured; and they are willing, whenever their own coast and harbours are safe, to aid Her Majesty's forces to preserve from aggression the Provinces in the rear.

But they view with profound distrust and apprehension schemes, recently propounded, by which it is proposed to transfer to the people of Canada the control of the Government, Legislation, and Revenues of this loyal and happy

Province, and they venture respectfully to crave from your Honourable House justice and protection:

That the Province of Canada lies as far from Nova Scotia as Austria does from England, and there exists no reason why a people who live at such a distance, with whom we have but little commerce, who have invested no capital in our country, who are unable to protect it, and are themselves shut off from ocean navigation by frost for five months of the year, should control our Legislation and Government:

That in 1864 the Government of Nova Scotia, without any authority from the Legislature, and without any evidence of the consent of the people, sent delegates to Canada to arrange in secret conference at Quebec a political union between the various Provinces. That these delegates concealed the result of their conference from the people until it became incidentally made public in another Province, and that, to this hour, they have never unfolded portions of the scheme having the most essential relation to the peculiar interests and local government of Nova Scotia subsequent to Confederation.

That the scheme, when at last made public, was received with great dissatisfaction in Nova Scotia; that the opposition to it has been constantly on the increase, and has been intensified by the conduct of the Government and the delegates, who now propose to call in the aid of your Honourable House to assist them to overthrow, by an arbitrary exercise of power, free institutions enjoyed for a century and never abused:

That the objections of the people to the proposed Confederation scheme affect not merely minor local details, but the radical principles of the plan. The people cannot recognize the necessity for change in their present tranquil, prosperous, and free condition. They cannot believe that the proposed Confederation with the distant Colony (Canada) will prove of any practical benefit, either for defence or trade; while, from the past history of that country, its sectional troubles, its eccentric political management and financial embarrassments, they have great reason to fear that Confederation would be to them a most disastrous change, retarding their progress, and rendering their prolonged connection with the Crown precarious if not impossible. Forming, as she does now, a portion of the Empire, Nova Scotia is already confederated with fifty other States and Provinces, enjoys free trade with two hundred and fifty millions of people living under one flag and owning the authority of one Sovereign. She has no desire to part with her self control, or to narrow her commercial privileges, by placing herself under the dominion of a Sister Colony, with an exposed frontier, frostbound for a third of the year, and with no navy to defend the Maritime Provinces when her ports are open.

The scheme of government framed at Quebec is unlike any other that history shows to have been successful. It secures neither the consolidation, dignity, and independent power of monarchy, nor the checks and guards which ensure to the smaller States self-government and controlling influence over the Federal authorities in the neighbouring Republic. By adopting the federal principle, sectionalism in the five Provinces is perpetuated; by the timid and imperfect mode in which that principle is applied the people, whose minds have been unsettled by this crude experiment, may be driven to draw contrasts and nourish aspirations of which adventurous and powerful neighbours will not be slow to take advantage; and the people of Nova Scotia have no desire to peril the integrity of the Empire, with the blessings they now enjoy, or to try new experiments, which may complicate foreign relations, and yet add no real strength to the Provinces it is proposed to combine.

The people object also the financial arrangements, as especially burdensome and unfair to this Province. Having long enjoyed the control and benefited by the expenditure of their own revenues, they cannot approve a scheme that will wrest the greater part of these from their hands, to keep up costly and cumbrous federal machinery, and to meet the liabilities of Canada.

For many years the commercial policy of Nova Scotia has been essentially different from that of Canada. The latter country, partly from necessity arising out of financial embarrassments, and partly as an indirect premium on her own manufactures, has adopted a tariff varying from 20 to 30 per cent. on imported goods.

Almost surrounded, as Nova Scotia is, by the ocean, her people are favourably situated for enjoying free commercial intercourse with every section of the British Empire and with those foreign countries open to her commerce by the enlightened policy of the Parent State: of this privilege she has availed herself by imitating, as far as local circumstances would permit, the liberal and free trade policy of the Mother Country—ten per cent. being the ad valorem duty collected under the Nova Scotia tariff on goods imported into the Province. The proposed scheme of union will give Canada, by her large preponderance in the Legislature, the power to shape the tariff for the whole Confederacy according to her inland ideas and necessities, so as to levy the same onerous duties on British goods imported into Nova Scotia as are now exacted by Canada.

That since the Confederation scheme has been announced there have been special parliamentary elections in three out of the eighteen counties of this Province, and in all three it has been condemned at the polls.

That in 1865 the scheme was condemned at nearly every public meeting held by the delegates to discuss it, and numerous petitions against its adoption were presented to the Provincial Parliament, and only one in its favour, until the leader of the Government declared the measure to be "impracticable."...

The undersigned, menaced by a measure that may be revolutionary, repose implicit confidence in the protection of the Imperial Parliament. They deny the authority of their own Legislature, invested with limited powers for a definite term, to deprive them of rights earned by their ancestors by the most painful sacrifices, wisely exercised and never abused for more than a century, and which they had no legitimate authority to alienate or break down. They believe that any scheme of government, framed by a committee of delegates and forced upon the Provinces without their revision or approval, would generate wide spread dissatisfaction among a loyal and contented people, who will not fail to reflect that no change can be made in the constitution of any of the neighbouring States which has not first been approved by the electors; and that important measures, affecting imperial policy or institutions, are rarely attempted till they have been submitted for acceptance or rejection by the people whose interests they are to affect....

## FURTHER READINGS

Beck, J. *Joseph Howe: Briton Becomes Canadian*. Montreal and Kingston: McGill-Queen's University Press, 1982.

Bolger, F. *Prince Edward Island and Confederation, 1863-1873*. Charlottetown: St. Dunstan's University Press, 1964.

Buckner, P., P. Waite, and W. Baker. "CHR Dialogue: The Maritimes and Confederation: A Reassessment." *Canadian Historical Review* 71, 1 (March 1990): 1-45.

Careless, J. *Brown of the Globe*. Toronto: University of Toronto Press, 1964.

Cook, R., Ed. *Confederation*. Toronto: University of Toronto Press, 1967.

Creighton, D. *The Road to Confederation: The Emergence of Canada 1863-1867*. Toronto: Macmillan, 1964.

Hiller, J. "Confederation Defeated: The Newfoundland Election of 1869." In *Newfoundland in the Nineteenth and Twentieth Centuries*, ed. J. Hiller and P. Neary. Toronto: University of Toronto Press, 1980.

Martin, G. *Britain and the Origins of the Canadian Confederation, 1837-1867.* Vancouver: University of British Columbia Press, 1995.

Martin, G., Ed. *The Causes of Canadian Confederation.* Fredericton: Acadiensis Press, 1990.

Moore, C. *1867: How the Fathers Made a Deal.* Toronto: McClelland and Stewart, 1997.

Morton, W. *The Critical Years: The Union of British North America, 1857-1873.* Toronto: McClelland and Stewart, 1964.

Owram, D. *Promise of Eden: The Canadian Expansionist Movement and the Idea of the West, 1856-1900.* 2nd ed. Toronto: University of Toronto Press, 1992.

Pryke, K. *Nova Scotia and Confederation, 1867-1871.* Toronto: University of Toronto Press, 1979.

Rawlyk, G. *The Atlantic Provinces and the Problems of Confederation.* Halifax: Breakwater Press, 1979.

Robertson, R. "Prince Edward Island Politics in the 1860s." *Acadiensis* 15, 1 (Autumn 1985): 35-58.

Silver, A. *The French Canadian Idea of Confederation, 1864-1900.* Toronto: University of Toronto Press, 1982.

Waite, P. *The Life and Times of Confederation, 1864-1867: Politics, Newspapers and the Union of British North America.* Toronto: University of Toronto Press, 1962.

Weale, D., and H. Baglole. *The Island and Confederation: The End of an Era.* Summerside: Williams and Crue, 1973.

*Sources*

## Chapter 1: "So Blind and So Ignorant": Looking into Other Eyes

Le Clerq's comments and those of the Micmac chief were reprinted in William Ganong (ed. and trans.), *New Relations of Gaspesia* (Toronto: The Champlain Society, 1910); for his general observations and his dialogue with Adario, see Lahontan, *Some New Voyages to North America* (London: H. Bonwicke, 1703).

## Chapter 2: "Advantages and Inconveniences": The Colonization of Canada

Champlain's account was reprinted in H. Bigger (ed.), *The Works of Samuel de Champlain*, Vol. 2 (Toronto: The Champlain Society, 1925). Pierre Boucher, *True and Genuine Description of New France Commonly Called Canada* (Paris: 1664) was translated and reprinted by E. Montizambert under the title *Canada in the Seventeenth Century* (Montreal: G.E. Desbarats, 1883). Talon's memoir can be found in *Rapport de l'Archiviste de la Province de Quebec 1930-31* (Québec: Imprimeur du Roi, 1931). Denonville's correspondence was reproduced in E.B. O'Callaghan (ed.), *Documents Relative to the Colonial History of the State of New York*, Vol. 9 (Albany: Weed Parson and Company, 1855).

Chapter 3: "An Afflicted People": The Acadians

The Acadian Memorial is reprinted in T. Atkins (ed.), *Selections from the Public Documents of Nova Scotia* (Halifax: C. Annand, 1869). The circular letter from Governor Lawrence to the Governors on the Continent, Halifax 1755, was reprinted in Public Archives of Canada, *Report*, II (Ottawa: King's Printer, 1905) as was Winslow's journal. The documents by Galerm can be found reproduced in N.F.S. Griffiths, *The Acadian Deportation: Deliberate Perfidy or Cruel Necessity* (Toronto: Copp Clark, 1969).

Chapter 4: "The Ruin of Canada": Last Decades of New France

Documents by Montcalm, Péan, and the untitled "Memoir" were reprinted in E.B. O'Callaghan (ed.), *Documents Relative to the Colonial History of the State of New York*, Vol. 10 (Albany: Weed Parson and Company, 1858). "Narrative of the doings during the Siege of Quebec, and the conquest of Canada by a nun of the General Hospital of Quebec transmitted to a religious community of the same order, in France" was first published in English in 1826 and most recently reprinted in Jean-Claude Hebert, *The Siege of Quebec in 1759: Three Eyewitness Accounts* (Québec: Ministry of Cultural Affairs, 1974).

Chapter 5: "Suffering Much by Toil and Want": Loyalists in Nova Scotia

The Marston diary can be found in W. Raymond (ed.), "Diary of Benjamin Marston," *Collections of the New Brunswick Historical Society*, 1909; Boston King's "Memoir" originally appeared in the *Methodist Magazine*, 1798; both of the Edward Winslow letters appear in W. Raymond (ed.), *Winslow Papers, 1776-1826* (Saint John: New Brunswick Historical Society, 1901); the E.S. document was reprinted in N. Mackinnon, "A Caustic Look at Shelburne Society in 1787," *Acadiensis* 17, 2 (Spring 1988).

Chapter 6: "The Abundant Blessings of British Rule": Quebec's New Administration

The Plessis sermon appears in H. Forbes (ed.), *Canadian Political Thought* (Toronto: Oxford University Press, 1977); "To the Editor of the Quebec Mercury," was published in *Le Canadien*, November 19, 1806; the excerpt from John Lambert comes from his book *Travels through Lower Canada and the United States of North America in the Years 1806, 1807 and 1808*, Vol. I (London: Richard Phillips, 1810); and the document by Gray appears in J. Hare and J. Wallot (eds.), *Ideas in Conflict* (Trois-Rivières: Editions Boreal Express, 1970).

## Chapter 7: "All is Gloomy": The War of 1812

The first three documents can be found in W. Wood (ed.), *Select British Documents of the Canadian War of 1812*, Vol. 3 (Toronto: Champlain Society, 1920-1928); M. Smith, *A Geographical View of the Province of Upper Canada, and Promiscuous Remarks upon the Government* (Hartford: Hale and Hosmer, 1813); and William Dunlop, "Recollections of the American War 1812-14," *The Literary Garland*, June to November 1847. John Strachan, *Report of the Loyal and Patriotic Society of Upper Canada to Thomas Jefferson, January 30, 1815* (Montreal: William Gray, 1817) was reprinted as an appendix in W. Coffin, *1812: The War and Its Moral* (Montreal: John Lovell, 1864). The memoire by Bédard is reproduced in Y. Lamonde and C. Corbo (eds.), *Le Rouge et le Bleu: Une Anthologie de la Pensée Politique au Québec de la Conquête á la Revolution Tranquille* (Montreal: Les Presses de L'Université de Montreal, 1999).

## Chapter 8: "A Train of Undisguised Violence": North West Company vs. Hudson's Bay Company

See Thomas Douglas, Earl of Selkirk, *The Memorial of Thomas Earl of Selkirk* (Montreal: Nehum Mower, 1819). Copies of correspondence by William McGillivray and E. Coltman's final report can be found in Great Britain, House of Commons, *Papers Relating to the Red River Settlement* (London: 1819).

## Chapter 9: "For the Sake of Humanity": Newfoundland and the Beothuk

All of these documents were reprinted in J.P. Howley (ed.), *The Beothuks or Red Indians: The Aboriginal Inhabitants of Newfoundland* (Cambridge: Cambridge University Press, 1915).

## Chapter 10: "Our Robinson Crusoe Sort of Life": Three Women in Upper Canada

Susanna Moodie, *Roughing It in the Bush* (London: Richard Bentley, 1852); Catharine Parr Traill, *The Backwoods of Canada* (London: Charles Knight, 1836).

## Chapter 11: "The Long and Heavy Chain of Abuse": Political Crisis in Lower Canada

"The Six Counties Address" was reprinted in H.D. Forbes (ed.), *Canadian Political Thought* (Toronto: Oxford University Press, 1977); the Nelson document appears in Lamonde and C. Corbo (eds.), *Le Rouge et le Bleu: Une Anthologie de la Pensée Politique au Québec de la Conquête á la Revolution Tranquille* (Montreal: Les Presses de L'Université de Montreal,

1999); Durham's comments can be found in C. Lucas (ed.), *Lord Durham's Report on the Affairs of British North America* (Oxford: Clarendon Press, 1912).

## Chapter 12: "Most Horrible and Heartless": Irish Immigration

Great Britain, House of Commons, *Papers Relative to Emigration* (London: 1847) contain copies of the accounts by Stephen de Vere, G.M. Douglas, W. Boulton, and H. Perley.

## Chapter 13: "A Great Humbug": British Columbia's Gold Rush

Major's account appeared in *British Columbia Historical Quarterly* IV (July 1941), while C.C. Gardiner's is found in *British Columbia Historical Quarterly* I (1937). The third excerpt is from Matthew Macfie, *Vancouver Island and British Columbia* (London: Longman, Green, Longman, Roberts and Green, 1865).

## Chapter 14: "The Sweet Zephyrs of British Land": The Black Experience

With the exception of Mary Cary's *A Plea for Emigration* (Detroit: George Patterson, 1852) and S. Howe, *The Refugees from Slavery in Canada West: Report to the Freedmen's Inquiry Commission* (Boston: Wright and Potter, 1864), copies of the other documents in this chapter can be found in C. Ripley (ed.), *The Black Abolitionist Papers*, Vol. 2 (Chapel Hill: University of North Carolina Press, 1986).

## Chapter 15: "Like Snow Beneath an April Sun": Mid-Nineteenth Century Native Dissent

The Paul *et al.* petition was included in R. Whitehead, *The Old Man Told Us: Excerpts from Micmac History, 1500–1950* (Halifax: Nimbus, 1991). Other excerpts are from P. Jones, *History of the Ojebway Indians* (London: A.W. Bennett, 1861) and "To the Chiefs and People of Several Indian Tribes Assembled in General Council at Orillia, July 31, 1846, *Minutes of the General Council of Chiefs and Principal Men* ... (Montreal: 1846). The document by Chief Peau de Chat was found in P. Petrone (ed.), *First People, First Voices* (Toronto: University of Toronto Press, 1983); Peguis to the Aborigines Protection Committee, 1857 appears as an appendix in Great Britain, House of Commons, *Report from the Select Committee on the Hudson's Bay Company* (London: 1857).

## Chapter 16: "The Bold Scheme": Confederation

Speeches by Cartier and Brown were reprinted in *Canada, Confederation Debates* (Ottawa: King's Printer, 1951); Howe's address was recorded in J.A. Chisholm (ed.), *The Speeches and Public Letters of Joseph Howe*, Vol. II (Halifax: 1909); the petitions from Prince Edward Island and Nova Scotia were reprinted in Great Britain, House of Commons, *Correspondence Respecting the Proposed Union of the British North American Provinces* (London: 1867).